Crim Pro 360°

CRIM PRO 360°

Criminal Procedure
The Investigation Process

ADAM M. GERSHOWITZ
Associate Dean for Academic Affairs and
Hugh & Nolie Haynes Professor of Law
William & Mary Law School

CAROLINA ACADEMIC PRESS
Durham

Library of Congress Cataloging-in-Publication Data

Names: Gershowitz, Adam M., author.
Title: Crim pro 360° : criminal procedure: the investigation process / Adam M. Gershowitz.
Other titles: Crim pro three hundred sixty
Description: Durham : Carolina Academic Press, 2021.
Identifiers: LCCN 2021028842 | ISBN 9781531021863 (paperback) | ISBN 9781531021870 (ebook)
Subjects: LCSH: Criminal investigation—United States—Examinations, questions, etc. | Criminal procedure—United States—Examinations, questions, etc. | Searches and seizures—United States—Examinations, questions, etc. | Self-incrimination—United States—Examinations, questions, etc. | Exclusionary rule (Evidence)—United States—Examinations, questions, etc.
Classification: LCC KF9619.85 .G47 2021 | DDC 345.73/05076—dc23
LC record available at https://lccn.loc.gov/2021028842

Carolina Academic Press
700 Kent Street
Durham, North Carolina 27701
(919) 489-7486
www.cap-press.com

Printed in the United States of America

For Andrea Gershowitz, who really loves books.

Table of Contents

Preface

This book is designed to help you learn all of the core concepts in your course on Criminal Procedure: The Investigative Process. It includes broad coverage of the Fourth Amendment rules governing search and seizure and the Fifth Amendment rules for coerced confessions and the *Miranda* doctrine. It also covers interrogations under the Sixth Amendment and lineups, which many professors also teach in their criminal procedure courses.

This book is not filled with long descriptions of why the Supreme Court reached the decisions it did or how the law might be improved. You will not find lengthy discussions of cases or pages of citations. Time is short. You are busy. This book cuts to the chase and teaches you the law in an extremely succinct way. How does it do that?

First, I have provided a step-by-step roadmap for tackling Fourth Amendment and Fifth Amendment questions. This book walks you through the exact questions you should ask as you are taking an exam and the order in which you should ask them. Then I break down the topics into discrete chapters the way you would find them on a syllabus. Inside each chapter you will find an overview of the law that helps you to learn it and *remember* it. Each chapter starts with the big-picture rule, followed by bullet points with the critical rules and exceptions you need to know. Then I provide a short narrative description of how those rules fit together. Thereafter, I show you the exam traps that professors like me use to determine which students understand the rules.

Most importantly, this book gives you a lot of opportunities to practice your knowledge. In the pages that follow, you will find more than 200 multiple-choice questions that cover each of the core topics from the course. Finally, there are seven essay questions and an answer key that will help you to practice what you have learned and see what issues you missed. These multiple-choice and essay questions come directly from exams I have given at three different law schools.

There are many books about criminal procedure. Some are a mile deep, with a ton of details about the rules, but no opportunity to practice and see if you understand. Other books offer practice questions without explaining the law. This book is designed to hit the sweet spot by being a complete 360° guide to the rules you need to know, while also giving you a lot of practice questions—both multiple-choice and essay—so that you can go into your exam confident that you know the material and can ace your exam.

Crim Pro 360°

Roadmap for Search and Seizure Problems

The Fourth Amendment is only 54 words long, but the Supreme Court has made the law of search and seizure very complicated. Most of your criminal procedure course will be mired in details about how much suspicion the police need and which exception to the warrant requirement should apply. You will need to learn all of these details, but in doing so it is important not to lose sight of the big picture. Your job on a criminal procedure exam is not just to analyze warrant exceptions. Your job is to determine whether the evidence should be admitted or suppressed. And to do that you must not forget the other steps of analysis.

Below are the eight big-picture steps that you should think about as you determine whether evidence will be admissible. Think of these eight steps as a subway line. You do not want to just consider a couple of steps in the middle. Sure, a lot of people get off the train at Penn Station or Times Square. And in a criminal procedure course, a lot of the action revolves around which exceptions to the warrant requirement might apply. But there are other subway stops and other Fourth Amendment points of analysis. A common error that students make is to get on the train in the middle, rather than taking the whole ride and analyzing all of the steps. As you answer multiple-choice questions or essay questions, be sure to run through each of the eight steps set out below in order to determine whether evidence should be admitted or suppressed.

1. Was a **Government Actor** involved?

- The Fourth Amendment only protects against actions by government agents.
- There is no Fourth Amendment violation when a private person invades your privacy, even if their actions were outrageous.

- The Fourth Amendment does apply, however, when a police officer directs a private person to search or seize on behalf of the government.

2. Was There a **Search**?

- The Supreme Court has decided that some actions by the police are not searches, even though it might seem like a search to the average person.
- If there has been no search, the police can do whatever they want—with no reasonable suspicion, probable cause, warrant, or an exception to the warrant requirement.
- The main test for determining whether there was a search is to ask whether the individual had a subjective expectation of privacy that was also objectively reasonable.

3. Was There a **Seizure**?

- Not every interaction with the police is a seizure for Fourth Amendment purposes.
- Sometimes when a person deals with the police, it is a "voluntary encounter" and therefore not a Fourth Amendment event.
- If the police have engaged in a seizure, you have to determine whether it is a detention (which will require only reasonable suspicion) or a full-scale arrest (which will require probable cause).

4. Was There a Valid **Warrant**?

- Police almost always need a warrant to enter a home to search or arrest.
- Police will sometimes need a warrant to arrest or search outside of the home.
- A search warrant must be based on probable cause.
- A search warrant must particularly describe the places to be searched and things to be seized.
- The police can only search for items listed in the warrant, although they can seize other items they find in plain view.
- The police must knock and announce their presence before executing a warrant, but there are some big exceptions to that rule.

5. If There Was No Warrant, Did an **Exception to the Warrant Requirement** Apply?

- The warrantless searches and seizures that occur most often in real life and on law school exams are:
  - Consent

  - Exigent circumstances
  - Automobile exception
  - Searches incident to arrest
  - *Terry* stops
  - *Terry* frisks for weapons
  - Inventories
  - DWI checkpoints
  - School searches

- Police can conduct some warrantless searches and seizures with *no suspicion*. The most common situations are:
  - Consent searches
  - Inventory searches
  - DWI checkpoints
  - Border checkpoints
- In other scenarios, police must demonstrate *reasonable suspicion* to conduct a warrantless search or seizure. This is a low level of suspicion that in turn allows the police to conduct a limited search or a limited seizure. The most common scenarios are:
  - Traffic stops
  - Temporary detentions of people walking on foot so that police can investigate possible criminal activity
  - Pat-downs of the outer layer of clothing (if there is reasonable suspicion that suspect is armed and dangerous)
  - Cursory inspections of a car to make sure there are no weapons
  - Quick sweeps of a house to make sure there are no people hiding who could harm the officers
- Many searches and seizures require *probable cause*. This level of suspicion allows full-scale searches and seizures, such as:
  - Arrests outside the home
  - Automobile searches
  - Searches of homes, cars, or other locations based on exigent circumstances

6. Is There Standing to Challenge the Search or Seizure?

- It is not enough that the police searched or seized improperly.
- To suppress evidence, the defendant must demonstrate that her personal Fourth Amendment rights have been violated.

7. Does the **Exclusionary Rule** Apply?

- If the police have discovered evidence as a result of an illegal search or seizure for which the defendant has standing, the court should exclude the evidence.
- If the police searched illegally and found no evidence at first, but later discovered evidence, you should consider whether the fruit of the poisonous tree doctrine should apply.

8. Does an **Exception to the Exclusionary Rule** Apply?

- The Supreme Court has recognized multiple exceptions to the exclusionary rule. The most important ones for your criminal procedure course are the:
  - Good Faith Exception
  - Inevitable Discovery Exception
  - Independent Source Exception
  - Attenuation Exception

As you proceed through your criminal procedure course (and your exam!), run through each of these eight steps. Remember that you can correctly identify which exception to the warrant requirement should apply, but still miss a substantial portion of the question if you don't analyze the other steps.

STEP 1
Was a Government Actor Involved?

Chapter 1: Government versus Private Actors

The first step in any Fourth Amendment question is the easiest. Determine whether it was a government actor who conducted the search or seizure. Although this issue comes up rarely, you should be sure not to skip it. Chapter 1 explains who counts as a government actor.

CHAPTER 1
Government versus Private Actors

THE RULE: For a search or seizure to be covered by the Fourth Amendment, it must be carried out either by (1) a government actor; or (2) a person acting at the direction of a government actor.

Critical Points

- The Fourth Amendment applies to searches by public actors.
- Public actors are usually police officers, but they could also be other governmental employees such as teachers, firefighters, or even public utility employees.
- The Fourth Amendment applies to searches by private individuals who are acting at the direction of government employees.
- The Fourth Amendment does not apply to purely private searches.

OVERVIEW OF THE LAW

The Fourth Amendment is a protection against *government* overreach. Thus, when a government employee conducts an unreasonable search or seizure, there will be a Fourth Amendment violation that may result in the suppression of evidence.

When we think of searches and seizures, we normally think of the local police, or perhaps the FBI or the DEA. But it is not just the police who are government agents. Teachers, firefighters, public utility workers (such as a public gas company) and many others work for the government. When one of these government employees conducts a search or seizure it is covered by the Fourth Amendment, just as if it had been done by a police officer.

The Fourth Amendment also applies when government employees direct a private person to conduct a search or seizure. In these cases it is the private person who takes the action, but because they are doing so at the direction of the government, those searches are also covered by the Fourth Amendment.

The Fourth Amendment does not apply to purely private searches, however. When a private actor conducts a search or seizure there cannot be governmental overreach and thus there can be no Fourth Amendment violation. Private security guards, private school teachers, and anyone else whose paycheck comes from a private business cannot commit a Fourth Amendment violation.

EXAM TRAPS TO AVOID

- *Public Employees Who Don't Look Like the Police*: Don't be fooled into ignoring the Fourth Amendment just because the person does not look like a police officer. A public utility officer who checks for gas leaks (and other public employees) can commit a Fourth Amendment violation.
- *Private Security*: A private security officer—even one who illegally detains an individual or improperly searches his car—cannot commit a Fourth Amendment violation.
- *The Private Actor Who Transforms into a Public Actor*: A purely private actor (who originally could not have committed a Fourth Amendment violation) can become a public actor if she begins acting at the direction of a law enforcement officer.

MULTIPLE-CHOICE QUESTIONS

Question 1

Yasmyn lives in Kingsland, a beautiful, gated community. Kingsland has its own private security force that patrols the neighborhood. The security officers wear uniforms and drive marked security cars. When anyone buys a home in Kingsland they sign a covenant that they agree to be bound by the authority of the Kingsland officers. The covenant empowers the officers to conduct searches and seizures, although only in compliance with the law of the Fourth Amendment. All Kingsland officers take a course in criminal procedure at the nearby law school. A Kingsland officer stopped Yasmyn for speeding, and searched the trunk of her car without probable cause. The officer discovered drugs in the trunk and turned the drugs over to the police. Yasmyn has moved to suppress the drugs. Which of the following is correct?

A) The court should suppress the drugs because the officer searched the trunk without probable cause.

B) The court should suppress the drugs because a court is a public entity and admitting illegally seized evidence is a state action.

C) The court should admit the drugs because the Kingsland officer was acting in a purely private capacity.

D) The court should admit the drugs because the Kingsland officer appeared to be a public police officer based on the uniform and marked car.

E) The court should admit the drugs because all of the community residents, including Yasmyn, had agreed to give the officer search and seizure authority, although only if the officer complied with the Fourth Amendment, which he didn't.

Question 2

Hillary is a student at St. Andrews Presbyterian High School, a private religious school. Multiple students have told Hillary's homeroom teacher, Ms. Sloan, that Hillary has been selling OxyContin pills in the bathroom. After school is over and all the students have gone home, Ms. Sloan asks the custodian to open Hillary's locker. Inside, Ms. Sloan finds a bottle of OxyContin pills, and she brings the pills to the police station. The officers said, "Oxy possession cases are hard to prove. We need distribution evidence. Here's what you do. Tomorrow you should follow her into the bathroom. That's where the kids usually do the dealing." The next day, when Hillary and another student both ask to go to the bathroom during homeroom, Ms. Sloan follows them into the bathroom. Hillary and the other student were standing at the sink and Ms. Sloan grabbed Hillary and slammed her against the wall. Ms. Sloan proceeded to conduct an invasive and unpleasant strip search. Ms. Sloan discovered a bag of cocaine inside of Hillary's underwear, and she turned this evidence over to the police. Hillary has moved to suppress all of the evidence. What result?

A) The OxyContin pills and the cocaine should definitely both be admitted because they resulted from a search by a private actor.

B) The OxyContin pills should be admitted because they were from a private search, but the court should remain open to suppressing the cocaine as a government directed search.

C) The OxyContin pills should be admitted because they were from a private search, but the cocaine should be admitted because it was found from an "invasive and unpleasant" search following Hillary being "slammed against the wall," all of which are so excessive as to transform a private party search into a Fourth Amendment violation.

D) The OxyContin pills and the cocaine should be suppressed because Ms. Sloan was acting at the direction of law enforcement.

Question 3

After serving for 25 years in the Colonial City Police Department, Officer Herman retired with distinction. The City of Colonial often hires retired police officers to work in its buildings and it quickly offered Herman a job as a school security guard at Colonial High School. During his first day on the job, the school immediately put Herman to work in the school. Herman became suspicious that a student was selling drugs. Herman unlocked the student's locker while he was in class and took his car keys from the locker. Herman then walked out of the school, found the student's car parked across the street, used the keys to unlock the vehicle, and searched the car. Herman found drugs in the car. The student has moved to suppress the drugs. Assume there was no probable cause to search the car. What result?

A) The drugs should be admitted because Herman is no longer a police officer; thus, he is a private actor who is not covered by the Fourth Amendment.

B) The drugs should be admitted because Herman conducted the search off school property.

C) The drugs should be suppressed because Herman is a public actor.

D) The drugs should be suppressed because even though he was a private actor, Herman was not properly trained.

ANSWERS TO MULTIPLE-CHOICE QUESTIONS

Answer to Question 1

Answer A is incorrect. The search was improper because there was no probable cause. But the officer is not a government agent and thus is not covered by the Fourth Amendment.

Answer B is incorrect. A court's decision to admit evidence that would have been a Fourth Amendment violation if it had been seized by a government actor does not transform a private search into a Fourth Amendment violation.

Answer C is correct. The Kingsland officer is a private party and cannot commit a Fourth Amendment violation.

Answer D is incorrect. The controlling factor is not whether the actor appears to be a government employee, but instead whether the actor *is* in fact a government employee.

Answer E is incorrect. The residents of a community cannot make a private party into a government actor covered by the Fourth Amendment by signing a real estate covenant.

Answer to Question 2

Answer A is incorrect. The OxyContin was found during a private search. But it is not clear that the cocaine was "definitely" found from a private search. Ms. Sloan was arguably acting at the direction of law enforcement when she found the cocaine. Because it is possible that a court could conclude the cocaine was found when Ms. Sloan searched and seized pursuant to law enforcement direction, this answer is not correct.

Answer B is correct. The OxyContin was found during a private search. Remember that Ms. Sloan works at a "private religious school." But it is arguable that Ms. Sloan was acting pursuant to police direction when she slammed Hillary against a wall and conducted the invasive search.

Answer C is incorrect. A search by a private party does not become a Fourth Amendment violation based on the severity of the actions of the private party.

Answer D is incorrect. It is possible that the search in the bathroom that led to the cocaine was at the direction of law enforcement, but that could not be said of the search that led to the discovery of the OxyContin pills. Ms. Sloan's initial search of the locker was not directed by law enforcement and was thus a private party action not covered by the Fourth Amendment.

Answer to Question 3

Answer A is incorrect. It is true that Herman is no longer a police officer and he would therefore no longer be a governmental actor in that capacity. But he is working for a public school and is thus a governmental actor. His conduct is therefore covered by the Fourth Amendment.

Answer B is incorrect. Herman was working in his capacity as a school security guard when he searched the car.

Answer C is correct. While Herman is no longer a police officer, he is a public employee working at a public school. He is thus a governmental actor covered by the Fourth Amendment.

Answer D is incorrect. A private actor's conduct does not become a Fourth Amendment violation because he received no training from his employer. In any event, Herman is not a private actor because he was working for a public school.

STEP 2
Was There a Search?

Chapter 2: Defining What It Means for the Police to Search

The second step in Fourth Amendment analysis is to ask whether the police have conducted a search. The main test for determining whether a search has occurred is whether the person had a subjective expectation of privacy that was objectively reasonable. The Supreme Court has also indicated that police can search by physically trespassing.

You should not begin to address topics such as probable cause, search warrants, or the numerous exceptions to the warrant requirement until first determining that a search occurred. If there was no search, police do not need to justify their actions at all. No search means there was no Fourth Amendment event and the evidence will be admissible regardless of whether there was probable cause, a warrant, or an exception to the warrant requirement.

CHAPTER 2
Defining What It Means for the Police to Search

THE RULE: The primary test for whether there was a search under the Fourth Amendment is whether the police invaded a subjective expectation of privacy that was objectively reasonable. An alternative test sometimes used by the Supreme Court is whether the police engaged in a physical trespass. If there was no search, there was no Fourth Amendment event and the evidence will be admissible, regardless of whether the police had suspicion or a warrant.

Critical Points

- *Primary Test*: The primary test for whether there has been a search is the "*Katz* test," which comes from Justice Harlan's concurring opinion in *Katz v. United States* (1967). The *Katz* test asks whether the defendant has a subjective expectation of privacy and whether that expectation was objectively reasonable. In practice, the subjective expectation prong is almost always met. Therefore, the whole ball game is whether there is an objectively reasonable expectation of privacy.
- *Alternative Test*: An alternative test used by the Court asks whether the officers engaged in a physical trespass to property.
- *Technology and the Home*: In a case where the police pointed a thermal imaging device at a home to gauge the heat level inside to see if marijuana was being grown, the Court relied on the fact that the device was not "in general public use." How widely available the technology is can play a role in whether the police conduct is a search.
- *Third Party Doctrine*: When a person knowingly makes information available to a third party, she runs the risk that the third party will share that information with the government. Thus, people do not have a reasonable

expectation of privacy in information conveyed to third parties. When police get information from third parties there is no search.

- *Exception to Third Party Doctrine*: When the government accesses historical cell site location data from cell phone towers, that is a search. Even though the individual has made that information available to a third party (the cell phone provider) cell phone data allows the government to develop a detailed record of exactly where a person has been and is thus different from other third party cases. Therefore it invades a reasonable expectation of privacy, and is a search.
- *Open Fields versus Curtilage*: The police do not conduct a search when they enter on open fields, but they do conduct a search if they set foot on the curtilage. The following factors are important in distinguishing between open fields and curtilage:
  - Proximity to the house.
  - Whether the area the police entered is fenced in with the house.
  - What the property is used for.
  - Steps taken by the owner to keep the property private.
- The Supreme Court has decided that the following police tactics are searches:
  - Trespassing on the driveway of private property (*Collins v. Virginia* (2018))
  - Drug-sniffing dogs on the porch of a house (*Florida v. Jardines* (2013))
  - Blood draws (*Missouri v. McNeeley* (2013))
  - Attaching a GPS device to a car (*United States v. Jones* (2010))
  - Manipulating luggage with fingers on a public bus (*Bond v. United States* (2000))
  - Pointing a thermal imaging device at a house to gauge the temperature inside, because the device was not in general public use (*Kyllo v. United States* (2001))
  - Gathering historical cell site location data from a third party (*Carpenter v. United States* (2018))
- The Court has decided that these police tactics are *not* searches:
  - Pen registers (*Smith v. Maryland* (1979))
  - Acquiring bank records from a third party (*United States v. Miller* (1976))
  - Aerial surveillance in lawful airspace (*California v. Ciraolo* (1986))
  - Rifling through trash left at the curb (*California v. Greenwood* (1988))
  - Trespassing in open fields (*Oliver v. United States* (1984))
  - Use of undercover informants (*Hoffa v. United States* (1966))
  - Drug-sniffing dogs in public places (*United States v. Place* (1983))

OVERVIEW OF THE BLACKLETTER LAW

The Fourth Amendment forbids unreasonable "searches." It is therefore crucial early on in your analysis to figure out whether the police action was in fact a search. If the police have searched, you have to proceed through the other Fourth Amendment steps, such as whether there was probable cause and a valid warrant. But if the police conduct is not a search, your work is done. If the officers have not searched (or seized), they could not have violated the Fourth Amendment.

Unfortunately, the Supreme Court has not offered a clear set of rules for determining whether the police have conducted a search. The primary test—arising from Justice Harlan's concurring opinion in *Katz v. United States* (1967)—asks (1) whether the person has a subjective expectation of privacy in the area searched; and (2) whether society recognizes that privacy interest to be objectively reasonable. The first prong is usually very easy. The defendant will ordinarily testify or otherwise demonstrate that she sought to keep the item or area private and away from public view. In almost all cases, the defendant can make a plausible claim that she has a subjective expectation of privacy. The real action is at the second prong—whether the person's privacy expectation is objectively reasonable. To be objectively reasonable, an expectation of privacy must be one that society is prepared to accept. A defendant might believe that airplanes won't conduct surveillance of her backyard, or that police will not go through trash she left at the curb. But the Court has concluded that society would not find such expectations to be reasonable.

Whether the defendant had a reasonable expectation of privacy is a case-by-case inquiry. Nevertheless, the Court has decided some high-profile cases that can give us some categorical guideposts. Before reviewing these cases, it is important to recognize that your professor can create a fact pattern that roughly resembles a Supreme Court decision, but change a few facts that may change the outcome. So use these Supreme Court decisions as guideposts and always analyze each case according to its own facts.

Let's start with the third party doctrine and so-called "false friends." When a person gives information to another, they are typically giving up any reasonable expectation of privacy. For example, if I tell my best friend a secret, I am taking the risk that the friend will blab it to others. I even run the risk that my friend could be wearing a wire or recording me on his smartphone. The same logic applies to businesses. If I use my American Express card to charge sports tickets or pharmacy prescriptions, I am giving away information about myself to a third party—the credit card company. For this reason, the Supreme Court has adopted the so-called "third party doctrine," which holds that a person has no reasonable expectation of privacy in information shared with others. When the police seek information from a third party—whether it is a friend, your bank, the phone company, or someone else—they are not conducting a search for Fourth Amendment purposes. (The bank might still insist on the police getting a subpoena, but that it not a Fourth Amendment issue you have to worry about.)

There is one major exception to the third party doctrine. In *Carpenter v. United States* (2018), the Supreme Court held that it is a Fourth Amendment search when the police procure historical cell site location data from a third party. The reason is that cell phone data can provide an extremely detailed picture of the exact movements of an individual over a long period. That level of invasive government surveillance was apparently more than the Court could stomach and they therefore found it to be different from other third party cases.

Another important "is it a search" question concerns the difference between open fields and curtilage. Open fields are privately owned lands that are typically undeveloped and aren't lived on. For example, farmland that stretches for acres behind a farmhouse is an open field. Curtilage is the area around the house that is treated like part of the home. When the police go onto open fields they are *not* conducting a search. When they go onto the curtilage they *are* conducting a Fourth Amendment search. The hard question is: how do you tell the difference between open fields and curtilage? The Court has identified a few factors: (1) the closer the land is to the house the more likely it is to be curtilage; (2) if the area is enclosed in the same fence as the house it is more likely to be curtilage; (3) if the property is used for traditional living activities it is more likely to be curtilage; and (4) the more steps the owner has taken to keep it private the more likely it is to be curtilage. You should use these factors for cases in which an officer has walked onto land. If it looks like the officer is on the curtilage, then the police have searched. If it looks like the officer is walking through an open field, it is not a search.

Notice that up until now we have been talking about officers *walking* onto the curtilage or an open field. There are different rules when the police conduct an investigation from the air. The Supreme Court has held that aerial surveillance is not a search when the plane or helicopter is flying at a lawful height. So if police fly over your back porch and see that you are selling drugs on the curtilage of your property, it is not a search. In short, aerial surveillance will usually not be a search as long as the plane or helicopter is flying in navigable air space.

It is possible, however, that aerial surveillance could be a search if the police are using rare technology. The Supreme Court has indicated that using technology that is not in general public use can be considered a search. In *Kyllo v. United States* (2001), officers pointed a thermal imaging device (which measures heat) at a house in order to determine that one of the rooms was very hot. The information from the thermal imaging device helped to create probable cause to believe the occupants were using very hot grow lights to illegally grow marijuana in the house. The Court held that the police action was a search because the police used an item not in general public use to gather intimate details about the inside of the house that they would not otherwise be able to discover. Although *Kyllo* is a case about thermal imaging devices, the idea that tools not in general public use make something more likely to be a search is relevant to other possible police tactics.

Given that police budgets are limited, in the real world the police do not have a lot of high-tech gadgets that are unavailable to the public. So it's important to consider some low-tech investigative techniques. The Supreme Court has held that if police rummage through garbage left at the curb that they have not conducted a search. When you throw out your garbage you have knowingly exposed it to the public. While most people do not go around rummaging through other people's trash, it does happen. Put simply, a person cannot reasonably expect to maintain privacy in garbage they throw out at the curb.

A similar low-tech investigative technique is the use of drug-sniffing dogs. Police regularly walk drug-sniffing dogs through airport terminals and around cars at traffic stops. The Supreme Court has held that the use of a drug-sniffing dog in a public location is not a search. The reason is that drug dogs are sniffing for illegal substances. And a person has no legitimate privacy expectation in illegal substances. Matters would of course be different if the officers forced the person to open their luggage or their vehicle's trunk to let the dog search inside. People have a reasonable expectation of privacy in closed containers. But in the average dog-sniffing case no containers are being opened. Instead, the dog is only sniffing the outside of the luggage or the vehicle. As noted above, a person cannot have a reasonable expectation of privacy in things they expose to the public. Moreover, while dogs are better able to smell odors than humans—thus arguably making them sense-enhancing technology—dogs are pretty common and thus can be considered to be in general public use.

Drug-sniffing dogs provide a nice segue to talk about the other test the Supreme Court sometimes uses to determine whether or not a search has occurred. In a small number of cases, the Court has focused on whether the police have engaged in a physical trespass to property. For example, in *United States v. Jones* (2010), police placed a GPS tracker on a suspect's vehicle and then saw what locations he went to. The Court concluded that this constituted a search because the police had trespassed on Jones's property when they attached the GPS tracker to the vehicle.

The other major case involving physical trespass involved a drug-sniffing dog. In *Florida v. Jardines* (2013), the police received a tip that marijuana was being grown in a house. To investigate, the officers walked a drug-sniffing dog on the front porch of the house. The Court held that this was a search because the officer (and dog) had physically trespassed on the curtilage of private property. Of course, people such as FedEx drivers, food delivery workers, and neighbors regularly walk onto the porches of houses that are not their own. How are they different from the drug-sniffing dog? The answer is that we do not typically think of neighbors and delivery drivers as trespassing—they have an implied license from the homeowner to come onto the property. A police officer and her drug-sniffing dog have no such license from the homeowner to wander around on the porch looking for incriminating evidence. Thus, a police officer bringing a drug-sniffing dog onto the porch to sniff for drugs is physically trespassing.

The reasonable expectation of privacy test is the more commonly used approach for determining whether there has been a search. But you also must consider the physical trespass test. If the police action invades a reasonable expectation of privacy *or* if it amounts to a physical trespass, the police have conducted a search.

The cases outlined above are the most high-profile questions about whether there has been a search. Your professor might cleverly dream up a different set of facts that has never been evaluated by the Supreme Court. So it is important not just to understand the outcomes of the cases discussed above, but also the key principles that underlie them.

Finally, if you've made it this far you've probably noticed that there are some inconsistencies here. Police can trespass in open fields, but not on the front porch. It violates a reasonable expectation of privacy for police to ignore airspace laws and fly too low, but it does not violate a reasonable expectation of privacy to rummage through garbage on the curb (which almost certainly violates some civil rule or regulation in most towns). Unfortunately, the Supreme Court has made a mess of this area of law and we have to live with the inconsistencies. On an essay question, you can use the inconsistencies to your advantage by arguing both sides: "on the one hand, on the other hand."

EXAM TRAPS TO AVOID

- The facts of any Supreme Court decision can be altered slightly in a way that could change the outcome. For instance, in *Kyllo v. United States* (2001), the Supreme Court held that pointing a thermal imaging device at a home was a search because it provided intimate information about the inside of a home by using a device not in general public use. More than two decades later, thermal imaging devices are much cheaper. If your exam question says a thermal imaging device can now be purchased at Target or Wal-Mart for $100, it might now be in general public use and therefore its use might no longer be a search. Or if the officer aimed the thermal imaging device at a barn rather than a home, it might not be giving intimate details and therefore no longer be a search. Do *not* assume that just because your exam question looks mostly like a Supreme Court case you studied that the answer on the exam has to be identical to the Supreme Court case.
    - Example: While aerial surveillance in lawful airspace is not a search, the outcome might be different if the plane or helicopter was flying lower than legally permitted.
    - Example: While police looking through garbage left at the curb is not normally a search, the outcome might be different if the homeowner put up barriers to prevent the public from accessing the garbage.

- The *Katz* reasonable expectation of privacy test and the physical trespass test are two different ways in which courts can find a police action to be a search. This is an "or" situation, not an "and" situation. If one of the tests is implicated, that is enough. You do not need to find both a reasonable expectation of privacy and a physical trespass to conclude that there was a search.

MULTIPLE-CHOICE QUESTIONS

Question 4

Police believe that Max and Spencer were involved in a criminal conspiracy to shake down local businesses. The police believe that Max and Spencer threatened the businesses with property damage (and the owners with personal injury) unless they paid them $200 a week. Police arrest Max and tell him they will charge him with several crimes. Max agrees to wear a wire in exchange for having the charges against him dropped. The goal of wearing a wire is to record Spencer admitting to criminal activity. The next day, Max goes to Spencer's house and Spencer invites him inside. Max then starts to talk about which business they will threaten next. Spencer makes incriminating statements. The police arrest Spencer and he moves to suppress the statements as the product of an illegal search. What result?

A) The statements should be suppressed because the agents effectively entered Spencer's house without a warrant.

B) The statements violate the Fourth Amendment because the police did not get a wiretap authorization from a court before recording Spencer.

C) The statements are not a Fourth Amendment violation because they fall under the third party doctrine.

D) The statements are not a search because Spencer does not have a subjective expectation of privacy.

Question 5

Police are investigating Larissa for money laundering and other financial fraud. Larissa runs several seemingly legitimate businesses. The officers are confident that she is reporting far more money from those businesses than would be possible. Accordingly, they are pretty sure that she is making money illegally somehow and then taking the cash to the seemingly legitimate businesses to launder it. To find out where she is coming from and going to, the officers hatched a plan. They put an undercover officer in a highway toll booth near where Larissa usually exits the highway. When Larissa drove through the toll booth and paid the toll, the undercover officer took a GPS tracker and dropped it onto the roof of Larissa's car without her noticing. Thereafter, the officers only had to monitor the tracker for less than an hour before it led them to the location where Larissa was running an illegal drug operation. Larissa claims that the police conducted an illegal search. Is she correct?

A) No, this could not have been a search because the officer never touched her vehicle.

B) No, this could not have been a search because Larissa interacted with an undercover officer and thus did not know that she was dealing with the police.

C) No, this could not have been a search because the police only monitored the GPS tracker for less than an hour.

D) Yes, this was a search because the police physically trespassed on Larissa's property.

E) Yes, this was a search because Larissa had a reasonable expectation of privacy that no one would follow her car while she was driving.

Question 6

Jill has invented a new smartphone app that she calls "Braeburn." The popular Braeburn app enables the user to continuously track the location of any person based on their phone number. The Braeburn app will tell you, with an accuracy of about 10 feet, exactly where the phone is located. Last week, police downloaded the Braeburn app and used it to track Dani, whom they had reasonable suspicion to believe was a drug courier. With the help of the Braeburn app, police trailed Dani to the apartment of a local drug dealer named Sven. While Dani was in Sven's apartment for 90 minutes, police got a warrant. They entered the apartment and eventually arrested Dani and Sven. If Dani challenges her arrest, which of the following would be correct?

I. The police have engaged in a physical trespass and therefore conducted a search under *United States v. Jones.*

II. The police may have engaged in a search under the *Katz* test.

III. The police have not engaged in a search because the physical trespass test has replaced the *Katz* test for cases of long-term monitoring under *United States v. Jones.*

IV. The police have not engaged in a search because Braeburn was designed by a private entrepreneur and thus there is no state action.

A) I only.

B) II only.

C) I and II only.

D) III only.

E) IV only.

Question 7

The FBI has been investigating Jonathan for possible terrorist activities. In particular, the FBI fears that Jonathan, a disgruntled physicist who was recently fired from NASA, may be trying to enrich uranium to build a bomb. The FBI has tried to investigate further, but they have been unsuccessful. Jonathan refuses to cooperate and has erected a 10-foot fence around his property, thus preventing the agents from getting a look at what is going on. Without first procuring a warrant, the FBI agents rent a plane and fly over Jonathan's backyard in navigable airspace at a height of 2,000 feet. Using a smartphone camera, the agents photograph the backyard and take pictures of large marijuana plants, which are illegal under federal law. Based on the photos, the agents procure a warrant to search Jonathan's house for drugs. Inside the house, the agents find in plain view evidence linking Jonathan to a terrorist organization. Jonathan is prosecuted for providing material support to terrorists. Which of the following is correct?

A) The terrorism evidence inside Jonathan's house must be suppressed because the airplane flyover was a search without probable cause.

B) The terrorism evidence inside Jonathan's house must be suppressed because the search for drugs was pretextual (as demonstrated by the fact that there was no subsequent prosecution for the marijuana plants), and the agents cannot execute a warrant based on a pretextual desire to find evidence not listed in the warrant.

C) The terrorism evidence inside Jonathan's house should be admitted because the airplane flyover was not a search and therefore the subsequent warrant was not tainted.

D) The terrorism evidence inside Jonathan's house should be admitted because even though the airplane flyover was a search without probable cause, the public safety exception excuses the lack of probable cause due to the enormous danger posed by enriched uranium.

Question 8

Assume the same facts as Question 7 above. For purposes of this question, though, imagine that the FBI agents could not see much at 2,000 feet in the air because of bad visibility. As such, the agents lowered the plane to 1,000 feet. The pilot said it was safe to fly at that height, though he recognized it violated civil airspace rules to take the plane below 1,200 feet in that location. By using binoculars, the officers were able to see the marijuana growing and subsequently procured a search warrant that led to the police finding incriminating evidence. Should the evidence be suppressed?

A) Yes, because the plane violated the airspace rules, which means the agents conducted an unlawful search during the flyover.

B) Yes, because the agents had to use binoculars to see the marijuana. Binoculars are sense-enhancing technology and therefore their use constitutes a search.

C) No, because although the plane violated the navigable airspace rules, those are civil regulations, not criminal laws.

D) No, because the pilot flew the plane at a safe altitude and thus the agents behaved reasonably.

Question 9

Mallory and Alan began dating a few years ago and recently got engaged. Mallory and Alan have a lot in common, including a love of horror films, romantic comedies, and cocaine. During the workweek, Mallory would often send Alan emails about plans for the weekend. These messages were usually lists of possible films to go to, movie times, and excerpts from movie reviews. Occasionally, Mallory would send an email that discussed where they might get some cocaine after the movie. Last week, Alan was arrested for breaking and entering. Realistically, Alan faced only a couple of weeks in jail if convicted, but because he had plans to apply to law school, he was very concerned that a conviction would destroy his chances of being admitted. Prosecutors offered to drop the charges if he produced evidence of someone committing a more serious crime. Reluctantly, Alan gave prosecutors the emails from Mallory about her cocaine purchases. Police arrested Mallory for cocaine possession and she currently faces up to two years in prison. Mallory has moved to suppress the email messages. What result?

A) Prosecutors should be allowed to use the email messages because she made them available to a third party and thus ran the risk of them becoming publicly available.

B) Prosecutors should be allowed to use the email messages because a person never has a reasonable expectation of privacy in written materials.

C) Prosecutors should not be allowed to use the email messages because she clearly intended to keep them private and she maintains a reasonable expectation of privacy because they were only disclosed to one other person.

D) Prosecutors should not be allowed to use the email messages because even though a person ordinarily waives their expectation of privacy by turning information over to a third party, in this case the third party was her fiancé, which created an added expectation of privacy.

Question 10

Police have received a tip that there is a heroin ring operating out of a local grocery store. They also see a lot of suspicious activity in the parking lot, which further heightens their suspicions. The officers do not know if it is the employees or people posing as customers who are dealing drugs. To gather more information, one officer brings his trained, drug-sniffing dog to the grocery store. The officer walks the dog through the dairy aisle and it sniffs numerous shoppers as they are picking up their milk. When Elsa walks past, the dog sits down in front of her, which is a signal that she has drugs on her. The officers ask Elsa if she is involved in the heroin distribution and she blurts out "I don't sell the drugs, I was just here to buy a small bit." Elsa takes the heroin out of her pocket and hands it to the officer. Elsa later moves to suppress her incriminating statement and the drugs on the grounds that the use of the drug-sniffing dog was unconstitutional. What result?

A) The use of a drug-sniffing dog was a search because it invaded Elsa's reasonable expectation of privacy.

B) The use of a drug-sniffing dog was a search because it sniffed "numerous shoppers" without any individualized suspicion.

C) The use of a drug-sniffing dog can never amount to a search no matter where police bring the dog.

D) The use of a drug-sniffing dog was not a search here because it did not invade Elsa's reasonable expectation of privacy.

Question 11

Officer Chase is on patrol and drives past a house that raises his suspicions. The grass in front of the house has not been mowed for weeks and it seems that an unusual number of people are milling about in front of the house. After the people standing in front of the house leave, Officer Chase takes his drug-sniffing dog (Charlie) out of the police vehicle and walks Charlie up to the front porch of the house. Charlie walks around the porch and sniffs the ground. Charlie is trained to alert to drugs by sitting down. Charlie does not alert to drugs at this time. Officer Chase assumes his hunch was wrong and turns to walk back to his police car. Just then, the front door of the house opens. (The occupants didn't realize anyone was on the porch when they opened the door.) Charlie walked over to the front door and immediately sat down. Based on Charlie's alert, a magistrate later issued a search warrant for the house and police found cocaine. Which of the following is correct?

A) Because the occupants of the house opened the door, the cocaine is admissible because it falls under the plain smell doctrine.

B) The cocaine is admissible because no search warrant was necessary for use of the drug-sniffing dog.

C) The cocaine is inadmissible because Officer Chase and Charlie have committed a physical trespass to property.

D) The cocaine is inadmissible because a person cannot have a reasonable expectation of privacy in the porch since mail carriers, salespeople, delivery drivers, and various other people regularly walk onto the porch.

Question 12

Police have been investigating a string of small-time burglaries. The officers believe they have probable cause to link Hank to the burglaries. The officers conduct surveillance of Hank's residence, and they are confident that he is not aware of their surveillance. After Hank leaves for work, the officers decide to have a look around Hank's property. The officers walk into the backyard, which is enclosed by a fence and has a couple of trees, some patio furniture, and a windowless tool shed. The officers are immediately interested in the tool shed. They walk back to it and see that the door is unlocked and slightly ajar. The officers stick their heads in the open tool shed door and crane their necks to see what is inside. Inside they see numerous items that were taken during the burglaries. Hank moves to suppress the items in the tool shed. How should the court rule?

A) The court should suppress the items in the tool shed because while the officers were allowed to look in the backyard and walk toward the shed, they were not permitted to stick their heads inside.

B) The court should suppress the items in the tool shed because the officers searched in the curtilage without a warrant.

C) The court should admit the evidence because the tool shed was in an open field and thus the police did not search.

D) The court should admit the evidence because the door of the tool shed was ajar and thus the police did not have to conduct a search to see what was inside.

Question 13

Police are investigating a different set of burglaries. Their primary suspect is Allison, who is known as the smartest person in town. Allison lives on a 90-acre ranch and the officers figure that no one as smart as Allison would keep stolen property in her house when she could hide it elsewhere. In the late afternoon, police drive to Allison's ranch. They walk up to a no trespassing sign that is about 200 yards away from Allison's house. The officers look at the sign and say, "Oh, forget this nonsense," and then walk past the sign. The officers keep walking for about a mile through undeveloped land. After walking a mile without seeing any crops, the officers get to an area where crops are growing. The police find it strange that the crops would be so far away from anything else so they decide to look closely through the area. On the ground in the middle of the field of crops the officers find property stolen from the burglaries. Allison has moved to suppress the stolen property. How should the court rule?

A) The court should suppress the stolen property because the officers trespassed.

B) The court should suppress the stolen property because Allison had a reasonable expectation of privacy and the police searched without a warrant.

C) The court should suppress the stolen property because the officer's comment, "Oh, forget this nonsense," shows that he was aware he was violating the Fourth Amendment.

D) The court should admit the stolen property because although the police trespassed they were in an open field.

E) The court should admit the stolen property because the stolen property might have been visible from an airplane flying in navigable airspace.

Question 14

DEA agents have learned that drug couriers are using Amtrak trains to transport cocaine from Miami to New York City. When a train stops in Washington, D.C., for a one-hour break (so that passengers can get off and grab lunch) agents board the train. The agents walk through the train car and begin asking passengers if they have luggage in the overhead rack. Sam tells the agents, "My suitcase is the green one in back. You can look in it if you want." The agents find Sam's eagerness to volunteer his suitcase to be strange so they take him up on his offer to look through it. The officers see the green suitcase behind a red bag that belongs to another passenger. Without asking the owner of the red bag, the officers gently move it to the side so that they can reach Sam's green suitcase. As they move the red bag, a large brick of cocaine falls out of it. The police seize the cocaine, learn the bag belongs to Winston (who is sitting one row behind Sam), and arrest Winston. Which of the following is correct?

A) Police have conducted a search of Winston's bag because they moved it.

B) Police have conducted a search of Winston's bag because the contents came out.

C) Police have not conducted a search of Winston's bag because it is not objectively reasonable to believe your suitcase will never be touched or moved on public transportation.

D) Police have not conducted a search of Winston's bag because it was not possible for Winston to have a subjective expectation of privacy.

Question 15

Assume the same facts as Question 14. For purposes of this question, though, imagine that when police moved the red bag they were surprised by how heavy it was. One of the agents moved her fingers back and forth over the outside of the bag (using her forefinger and her thumb) to feel one of the objects inside. The officer recognized the object to be a handgun. Under federal law, a passenger may not carry a firearm on an Amtrak train. Prosecutors subsequently prosecute Winston for a firearms offense. Winston claims that the agents conducted an impermissible search. Did the agents search?

A) Yes, the agent searched because she manually manipulated the bag with her fingers.

B) Yes, the agent searched both when she moved the bag and when she manually manipulated the contours of the bag.

C) No, the agents did not conduct a search because Winston's bag was on a public train and no reasonable person can expect the bag won't be manipulated.

D) No, the agents did not conduct a search because they were only frisking the bag for weapons.

ANSWERS TO MULTIPLE-CHOICE QUESTIONS

Answer to Question 4

Answer A is incorrect. Although Max is working at the direction of law enforcement, he entered Spencer's house with Spencer's permission.

Answer B is incorrect. Police do not need a wiretap in this situation to comply with the Fourth Amendment.

Answer C is correct. By willingly sharing information, Spencer runs the risk that Max will share the information with law enforcement. The third party doctrine means that Spencer has no reasonable expectation of privacy in what he conveys to another. Max is a "false friend."

Answer D is incorrect. Spencer likely believed that the things he told Max would be kept private. He therefore probably does have a subjective expectation of privacy. But that is not the only part of the test. Spencer's expectation must also be objectively reasonable. And because of the third party doctrine, his expectation is not reasonable in this situation.

Answer to Question 5

Answer A is incorrect. It is factually true that the officer did not touch the vehicle. But that is not the relevant inquiry. The police attached a device to the vehicle. In *United States v. Jones* (2010), the Supreme Court held that attaching a tracking device is a physical trespass and a search.

Answer B is incorrect. Larissa does not have to know she is dealing with the police for it to be a search. The question is whether the police officers invaded a reasonable expectation of privacy or whether they physically trespassed, not whether they were wearing their uniform when they did so.

Answer C is incorrect. The key point is that the police physically trespassed on Larissa's vehicle. The fact that it took less than an hour to find what they were looking for does not eliminate the physical trespass.

Answer D is correct. The police officer physically trespassed on Larissa's vehicle when she dropped the GPS tracker onto the vehicle. That physical trespass is a search.

Answer E is incorrect. Larissa does not have a reasonable expectation of privacy that she will not be followed when she is driving out in the open on public roads. Because her movements are exposed to the public, Larissa cannot reasonably expect that they are private. Larissa has still been subjected to a search, but it is because she was subjected to a physical trespass, not because her reasonable expectation of privacy was violated.

Answer to Question 6

Answer A is incorrect. The officers did not engage in a physical trespass because they never accessed private property without a license to do so. The police did not install the app on Dani's phone. They installed it on their own phone.

Answer B is correct. It is possible that the officers violated Dani's reasonable expectation of privacy. Dani likely has a subjective expectation of privacy that she will not be tracked. However, is that expectation reasonable if the app is widely used by the public? The question says the app is "popular." On the other hand, the *Carpenter* decision said the third party doctrine is not appropriate when it permits detailed surveillance of a person's location over a long period. In short, it is unclear whether using the Braeburn app is a search, thus making this the best answer choice.

Answer C is incorrect. As noted in the explanation above, the officers did not engage in a physical trespass to Dani's property. Accordingly, numeral I cannot be correct and by implication Answer C is incorrect.

Answer D is incorrect. The physical trespass test has not replaced the *Katz* reasonable expectation of privacy test. The Supreme Court utilizes both tests.

Answer E is incorrect. It is true that a private company designed the app. But that does not mean the police do not search when they use it. Private companies design thermal imaging devices, airplanes, and various other items that the police might use to conduct surveillance. Police actions are not exempted from being a search simply because the police did not build the device.

Answer to Question 7

Answer A is incorrect. The Supreme Court has held that flying a plane or helicopter within navigable airspace to collect evidence is not a search.

Answer B is incorrect. The FBI's motives for conducting the search for drugs in the house are not controlling. If the officers had a valid warrant (which it appears they did) then the search will be valid irrespective of what they hoped to find.

Answer C is correct. The Supreme Court has held that when a plane or helicopter is in navigable airspace, the government does not conduct a search. Here the question tells us that the plane was flying at 2,000 feet in "navigable airspace." Accordingly, the evidence gathered from the plane could be used to obtain a valid search warrant.

Answer D is incorrect. First, the airplane flyover was not a search. Second, there is no public safety exception to the Fourth Amendment. There is an exigent circumstances exception, but the FBI would still need to have probable cause in order to claim exigent circumstances. This answer choice says there is no probable cause, however.

Answer to Question 8

Answer A is correct. The Supreme Court has held that it is not a search when police gather evidence from an airplane flyover if they are in navigable airspace. Here the plane was well below navigable airspace. It is therefore likely a search.

Answer B is incorrect: The binoculars improved the agents' view, but that does not mean they engaged in a search. Binoculars are in general public use; they can be bought in many stores and millions of people have them. Accordingly, individuals have no reasonable expectation of privacy not to be viewed with binoculars.

Answer C is incorrect. In focusing on whether a plane was in navigable airspace the Court never required that the airspace rules be criminal rules, as opposed to civil regulations. Indeed, the Supreme Court regularly looks to sources other than the criminal law to determine whether a person has a reasonable expectation of privacy. For example, in *Katz* itself, the Court noted that when a person puts a quarter in a phone booth and closes the door they "pay the toll," giving them privacy. Courts look to societal expectations like that, not just criminal laws, to determine if an expectation of privacy is reasonable.

Answer D is incorrect. The key question is not whether the agents were at a safe altitude for themselves in the plane, but whether they invaded the homeowner's reasonable expectation of privacy.

Answer to Question 9

Answer A is correct. When Mallory emailed the information about the cocaine to Alan she made it available to a third party. When a person exposes information to a third party (with the exception of cell phone location data) they no longer have a reasonable expectation of privacy in it.

Answer B is incorrect. If Mallory wrote notes in her personal diary, for example, and never provided that information to a third party, she would have a reasonable expectation of privacy. Written information that is not exposed to the public is protected by the Fourth Amendment.

Answer C is incorrect. While Mallory has a subjective expectation of privacy, it is not one that society is prepared to recognize as reasonable. When you communicate information to a third party, you run the risk that they will turn that information over to law enforcement.

Answer D is incorrect. The fact that Mallory and Alan were engaged does not change the third party doctrine. Mallory still made information available to a third party and ran the risk that he would turn it over to law enforcement. Just because two people are engaged does not mean that one person will not sell the other out to the police for their own personal benefit.

Answer to Question 10

Answer A is incorrect. Drug-sniffing dogs smell only contraband. The dog then either alerts that there are illegal drugs or does not alert. The police therefore do not discover private information about a person that a person reasonably expects to keep private. Thus, the dog sniff—by itself—does not invade a reasonable expectation of privacy. Moreover, in this case, Elsa is in a public location and does not have a reasonable expectation of privacy in the place where she is located.

Answer B is incorrect. The use of a drug-sniffing dog does not become a search simply because the dog sniffs many people. Drug-sniffing dogs in airports often sniff many people and things. This does not create a reasonable expectation of privacy for any one person.

Answer C is incorrect. This answer choice is too broad. While people do not have Fourth Amendment protection with respect to the use of a drug dog in public areas, they do have a Fourth Amendment protection with respect to other areas. For instance, police cannot simply bring a drug-sniffing dog onto the porch of a person's home.

Answer D is correct. A drug-sniffing dog only gathers information about the smell of illegal drugs. The dog is not gathering private information in which a person has a reasonable expectation of privacy. As such, Elsa does not have a reasonable expectation of privacy not to have the dog sniff near her in a public location.

Answer to Question 11

Answer A is incorrect. While it is true that the house door was open, the drug-sniffing dog did not smell the cocaine from the street. The dog was able to alert because it was on the porch. For the plain smell doctrine to be applicable, the dog must be lawfully present to begin with. Here, Officer Chase and the drug dog were trespassing on the porch.

Answer B is incorrect. Police do not need a search warrant to use a drug-sniffing dog in some situations. Police can walk a drug dog around luggage in the airport or around a car that is lawfully stopped. But this situation is different. The Supreme Court has held that walking a drug-sniffing dog onto the porch of a house without being invited there amounts to a trespass.

Answer C is correct. The facts of this case are nearly identical to *Florida v. Jardines* (2013), in which the Court held that bringing a drug-sniffing dog onto the porch of a house amounts to a physical trespass and is therefore a search.

Answer D is incorrect. It is true that lots of people walk up to the front door of houses every day, including delivery drivers and mail carriers. The Supreme Court distinguished these people on the grounds that they are invited licensees. By contrast, the homeowner never extended a license—either express or implied—for the police to bring a drug-sniffing dog onto their private property.

Answer to Question 12

Answer A is incorrect. The officers did not have the right to walk into the backyard and walk toward the shed. The backyard is inside the fence and therefore appears to be within the curtilage of the house. Walking in the backyard and walking to the shed is a search. Because the police have searched in the curtilage of the house without a warrant (and without an exigency because Hank was "not aware of their surveillance"), the police have conducted a search.

Answer B is correct. The tool shed is likely within the curtilage of the house. The shed is inside of the fence. And the description of the backyard makes it sound like a normal-sized backyard. By searching in the curtilage without a warrant or exigent circumstances (because Hank was "not aware of their surveillance"), the police have violated the Fourth Amendment.

Answer C is incorrect. Hank's backyard does not appear to be an open field. It is a standard backyard (with a swing set and patio furniture), next to the house, and it is enclosed by a fence. This description strongly suggests the shed is in the curtilage, not an open field.

Answer D is incorrect. Even though the door is open, the police had to stick their heads inside the door in order to see what was inside. Entering the structure is therefore a search. Additionally, the police had already committed a Fourth Amendment violation by walking to the tool shed.

Answer to Question 13

Answer A is incorrect. It is true that the police officers trespassed, but they did so in an open field. Importantly, the question says that the no trespassing sign was 200 yards from the house. Moreover, the officers walked for a mile to get to the area where they found the evidence. These large distances signal that the question is about an open field, not curtilage. Accordingly, the fact that the officers trespassed does not make this situation a search.

Answer B is incorrect. Allison would have a hard time arguing that she has a reasonable expectation of privacy in an area that is a mile from her home where crops are grown. The fact that the officers had to walk through undeveloped land to get to this spot furthers the conclusion that Allison lacks a reasonable expectation of privacy. Finally, note that there is no structure at this location—no house, not even a barn or a shed.

Answer C is incorrect. The subjective intent of the officer is not relevant. Whether there is a Fourth Amendment violation in this circumstance turns on whether there is a search, not whether the officer believed he was doing something wrong.

Answer D is correct. As noted above, it is true that the police officers trespassed, but they did so in an open field. A number of facts in the question point to this being an open field, not the curtilage. First, the no trespassing sign where the officers entered the property was 200 yards from the house. That is two football fields away from the home—a long distance. Second, the officers walked for a mile to get to the area where they found the evidence. Third, the area that the police searched was undeveloped. There was no house, barn, or shed—or anything that could arguably be construed as an area that a person wanted to keep private from others. All of these facts suggest that the police entered an open field. Police do not conduct a search when they enter onto open fields.

Answer E is incorrect. That the police might have been able to see the stolen property from an airplane (which is unlikely given that it was on the ground surrounded by crops) is not relevant. We must assess what the police actually did, not what they could have done.

Answer to Question 14

Answer A is incorrect. The Supreme Court held in *Bond v. United States* (2000) that when police manipulate the contours of a bag they have conducted a search. The agents have not done that here. They have only "gently move[d] it to the side." The Supreme Court recognized that there was a difference between moving a bag (which is not a search) and manipulating the contours of the bag (which is a search). In *Bond*, the Supreme Court explained: "When a bus passenger places a bag in an overhead bin, he expects that other passengers or bus employees may move it for one reason or another. Thus, a bus passenger clearly expects that his bag may be handled. He does not expect that other passengers or bus employees will, as a matter of course, feel the bag in an exploratory manner."

Answer B is incorrect. The fact that something fell out of the bag does not, by itself, make these events a search. Whether something is a search turns on the actions of the police officers, not what happened to the contents of the bag.

Answer C is correct. As explained above in response to Answer A, the Supreme Court recognized that a passenger cannot have a reasonable expectation of privacy in this situation because "[w]hen a bus passenger places a bag in an overhead bin, he expects that other passengers or bus employees may move it for one reason or another. Thus, a bus passenger clearly expects that his bag may be handled." Accordingly, it could not have been objectively reasonable for Winston to believe his bag would not be touched or moved.

Answer D is incorrect. A passenger can have a subjective expectation of privacy if they personally wished for the item to remain private. By putting his belongings in an opaque bag, Winston likely expected them to remain private. While Winston had a subjective expectation of privacy, his expectation was not objectively reasonable.

Answer to Question 15

Answer A is correct. The Supreme Court held in *Bond v. United States* (2000) that manually manipulating the contents of a suitcase (even from the outside) is a search.

Answer B is incorrect. While manually manipulating a suitcase is a search, the Court observed in *Bond v. United States* (2000) that simply moving a suitcase on public transportation is not a search.

Answer C is incorrect. The Supreme Court has held the opposite. Passengers, even on public transportation, can have a reasonable expectation of privacy that officers and other passengers won't manipulate their luggage by feeling it in detail with their fingers.

Answer D is incorrect. First, it does not appear that the agent was simply frisking the luggage. Rather, the agent was manipulating the bag with her finger to figure out what was inside. As we will explore in Chapter 15, this action goes beyond a frisk. Moreover, a frisk is still a search (albeit a less invasive one).

STEP 3
Was There a Seizure?

Chapter 3: Voluntary Encounters versus Detentions versus Arrests

The Fourth Amendment forbids unreasonable searches *and seizures.* We must therefore determine whether a seizure occurred. If there was a seizure, we then must determine what kind of seizure it was.

Chapter 3 sets out three situations: voluntary encounters, detentions (*Terry* stops), and arrests. Voluntary encounters are not seizures under the Fourth Amendment and therefore the police do not have to point to any suspicion to justify them. *Terry* stops are limited detentions that require reasonable suspicion. Arrests are full-scale seizures that require probable cause. Chapter 3 explains how to identify the differences between voluntary encounters, *Terry* stops, and arrests.

If you conclude that there has only been a voluntary encounter, you have no more work to do. The police action is lawful.

If you conclude that the police have conducted a *Terry* stop, you will need to determine whether the officers had reasonable suspicion. Chapter 14 reviews *Terry* stops and reasonable suspicion in detail.

If you conclude that the police have conducted an arrest, you must analyze whether the officers had probable cause. Chapter 4 reviews the probable cause standard in detail.

CHAPTER 3

Voluntary Encounters versus Detentions versus Arrests

THE RULE: Not every interaction with the police is governed by the Fourth Amendment. If you have a "voluntary encounter" with the police, that is not a seizure and therefore the police do not need to demonstrate any suspicion. If the police go further and do conduct a seizure, it could be either a detention (a *Terry* stop) or an arrest. Detentions require reasonable suspicion. Arrests require probable cause.

Critical Points

- This Chapter Will Help You Determine the Differences Between:
  - Voluntary encounters, which require no suspicion;
  - Detentions (*Terry* stops), which require reasonable suspicion; and
  - Arrests, which require probable cause.
- Voluntary Encounters
  - People engage in voluntary encounters with the police thousands of times per day in the United States. Voluntary encounters are not seizures and therefore are not covered by the Fourth Amendment.
  - Voluntary encounters can involve police asking questions about criminal activity, such as "We see you are flying to a known drug city. Can we search your luggage?"
  - Standard: If a reasonable person would feel free to leave the situation, it is a voluntary encounter, not a seizure.
  - No Suspicion: Police do not need any suspicion to talk with a person during a voluntary encounter.

- *Terry* Stops (Also Called "Detentions")
  - A *Terry* stop is a limited detention. A person who has been detained is not free to leave. She has been seized.
  - *Terry* stops occur in various situations:
  - Traffic stops are *Terry* stops.
  - An officer detaining a person on the street and preventing them from leaving is a *Terry* stop.
  - An officer using physical force to stop a person is a *Terry* stop.
  - An officer verbally ordering a person to stop is also a *Terry* stop if the person in fact stops.
  - Standard: To conduct a *Terry* stop, the police need reasonable suspicion—a standard less than probable cause—that criminal activity has happened, is currently happening, or is about to happen.
  - *Distinguishing between voluntary encounters and* Terry *stops*: The following factors make it more likely that the police have conducted a *Terry* stop, as opposed to a voluntary encounter:
    - Several officers are present.
    - An officer has brandished (i.e., shown) a weapon.
    - An officer has physically touched the individual.
    - An officer has used intimidating language or a loud tone of voice.
    - The individual has asked to leave and the officer has said "no."
    - (*Terry* stops are explored in more detail in Chapter 14.)
- Arrests
  - An arrest is a full-scale seizure.
  - Standard: Police must have probable cause to make an arrest.
  - Distinguishing between *Terry* stops and arrests: The following factors make it more likely that the police have made an arrest, as opposed to a *Terry* stop:
    - Moving the person from where they were stopped to a new location.
    - Handcuffing the person.
    - Pointing a gun at the person.
    - Locking the person in the back of a police car.
    - Refusing to let the person leave for a long time.
  - The police do *not* have to specifically say "You're under arrest" in order for it to qualify as an arrest.

- The police do not need any suspicion to conduct a voluntary encounter, but the person is free to leave their interaction with the police at any time.
- The police need reasonable suspicion of criminal activity to conduct a *Terry* stop. The person is not free to leave, but their liberty is not as restricted as it would be for a full arrest.
- The police need probable cause to make an arrest.

OVERVIEW OF THE BLACKLETTER LAW

Courts are frequently called on to decide if police had enough reasonable suspicion to stop and frisk someone or whether they had enough probable cause to conduct an arrest. In Chapter 4 we will explore probable cause. And in Chapters 14 and 15 we will analyze when reasonable suspicion exists to stop and frisk individuals.

Before getting to whether the reasonable suspicion or probable cause standards are satisfied, we must first figure out whether a person has been seized. And if they have been seized, whether it is a *Terry* stop or a full-scale arrest. Accordingly, we need to understand the differences between voluntary encounters (which require no suspicion), *Terry* stops (which require reasonable suspicion), and arrests (which require probable cause). In short, how do we tell the differences between each of these? Unfortunately, courts have to make case-by-case determinations. And your criminal procedure exam will likely require you to do the same. Here are some basic guideposts.

A voluntary encounter with the police occurs when a reasonable person would feel free to leave. If police walk up to a person in a public place and begin to talk to them—even to ask pointed questions—that situation is probably a voluntary encounter. Indeed, if a pair of officers walk up to a person and start to quiz them about where they are going and whether they have drugs in their bag, that is also a voluntary encounter. If the police officer then asks for consent to search the person's backpack, that is still probably a voluntary encounter. The reason is that courts—perhaps unrealistically—expect that a reasonable person would feel free to say to the police "I don't want to talk with you any longer," or "No, I do not give you consent to search my bag." The Supreme Court believes that a person who is dealing with the police out in the open would feel free to simply walk away from them.

So when does an encounter cease to be voluntary and instead become a detention—what we call a *Terry* stop? First, imagine situations in which we are certain that a person would not be free to leave. We all know that when a police officer turns on her sirens and lights and signals for a driver to pull over that the driver cannot simply ignore the officer. When an officer pulls you over and asks for your license and registration, you cannot simply drive away. A traffic stop is thus very clearly not a voluntary encounter, but it also does not rise to the level of an arrest. The driver is not handcuffed or locked in the back of a police car. And traffic stops are usually pretty brief. The driver's liberty is only somewhat restricted. A traffic stop is therefore a detention—a *Terry* stop.

Another easy *Terry* stop case is one in which the officer physically stops a person from moving, or orders a person to stop moving and the person complies. In these cases, a person obviously would not feel free to leave because a police officer's hands are on them, or because they stopped moving when an officer told them to do so.

There are also hard cases in which it is debatable whether the person was subject to a *Terry* stop or whether it was just a voluntary encounter. It is more likely to be a *Terry* stop if more than three officers are present, an officer has brandished a weapon, an officer has physically touched the individual, an officer has used intimidating language or a loud tone of voice, or the individual has asked to leave and been told no.

The next (sometimes difficult) question is whether the police have conducted a *Terry* stop or an arrest. Obviously, when police announce "You're under arrest" and take the person into custody we know that the individual has been arrested and that the police must have probable cause rather than the lower reasonable suspicion standard. But how do you determine whether it is a *Terry* stop or an arrest if the exam question does not explicitly say it? The answer is to look for facts that show whether a person's liberty has been restrained to an extent consistent with an arrest. The following facts make it more likely that the police have made an arrest rather than a *Terry* stop: handcuffing the individual, taking the individual to the police station, moving the individual from where they were stopped to a different location, pointing a gun at the individual, locking the individual in the back of a police car, or refusing to let the individual leave for a long time. The more of these factors that are present, the more certain it becomes that the police have made an arrest and that they need probable cause to justify it.

EXAM TRAPS TO AVOID

- Just because police have approached a person and are asking them uncomfortable questions about criminal activity does not mean the police need reasonable suspicion or probable cause. It may be a voluntary encounter that does not require any suspicion.
- Just because police have detained a person at a traffic stop does not mean they need probable cause. A traffic stop is usually a *Terry* stop requiring only reasonable suspicion.
- Just because the police never said "You're under arrest" does not mean the situation is not the functional equivalent of an arrest, thus requiring probable cause.

MULTIPLE-CHOICE QUESTIONS

Question 16

Tricia recently got her driver's license. She is an honors student finishing up high school and was on her way home from school, traveling at the speed limit. Police turn on their siren and pull her over. When the officer comes to her window, Tricia asks, "Did I do anything wrong?" and the officer responds, "No. We wanted to reward you for doing an excellent job as a new driver. We're doing a new program sponsored by local businesses. Today, Jimmy's Famous Cookies is giving out free cookies to the first 10 people we see doing an excellent job driving. Here is your prize." The officer hands Tricia a box of cookies and tells her to keep up the good work. This entire series of events took less than two minutes. How would you describe this situation?

A) This a is a voluntary encounter because it is for a friendly purpose and thus requires no suspicion.

B) This is a voluntary encounter because it is extremely brief and thus requires no suspicion.

C) This is a *Terry* stop requiring reasonable suspicion.

D) This is the functional equivalent of an arrest requiring probable cause.

Question 17

Police see Danilo driving across lanes of traffic and suspect that he is driving drunk. The officers pull him over and smell alcohol on him. The officers handcuff him and place him in the back of the police car. When he is first placed in the police car, Danilo says, "I haven't done anything wrong. You can't arrest me." The officer responds, "We're not arresting you, calm down." The officers call to other officers who have a portable Breathalyzer in their patrol car. Those officers arrive about two hours later and ask Danilo to take the Breathalyzer test. Danilo blows a .01, well below the legal limit. Danilo says, "I've been trying to tell you, I just had some mouthwash because I was about to go on a date. I haven't had any alcohol." The officers then notice a bottle of mouthwash in the back of the car. Knowing that mouthwash can sometimes smell like alcohol, they decide to let Danilo go. Which of the following is correct?

A) Danilo has been subjected to a *Terry* stop because he was not free to leave.

B) Danilo has been subjected to a *Terry* stop, rather than an arrest, but only if the officers subjectively believed that they were not arresting him.

C) Danilo has not been subjected to arrest because the officer specifically told him he was not under arrest.

D) Danilo has been subjected to an arrest because his liberty has been restricted consistent with an arrest.

E) Danilo has been subject to an arrest because he was forced to take a Breathalyzer test.

Question 18

Caden is on a Greyhound bus traveling from Florida to Maine. The bus stops in Washington, D.C., to let the passengers take a one-hour lunch break. The passengers get off the bus around noon and are told to be back on by 1:00 p.m. At 12:45 p.m., three officers board the bus. Two of the officers stand near the back of the bus. The other officer walks down the aisle, stopping to talk to passengers. The officer asks each passenger where they are going. The officer also explains that Greyhound buses are often used to transport drugs from Florida to the rest of the country. The officer asks each of the passengers whether they were carrying any illegal drugs. When the officer gets to Caden, the officer asks where Caden is going and whether he is carrying any drugs. Caden answers "No," but his hands are shaking and he seems very nervous. The officer says, "Great, can I search your bag just to be sure you are telling the truth?" Caden doesn't want the officer to look through his bag, but he consents to the search. The officer finds heroin inside and arrests Caden. Which of the following is correct?

A) The court should suppress the evidence because the officers engaged in a *Terry* stop without reasonable suspicion.

B) The court should admit the evidence because Caden voluntarily spoke to the officers and consented to a search of his bag.

ANSWERS TO MULTIPLE-CHOICE QUESTIONS

Answer to Question 16

Answer A is incorrect. The officer turned on a siren and pulled Tricia over. For it to be a voluntary encounter, a reasonable person in Tricia's situation would have had to feel free to leave. When police activate their siren and instruct people to pull over, reasonable people do not simply drive away.

Answer B is incorrect. A *Terry* stop can be very brief. In separating a voluntary encounter from a *Terry* stop, the determinative factor is not how many minutes the event lasts, but instead whether a reasonable person would feel free to leave.

Answer C is correct. The officer has pulled Tricia over. Although the police have conducted a stop for a nice reason, that does not change the fact that they have detained Tricia. When the officers turned on their sirens and signaled for her to pull over, they detained her.

Answer D is incorrect. Traffic stops are ordinarily *Terry* stops, not arrests. That is true in this case. A reasonable person in Tricia's position would not feel free to leave, which is the standard for a *Terry* stop. For the situation to rise to the level of an arrest, we would have to see things like handcuffs, pointing a gun, locking Tricia in the back of a police car, or a detention that went on for a long time. None of those is present here.

Answer to Question 17

Answer A is incorrect. This situation exceeds a *Terry* stop and is much more akin to an arrest. Danilo is handcuffed in the back of a police car for "about two hours."

Answer B is incorrect. The subjective belief of a police officer is irrelevant. We determine whether a seizure is an arrest or a *Terry* stop by looking objectively at the facts of the situation, not what the police officer believed.

Answer C is incorrect. What the officer told Danilo is not controlling. Given that Danilo is handcuffed and locked in the back of a police car for about two hours, this looks like an arrest.

Answer D is correct. Danilo is handcuffed and has been locked in the back of a police car for "about two hours." This looks very much like an arrest.

Answer E is incorrect. According to the facts, Danilo was not forced to take the Breathalyzer test; he was "asked" to take it. Moreover, encouraging someone to take a Breathalyzer test would not automatically transform a situation from a *Terry* stop into an arrest.

Answer to Question 18

Answer A is incorrect. The officers did not engage in a *Terry* stop. See *United States v. Drayton* (2002). According to a majority of the Supreme Court, a reasonable person in Caden's position would have felt free to leave.

Answer B is correct. According to the Supreme Court, this is a voluntary encounter. The police are free to walk up to people and ask them questions. According to the Supreme Court, a reasonable person in Caden's situation would have felt free to decline the officer's request for consent and to terminate the encounter.

STEP 4
Was There a Valid Warrant?

Chapter 4: Probable Cause
Chapter 5: Particularity
Chapter 6: The Knock and Announce Rule

Once we have concluded that there was a search or seizure, we must next determine whether it was reasonable. A search or seizure can be reasonable if there was a valid warrant.

To have a valid warrant, the police must have probable cause. Chapter 4 explains the ways in which police can demonstrate probable cause.

In addition to probable cause, a warrant must particularly describe the places to be searched and the items to be seized. Chapter 5 explains the particularity doctrine and the common ways in which warrants fail the particularity requirement.

When police execute a warrant they usually (though not always) are obligated to knock and announce. Chapter 6 describes the knock-and-announce rule and the very broad exceptions to that rule.

CHAPTER 4
Probable Cause

THE RULE: To conduct an arrest and most full-scale searches, police must demonstrate probable cause. Probable cause is more than a hunch and more than the reasonable suspicion needed to stop and frisk, but it is less than a preponderance of the evidence.

Critical Points

- *When Needed*: Probable cause is necessary for:
  - Search warrants
  - Arrest warrants
  - Warrantless arrests
  - Warrantless searches based on exigent circumstances
  - Warrantless searches based on the automobile exception
  - Warrantless plain view seizures
  - Warrantless plain touch doctrine
- *Types of Evidence*: Probable cause can be based on information from officers, informants, and others. It can be based on hearsay, physical evidence, video recordings, police observations, and a wide variety of other sources.
- *Level of Suspicion*: Probable cause is more than a hunch and more than the reasonable suspicion needed for a brief stop or frisk. But it is far less than proof beyond a reasonable doubt or even a preponderance of the evidence.
- *Objective Standard*: It does not matter if the officers believe there is enough suspicion. Probable cause is determined from an objective standpoint by

asking whether a reasonable police officer would believe the circumstances create enough suspicion.

- *Common Testing Scenarios:*
  - *Informants and probable cause*: Courts judge whether an informant's tip can create probable cause by assessing: (A) the reliability of the informant and (B) the informant's basis of knowledge. Courts use a totality of the circumstances test. Thus, if one of the prongs is weak (e.g., we know little about the informant's reliability), it can be made up for if the other prong is strong (e.g., the informant has a strong basis of knowledge because she saw the crime occur).
  - *Drug-sniffing dogs*: When a trained drug dog alerts its handler that there are drugs in a vehicle, that alert can be sufficient—by itself—to create probable cause. Ordinarily, if the drug dog has been certified by a bona fide organization, courts will find the dog to be trustworthy. However, defendants can raise challenges to the certification or the dog's reliability in the field in an attempt to show the dog's alert cannot be considered trustworthy.
  - *Probable Cause to Search Can Become Stale*: Probable cause to search a location can become stale if the information is old. For example, a tip that contraband is in the back of a car might initially create probable cause to search the car, but if days pass it may no longer be reasonable for police to believe the stolen items are still in the car.
  - *Probable Cause to Arrest Does Not Become Stale*: When police have probable cause to arrest, they can ordinarily continue to rely on it days, weeks, or even months later.

OVERVIEW OF THE BLACKLETTER LAW

For many searches (though certainly not all) police must demonstrate probable cause. Police need probable cause to obtain a warrant—either a search warrant or an arrest warrant—and to conduct a warrantless arrest. Probable cause is also required for police to invoke some of the exceptions to the warrant requirement: exigency, automobile, plain view, and plain touch.

At the outset, it is important to put into perspective the amount of suspicion necessary to demonstrate probable cause. Probable cause is more than a hunch (which does not authorize any type of search or seizure). It is more than reasonable suspicion (which permits stops and frisks in some situations (see Chapters 14 and 15)). Probable cause is less than the preponderance of the evidence standard in civil cases, and it is far less than the beyond a reasonable doubt standard necessary to convict a defendant at trial.

The next thing to think about is how to demonstrate that probable cause exists. Probable cause is an amorphous concept. Whether there is probable cause is therefore heavily fact-dependent. With the exception of informants (discussed below), courts do not ordinarily have multifactor tests with specific legal questions that tell us whether there is probable cause. Rather, courts simply look at the facts presented by an officer and determine if the information is sufficiently trustworthy to lead a reasonable person to conclude that a suspect has committed a criminal offense (and can be arrested) or that a specific item will be found in the place to be searched (thus authorizing a search).

Although your law school course might have focused heavily on whether an informant's tip creates probable cause, it is important to recognize that many other situations can also give rise to probable cause. In the simplest case, police officers observe criminal activity with their own eyes and can easily demonstrate probable cause. Police might also develop probable cause based on paper records, video recordings, physical evidence (such as blood, hair, breath, or fingerprints), and numerous other types of evidence.

In your criminal procedure course, you likely devoted some time to studying whether an informant's tip can create probable cause. In part this is because police regularly utilize informants. Professors also discuss informants because it is one of the few areas in which there is a specific test for determining probable cause. The Supreme Court has long focused on two factors in determining whether a tip from an informant can create probable cause: (A) reliability; and (B) basis of knowledge.

An informant (including an anonymous informant) can be reliable if she has given correct information in the past. It is common in the real world (and on law school exams) to see a police officer say "This informant has given us three prior tips and all of them turned out to be correct." An informant can also be reliable if she is a credible member of the community. For instance, your criminal procedure professor is likely a member of the bar who is well-respected and has no incentive to lie. She is therefore reliable even if she has never given police information in the past.

The basis-of-knowledge prong focuses on how the informant knows the information he is providing to the police. The best basis of knowledge is when an informant has firsthand knowledge because he saw the events happen. But in some cases an informant can also have an adequate basis of knowledge if he learned about the incriminating information secondhand. Finally, sometimes the officers do not learn how an informant acquired the incriminating information. Courts will nevertheless find a basis of knowledge if the officers are able to verify some of the details from the informant's tip.

For many years, the Supreme Court used a fairly rigid test and required a minimum showing of reliability and basis of knowledge before an informant's tip could give rise to probable cause. In *Illinois v. Gates* (1983), however, the Supreme Court switched to a totality of the circumstances test that makes it easier for the government to demonstrate probable cause from an informant's tip. Basis of knowledge and reliability are still two important factors, but courts no longer have to analyze them as two independent factors. If one factor is weak, the other factor, if strong, can make up for it. For example, if an informant comes forward with highly detailed information that suggests a strong basis of knowledge and the police are able to confirm that information, the court can find probable cause even if there is little information about the informant's reliability.

Another frequent probable cause situation involves drug-sniffing dogs. When police have lawfully stopped a vehicle, they can walk a drug dog around the car so long as they do not prolong the detention. If the drug dog alerts to drugs—often by sitting down in front of a part of the car—the dog's alert can create probable cause for the police to search the vehicle. Thus, what started as a simple stop of a vehicle can turn into probable cause to search the vehicle under the automobile exception (See Chapter 10 for a discussion of the automobile exception). Defendants often move to suppress the evidence on the ground that the drug dog was not qualified or trustworthy enough to generate probable cause. The Supreme Court has held that the dog's trustworthiness can be established if it has been certified to identify drugs by a bona fide organization. Defendants are then free to try to challenge the certification by suggesting the organization's standards were too lax, or by pointing to evidence from the field that the dog is often wrong.

Although courts use the same probable cause standard for arrests and searches, there is one important distinction to remember. Probable cause to *search* can become stale if too much time goes by. Imagine that an informant tells police that drug dealers are running an open-air drug market in the courtyard of an apartment complex. The informant—who has been reliable six times in the past—says the main stash of drugs is being kept in apartment 1F. The officers wait three weeks before seeking a warrant, though. But drug dealers typically move stash houses frequently so that the police (and other drug gangs) will not find the stash of drugs. While the informant's tip might have created probable cause to search the apartment three weeks ago, that probable cause is now stale. By contrast, probable cause to *arrest* does not become stale. If the informant had told the police that he had seen a person selling drugs in the courtyard, the police would still have probable cause to arrest him three weeks later.

EXAM TRAPS TO AVOID

- Beware of an informant who has no basis of knowledge or absolutely no indicia of reliability. Those informants likely cannot create probable cause by themselves.
- Just because an informant has weak reliability/credibility, that does not mean their information cannot give rise to probable cause. Weak reliability can be made up for with a strong basis of knowledge, and vice versa.

- If a police officer observes a crime, that alone can create probable cause to search or arrest.
- Ignore the personal views of a police officer as to whether there is probable cause. Courts judge probable cause based on objective standards, not one officer's view.
- Just because there is probable cause to arrest a person does not necessarily mean there is probable cause to search a nearby location, and vice versa.
- Police do not need detailed data about a drug dog's prior performance to rely on a dog's alert to establish probable cause.

MULTIPLE-CHOICE QUESTIONS

Question 19

While on patrol, police officers observe Cathy handing a man what looks like a small bag with her left hand and then taking cash from the man with her right hand. The officers continue watching and 10 minutes later they see another man walk up to Cathy. The same events occur—Cathy hands the man a small bag with her left hand and takes cash with her right hand. Moments later, the officers surprise Cathy and take her into custody. After Cathy waives her *Miranda* rights, the officers ask Cathy what was in the plastic bags. Cathy says, "I confess I was dealing heroin. If you let me go though, I can give you the supplier. I get the drugs directly from him. His name is Joe. He meets me in his garage at 123 State Street. He hides the drugs in a bag of potting soil in the garage." The officers feel bad for Cathy and let her go free. The officers then write up an affidavit that says "We have learned from an informant that Joe is a drug supplier who lives at 123 State Street and that his supply of drugs is kept in the garage. The informant has directly seen the drugs in a bag in the garage." Based on these facts, should the magistrate issue a search warrant for the garage at 123 State Street?

A) The magistrate should issue the warrant because Cathy has a strong basis of knowledge, which is the primary test for assessing probable cause.

B) The magistrate should issue the warrant because the officers have confirmed Cathy's tip and thus have demonstrated probable cause.

C) The magistrate should be reluctant to issue the warrant because while Cathy has a strong basis of knowledge, there is no reason to believe her tip is reliable.

D) The magistrate should not issue the warrant because the police caught Cathy in criminal activity and someone involved in criminal activity cannot be a reliable informant.

E) Both C and D.

Question 20

Assume the same facts as Question 19, but also assume that, as they were talking with Cathy, the officers called one of their colleagues, Officer Charles. Officer Charles let his colleagues know that Cathy had previously given a tip about a drug supplier and that Cathy's tip had been correct. On the other hand, Officer Charles explained that when he tried to use Cathy as an informant on another occasion, Cathy ran away from him. The officers submit the same affidavit to the magistrate as in Question 19, except this time they include the information about Cathy's prior tip and her prior interactions with Officer Charles. What result?

A) The magistrate should not issue a warrant because Cathy's reliability is still weak, and a robust level of reliability is necessary for an informant's tip

B) The magistrate should not issue a warrant because Cathy's flight from Officer Charles indicates her dishonesty.

C) The magistrate should probably issue the warrant because under a totality of the circumstances test, Cathy's strong basis of knowledge balances out the weaker reliability prong.

D) The magistrate should issue the warrant because Cathy's correct tip from the past creates a rebuttable presumption that her tip in this instance creates probable cause. In this case, there is nothing to rebut the presumption.

Question 21

Officer Hyde has been working undercover to infiltrate a street gang that sells drugs. After spending a few days with the gang, Officer Hyde documents his observations in an affidavit and applies to a magistrate for an arrest warrant for three members of the gang and for a search warrant for 123 Main Street, which Officer Hyde says is the stash house. Officer Hyde's affidavit explains how he has been working undercover in the gang for days and that he has seen the three members of the gang getting drugs out of the stash house at 123 Main Street. This is the only information submitted to the magistrate. Should the magistrate find enough probable cause to issue the warrant?

A) No, there is not enough for probable cause because we do not have enough evidence to indicate whether Officer Hyde is reliable.

B) No, there is not enough for probable cause because both the basis of knowledge and reliability prongs are lacking.

C) Yes, there is probable cause because Officer Hyde has a strong basis of knowledge and he is reliable.

D) Yes, there is probable cause because when a witness says they observed a crime, that is always sufficient to create probable cause.

E) There is probable cause for the search warrant, but not the arrest warrant.

Question 22

Officer Palmer pulls over a driver who was speeding. Officer Palmer notices that the driver seems nervous. She asks the driver if he has any drugs in the car. The driver answers "No," but his voice is trembling a little. Officer Palmer then says, "Well, if you don't have any drugs in the car, would you mind if I searched through your trunk?" The driver said—with his voice trembling even more now—"No. You can't have consent to search my trunk." Officer Palmer was very suspicious at this point and searched the trunk of the car and found drugs. Should the drugs be admitted or suppressed?

A) The drugs should be suppressed because even though the nervousness plus the refusal to grant consent might amount to probable cause generally speaking, there was no specific probable cause to search the trunk.

B) The drugs should be suppressed because nervousness by itself does not give rise to probable cause, and refusal to grant consent cannot be counted toward finding probable cause.

C) The drugs should be admitted because the driver's refusal to consent, combined with his nervous demeanor, creates probable cause.

D) The drugs should be admitted because Officer Palmer was "very suspicious," which is greater than the standard necessary to establish probable cause.

Question 23

Officer Stone notices two young men with trench coats walking funny as they leave the Disney Store in the mall. Officer Stone has been a patrol officer for more than 30 years and has arrested hundreds of people for theft. Based on his experience and intuition, Officer Stone stops the two men, frisks them, and feels a soft puffy object in the pocket of one of the men. Officer Stone guesses that the man had stolen a stuffed animal from the Disney Store. He reaches into the coat pocket and sure enough, he pulls out a stolen Mickey Mouse stuffed animal. Officer Stone arrests the man for shoplifting and the defendant has moved to suppress. What result?

A) The stuffed animal should be suppressed because Officer Stone needed probable cause to stop the men and he did not have it.

B) The stuffed animal should be suppressed because Officer Stone needed probable cause to pull the stuffed animal out of the coat pocket and he did not have it.

C) The stuffed animal should be admitted because Officer Stone's experience, intuition, and the behavior of the men in the trench coats gave him probable cause.

D) The stuffed animal should be admitted because Officer Stone did not need probable cause since he found the evidence during a stop and frisk that requires only reasonable suspicion.

Question 24

Officer Chase and Officer Ryder are on patrol and have their drug-sniffing dog, Marshall, in the back seat. The officers pull over a car that is speeding. While Officer Chase speaks with the driver and runs a check on her license to make sure there are no outstanding warrants, Officer Ryder walks Marshall (the drug-sniffing dog) around the stopped vehicle. Marshall sits down by the trunk, which he is trained to do when he smells illegal drugs. Based on Marshall's alert, Officers Chase and Ryder search the trunk of the car and find cocaine. Which of the following is correct?

A) The cocaine is admissible because the dog alert created probable cause.

B) The cocaine is admissible because the traffic stop supplements the dog alert to create probable cause.

C) The cocaine is inadmissible because the police lacked probable cause to walk the drug-sniffing dog around the vehicle.

D) The cocaine is inadmissible because the alert by the drug-sniffing dog, by itself, cannot give rise to probable cause.

Question 25

Assume the same facts as Question 24 above. The defense lawyer asks the prosecutor to turn over records of Marshall's accuracy in the field. The prosecutor responds that there are no records of Marshall's accuracy. Instead, the prosecutor provides documentation showing that Marshall successfully completed a 120-hour course last year given by a private company—K-9 Narcotics Detection School. The defense lawyer moves to suppress the drugs on the grounds that the officers did not have probable cause. How should the court rule?

A) The court should suppress the drugs because the prosecution needs some documentation of Marshall's accuracy (and inaccuracy) in the field to rely on him for probable cause.

B) The court should suppress the drugs because while successful completion of drug-dog certification program can be sufficient to establish probable cause, the program must be run by a law enforcement agency, not a private company.

C) The court should overrule the suppression motion because when a bona fide organization has certified a drug dog, that certification is sufficient and not subject to refutation.

D) The court should overrule the suppression motion because when a bona fide organization has certified a drug dog, that certification is sufficient, absent conflicting evidence such as problems with the training, prior inaccuracy in the field, or circumstances surrounding the particular alert at issue.

Question 26

Police receive a tip from a trusted informant that a 1986 Honda Accord with license plate ABC-789 has been involved in transporting drugs. The informant—who has been right 10 times in the past—told the police that he and Walter loaded drugs into the trunk that morning. After receiving the tip, officers locate the Honda Accord and pull it over. The officers note that Walter is driving the vehicle and that another person who they have no information about—Hank—is sitting in the passenger's seat. The officers order both men out of the vehicle and take the car keys from Walter. The officers then place the key into the trunk lock and use it to open the trunk. Inside the trunk they find a kilogram of cocaine. The officers arrest both Walter and Hank. Which of the following is correct?

A) There was probable cause to search the trunk only, but not to arrest anyone.

B) There was probable cause to search the trunk and to arrest Walter.

C) There was probable cause to search the trunk and to arrest both Walter and Hank.

D) There was probable cause to search the trunk and to arrest both Walter and Hank, but because the police received the tip from the informant in the morning, they had time to get a warrant and thus the warrantless search and arrests are invalid.

Question 27

Assume the same facts as Question 26 above. This time, however, assume that the informant told the officers that Walter and one other person placed drugs inside a 1986 Honda Accord in the center console between the driver's seat and the front passenger's seat. When the officers stopped the vehicle and searched the center console, they found a bag of drugs. The officers arrested Walter (who was in the driver's seat) and Hank (who was in the front passenger's seat). Do the officers have probable cause to arrest Hank now?

A) Yes, because there is probable cause to believe Hank could be in control of the drugs.

B) No, because the drugs can only belong to one person and there is more probable cause to link Walter to the drugs.

Question 28

DEA agents have been following Vincent because an informant tipped them off that he is a drug dealer and that he regularly flies drugs from one side of the country to the other. The agents observe that Vincent has paid cash for a one-way flight to Miami, a known drug city, and that he is acting suspiciously by looking around very nervously. A trained drug-sniffing dog smells Vincent's luggage (which is on the floor next to him) and the dog alerts, indicating that the luggage contains drugs. The DEA agents ask Vincent to voluntarily accompany them to the DEA office in the airport. They do not place him under arrest. In the DEA office, the agents begin to look through Vincent's bag and they find four packets of cocaine. Before trial, Vincent moves to suppress the cocaine. How should the court rule?

A) The court should deny Vincent's motion because the agents had probable cause to believe Vincent was involved in drug activity and the alert from the drug-sniffing dog gave them probable cause to believe the luggage contained narcotics.

B) The court should deny Vincent's motion because Vincent's silence in the DEA office amounted to consent to search his bag.

C) The court should grant Vincent's motion because the agents did not have a warrant to search the bag and the search did not fall under any of the warrant exceptions.

D) The court should grant Vincent's motion because the agents had no probable cause to believe Vincent's bag contained narcotics.

ANSWERS TO MULTIPLE-CHOICE QUESTIONS

Answer to Question 19

Answer A is incorrect. While an informant's tip is judged under a totality of the circumstances test and a strong basis of knowledge can make up for weak reliability prong, here there is zero evidence that Cathy is reliable. There is no evidence that she has given reliable information in the past and she has an incentive to lie to get out of trouble. None of this demonstrates reliability.

Answer B is incorrect. Nothing in the question indicates that the officers have confirmed any of the details in Cathy's tip.

Answer C is correct. Cathy does have a strong basis of knowledge because she claimed to see the drugs in the garage firsthand and has provided a lot of details about her observation. As explained above, however, there is nothing in the question to indicate that Cathy is reliable or that police have confirmed the details Cathy provided.

Answer D is incorrect. Police regularly rely on informants who have been caught engaging in criminal activity. Because police are trying to catch criminals, they often have to rely on other people who have engaged in criminal activity to act as informants.

Answer E is incorrect because Answer D is incorrect.

Answer to Question 20

Answer A is incorrect. Under old Supreme Court rulings, this might have been correct. But pursuant to the Supreme Court's decision in *Illinois v. Gates* (1983), the two prongs (basis of knowledge and reliability) are no longer rigid requirements. If the reliability prong is weak, it can be offset (and probable cause demonstrated) if the basis of knowledge prong is strong. The reverse (strong reliability and weak basis of knowledge) is also true.

Answer B is incorrect. That an informant did not wish to talk with an officer and ran away does not necessarily indicate that the informant is dishonest and unreliable.

Answer C is correct. As indicated above, the totality of the circumstances test adopted in *Illinois v. Gates* provides that weakness in one prong can be offset by strength in the other prong. Here, Cathy has a strong basis of knowledge because she personally saw the drugs in the garage and provided details about her observation. This strong basis of knowledge can offset weak reliability.

Answer D is incorrect. The law does not recognize a rebuttable presumption that because an informant was right in the past, their current tip creates probable cause in this case. Even if an informant was correct in the past, the court must still assess their basis of knowledge and reliability in this instance.

Answer to Question 21

Answer A is incorrect. Police officers are generally considered to be reliable. Courts expect that the officers are law-abiding citizens who are honest. Accordingly, we do not need additional evidence (such as giving correct tips in the past) to determine that a police officer is reliable.

Answer B is incorrect. Officer Hyde has a strong basis of knowledge. He was undercover in the street gang and he personally saw the suspects go into the stash house and come out with drugs. As noted above, Officer Hyde is also reliable.

Answer C is correct. As a police officer, we have reason to believe Officer Hyde is reliable. His basis of knowledge is also strong because he observed the suspects getting drugs out of the stash house. Officer Hyde's affidavit thus supports a finding of probable cause.

Answer D is incorrect. While a witness's observation of a crime would normally create probable cause, that is not always true. If a witness had severe vision problems or multiple convictions for crimes of honesty (e.g., perjury or theft) a judge might well conclude that the witness was not reliable.

Answer E is incorrect. There is not a higher standard of probable cause for police to arrest someone than to conduct a search. In this case, the same evidence—the suspects taking drugs out of the stash house—creates probable cause for both the arrest and search warrants.

Answer to Question 22

Answer A is incorrect. Refusal to grant consent is a constitutional right. It cannot be counted as an incriminating factor toward probable cause. The first part of the answer choice is therefore incorrect.

Answer B is correct. Courts have recognized that many people become nervous when they interact with the police. Nervousness by itself cannot create probable cause. And, as noted above, refusal to grant consent is also not considered suspicious.

Answer C is incorrect. For the reasons explained above, consent cannot be counted toward probable cause. Thus, we are left only with nervousness. And nervousness by itself is not sufficient to create probable cause.

Answer D is incorrect. The subjective view of the officer is not relevant. While Officer Palmer may personally have been very suspicious, courts do not determine probable cause based on the feelings of the officers. Instead, probable cause is determined from an objective standpoint.

Answer to Question 23

Answer A is incorrect. Officer Stone did not need probable cause to stop the men. If he had reasonable suspicion that criminal activity was afoot (see Chapter 14 on *Terry* stops) he could conduct a brief investigatory stop with less than probable cause.

Answer B is correct. While police can conduct a brief stop with reasonable suspicion of criminal activity, and a frisk with reasonable suspicion that the person is armed and dangerous, that does not mean the officers can reach into a pocket during the frisk. Officer Stone felt a soft puffy object and there is no plausible way this could be considered a weapon, nor was it immediately incriminating because Officer Stone could only "guess" that it was a stuffed animal. As such, the officer would need probable cause (and a warrant) to search and remove it from the man's pocket. Officer Stone did not have that probable cause.

Answer C is incorrect. This answer is tempting. The standard for probable cause is not high. But it is not so low that a hunch or even reasonable suspicion will qualify. Here, Officer Stone seems to have a hunch based on his years of experience and intuition. But that, even when combined with strange movements, is probably not enough to create probable cause.

Answer D is incorrect. Even if Officer Stone had reasonable suspicion that the men were armed and dangerous (which does not seem to be the case), when he felt the soft puffy object he did not immediately recognize it to be a weapon or contraband. Accordingly, he cannot reach into the pocket with less than probable cause to remove it.

Answer to Question 24

Answer A is correct. A dog alert can give rise to probable cause. Here, Marshall has clearly indicated finding drugs through his trained behavior. Police therefore have probable cause to believe there are drugs in the trunk and can conduct a warrantless search of the trunk under the automobile exception (See Chapter 10).

Answer B is incorrect. The dog alert alone can create probable cause. The traffic stop does not add anything to the probable cause analysis, though, because the driver was stopped for speeding, which has no connection to whether there are drugs in the trunk.

Answer C is incorrect. If a vehicle is lawfully detained and the officer does not extend the detention unjustifiably, police can walk a drug dog around the vehicle. Here, police had grounds to stop the car (speeding) and they were permitted to run a check for outstanding warrants. The officers did not needlessly extend the detention. Accordingly, the use of the drug-sniffing dog was permissible.

Answer D is incorrect. An alert by a drug dog is sufficient, by itself, to create probable cause.

Answer to Question 25

Answer A is incorrect. The Supreme Court has held that information about a drug dog's accuracy in the field is not required.

Answer B is incorrect. The Supreme Court has not required that drug dogs complete a certification program that is run by a governmental agency as opposed to a private company.

Answer C is incorrect. The completion of a certification program can be sufficient to conclude that a drug dog is trustworthy. However, the defendant must also have the opportunity to challenge the dog's trustworthiness. The defendant can do this in multiple ways, including by challenging the quality of the certification program or by pointing toward the dog's inaccuracy in the field.

Answer D is correct. When a drug dog has been certified by a bona fide organization, the dog can be considered trustworthy unless there is conflicting evidence that sufficiently casts doubt on the dog's trustworthiness.

Answer to Question 26

Answer A is incorrect. The informant's tip ties Walter to the drugs. Additionally, as the driver of the car, it is likely that Walter is in control of the trunk. He is therefore in control of the drugs found in the trunk.

Answer B is correct. The informant's tip creates probable cause to search the trunk of the vehicle (and the automobile exception eliminates the need for a search warrant). The informant's tip alone (and certainly in connection with finding drugs in the trunk) provides probable cause to arrest Walter. Because Walter is arrested in public, no warrant is necessary.

Answer C is incorrect. While police can search the trunk and arrest Walter, there is no probable cause to arrest Hank. The informant said nothing about anyone other than Walter loading drugs into the trunk. Additionally, this is an old car with an old-fashioned key. So far as we know, Walter is the only one with the key to the trunk. It is therefore difficult to make the case that Hank is in control of the drugs in the trunk. Thus, while there is probable cause to search for the drugs and arrest Walter, that does not mean there is probable cause to arrest Hank.

Answer D is incorrect. The officers do not need a search warrant if they can invoke the automobile exception (see Chapter 10), and they do not need an arrest warrant for a public arrest. While they may have had a sufficient amount of time to procure such warrants, the officers are not required to do so.

Answer to Question 27

Answer A is correct. The Supreme Court has upheld an arrest of multiple people in a vehicle when it was plausible to conclude that any of them could be in control of drugs found in the passenger compartment.

Answer B is incorrect. More than one person can be in constructive possession of drugs inside of a vehicle. Because it was entirely possible that Hank was in control of the drugs found next to him in the center console, the police had probable cause to arrest him. That there was also evidence to link Walter to the drugs does not eliminate probable cause to believe Hank is also in constructive possession.

Answer to Question 28

Answer A is incorrect. The agents did have probable cause because of the tip from the informant, the one-way ticket, the nervous behavior, and the alert from the drug-sniffing dog. However, police cannot search personal items simply because they have probable cause. They also need a warrant or an exception to the warrant requirement and neither is present here.

Answer B is incorrect. As we will see in Chapter 8, consent can be an exception to both probable cause and the warrant requirement. However, consent cannot be presumed based on silence. Nothing in this question indicates that Vincent has given consent.

Answer C is correct. While the officers have probable cause, it is important to remember that probable cause is not enough to conduct a search. Police must also have a warrant or an exception to the warrant requirement. Neither is present here.

Answer D is incorrect. There is more than enough evidence to create probable cause for a search of Vincent's luggage. The agents have a tip from an informant that can be somewhat verified. (Vincent is flying across the country.) A one-way ticket is not always for an illicit purpose, but it is suspicious. Vincent is acting nervous. And, most importantly, the alert by a trained drug-sniffing dog is strongly indicative of criminal activity. Taking all of this information together, the officers have more than enough to demonstrate probable cause.

CHAPTER 5
The Particularity Requirement

THE RULE: Magistrates may not issue general warrants that do not provide guidance to police officers. To be valid, a warrant must particularly describe the places to be searched and the items or persons to be seized.

Critical Points

- The warrant should provide enough detail that police officers will not be generally rummaging.
- A search warrant should describe the place to be searched in enough detail to guide the police officer.
- For a single-family home, the search warrant can simply identify the address of the home.
- For apartments, duplexes, and other types of buildings, the search warrant may have to provide more detail about the place to be searched.
- A search warrant should describe the items to be seized in enough detail that police officers will not be exercising discretion in deciding what to seize.
- A search warrant for an electronic device does not have to impose search protocols specifying the apps or functions on the phone that can be searched.

OVERVIEW OF THE BLACKLETTER LAW

The Fourth Amendment requires that warrants particularly describe the places to be searched and the items or persons to be seized. The particularity requirement was designed to protect against general warrants that would allow government agents to indiscriminately rummage through a suspect's personal effects.

A search warrant authorizes the police to search for evidence and it must particularly describe the area where the evidence is likely to be found. If police have probable cause that a suspect is dealing drugs, that does not mean that a magistrate can automatically issue a search warrant for the suspect's house, office, car, and person. Rather, the warrant must only authorize a search of the areas for which there is probable cause and it must particularly describe those areas so that the officers executing the warrant will know exactly where to search.

If there is probable cause to believe the suspect has drugs in her house, the warrant need only identify the address of the house. It does not have to describe the house in detail, nor does it have to specify where in the house that the police officers can look. This is because drugs can be hidden in many places in a home.

By contrast, if the officers have probable cause to search the suspect's car, the description of the vehicle should be more detailed than simply saying "suspect's car." And if the probable cause is only for the trunk of the car, the warrant should specify that the police can only search the trunk.

The particularity requirement is difficult to apply when police procure a warrant to search an electronic device. Because electronic data can be hidden anywhere on a computer or cell phone, it is very hard for officers to narrow down in advance the area that should be searched. While a few courts have required the warrant to include search protocols establishing the steps police must take when searching an electronic device, most courts do not impose such limits. Instead, courts typically let officers search through enormous amounts of data to find the needle in the electronic haystack.

EXAM TRAPS TO AVOID

- A search warrant must describe stolen property in sufficient detail. Simply calling the items "stolen property" with no further description will violate the particularity requirement.
- While general rummaging and fishing expeditions likely raise particularity problems for physical searches, police have broad authority in searching electronic devices. Successful particularity challenges to searches of electronic devices are rare.
- If a warrant provides little or no description of an apartment or duplex and it is not clear which unit the police should be searching, there may be a particularity problem.

MULTIPLE-CHOICE QUESTIONS

Question 29

Police have been investigating a theft from an electronics store. The officers have probable cause to believe that Nina stole a 27-inch monitor, a laptop, a tablet computer, and a smart watch. The lead officer signs an affidavit that says "The officers have observed surveillance video from three different cameras and spoken to two witnesses who saw Nina walk out with the 27-inch monitor and the laptop, tablet, and smart watch." The officer submits the affidavit to the magistrate and requests a warrant. The magistrate reviews the affidavit and signs a warrant authorizing a "search of 123 Clark Street, the home of Nina Nellers, to search for and seize a 27-inch monitor, a laptop, and other stolen electronics." The officers execute the warrant later that day. After finding the stolen monitor, laptop, and tablet, the officers proceed to search for the smart watch. The officers look inside a small box that is just large enough to hold a watch, but instead of a watch they find a small bag of cocaine. Nina has moved to suppress the cocaine. What result?

A) The judge should suppress the cocaine because neither the cocaine nor the watch was described in the warrant and the officers had no other reason to look in the small box.

B) The judge should suppress the cocaine because the police were only allowed to search for electronics and cannot seize cocaine.

C) The judge should admit the cocaine because it was in a box that could have held the stolen smart watch.

D) The judge should admit the cocaine because it is contraband and thus the police can seize it regardless of whether it is listed in the warrant.

The Following Facts Apply to Questions 30–33.

Peter is wandering around a fancy clothing store and he follows a woman into the dressing room. A few minutes later, the woman runs out of the dressing room and says, "Some pervert followed me into the dressing room and then put his cell phone under the dressing room door so that he could take pictures of me while I was changing." By the time the police arrived at the clothing store, Peter had already fled. The victim provided the police with a good description of Peter. In reviewing the security camera footage, the officers also saw that Peter had stolen an expensive pair of shoes as he fled the store. The officers quickly determined Peter's full name and address and that his cell phone was an older model smartphone. The magistrate issued a combination arrest and search warrant that authorized the police to enter the home of Peter Parker, 101 Double Lane, to arrest him and to seize his smart phone so that it could be searched for "photos indicating peeping on women in the dressing room."

The officer then searched 101 Double Lane and found a smartphone and a full-sized tablet computer. As he was leaving 101 Double Lane, the officer tripped over some shoes and realized they were the shoes that Peter had stolen from the clothing store. The officer seized the shoes.

Question 30

For purposes of this question, assume that the officer searched the smartphone at the police station. The officer did not simply look at the photo apps on the smartphone, but instead used a sophisticated computer device to download the entire contents of the phone. While looking for the photos of the woman in the dressing room, the officer came across child pornography. Peter has moved to suppress. How should the court rule?

A) The child pornography should be suppressed because the warrant did not describe with particularity the items to be searched or seized.

B) The child pornography should be suppressed because the warrant only authorized a search for evidence of peeping in the dressing room, not for child pornography.

C) The child pornography should be suppressed because the warrant did not provide the officers with guidance on what procedure to follow in conducting the electronic search.

D) The child pornography should be suppressed because police may not download the full contents of an electronic device prior to searching it.

E) None of the above.

Question 31

For purposes of this question, assume that after finding child pornography on the smartphone that the officer proceeded to conduct a search of the full-sized tablet. After a few minutes of searching, the officer found a photo on the tablet of Peter holding an illegal machine gun. Peter moves to suppress the incriminating firearm photo. What result?

A) The firearm photo is admissible because the officer had probable cause to look for child pornography and came across the incriminating firearm photo inadvertently.

B) The firearm photo is inadmissible because the tablet was not listed in the warrant and thus could not be searched.

Question 32

For purposes of this question, focus on the stolen shoes that the officer tripped over as he was leaving 101 Double Lane. Peter has moved to suppress the shoes. How should the court rule?

A) Admit the shoes because the officer was lawfully present, the shoes were contraband, and they were in plain view.

B) Suppress the shoes because they were not listed in the warrant (which only authorized the police to seize the smartphone).

Question 33

For purposes of this question, assume that when the two police officers arrived at 101 Double Lane to execute the warrant, they learned for the first time that it was a duplex. There was a 101A Double Lane and a 101B Double Lane. The officers were not sure whether Peter lived in 101A or 101B. So they split up and decided to enter both units. The first officer entered 101A and the second officer entered 101B. It turns out that Peter lived in 101A. When the first officer entered 101A, he quickly found and arrested Peter. As the first officer was arresting Peter in 101A, the other officer was searching for Peter in 101B. When the officer entered the kitchen of 101B, she saw a bag of cocaine as well as drug paraphernalia on the kitchen table. The officer seized the drugs and the paraphernalia. Subsequently, the prosecutor charged the only resident of 101B—Paula— with various drug crimes. Paula has moved to suppress. How should the court rule?

A) The court should suppress the evidence because the warrant only authorized the police to enter Peter's house and the officers should have investigated further to determine whether Peter resided in 101A or 101B.

B) The court should suppress the evidence because the warrant did not authorize the police to search for or seize drug evidence.

C) The court should admit the evidence because the warrant authorized the police to enter 101 Double Lane, which they did.

D) The court should admit the evidence because Paula lacks standing to challenge a validly issued warrant.

E) The court should admit the evidence because even though the warrant was flawed the officers executed it in good faith.

ANSWERS TO MULTIPLE-CHOICE QUESTIONS

Answer to Question 29

Answer A is correct. The officers had probable cause to believe Nina had stolen a smart watch. If the warrant had included the smart watch, the officers could have searched any container large enough to contain a smart watch. But the warrant failed to list the smart watch. The phrase "other stolen electronics" is too general to satisfy the particularity requirement. Because the officers had already found all of the other evidence listed in the warrant and because all of the other evidence listed in the warrant was too large to fit in the small box, there was no reason for the officers to search in the small box. Accordingly, the officers were not permitted to search the small box. They were therefore not lawfully searching when they discovered the cocaine and it should be suppressed.

Answer B is incorrect. If the officers had been lawfully searching when they came across the cocaine, they could have seized it under the plain view doctrine. Cocaine is immediately incriminating and the police would have been lawfully present had they been searching properly (see Chapter 13). As noted above, however, the police were not lawfully searching when they opened the box.

Answer C is incorrect. As explained in response to Answer A, the police did not have authority to look in the small box. Nothing in the warrant authorized a search for the smart watch. The warrant did reference "other stolen electronics," but that phrase is too general to satisfy the particularity requirement.

Answer D is incorrect. Cocaine is contraband that police can seize even if it is not identified in the warrant. However, to seize the cocaine, the police must have been searching properly when they found it. Because the warrant did not authorize a search of a small box, the officers were not searching lawfully when they encountered the cocaine.

Answer to Question 30

Answer A is incorrect. The warrant identified the particular cell phone the police were to seize and eventually search. It also identified the type of evidence that the officers were to look for: "photos indicating peeping on women in the dressing room."

Answer B is incorrect. While the warrant did limit the search to evidence of peeping in the dressing room, the officers came across the child pornography while searching for the peeping evidence and thus the child pornography was in plain view and could be seized.

Answer C is incorrect. A handful of courts have imposed search protocols for electronic searches requiring that police follow particular steps when searching electronic devices. But almost all courts have rejected this approach and allow police officers wide discretion in how to carry out the search of electronic devices.

Answer D is incorrect. Because of the difficulty of looking through electronic devices one file or image at a time and the risk that evidence could be overlooked or mistakenly deleted, courts have allowed officers to download the full contents of an electronic device prior to searching it.

Answer E is correct because all of the other answer choices are wrong.

Answer to Question 31

Answer A is incorrect. Finding child pornography on one electronic device might create probable cause to believe there is child pornography on other electronic devices found at the same residence. But the warrant was issued only for the smart phone and only to search for photographic evidence that Pete was peeping into dressing rooms. The warrant therefore cannot authorize a search of another device (the tablet) for other evidence (child pornography).

Answer B is correct. The warrant authorizes a search for peeping evidence on the smartphone. To search the tablet for evidence of child pornography, the officers must return to the magistrate and seek a new warrant that particularly describes the items to be searched for, i.e., child pornography.

Answer to Question 32

Answer A is correct. The warrant authorized the police to seize the smart phone, but said nothing about the shoes. This was likely an error on the part of the police officer who requested the warrant or the judge who issued it. But the error only prevents the police from searching for the shoes in order to seize them. If the officer instead accidentally comes across the shoes while complying with the warrant, then the officer can seize the shoes. The reason is that in this case the officer knows that the shoes are stolen property. Under the plain view doctrine (see Chapter 13) an officer may seize items that are immediately incriminating if the officer is lawfully present when he sees the incriminating items. Thus, while the warrant does not specifically authorize the officer to seize the shoes, the officer can do so under the plain view doctrine.

Answer B is incorrect. For the reasons explained above, the failure to list certain contraband in the warrant is not fatal in this situation. While police cannot search specifically for items not listed in the warrant, they can seize contraband that they come across while properly executing the warrant and searching for items listed in the warrant.

Answer to Question 33

Answer A is correct. If the officers accidentally entered the wrong unit and seized the drug items, the evidence would likely have been admissible. (See *Maryland v. Garrison* (1987)). But here the officers knew *before* they entered that there were two units and that Peter resided in only one of the two units. The officers should have investigated further to determine which unit belonged to Peter.

Answer B is incorrect. Had the officers entered the apartment lawfully they would have been permitted to seize stolen property found in plain view, even if it were not listed in the warrant.

Answer C is incorrect. The officers recognized—prior to entering—that only one of the two units belonged to Peter. The officers thus should have investigated further to determine which unit belonged to Peter because the warrant only intended to authorize an entrance into Peter's home.

Answer D is incorrect. As explained in Chapter 20, Paula has standing to challenge a search of her own home. Paula has a reasonable expectation of privacy in her own home.

Answer E is incorrect. Because the officers recognized—before entering—that Peter did not reside in both units, the officers did not proceed in good faith. The search of 101B was not due to an accident or mistake, but instead because the officers chose to enter before clarifying the situation.

CHAPTER 6
The Knock and Announce Rule

THE RULE: Before executing a warrant, police are supposed to knock and announce their presence and wait for admittance before entering. However, if the officer has reasonable suspicion that knocking and announcing would be dangerous or would allow the suspect to destroy evidence, the officers need not knock and announce.

Critical Points

- The Fourth Amendment requires police to knock and announce their presence before entering a residence to execute a search or arrest warrant.
- Police do not have to knock and announce, however, if they have reasonable suspicion that doing so would be dangerous or if it would enable a suspect to destroy evidence.
- Violations of the knock and announce rule do not lead to the exclusion of evidence.

OVERVIEW OF THE BLACKLETTER LAW

The text of the Fourth Amendment does not mention an obligation for the police to knock and announce their presence when executing a warrant. Nevertheless, the Supreme Court has held that the "reasonableness" language in the Fourth Amendment requires the police to knock and announce before executing a warrant. There are logical reasons for the police to knock and announce. First, and most importantly, it protects human life. If police barged through the door, the occupant might not realize it was the police and needless violence could ensue. Second, the knock and announce rule prevents the unnecessary destruction of property. Put simply, police will not need to knock down the door if the occupant opens it. Third, the knock and announce rule enables people to get dressed so that they will not be humiliated by having police barge through the door and find them undressed.

While there are good reasons for a knock and announce requirement, there are also reasons not to require it in all cases. Police often have search warrants or arrest warrants for dangerous people. If the police knock on the door and announce that they are standing outside, the dangerous people may shoot or otherwise attack the officers. Or the people inside may try to destroy evidence while the police are waiting outside. Accordingly, the Supreme Court has recognized an exception to the knock and announce rule. When police have reasonable suspicion that knocking and announcing their presence would be dangerous or would result in the destruction of evidence, the police need not knock and announce.

Finally, although the Supreme Court has said that the Fourth Amendment requires police to knock and announce in many instances, the Court has also held that violations of the rule will not lead to exclusion of evidence. As described in Chapter 21, the exclusionary rule provides that illegally seized evidence will not be admissible. There are various exceptions to the exclusionary rule, however. The Supreme Court has held that lower courts should not suppress evidence found after a knock and announce violation if the police executed an otherwise valid warrant.

EXAM TRAPS TO AVOID

- The police cannot simply claim that they fear violence or destruction of evidence. The officers must have reasonable suspicion that knocking and announcing would be dangerous or result in the destruction of evidence.
- Failure to knock and announce can be a Fourth Amendment violation, but the exclusionary rule does not apply to knock-and-announce violations and thus the evidence will not be suppressed.

MULTIPLE-CHOICE QUESTIONS

Question 34

Police have a valid warrant to arrest Avon and Marlo for dealing large quantities of heroin out of a drug house. The officers proceed to the house. At 4:00 a.m., the officers go to the front door, see a few lights on inside the house, and kick in the door without knocking and announcing their presence. Inside the officers find that Avon and Marlo are just getting up (apparently from sleeping) in response to the noise of the door being kicked in. The officers handcuff both men and arrest them. Which of the following is correct?

I. The police were not obligated to knock and announce because of the risk that Avon and Marlo could be dangerous to the officers.

II. The police were not obligated to knock and announce because of the risk of destruction of evidence.

III. The police were not obligated to knock and announce because they had a valid arrest warrant.

IV. The police were obligated to knock and announce because it was the middle of the night and there was no risk of danger or destruction of evidence.

A) I only

B) I and II only

C) I, II, and III only

D) IV only

Question 35

Police have a valid warrant to arrest Oliver for tax evasion. Oliver is an anti-gun political activist with a clean criminal record. Oliver lives alone, and officers staking out his residence have not seen anyone besides Oliver enter the house. When the officers execute the arrest warrant, they do not knock and announce. They use a battering ram to take down the front door. The officers then enter the residence and find Oliver standing there pointing an unregistered handgun at them. The officers tackle Oliver to the ground before he can shoot his weapon. The officers then arrest him. In addition to the tax evasion charge, the prosecutors have added a charge for illegal weapons possession. Which of the following is correct?

A) The handgun is not admissible because the police failed to knock and announce their presence.

B) The handgun is admissible because the knock and announce rule applies to search warrants, not arrest warrants.

C) The handgun is admissible because the exclusionary rule does not ordinarily apply when the police violate the knock and announce rule so long as they had a valid warrant.

D) The handgun is admissible because even though police lacked reasonable suspicion to believe that Oliver posed a danger, it turns out that he did in fact have a handgun.

ANSWERS TO MULTIPLE-CHOICE QUESTIONS

Answer to Question 34

Roman numerals I and II are correct answers. Police are not obligated to knock and announce if doing so would create danger for the officers or would risk the destruction of evidence. In the case of a drug house—especially one selling "large quantities of heroin"—the police will have reasonable suspicion of danger to themselves as well as destruction of evidence. To protect a drug house, dealers typically have to use weapons. Thus it is reasonable for police to believe that Avon and Marlo would have weapons and might shoot. Additionally, if police announced their presence, Avon and Marlo might try to destroy the drug evidence against them.

Roman numeral III is incorrect. The existence of a warrant does not eliminate the need to knock and announce. To the contrary, the Supreme Court has held that, absent reasonable suspicion of danger or destruction of evidence, police must knock and announce before executing a warrant.

Roman numeral IV is also incorrect. Although it is more likely that suspects are sleeping at 4:00 a.m. and that they would not be in a position to harm officers or destroy evidence, that is not always the case. Police can still have reasonable suspicion that there will be danger or destruction of evidence. In this case, the officers saw multiple lights on inside the house, which could cause a reasonable officer to believe the suspects were awake.

Accordingly, Answer B is the correct answer choice.

Answer to Question 35

Answer A is incorrect. The exclusionary rule does not ordinarily apply to violations of the knock and announce rule.

Answer B is incorrect. The knock and announce rule applies to both search warrants and arrest warrants.

Answer C is correct. It appears that the police violated the knock and announce rule. There was no reasonable suspicion that Oliver posed a danger to the officers because they believed he was opposed to weapons and because the officers were sure no one else was in the house. Moreover, there is no reason to believe Oliver would be able to destroy any evidence if the officers knocked and announced. However, the exclusionary rule does not ordinarily apply to violations of the knock and announce rule.

Answer D is incorrect. In assessing whether the knock and announce rule applies, we must look at the moment when the officers decided to enter without knocking and announcing. At that moment, the police lacked reasonable suspicion to believe that Oliver would be armed and dangerous to them. The fact that the officers learned *after they entered* that Oliver was in fact armed is not the relevant inquiry.

STEP 5
If There Was No Warrant, Was There an Exception to the Warrant Requirement?

Chapter 7: Exigent Circumstances
Chapter 8: Consent
Chapter 9: The Search Incident to a Lawful Arrest
Chapter 10: The Automobile Exception
Chapter 11: Search of a Vehicle Incident to Arrest
Chapter 12: The Inventory Exception
Chapter 13: The Plain View Exception
Chapter 14: Terry *Stops*
Chapter 15: Terry *Frisks*
Chapter 16: Drunk Driving, Drug, and Other Checkpoints
Chapter 17: Border Searches
Chapter 18: School Searches
Chapter 19: DNA Swabs and Routine Booking Procedures

A search or seizure can be reasonable if the police have a valid warrant (See Step 4). If there is no warrant, however, the next step is to determine whether an exception to the warrant requirement applies. If police act pursuant to a warrant exception, the search or seizure will also be reasonable.

Step 5 requires you to consider more than a dozen heavily tested exceptions to the warrant requirement. Some of these exceptions require probable cause, while others require only reasonable suspicion. And still some others do not require any suspicion at all.

CHAPTER 7
Exigent Circumstances

THE RULE: Police can conduct a warrantless search if they: (1) have probable cause; and (2) can demonstrate exigent circumstances, which include hot pursuit, an escaping suspect, imminent destruction of evidence, or a public safety need.

Critical Points

- *Exception to the Warrant Requirement, but Not Probable Cause*: The police still need probable cause to invoke the exigency exception.
- *Common Cases*: Exigent circumstances usually involve hot pursuit, imminent destruction of evidence, escape, or public safety.

OVERVIEW OF THE BLACKLETTER LAW

When there is an exigency, police may search without a warrant. But an exigency alone is not sufficient. Police must still have probable cause. The exigent circumstances exception is only an exception to the warrant requirement. The Supreme Court has recognized three types of exigent circumstances: (1) hot pursuit and escape; (2) imminent destruction of evidence; and (3) public safety. Let's take them one at a time.

1. Hot Pursuit and Escape

Police ordinarily need a warrant to enter a suspect's home to make an arrest, but they do not ordinarily need a warrant to arrest a person in public. If officers attempt to arrest a person in public without a warrant and the suspect flees, the officers can pursue him. Once the officers are in "hot pursuit" they are not obligated to stop if the suspect makes it to his home and shuts the front door. Real life does not resemble a game of freeze tag in which a person is safe if they reach home base. An officer in hot pursuit of a fleeing suspect ordinarily does not have to procure a warrant before entering a home. Note again, though, that the officer still needs probable cause.

The same logic applies to escape. If police have probable cause to arrest a suspect and they reasonably believe the suspect is about to escape, the officers can utilize the exigent circumstances exception to enter a home to arrest him.

2. Imminent Destruction of Evidence

When a suspect is about to destroy evidence, police do not need to run to a magistrate for a warrant and hope they make it back in time. Imminent destruction of evidence is an exigent circumstance that allows police to enter the premises without a warrant.

One of the most common destruction of evidence situations occurs when police are investigating drug activity and hear suspects inside the home trying to flush or otherwise destroy evidence. The exigent circumstances exception allows the police to enter without a warrant. Another common situation involves drunk driving. Blood-alcohol levels dissipate over time, so if a DWI suspect refuses to consent to a breath or blood sample, evidence of their intoxication slowly disappears during the time it would take for the officer to get a warrant to draw their blood. The Supreme Court has held that ordinarily police have to get a warrant before ordering a blood draw in a drunk-driving case. But the Court also recognized that in some rare cases it is impractical to get a warrant. For example, in a rural community with limited access to magistrates it might be impossible to procure a warrant in the middle of the night. The Court therefore indicated that while there is no per se exigency exception for drunk-driving cases, exigent circumstances could exist in some cases.

3. Public Safety

Police can also invoke the exigent circumstances exception to the warrant requirement to protect public safety. For example, in *Brigham City, Utah v. Stuart* (2006), officers responded to a noise complaint and could see a physical fight happening inside of the home. The officers had no warrant to enter the house but did so anyway to stop the fight. The Court upheld the warrantless entry because ongoing violence was an exigent circumstance and the officers were objectively reasonable in believing they needed to stop the violence. In addition to ongoing violence, the public safety rationale would also apply to explosives.

EXAM TRAPS TO AVOID

- Police must have probable cause to invoke the exigent circumstances exception. Do not be fooled by a question in which there is an obvious exigency but no probable cause.

MULTIPLE CHOICE QUESTIONS

Question 36

At 9:15 p.m., police receive a call that a gas station on the corner of Main and Smith Streets has just been robbed at gunpoint by three men. The report indicates that the men were wearing masks and that they were driving a grey Toyota Camry with a license plate containing the letters "AFZ." At 9:22 p.m., two officers spot a grey Toyota Camry with license plate "AFZ-407" about four miles from the scene of the crime. The officers turn on their sirens and follow the Camry for less than a minute when they see it turn into a driveway. The officers then see three men get out of the car and run into the house. One of the men looks like he is holding a mask, and a second man is clearly carrying a bag. The officers decide to follow the men into the house. With weapons drawn, and without knocking or announcing their presence, the officers bust through the front door and tackle the man holding the mask and the other man, who was holding the bag. In arresting the two men, the officers find cash from the robbery. The defendants move to suppress the evidence as the fruit of an unlawful arrest. How should the court rule?

A) The suppression motion should be denied because while the arrest might be unlawful for lack of a warrant, there was still probable cause and therefore the court should not suppress evidence that is subsequently discovered.

B) The suppression motion should be denied because police were entitled to make a warrantless entry under an exigency theory.

C) The suppression motion should be granted because the police were obligated to procure a warrant before entering the home.

D) The suppression motion should be granted because the police lacked probable cause to link the men to the robbery.

Question 37

Officer Chase was on patrol and drove past a house that raised his suspicions. The grass in front of the house had not been mowed for weeks and it seemed that an unusual number of people were milling about in front of the house. After the people standing in front of the house left, Officer Chase walked on the brick-lined path from the street to the front door of the house to make sure everything was all right. Although there was a doorbell and a door knocker on the front door, Officer Chase did not use either. Instead, he pounded on the front door and yelled very loudly "This is the police!" About 30 seconds later, Officer Chase smelled fire and surmised that the occupants of the house were burning evidence. Officer Chase then entered the house without a warrant. Inside he found a large-scale methamphetamine operation. The occupants moved to suppress the evidence found inside the house. How should the court rule?

A) The court should suppress the evidence because Officer Chase physically trespassed on the porch in violation of the Fourth Amendment.

B) The court should suppress the evidence because, by banging on the door and yelling "This is the police!" Officer Chase probably intended to trick the occupants into destroying evidence or fleeing.

C) As long as there is probable cause, the court should admit the evidence because Officer Chase was justified in entering the house based on exigent circumstances.

D) The court should admit the evidence because, even though Officer Chase tricked the occupants, he acted in good faith.

Question 38

Officer Vance is on patrol in Chicago, Illinois. Around 11:00 p.m., Officer Vance pulls over a vehicle for weaving all over the road. Officer Vance suspected that the driver—Roger Refusal—was intoxicated and asked him to submit to a Breathalyzer test. Roger refused the Breathalyzer test. Officer Vance called the magistrate on duty to request a warrant to draw blood from Roger. The judge's assistant put Officer Vance on hold and said, "The judge is busy. He'll get back to you in about 20 minutes or so." When 20 minutes came and went, Officer Vance grew impatient, worried that Roger's blood-alcohol level was dropping with each passing minute and that the judge might not call back immediately. Officer Vance took Roger to a nearby hospital and ordered a nurse to draw his blood. Which of the following is correct?

A) The warrantless blood draw is very likely unconstitutional because it was possible to get a warrant under the circumstances.

B) The warrantless blood draw is always unconstitutional because an invasive search for bodily fluids always requires a warrant.

C) The warrantless blood draw is covered by exigent circumstances because Officer Vance waited 20 minutes and thus acted in good faith.

D) The warrantless blood draw is covered by exigent circumstances since Roger's blood-alcohol level was dissipating and evidence was disappearing.

Question 39

Assume the same facts as Question 38. However, this time Officer Vance was on patrol in Bland County, Virginia, which has a population of less than 7,000 people. Around 2:00 a.m., Officer Vance pulled over a vehicle that was weaving all over the road. Officer Vance suspected the driver—Roger Refusal—was intoxicated and asked him to submit to a Breathalyzer test. Roger refused the Breathalyzer test. Officer Vance called *the* Bland County Magistrate (there is only one magistrate in the county) to issue a search warrant for a blood draw. The magistrate's husband informed Officer Vance that the Magistrate was very ill that night and that she would call back "if she feels up to it." Officer Vance thought for a few minutes and then decided to make the 45-minute drive to the Bland County Hospital where a nurse could draw Roger's blood. When the nurse asked Officer Vance if he had a warrant, Officer Vance responded: "Don't need one. There are exigent circumstances." Which of the following is correct?

A) The blood draw is constitutional because blood-alcohol levels dissipate over time, thus creating a per se exigency.

B) The blood draw may be constitutional, although the outcome likely turns on factual questions such as whether a neighboring magistrate could have lawfully issued a warrant and the time it would take to procure that warrant.

C) The blood draw may be constitutional, but only if an officer subjectively concluded that there was not enough time to get a warrant.

D) The blood draw is unconstitutional because physical entry into the body is the most invasive type of search and can only be conducted if a proper warrant has issued.

Question 40

On Monday night, two men kidnapped a child of wealthy parents. The kidnappers contacted the parents and told them that they would kill the child if the parents did not pay a $1 million ransom. The police have been furiously investigating and they believe that one of the kidnappers may be Ryan. The officers stake out the grocery store and other places where Ryan ordinarily goes. On Wednesday morning, the officers see Ryan enter the grocery store and immediately detain him and question him. The officers ask him whether he's involved in the kidnapping and he says, "How did you know? Wait, no. I'm not involved. I mean, it's not my fault. The other guy made me do it. He was texting me threatening messages." The officers ask Ryan where the child is being held and Ryan says, "I'm not telling you anything else." The officers arrest Ryan and remove his cell phone from his pocket. The officers begin looking through the cell phone in the hopes of finding any evidence that will lead them to the child. In Ryan's text messages, the officers discover a chain of messages that show not only that Ryan was involved but that he was the mastermind of the operation. Eventually the police locate the child, who is safe, and prosecutors charge Ryan with kidnapping. Ryan moves to suppress the text messages as the result of an unlawful search. What result?

A) The text messages are admissible as a valid search incident to arrest.

B) The text messages are admissible under the exigent circumstances doctrine.

C) The text messages are not admissible because the Supreme Court has explicitly held that warrantless cell phone searches are always unconstitutional.

D) The text messages are not admissible because police failed to read Ryan his *Miranda* rights before finding the text messages.

ANSWERS TO MULTIPLE-CHOICE QUESTIONS

Answer to Question 36

Answer A is incorrect. The arrest is lawful here because the officers have probable cause and they can claim exigent circumstances because they were in hot pursuit.

Answer B is correct. Because the officers were in hot pursuit, they can enter the home without a warrant under an exigent circumstances rationale.

Answer C is incorrect. Because the officers were in hot pursuit, the officers do not need a warrant.

Answer D is incorrect. The officers saw a car that matched the make and color of the getaway vehicle. The officers were also able to match a substantial portion of the license plate numbers. Further, the officers saw a man holding a mask. Taken together, this amounts to probable cause.

Answer to Question 37

Answer A is incorrect. Because Officer Chase walked on the brick-lined path to the front door to check to make sure everything was all right, Officer Chase has not trespassed. Walking to the front door to check out the situation is constitutional.

Answer B is incorrect. The subjective intent of the officer is not ordinarily relevant in Fourth Amendment analysis and it is not relevant here. In a similar case, the Supreme Court rejected the argument that evidence should be suppressed because the officer created the exigency by banging loudly on the front door.

Answer C is correct. If Officer Chase reasonably believes the occupants are burning evidence, he may enter the house without a warrant to prevent the destruction of evidence.

Answer D is incorrect. The good faith exception is ordinarily not applicable in cases where the police acted without a warrant. The key question is whether there was an exigency (not what the subjective views of the officer were).

Answer to Question 38

Answer A is correct. The Supreme Court has indicated that warrantless blood draws will rarely be permissible under the exigent circumstances doctrine. The rare cases mostly involve situations in which it was not possible to find a magistrate to issue a warrant. Officer Vance was in a large jurisdiction that likely has many magistrates. Indeed, Officer Vance had located a magistrate who was on duty and was told he would call back shortly. Under the totality of the circumstances, it is very unlikely that a court would find exigent circumstances for a warrantless blood draw.

Answer B is incorrect. This answer misstates the law. A warrantless blood draw will rarely qualify as an exigent circumstance. But that does not mean it is "always unconstitutional." In some cases—when the suspect is unconscious or it would be impossible to reach a magistrate—a warrantless blood draw may be constitutional.

Answer C is incorrect. The good faith exception almost never applies to warrantless searches. Moreover, Officer Vance did not act in good faith. There was still time for the magistrate to call back and Officer Vance should have waited.

Answer D is incorrect. This answer misstates the law. A suspect's blood-alcohol level is always dissipating in the bloodstream. But the Supreme Court has recognized in almost all cases that a dissipating blood-alcohol level is not a sufficient justification for a warrantless blood draw.

Answer to Question 39

Answer A is incorrect. The Supreme Court has rejected a per se exigency rationale for warrantless blood draws. To the contrary, the Court has signaled that warrantless blood draws should be quite rare.

Answer B is correct. Normally, warrantless blood draws are unconstitutional. However, in a small county with a single magistrate who is indisposed it is likely that the officer has no other alternative in order to preserve the evidence. A warrantless blood draw might be unconstitutional, however, if the officer could procure a warrant from a judge in a neighboring county.

Answer C is incorrect. Fourth Amendment law almost never turns on the subjective intent of the officer. In this case, the officer's personal view is not relevant.

Answer D is incorrect. This statement is mostly true, though not entirely. The Supreme Court has authorized warrantless blood draws when a suspect is unconscious and also when it would not be possible for the police to procure a warrant.

Answer to Question 40

Answer A is incorrect. The Supreme Court held in *Riley v. California* (2014) that the police cannot search a cell phone incident to arrest.

Answer B is correct. While police may not search a cell phone incident to arrest, the Supreme Court left open the possibility that cell phone searches could be justified under the exigent circumstances exception. The need to save a kidnapped child qualifies as an exigent circumstance.

Answer C is incorrect. As noted above, police may not search a cell phone incident to arrest, but it is possible for officers to search a cell phone subject to some other exceptions to the warrant requirement.

Answer D is incorrect. Ryan may not have been in custody when he was questioned, in which case the *Miranda* warnings would not have been required (see Chapter 29). The *Miranda* warnings also might not have been required in this case because of the public safety exception (see Chapter 31). In any event, even if the police violated *Miranda* and Ryan's statements in the grocery store would be suppressed, the fruit of the poisonous tree doctrine does not apply to subsequent evidence found as a result of a *Miranda* violation. (see Chapter 34). Accordingly, the text messages would likely be admissible even if there were a *Miranda* violation.

CHAPTER 8
Consent

THE RULE: When a person voluntarily consents to a search of their person, home, vehicle, or other item, officers can search without having probable cause or a warrant.

Critical Points

- *Exception to Probable Cause and Warrant Requirement*: Police do not need probable cause or a warrant to search if they have consent.
- *Test for Valid Consent*: Consent must be given freely and voluntarily. This is judged by a totality of the circumstances test.
- *No Right to Be Told You Can Refuse Consent*: When an officer asks for consent to search, the officer does not have to say the person can refuse.
- *Police Cannot Coerce Consent*: If police threaten a person—by brandishing a weapon or threatening physical harm—consent cannot be voluntary.
- *Scope of Consent*: When a person gives consent, police can search anywhere that it would be reasonable to believe the consent extended to.
- *Refusing to Give Consent Does Not Create Probable Cause*: Individuals have a constitutional right not to give an officer consent to search. If a person invokes their constitutional right to refuse consent, that does not create suspicion that the police can use against them.
- *Third Parties Can Grant Consent*: A third party (for example, your spouse) can grant consent to search a common area that you share.
- *Physically Present Objecting Cotenant Can Block Third-Party Consent*: A third party cannot grant valid consent if the other occupant of the house is physically present and refuses to grant consent.

- *Apparent Third-Party Authority*: If police reasonably believed that a third party had the authority to grant consent, but the officers were wrong, the evidence is still admissible.
- *Revoking Consent*: A person who has granted consent can revoke it at any time (though any evidence found up to that point is admissible).

OVERVIEW OF THE BLACKLETTER LAW

Police conduct millions of searches each year, and they rely on consent more than any other exception to the warrant requirement. Consent is an exception to both probable cause and the warrant requirement. Police can ask for consent to search even if they have no suspicion whatsoever. There are four big consent topics that you are likely to see on an exam:

1. Was consent validly given?
2. What locations could the officers search in light of that consent? This is known as the scope of consent.
3. Can third parties grant or block consent to search?
4. What happens when a person declines or revokes consent?

1. Was Consent Validly Given?

In determining whether consent was validly given, courts look to the totality of the circumstances. The test is whether the individual freely and voluntarily consented to the search. If the police officer coerced the individual into consenting, then consent was not freely and voluntarily given.

For example, consent might be coerced if (A) the officer brandished a weapon while asking for consent. Consent might also be coerced if (B) the officer lied about the prospect of getting a warrant and *falsely* told the individual that "if you don't consent to let me search, then the magistrate will give me a warrant and we'll do it the hard way." Consent could also be coerced if (C) numerous officers surround the individual while asking for consent.

The difficulty with a totality of the circumstances test is that small variations in the facts might change the outcome. Consider a variation on scenario (A) above: If the officer asked for consent while resting her hand on her firearm but did not remove the weapon from the holster, then consent might not have been coerced. Or consider a variation on scenario (B): If the officer truthfully told the individual, "Look, I have probable cause to search your purse and a judge will surely issue a warrant, but if you consent we can skip that time-consuming step," this might not be coercive. Finally, consider a variation on scenario (C) that might not be coercive: Imagine that an officer is talking with a pedestrian and asks for consent just as another patrol car stops to make sure the first officer has everything under control. Multiple officers are now on the scene, but they are not surrounding the individual in a threatening way.

In short, whether consent was freely and voluntarily given is a classic law school essay question in which the facts matter greatly and the answer is sometimes debatable.

There is one rule about voluntariness and consent that is bright-line and clear. Police are under no obligation to tell an individual that he has the right to refuse consent.

2. What Is the Scope of Consent?

Once you have determined that a person has given valid consent, the next question is: what areas the officer can search based on that consent? The main rule is that police can search any location where it is reasonable to believe the consent extended. The key things to focus on in assessing the scope of consent are: (A) What is the officer looking for? and (B) What did the officer tell the person when asking for consent? If an officer asked for consent to look for a large object (e.g., a stolen television), then consent would extend to the trunk, but not small compartments in a backpack found in the trunk. By contrast, imagine that the officer said, "I'm looking for drugs, can I search your trunk?" and the individual responded, "Go ahead." In that case it is reasonable to believe consent extended to any location in the trunk that could hold drugs. So officers could open the backpack and any small, zippered compartments in the backpack because they could hold drugs.

A second key rule with respect to the scope of consent is that general consent ordinarily does not grant police the authority to break, rip, or destroy items to look inside of them. This means that if police have consent to search a vehicle, they cannot rip the upholstery in order to look inside the seats. It also means that if officers come across a sealed or locked container that the officers cannot break the lock or tear the seal. To break, rip, or tear, the officers usually need to get specific consent to do so.

3. Can Third Parties Grant or Block Consent to Search?

Police sometimes rely on the consent of third parties. A third party can consent to the search of property if she has common authority over the property. For example, a wife might consent to the search of a home she shares with her spouse. If the police then find incriminating evidence that implicates the spouse, the evidence is admissible against the spouse, even if the spouse never personally gave consent.

Sometimes when police rely on consent from a third party they make a mistake. The officers think that the third party has common authority over the property, but the third party has no such authority. The third party might simply be a temporary guest with no authority over the house. To take a salacious example, imagine that Jim goes out to a bar one night, meets Pam, and that they go back to Jim's house and spend the night together. The next morning, the police knock on Jim's door and

Pam answers the door half-awake and half-dressed. The officers ask her for consent to search and she says, "Go ahead." The officers find incriminating evidence before Jim even wakes up. Pam did not have common authority over the property to give third-party consent—she is not on the lease, has no key, keeps no property at the house, and in fact had never been there until 12 hours ago. Nevertheless, the evidence found as a result of Pam's consent is admissible against Jim anyway. The reason is that Pam had "apparent authority." As long as the officers reasonably believed that Pam (or any other third party) had common authority over the property, they could rely on her consent even if it turns out that Pam lacked the power to grant such consent.

The other third-party situation that is commonly tested is when one occupant grants consent while the other refuses consent. The Supreme Court has held that when a cotenant is physically present and objects to a search, the officers cannot rely on the consent of the other cotenant. In other words, when two parties are present and disagree about whether to let the police search, there can be no valid consent. Police have two ways around this problem. The first way is to wait until the objecting cotenant is no longer physically present. Officers can simply wait for the objecting cotenant to go to work, the gym, the grocery store, or anywhere else and then the officers can ask for consent again from the more cooperative cotenant. Second, if the physically present objecting cotenant has broken the law (for instance, committed domestic violence) the officers can arrest him, remove him from the scene, and then ask the remaining cotenant to grant consent. In short, a physically present objecting cotenant cannot block a consent search forever. Once he has left the premises, the officers can simply ask the other tenant (who wanted to grant consent in the first place) to give her consent again.

4. Refusing to Give Consent or Revoking Consent

Because individuals have a constitutional right not to be searched in violation of the Fourth Amendment, they cannot be penalized for refusing to consent to a search. For that reason, a person's refusal to consent to a search cannot create (or help to create) suspicion for a search. Put simply, refusal to give consent is not incriminating and cannot create reasonable suspicion or probable cause.

Revoking consent is also not supposed to be incriminating. An individual who has granted consent to search is always free to assert their Fourth Amendment rights in the middle of the search and to revoke their consent. Of course, any evidence the police found before consent was revoked will be admissible. But the act of revoking consent cannot create probable cause or reasonable suspicion for the police to continue searching.

In reality, many people may believe that it will be suspicious and counterproductive for them to refuse to grant consent or to revoke consent they have already given. But courts are supposed to apply the law, not the perceptions of the public.

EXAM TRAPS TO AVOID

- *Arrest Does Not Prevent Consent*: Just because a suspect is being detained or is under arrest does not mean they cannot voluntarily give consent.
- *Physically Present Objectors Win*: If two physically present occupants of a residence disagree about whether to grant consent, the police cannot search under a consent theory.
- *Breaking Items Requires Specific Consent*: If a person gives consent for the police to "look around" their house or vehicle, that consent likely does not extend to breaking open items. Officers need to go back and ask specifically before they can open sealed or locked items.
- *Refusing or Revoking Consent Does Not Create Suspicion*: The government cannot claim that a person's refusal to grant consent or their decision to revoke consent creates probable cause or reasonable suspicion.

MULTIPLE CHOICE QUESTIONS

The following facts apply to Questions 41–44.

Officer Colin pulls over Erica for speeding. After writing her a ticket and telling her to drive more carefully, Officer Colin says, "Just one more thing. We've been having a lot of problems with drugs being transported up and down this road. I'd like to get a look in your trunk."

Question 41

For purposes of this question, assume that Erica does not say anything clearly in response to the officer and instead mumbles something under her breath. The officer then says, "I couldn't hear you. Are you going to let me look in the trunk or not?" Erica again doesn't say anything, but this time she nods her head up and down in response to the officer's question. The officer opens the trunk and immediately sees a brick of cocaine sitting in the middle of the trunk. Erica moves to suppress the cocaine. What result?

A) The cocaine should be suppressed because Erica never gave a verbal response indicating that she consented.

B) The cocaine should be suppressed because the officer asked multiple times, which amounts to coercion.

C) The cocaine should be admitted because Erica nodding her head up and down indicated consent.

D) The cocaine should be admitted because Erica's initial refusal to grant consent is incriminating and creates grounds for the officer to search the trunk under the automobile exception.

Question 42

For purposes of this question, assume that Erica is silent after Officer Colin asks to look in the trunk and that she starts to frown. Also assume that a nearby police vehicle (with Officers Paige and Paul) had already arrived as backup. Officer Colin calls over to the backup vehicle and asks Officers Paige and Paul to come over to Erica's car. Officer Colin says to Officers Paige and Paul, "I asked her for consent and she frowned at me." Officer Paige said, "Well maybe I should ask her and she'll have a better response for me." Officer Paige then turned to Erica and said, "You know we're just trying to do our job here and you're taking up a lot of our time." Erica then said, "Look all I've got in my trunk is a bunch of my kids' toys." Officer Paige immediately responded, "Well we'll see about that. Just go ahead and show us the toys and you can get on your way." Erica opened the trunk and the police immediately found cocaine. Erica moves to suppress the cocaine. How should the court rule?

A) The court should admit the cocaine because Erica voluntarily opened the trunk and thus granted consent.

B) The court should admit the cocaine because Erica never affirmatively rejected the request for consent.

C) The court should suppress the cocaine because the presence of three officers amounts to coercion.

D) The court should suppress the cocaine because under the totality of the circumstances, Erica's consent was coerced.

Question 43

For purposes of this question, assume that Erica says "yes" after Officer Colin asks to look in the trunk of her car. The officer opens the trunk and sees nothing out of the ordinary. Officer Colin then lifts up the spare tire so that he can look underneath. Beneath the spare tire, Officer Colin finds a small, sealed cardboard box. He breaks the seal, opens the box, and finds cocaine inside. Is the cocaine admissible?

A) The cocaine is inadmissible because Officer Colin did not have authority to look under the spare tire.

B) The cocaine is inadmissible because Officer Colin did not have authority to open the box.

C) The cocaine is admissible because Officer Colin had consent to look for drugs and drugs can fit in a small box.

D) The cocaine is admissible because Erica did not object as Officer Colin opened the box.

Question 44

For purposes of this question, assume that speeding is an arrestable offense and that Officer Colin arrested Erica for speeding. After handcuffing Erica and placing her in the back of the police car, Officer Colin said, "I'd like to search the trunk of your car for drugs. Can I look in the trunk?" Erica responded, "Um, I mean, I guess so, go ahead." Officer Colin finds drugs in the trunk. Which of the following is correct?

A) Consent is valid because Erica said "go ahead."

B) Consent is invalid because Erica wavered on granting consent; but it does not matter because the drugs are admissible under an automobile search incident to arrest.

C) Consent is invalid because Erica wavered on granting consent, but the drugs are admissible under the automobile exception.

D) Consent is invalid because Erica was unsure about whether she had to consent and the officer never told her she had the right to refuse consent.

E) Consent is invalid because Erica had been arrested, handcuffed, and placed in the back of the police car, which rendered the situation coercive and her consent involuntary.

Question 45

Harry and Wanda were happily married for 10 years. The eleventh year has not been so happy, though, and they are now in the process of getting divorced. One day they were furiously arguing and Wanda said, "I'm going to call the police and tell them they can search the garage and find all the property you've stolen from the burglaries you committed." Harry said, "You're the worst. I'm getting out of here before I say something I regret." Before he left however, Harry hung up a giant sign on the front door. It said: "My name is Harry. I am the co-owner and co-tenant of this house. And I do not give consent for any police officers to search, no matter what my wife Wanda says." When Wanda sees the sign, she says, "We'll see about that." Wanda calls the police and tells them about the stolen property in the garage. Officers arrive a few minutes later and Wanda gives consent for them to enter the house and look for stolen property. The officers read the sign that Harry left on the door and ask Wanda, "What is this?" Wanda lies and says it was made by her teenage children and is just a prank. The officers walk past the sign and enter the house. The officers find stolen property inside and later arrest Harry. Should the stolen property be admitted or suppressed?

A) The stolen property should be suppressed because a cotenant has objected to a search of the house.

B) The stolen property should be suppressed because Wanda's story about the teenagers making the sign is not plausible and the officers were obligated to clarify the situation before searching.

C) The stolen property should be admitted because there was no physically present co-tenant who objected when Wanda granted consent.

D) The stolen property should be admitted because as long as one tenant consents to the search of property it is irrelevant whether another cotenant objects.

Question 46

Assume the same facts as Question 45, except in this case Harry does not make a sign to put on the front door and he instead remains at the house until the police arrive. When the police arrive, Harry says, "I want to be crystal clear. I do not consent to a search of this house. You cannot come in here without a warrant." Wanda then came outside and told the police, "Harry just hit me. We're getting divorced and he's not taking it well. He slapped me in the face for no reason." The officers looked at Wanda's face and saw a bruise. They concluded Wanda was telling the truth and they arrested Harry and took him to jail. Thirty minutes later, the officers returned and (with Harry now incarcerated) they asked Wanda, "Will you give us consent to search the house for any property Harry might have stolen?" Wanda said "Yes." The officers went inside and found stolen property. Harry later moves to suppress the stolen property as the product of an unlawful search. Which of the following is correct?

A) The evidence should be suppressed because Harry was physically present when he objected to the search of the house.

B) The evidence should be suppressed because Harry's objection to a consensual search remains in effect until he revokes it.

C) The evidence should be admitted, but only if the officer returned the next day (regardless of whether Harry was still in jail) and obtains new consent from Wanda.

D) The evidence should be admitted because there was no physically present co-tenant who objected when Wanda gave consent to search the house.

Question 47

Fred and Mike live on the sixth floor of an apartment complex. Mike lives on the west side of the floor and Fred lives on the east side of the floor. Fred and Mike quickly became friends because they both love baseball. One July night, they decide to watch a New York Mets game at Fred's apartment. Fred and Mike have been drinking beer and around the seventh inning Fred realizes they are out of beer. Mike, who is lying on the couch and doesn't want to get up, throws his keys to Fred and says, "I've got beer in my fridge. Just go get it out of my apartment." Fred takes the keys, walks down the hall, and tries a couple of keys before getting the right one to unlock Mike's apartment. Fred then goes inside to pick up the beer. While Fred is inside Mike's apartment picking up the beer, there is a knock on the door. Fred answers the door and sees two uniformed police officers standing there. The officers say, "We've had reports of drug dealing in the stairwell at this end of the apartment complex. Do you mind if we check out your apartment for drugs?" Fred says, "Fine by me." The officers search the apartment—Mike's apartment—and find drugs. Police later arrest Mike and Mike moves to suppress the drugs found in his apartment. Which of the following is correct?

A) The drugs are not admissible because only Mike can consent to a search of his own apartment.

B) The drugs are not admissible because police never told Fred he had the right to refuse consent.

C) The drugs are not admissible because the police officers reasonably believed that Fred had the authority to consent to a search, but they were mistaken.

D) The drugs are admissible because Fred possessed the keys, which gave him the authority to consent to a search.

E) The drugs are admissible because the officers reasonably could have believed that Fred had authority to consent, even if he did not actually have that authority.

Question 48

In the middle of the semester, a professor announces to her students that she is actually an FBI agent investigating drug use on campus. The professor is armed and her gun is in a holster on her hip. The professor stands at the end of the third row of seats. For no reason in particular, she points to the student sitting in the middle of the third row and says, "Can I look in your backpack for drugs?" The student opens the backpack, which contains drugs. Which of the following is correct?

A) The drugs should be suppressed because the FBI agent has conducted a brief investigatory seizure without any reasonable suspicion.

B) The drugs should be admitted at trial because a reasonable person would have felt free to leave and therefore the drugs were discovered as a result of consent, not a seizure.

C) The drugs should be admitted because consent cannot be coerced when a large group of people is present.

D) The drugs should be admitted so long as the FBI agent had reasonable suspicion to search the bag.

Question 49

William, a philosophy professor, is pulled over for speeding, which is an arrestable offense. The officer asks William, "Will you open the trunk so I can take a look inside for drugs?" William is reluctant to open the trunk but does so in part because he does not think the officer will look in the zippered backpack where William keeps his cocaine. The officer opens the zippered backpack and finds the cocaine. Before trial, William moves to suppress the drugs. How should the court rule?

A) The drugs should be admitted because William gave his voluntary consent to a search of the trunk.

B) The drugs should be admitted because the officer can search the trunk pursuant to the automobile exception.

C) The drugs should be suppressed because the officer asked to search in a misleading way and never told William he had the right to refuse consent.

D) The drugs should be suppressed because William's consent to search did not extend to the zippered backpack.

ANSWERS TO MULTIPLE-CHOICE QUESTIONS

Answer to Question 41

Answer A is incorrect. Consent must be given freely and voluntarily, but that does not require the individual to give a verbal yes. Body language can be sufficient.

Answer B is incorrect. The officer did ask twice for consent. There is no rule that multiple requests automatically amount to coercion. Moreover, the second request was to clarify Erica's answer, which was inaudible. The second request does not appear to be coercive.

Answer C is correct. By nodding her head up and down, Erica has given affirmative consent.

Answer D is incorrect. Refusal to grant consent is a constitutional right and it is not incriminating. Even if Erica initially refused to grant consent (which is not what appears to have happened in the question) it would not create probable cause to invoke the automobile exception.

Answer to Question 42

Answer A is incorrect. This does not appear to be voluntary consent. Instead, it appears that the officers repeatedly pressured Erica to grant consent.

Answer B is incorrect. It is factually true that Erica never affirmatively rejected the request for consent. But that is not the standard. For the police to search without probable cause and a warrant, Erica must have affirmatively waived her Fourth Amendment rights. The burden is not on Erica to affirmatively reject the officers' request.

Answer C is incorrect. A large number of officers on the scene can sometimes create a coercive situation. But three officers is not an unusually large number and by itself is probably not sufficient to coerce consent.

Answer D is correct. When we combine multiple officers, repeated requests for consent, and confrontational questioning it is likely that a court would find consent to be coerced under the totality of the circumstances.

Answer to Question 43

Answer A is incorrect. The officer asked for consent to search for drugs and Erica granted that consent. Drugs are small and could be located under the spare tire. Consent therefore extends to that location.

Answer B is correct. General consent to search for items—including drugs—does not include the consent to break, rip, or destroy containers. To break, rip, or destroy a container in order to look inside, the officer needs further consent specific to that item. The officer did not procure that consent in this case.

Answer C is incorrect. While it is true that drugs can fit in a small box, the box was sealed. The officer only had consent to look in the trunk, not to break the seal of a box.

Answer D is incorrect. Erica never gave consent to search a sealed container. She is not obligated to monitor Officer Colin's search of the trunk and to object to the search of items she never consented to have the police search in the first place.

Answer to Question 44

Answer A is correct. Erica has provided voluntary affirmative consent.

Answer B is incorrect. Police cannot search the trunk of a car in a search of an automobile incident to arrest. Additionally, the officer has no reason to believe evidence of the crime of arrest (speeding) will be found in the vehicle (see Chapter 11).

Answer C is incorrect. Officer Colin has no probable cause to believe contraband or evidence is located in the trunk. Without probable cause, he cannot rely on the automobile exception. (See Chapter 10 for a discussion of the automobile exception.)

Answer D is incorrect. Police are not obligated to inform individuals that they have a right to refuse consent.

Answer E is incorrect. Just because Erica is under arrest, handcuffed, and in the back of the police vehicle does not mean that her consent has been coerced. The officer did not make a show of force or otherwise threaten her in order to procure her consent. Suspects who are under arrest can still give valid consent.

Answer to Question 45

Answer A is incorrect. For a cotenant to block another tenant's consent, he must be physically present when he objects. Harry's sign conveys his lack of consent, but he is not physically present.

Answer B is incorrect. Officers do not have an obligation to clarify the situation.

While Wanda lied about who wrote the sign, it does not matter because there is no physically present objecting cotenant.

Answer C is correct. To be able to block Wanda's consent, Harry has to be physically present when he objects.

Answer D is incorrect. This incorrectly states the rule. If a physically present cotenant objects to granting consent, the police cannot rely on the consent of the other tenant.

Answer to Question 46

Answer A is incorrect. The rule requires that there be a physically present cotenant who objects to a search at the time that another tenant is giving consent. When Wanda granted consent, Harry was in jail and not physically present to object.

Answer B is incorrect. The Supreme Court has never held that a cotenant's refusal to consent operates in perpetuity after they leave the premises.

Answer C is incorrect. The Supreme Court has not required officers to wait a full day after an objecting cotenant leaves the premises before requesting consent from a different cotenant.

Answer D is correct. The rule is that only a physically present cotenant can block another cotenant from giving consent to the police to search the premises. Because Harry was not physically present when Wanda gave consent, her consent is valid.

Answer to Question 47

Answer A is incorrect. Police can rely on consent given by a third party when it reasonably appears the third party has authority to grant consent, even if the third party has no such authority.

Answer B is incorrect. The police have no obligation to tell individuals that they have a right to refuse consent.

Answer C is incorrect. A mistake by the police will only eliminate a third party's consent if the officers are unreasonable in relying on that individual's consent.

Answer D is incorrect. Simply possessing the key to a location does not automatically give the person the authority to consent. Typically, a third party would need a greater connection to an apartment to have authority to give consent. For instance, if a third party regularly slept at the apartment and kept personal items there, that would make it more likely they had authority to grant consent.

Answer E is correct. Fred did not have authority to consent to a search of Mike's apartment, but the police did not know that. When the officers knocked, Fred opened the door and it would seem to a reasonable person that Fred lived there. Moreover, Fred never said anything that would make a reasonable officer think Fred lacked authority to consent.

Answer to Question 48

Answer A is incorrect. Although the officer is armed, this does not mean that a reasonable person would not feel free to leave. Individuals regularly encounter officers who have holstered weapons, and those individuals regularly feel free to leave their interactions with the officers.

Answer B is correct. The officer has not conducted a detention merely by being present with a firearm. In requesting consent, the officer asked a question of the student and the student responded by opening the backpack. The student consented to opening the backpack.

Answer C is incorrect. This answer choice is an overstatement. Police cannot procure valid consent through coercion. And it is surely harder to coerce consent when an individual is surrounded by a large group of people. But it is not true that the mere existence of a large group of people ever prevents coercion from occurring.

Answer D is incorrect. This answer choice suggests that there could not have been consent and that the only way to search the backpack is under the *Terry* doctrine. It is possible to procure consent, however. And even if the officer did not have consent, reasonable suspicion is not a sufficient basis to search the backpack. To search a backpack, the officer would have needed probable cause and a warrant or an exception to the warrant requirement.

Answer to Question 49

Answer A is correct. The officer made clear that he was searching for drugs when he asked William for consent to search the trunk. William granted consent without imposing any restrictions. A reasonable officer would thus have believed that consent extended to any place in the trunk where drugs could be held. The fact that William thought in his own mind that he was restricting the scope of consent is not sufficient to invalidate the search.

Answer B is incorrect. The officer pulled William over for speeding, not drugs. Nothing in the question indicates that the officer had probable cause to believe there were drugs in the trunk. Accordingly, the officer cannot invoke the automobile exception. (See Chapter 10 for a discussion of the automobile exception.)

Answer C is incorrect. The officer did not mislead William, and the officer is under no obligation to tell William that he has the right to refuse consent.

Answer D is incorrect. The officer indicated he was looking for drugs, and the backpack is certainly big enough that it could contain drugs. Accordingly, consent to search extended to the backpack.

CHAPTER 9

The Search Incident to a Lawful Arrest Exception

THE RULE: When police conduct a lawful custodial arrest, they can search the person of the arrestee as well as the area within her immediate reach. The police can conduct a full-scale search of everything except for a cell phone. No warrant is required and the police only need probable cause for a lawful arrest.

Critical Points

- The search incident to arrest doctrine is an exception to *both* probable cause and the warrant requirement.
- To invoke the exception there must be a lawful custodial arrest. If the suspect is not lawfully under arrest and in custody (or just about to be under arrest and in custody) then the exception does not apply.
- The police can search: (1) the person of the arrestee (for example, pockets and containers inside pockets); and (2) the area within the arrestee's immediate reach.
    - Police cannot search the electronic contents of a cell phone.
    - Police cannot conduct a body cavity search.
    - Police can search every other item on an arrestee or within his immediate reach.
- The search must be contemporaneous with the arrest.
    - The Supreme Court has never clearly defined "contemporaneous."
    - Searches that occur moments before and after arrest are usually contemporaneous. Searches of the area within the arrestee's immediate reach that police conduct hours after arrest are typically not considered contemporaneous.

OVERVIEW OF THE BLACKLETTER LAW

The search incident to arrest doctrine permits police to conduct a full-scale search of the body of the arrestee as well as the area within her immediate reach.

In searching the body of the arrestee, the police can search any item on the arrestee, with the exception of a cell phone. For example, police can reach inside of pockets. If the officer feels a crumpled-up piece of paper in the individual's pocket, the officer can open it. If the arrestee is wearing a purse or backpack, the officer can remove it from the arrestee's body, open the purse or backpack, and open any item inside. With the exception of searching through the electronic contents of a cell phone, the police can open and search *anything*. This is a bright-line rule designed to make matters very clear for police officers.

In searching the area within the arrestee's immediate reach, the rules are less clear. Courts uphold full-scale searches of areas that the arrestee could "immediately control" or grab an item from. If an arrestee is standing next to a car with an open trunk, their immediate reach would include the trunk. If an arrestee is standing in an office, their immediate reach would include the desk drawers or file cabinet that he could lunge toward. By contrast, if police arrest someone in a house, the officers cannot conduct a search of the entire house incident to arrest because that would exceed the arrestee's immediate reach.

A search incident to arrest must be the result of a lawful custodial arrest. First, consider the legality of the arrest. If the police did not have probable cause for the arrest, then the arrest would be unlawful and the evidence found as a result would not be admissible. There can be no valid search incident to arrest unless there was a lawful arrest that complied with the Fourth Amendment. Second, there must in fact be a custodial arrest. Police cannot search incident to a citation or a traffic ticket. If the police do not take the suspect into custody, there cannot be a search incident to arrest.

The arrest must be contemporaneous with that arrest. Normally this is not an issue because police conduct the search at the same time they make the arrest. But sometimes police officers conduct the search either before or after the arrest. A search occurring just before an arrest can still be a search incident to arrest because the Court does not want to micromanage the police by telling them how to proceed. Similarly, police can also conduct a search incident to arrest right after an individual is handcuffed or has been removed from the area. In other words, there is a general contemporaneousness requirement rather than a rigid one. But police cannot make an arrest and then return hours later to search the area under the search incident to arrest doctrine.

Even if all the other elements are met—(1) lawful arrest; (2) custodial arrest; (3) contemporaneous search; (4) of items on the person or within their immediate reach—the police still cannot search a cell phone under the search incident to arrest doctrine. In *Riley v. California* (2014), the Supreme Court held that cell phones are different from other containers because they hold vastly more information. If police come across a cell phone while conducting a search incident to arrest, they may seize the phone but not search it. To search a cell phone, police must either procure a warrant or find another exception to the warrant requirement (such as exigent circumstances).

The rationale for the search incident to arrest doctrine is twofold: (1) officer safety and (2) to prevent the destruction of evidence. The Supreme Court has repeatedly recognized the importance of officer safety. If police did not search a person at the time of arrest, that individual might be able to reach a gun, knife, or other weapon that could be used against the officers. The Court has also expressed concern about suspects destroying evidence. Even when police have a suspect in custody, they cannot watch her every second. A suspect who is under arrest and is facing the prospect of criminal charges has a strong incentive to destroy incriminating evidence. The Supreme Court therefore recognizes the importance of allowing police to search for evidence—including in hard-to-reach locations or small closed containers—when conducting an arrest.

While there are two underlying rationales for the existence of the search incident to arrest doctrine—danger to the officers and destruction of evidence—neither rationale need be present in a particular case. The search incident to arrest doctrine is automatic and police can invoke it even if there is no danger to the officer or risk of evidence destruction in the case at hand.

EXAM TRAPS TO AVOID

- *Unlawful Arrests*: Be sure that there is a *lawful* arrest. Do not assume that just because the question says a person was arrested that a subsequent search is valid. In order for the search incident to arrest to be valid, the arrest must be valid.
- *Noncustodial Situations*: Be sure that the individual has actually been subjected to a *custodial* arrest. If the police only ask a person to sit in the police car while they write her a ticket, that is not necessarily a custodial arrest and therefore a search would not fall under the search incident to arrest doctrine.
- *Lack of Contemporaneousness*: Be sure that the search is *contemporaneous* with the arrest. If the police are searching moments before or after an arrest, it is likely contemporaneous. If hours have passed since the arrest, a search of the immediate grabbing space is probably not contemporaneous.
- *Not within the Arrestee's Immediate Reach*: Be sure to analyze whether the area searched is within the arrestee's *immediate reach*. If the arrestee is in a small room (like a bathroom) the entire room may be within the arrestee's immediate reach. If the arrestee is in a larger room (like a living room) then the police may only be able to search a portion of the room.

MULTIPLE-CHOICE QUESTIONS

Question 50

After a thorough investigation, the police have probable cause to believe that Janet is involved in a recent diamond robbery that carries a possible 20-year prison sentence. The police know that Janet is home on Wednesday mornings and, after knocking and announcing their presence, wait for 30 seconds before pushing in the front door and arresting Janet in her kitchen. After placing Janet under arrest, the police search her person and find diamonds in her jacket pocket. The police later confirm the diamonds are from the diamond robbery they have been investigating. Janet moves to suppress the diamonds. How should the court rule?

A) The suppression motion should be granted because the diamonds are the fruit of an unlawful arrest.

B) The suppression motion should be granted because police cannot reach inside pockets when they search incident to arrest. They can only pat down the outer layer of the suspect's garment.

C) The suppression motion should be denied because the diamonds were discovered incident to a lawful arrest.

D) The suppression motion should be denied because the police were entitled to search anywhere in the house where the diamonds could have been hidden.

Question 51

Police have been investigating Ted for sexual misconduct. In particular, the officers believe that Ted is photographing young children at a swimming pool locker room when the children go in to change into their swimsuits. The police were alerted to Ted by an anonymous tip. The officers have confirmed that Ted—who has no children and does not live or work in the neighborhood—is often at the swimming pool on weekends when children are at the pool. The officers conduct surveillance and see Ted enter the locker room with his cell phone out and pointed at the children. When Ted exits the locker room, the officers arrest him for the crime of public indecency. The officers take Ted's phone and immediately open it to the photo application. The officers find photos of naked children. The officers do not search any further. Ted is charged with public indecency and possession of child pornography. Ted moves to suppress the photos. Which of the following is correct?

A) The photos are admissible because the phone was on Ted's person and could be fully searched incident to arrest.

B) The photos are admissible because the officers had reason to believe evidence related to the crime of arrest would be found on the phone.

C) The photos are admissible because the police searched no further than necessary by immediately opening the photo application on the phone and searching no further.

D) The photos are inadmissible because it was possible for police to seize and immobilize the phone while awaiting a warrant.

E) The photos are inadmissible because the crime of arrest was public indecency—not child pornography—and it was not reasonable to believe evidence of public indecency could be found on the phone.

Question 52

Officer Jones is parked on the highway, running his radar gun while traffic drives by. Most drivers are exceeding the speed limit by about five miles per hour, and Officer Jones does not pursue them. After letting about 100 speeding cars pass, Officer Jones clocks Steve, a young African American man, exceeding the speed limit by two miles per hour. Speeding is an arrestable offense that is punishable by up to a $500 fine, but no jail time. Officer Jones pulls over Steve, handcuffs him, and places him under arrest. Five minutes later, Officer Jones searches Steve incident to arrest, and finds cocaine in his pocket. If Steve appeals his conviction for cocaine possession, how should the court rule?

A) The conviction should be reversed because the officer's reason for stopping Steve was a pretextual cover for racial discrimination.

B) The conviction should be reversed because it is impermissible to search a defendant incident to arrest for a crime that does not carry any jail time.

C) The conviction should be reversed because the search incident to arrest occurred several minutes after the officer handcuffed Steve.

D) The conviction should be affirmed because there was a lawful basis for the stop and a lawful basis for the arrest.

Question 53

Police have probable cause to believe that Melanie has been dealing cocaine. The officers procure a valid arrest warrant for Melanie. Once they have arrived at Melanie's residence, the officers knock and announce their presence, but no one responds. The officers therefore break down the door and begin looking for Melanie in the house. They find her in her bedroom standing directly behind a desk. Because there are two other people in the house, the officers immediately handcuff Melanie and quickly escort her out of the house. Once outside, the officers search Melanie's person and feel a bulge around her stomach that is under her shirt. The officers immediately remove a bag of cocaine that was under Melanie's shirt and taped to her stomach. If Melanie moves to suppress the cocaine, how should the court rule?

A) The court should grant the motion to suppress because the search did not occur where Melanie was arrested and thus is not contemporaneous.

B) The court should grant the motion to suppress because the police cannot search underneath clothing.

C) The court should deny the motion to suppress because the police did not exceed the scope of a valid search incident to arrest.

D) The court should deny the motion to suppress because Melanie lacks standing since there was a valid arrest warrant.

Question 54

Imagine the same facts as Question 53 with the following variation. Two police officers entered Melanie's house to conduct the arrest. The first officer handcuffed Melanie and brought her outside. The second officer remained inside and searched the desk that Melanie had been standing behind. The second officer opened the desk drawer and found a bag of heroin hidden underneath a pile of papers. How should the court rule if Melanie moves to suppress the heroin?

A) The court should grant the motion to suppress because the police only procured an arrest warrant and not a search warrant.

B) The court should grant the motion to suppress because Melanie was no longer present when the officer searched and therefore there cannot be a valid search incident to arrest.

C) The court should grant the motion to suppress because while it would have been okay for the officer to open the desk drawer to look for a weapon, the act of moving the papers is too invasive and therefore not valid.

D) The court should deny the motion to suppress because the search incident to arrest doctrine is a bright-line rule that extends to the entire room where an individual is arrested.

E) The court should deny the motion to suppress because the desk drawer was within Melanie's immediate reach at the time of her arrest.

Question 55

For purposes of this question, assume that the police lawfully arrested Melanie for an earlier incident of cocaine distribution. When the officers began to handcuff Melanie, they removed a purse from her shoulder. The officers opened the purse and found a brush, a pack of gum, lip balm, tissues, and a wallet. The officers took out the pack of gum. They unwrapped the foil around the first piece of gum and found nothing but gum inside. The officers then unwrapped the foil around the second piece of gum and inside they found heroin rather than gum. Prosecutors have charged Melanie with possession of a controlled substance and she has moved to suppress the heroin. What result?

A) The heroin is admissible as a valid search incident to arrest.

B) The heroin is admissible as a valid search incident to arrest, but only because the crime of arrest was cocaine distribution and it was therefore reasonable to believe evidence of drugs might be found in her control.

C) The heroin is not admissible because police cannot open closed containers during a search incident to arrest.

D) The heroin is not admissible because even though police can initially open containers under a search incident to arrest, when they found nothing illegal after opening the foil around the first piece of gum they were obligated to stop searching.

ANSWERS TO MULTIPLE-CHOICE QUESTIONS

Answer to Question 50

Answer A is correct. Police need a warrant to make an arrest inside of a home. The question does not say that the police have a warrant. Because the arrest is unlawful, there can be no valid search incident to arrest.

Answer B is incorrect. Police *can* reach inside of pockets when searching incident to arrest. The search incident to arrest allows a full-scale search.

Answer C is also incorrect. The search was incident to arrest. But it was not a lawful arrest because there was no warrant to enter the home. Therefore the evidence must be suppressed.

Answer D is incorrect. Police cannot automatically search an entire house incident to arrest. The search is limited to the body of the arrestee and the area of their immediate reach. Typically, the arrestee's immediate reach will not extend to the entire house.

Answer to Question 51

Answer A is incorrect. The Supreme Court held in *Riley v. California* (2014) that police cannot search a cell phone incident to arrest.

Answer B is incorrect. This answer choice states the test from *Arizona v. Gant* (2009) for searching a vehicle incident to arrest. That test is not applicable to cell phone searches.

Answer C is incorrect. The search incident to arrest doctrine does not utilize a "no further than necessary" test.

Answer D is correct. Pursuant to the Supreme Court's decision in *Riley v. California* (2014), if police encounter a cell phone while searching incident to arrest, they may seize the phone while they procure a warrant to search it. The officers may not search the phone incident to arrest without a warrant.

Answer E is incorrect. This answer choice, like choice B, states the test for searching a vehicle incident to arrest.

Answer to Question 52

Answer A is incorrect. While the officer may have engaged in pretextual discrimination by stopping an African American driver after allowing other drivers to go past, the arrest is likely still lawful. Pursuant to the Supreme Court's decision in *Whren v. United States* (1996), courts must focus on whether there was an objectively valid reason for pulling over the driver. Because Steve was exceeding the speed limit, it is permissible for the officer to stop him. And because speeding is an arrestable offense, police may arrest him and search him incident to arrest.

Answer B is incorrect. Police may arrest someone and search them incident to that arrest even if the offense does not carry jail time. Police cannot search someone incident to a citation or a traffic ticket because that is not a custodial arrest. But here the question tells us that the officer arrested Steve.

Answer C is incorrect. While a search incident to arrest must be contemporaneous with arrest, it does not have to occur at the exact moment of arrest. Here only a few minutes passed between the arrest and the search. The search is still incident to arrest.

Answer D is correct. The stop is lawful because Steve was exceeding the speed limit. Because the officer made a custodial arrest, the police can search Steve incident to arrest.

Answer to Question 53

Answer A is incorrect. Police do not have to conduct the search incident to arrest at the exact moment or location of an arrest. They can move the suspect and conduct the search incident to arrest after the arrest. That is particularly true here, given that there are two other individuals in the home who could pose a risk to the officers.

Answer B is incorrect. While the search incident to arrest doctrine does not typically allow police to conduct invasive searches (such as body cavity searches), here the question tells us that police are immediately able to feel the package during an ordinary search incident to arrest. They can accordingly seize the drugs from under Melanie's shirt.

Answer C is correct. The cocaine was discovered during a lawful search incident to arrest.

Answer D is incorrect. Although there is a valid arrest warrant, that does not eliminate Melanie's standing to challenge the search of her person. Melanie has a reasonable expectation of privacy in her own body and thus has standing to challenge a search. (For a discussion of standing, see Chapter 20.) Although she has standing, though, her claim will fail because the police conducted a valid search incident to arrest.

Answer to Question 54

Answer A is incorrect. The police do not need a search warrant. If the police conduct a lawful custodial arrest, they can search incident to arrest without a search warrant.

Answer B is incorrect. A search incident to arrest must be contemporaneous with arrest, but delaying the search until a few moments after arrest is permissible. If the arrestee has been removed from the location in those few moments, it does not eliminate the officer's authority to search the area where she was located when the arrest occurred.

Answer C is incorrect. The search incident to arrest doctrine authorizes a full-scale search. The officers are not limited to looking for a weapon. Nor are officers restricted to only looking at the first visible layer of items. Officers can dig through the contents of a drawer and conduct a detailed and thorough search.

Answer D is incorrect. The search incident to arrest doctrine is a bright-line rule with respect to the search of the person (because the officer can search any item on the arrestee except a cell phone), but it is not a bright-line rule with respect to the area around an arrestee. In searching the area where an arrestee was located, the police can only search the area within the arrestee's immediate reach. In a very small room, the immediate reach may extend to the entire room. But in a medium-sized or larger room, the police cannot search the entire room incident to arrest. The area that can be searched is only the area within the arrestee's immediate reach.

Answer E is correct. The question tells us that Melanie was "standing directly behind a desk" (see Question 53). The desk drawer was therefore within Melanie's immediate reach and can be searched incident to arrest.

Answer to Question 55

Answer A is correct. When police make a valid arrest, they are permitted to search the person and the area within their immediate reach incident to arrest. That would certainly include the purse on Melanie's shoulder. In conducting the search incident to arrest, the officers can open any item, including closed containers. The officers are therefore permitted to open the package of gum and to open the individual foil wrappers around each piece of gum.

Answer B is incorrect. When police search a person incident to arrest they can automatically open all containers on the person and within their immediate reach. The officers do not need to have reason to believe evidence of the crime of arrest will be in a container before opening that container. (Note: This rule is different for searches of vehicles incident to arrest. As explained in Chapter 11, police can only search the passenger compartment of a vehicle incident to arrest when they have reason to believe evidence of the crime of arrest can be found in the vehicle.)

Answer C is incorrect. Police *can* open closed containers during a search incident to arrest.

Answer D is incorrect. Police can open all closed containers when searching incident to arrest. Just because they do not find contraband in the first (or second, or third) place they look does not mean that they have to stop searching incident to arrest.

CHAPTER 10
The Automobile Exception

THE RULE: When police have probable cause to believe that evidence will be found in a vehicle, they can search the area of the vehicle for which they have probable cause (usually the whole vehicle) without a warrant.

Critical Points

- The automobile exception is an exception to the warrant requirement but it is *not* an exception to the probable cause requirement. Police still need to demonstrate probable cause if they want to invoke the automobile exception.
- *Where and What Can the Police Search*
  - Usually (but not always) police can search the entire car because police typically have probable cause for the entire vehicle.
  - Sometimes the search is limited to only part of the vehicle: Be careful of situations in which the police only have probable cause for a specific portion of the vehicle. For example, if an informant tells police he knows there are drugs in the trunk of a car, that creates probable cause for the trunk only and thus the automobile exception only applies to the trunk.
- *When and Where Can the Police Search?* The police can conduct a warrantless search at the scene where they locate the vehicle, or they can tow the car to a safer location and conduct the search there. The automobile exception allows the officers to search the vehicle hours after they first encounter it.
- *Container Searches Are Permissible:* Police can search inside any container that is large enough to hold the evidence they are looking for.

- *Searching Locked Areas Is Permissible:* Police can break into locked areas (for example, the glove box) or locked containers inside a vehicle if they have probable cause to believe those locked areas or containers contain evidence.
- *Taking Apart the Car May Be Permissible:* Drug dealers sometimes hide drugs in gas tanks, the engine, inside of seats, and in other hidden compartments. If police have probable cause to believe that evidence is hidden in one of these unusual locations, they can take apart the engine, gas tank, or other area in order to search under the automobile exception.

OVERVIEW OF THE BLACKLETTER LAW

Police frequently search vehicles without a warrant, and professors frequently test whether evidence found during those warrantless searches is admissible. One of the main ways in which police justify searching vehicles is through what the Supreme Court has called the automobile exception to the warrant requirement. Under Supreme Court precedent that dates back almost a century, the Court has allowed warrantless searches of vehicles as long as the police have probable cause to believe that the vehicle contains evidence of criminal activity. The Court does not demand a search warrant to search vehicles because cars are mobile (and could thus disappear before the police come back with the warrant) and also because vehicles are heavily regulated and thus carry a lesser expectation of privacy than other property. The automobile exception is thus an exception to the warrant requirement. The automobile exception *does not* excuse the police from having to demonstrate probable cause. Indeed, the automobile exception focuses almost entirely on the question of probable cause.

Many situations can give rise to the probable cause police need to search a vehicle under the automobile exception. For example, an informant could tell police that there are drugs in the car. Or the police themselves could smell drugs when standing next to the car. Or a drug-sniffing dog could alert its handler that the dog smells drugs. The possibilities for finding probable cause to search a vehicle are numerous.

Once the police have probable cause, the next question is: where they can search based on that probable cause? In most cases, the automobile exception gives police authority to search the entire vehicle. The reason is that the probable cause the police have is not specific to any part of the vehicle. For example, if a reliable informant says, "Dan is selling heroin on the street and he keeps his supply in his Toyota Camry," that tip will likely create probable cause to search the entire Toyota Camry for heroin.

In other instances, however, police may only have probable cause to search a portion of the vehicle. For example, if the informant said, "Dan is selling heroin out of *the trunk* of his Toyota Camry" that tip would create probable cause only to search the trunk. The key point here is that the automobile exception extends to any location in the vehicle for which there is probable cause. Unlike the search incident to arrest exception (see Chapter 9), the automobile exception is not a blanket exception that automatically allows a search of the entire passenger compartment of the vehicle.

After determining which parts of the vehicle the police can search, the next question is whether police can open compartments or containers that they come across inside of the vehicle. For instance, if the police are searching under the automobile exception, can they open suitcases, briefcases, or backpacks? Can they look under the spare tire? Are they allowed to look in the glove compartment or small containers, such as jewelry box? The answer to all of these questions turns on what the police have probable cause to be searching for and the size of that item. You should ask yourself "could the item for which the police are searching fit in this container?" If the answer is "yes," then police can open the container and look inside. Consider two different-sized items: drugs and a shotgun. If the police have probable cause to search for drugs, they can likely open almost any container or compartment inside the vehicle because drugs are tiny and can fit inside of almost any container. By contrast, shotguns are long and can only fit in long spaces. If the police have probable cause to search for a shotgun, they can certainly look in the passenger compartment and the trunk (because the shotgun could fit there) but they cannot search the glove compartment or a jewelry box found in the trunk (because the shotgun could not fit in either of those locations). The key point is that the scope of an automobile exception search turns on what item the police have probable cause to search for and where that item could possibly be located.

A final common question for automobile exception searches is what happens if the police come across a locked container while searching a vehicle. The answer is that police can unlock or break into a container that is locked. The automobile exception operates a as a substitute for a search warrant. Thus, police can conduct any search under the automobile exception that they would be able to conduct with a search warrant. If police were executing a search warrant and came across a locked box, they would not simply say, "Oh well, it's locked, so I guess we'll just skip that." When executing a search warrant, police regularly break down doors or pry open locked containers. Because the automobile exception is a substitute for a search warrant, police can therefore break into closed and locked containers if they have probable cause to believe evidence may be inside.

EXAM TRAPS TO AVOID

- Do Not Assume the Police Can Search the Entire Car: The automobile exception does not automatically apply to the entire vehicle. Always check to make sure there is probable cause for the area of the car where the police are searching.
- Arrest of the Driver Is Not Relevant: The automobile exception does not apply just because the driver was arrested. A question may tell you that the

driver committed a traffic offense and was arrested. Or the question might say that there was a warrant out for the driver's arrest and that the police took him into custody. These scenarios do not automatically mean that the police can search the vehicle under the automobile exception. You must always ask: Is there probable cause to believe evidence of criminal activity will be found in the vehicle?

- Different from the Search of a Vehicle Incident to Arrest Exception: The automobile exception is different from the search of a vehicle incident to arrest exception. As explained later (see Chapter 11), the search of a vehicle incident to arrest exception almost never allows a search of the trunk, whereas the automobile exception usually allows a search of the trunk as long as there is probable cause.

MULTIPLE-CHOICE QUESTIONS

Question 56

The police have been conducting surveillance of Arnold and they have seen him carrying around a small box that is the size of a coffee mug. The police have probable cause to believe the box contains illegal drugs. While observing Arnold, the police never see him dispose of the box. Instead, they see Arnold get into his car. As Arnold is driving away from his home, the police stop his car, order him out of the car, and search the entire car, including the trunk, in order to find the box. The police find the box hidden under a spare tire in the trunk. The police open the box and find illegal drugs inside. Arnold moves to suppress the drug evidence. How should the court rule?

A) The court should grant Arnold's motion because the police did not have a warrant to search the car.

B) The court should grant Arnold's motion because even though the police did not need a warrant to search the car, they did need a warrant to open the container.

C) The court should deny Arnold's motion because the search falls within the automobile exception to the warrant requirement.

D) The court should deny Arnold's motion because the police had probable cause to arrest Arnold and inevitably would have found the drugs when they searched incident to arrest.

Question 57

Police receive a tip that Mary is selling drugs out of her car. Police follow Mary for a few hours and confirm that she is engaged in suspicious activity. Using binoculars, police see Mary hand a man a small bag of cocaine while simultaneously taking money from the man. Police then approach Mary as she is standing near her car. Police notice that the cap to the car's gas tank is open and that there is a small plastic bag hanging out of the gas tank. Police arrest Mary and search her person as well as the passenger compartment of the car and the trunk of the car. The police do not find any drugs. Police then tow the car to a mechanic and instruct the mechanic to take apart the car's gas tank. About four hours after Mary's arrest, the mechanic finds more than two dozen bags of cocaine in the gas tank. Are the bags of cocaine admissible against Mary under any warrant exception?

A) No, because you cannot search the gas tank of a vehicle incident to arrest.

B) No, because while you might be able to search the car under the automobile exception, you cannot tow it to another location to conduct the search.

C) Yes, because the police have conducted a valid search incident to arrest.

D) Yes, because there was probable cause to believe there was evidence in the gas tank and the search is therefore valid under the automobile exception.

Question 58

Police receive a tip that a bright red Tesla car with the license plate "CATCH ME" was seen fleeing the scene of a home burglary. A witness said the burglar left the home with a black bag and put it in the trunk of the Tesla. The next morning, two officers walk out of the police station toward their patrol car to begin their shift. As they reach their patrol car, the officers notice a red Tesla with the license plate "CATCH ME" lawfully parked one block up the street directly in front of the courthouse. No one was in the car. The officers opened the trunk of the car and found the black bag, which contained stolen jewelry. The defendant has moved to suppress the jewelry as the product of an unlawful search. Which of the following is correct?

A) The jewelry is admissible because the car is abandoned and thus is entitled to no Fourth Amendment protection.

B) The jewelry is admissible because the police do not need a warrant to search a vehicle if they have probable cause.

C) The jewelry is inadmissible given that the vehicle was only a block from the courthouse, thus making it practicable to obtain a search warrant.

D) The jewelry is inadmissible because there was no one in the vehicle, making it impossible for the vehicle to be moved and thus the automobile exception does not apply.

E) The jewelry is inadmissible because the automobile exception allows a warrantless search of the passenger compartment of the vehicle, but not the trunk.

Question 59

Two people robbed the First National Bank while dressed in all black and wearing ski masks. The robbers fled in a blue Honda Civic with license plate ABC-123. The police investigated and learned that the car was registered to Gary. Police go to Gary's apartment and knock on the door, but there is no answer. As the police are driving away from Gary's apartment, they see a blue Honda Civic with license plate ABC-123 parked about two blocks away. The officers get very close to the car window and look inside. They see a pile of black clothing and a ski mask on the floor of the back seat of the vehicle. There is no one near the car and it is the middle of the afternoon. The officers call a tow truck and have the vehicle towed to the police station. Four hours later, they search the car at the station and find not just the clothing and ski mask, but also a pile of money that had been stolen from the bank. The prosecution contends that the evidence is admissible under the automobile exception. If Gary moves to suppress, how should the court rule?

A) The court should admit the evidence because the officers had probable cause and do not need a warrant under the automobile exception.

B) The court should admit the evidence because the officers had probable cause and while they should have procured a warrant before searching the car at the police station, they acted in good faith.

C) The court should suppress the evidence because when the officers got "very close to the car window" and looked inside they searched without probable cause or a warrant.

D) The court should suppress the evidence because while the officers could have searched the car contemporaneously on the street when they located it, they cannot tow it to the station and search it four hours later.

Question 60

A highway patrol officer is investigating reports about a silver Porsche that was driving at almost 100 mph in the suburbs outside Richmond, Virginia. The officer has also received a report from a Richmond resident that her silver Porsche with license plate "VROOM 1" was recently stolen. While conducting regular surveillance in a suburb of Richmond, the officer drove past a house with a car in the driveway. The car was under a tarp so it was impossible to see the license plate or even what type of car it was. But the car was the same distinctive shape as a Porsche and the bottom of the car was exposed enough to see that the vehicle was silver. The officer walked onto the driveway, lifted the tarp a few inches so that she could see the license plate, which read "VROOM 1." At that moment, Karen came out of the house and said, "Hey, what are you doing?" The officer arrested Karen for possession of stolen property. Karen has alleged that the officer acted unconstitutionally. Which of the following is correct?

A) The officer acted lawfully because she had probable cause and moving the tarp is covered by the automobile exception.

B) The officer acted lawfully because Karen has no reasonable expectation of privacy because the property was stolen.

C) The officer acted unlawfully by trespassing on Karen's driveway, even if the car was in fact stolen.

D) The officer acted unlawfully because the automobile was covered by a tarp and thus was not mobile and could not fall under the automobile exception.

Question 61

Police are conducting surveillance of a street corner known for drug sales. There is a motor home parked on the corner. A motor home, or an "RV," as it is sometimes called, is a large vehicle that people can live in. This motor home is large enough that it almost surely has a bedroom, kitchen, and bathroom inside of it. The officers watch as Bailey stands in back of the motor home and talks with another person. Bailey takes what appears to be cash and gives the other person what appears to be a small plastic bag. The officers watch as Bailey does the same thing a few minutes later with another person. Thereafter, Bailey goes inside the motor home and comes out a moment later with what looks like more plastic bags. The police watch Bailey exchange the bags for cash with two other people. At that point, Bailey sees the officers watching from across the street, and she takes off running with the keys to the motor home in her hand. The officers approach the motor home, which is unlocked. They go inside and search it from top to bottom. The officers find a large amount of heroin inside. The officers later capture and arrest Bailey a few hours later. Bailey contends that the search of the motor home was unlawful. Which of the following is correct?

A) The search does not fall under the automobile exception because a motor home (with a bedroom, bathroom, and kitchen) is a home that cannot be searched without a warrant.

B) The search is unlawful because police lacked probable cause to claim the automobile exception.

C) The search is unlawful. The police cannot invoke the automobile exception because Bailey left the scene "with the keys to the motor home in her hand" and thus the motor home could not have been driven away.

D) The search is lawful because the police can search the motor home without a warrant under the automobile exception.

E) The search is lawful because it is a search incident to arrest.

Question 62

Alan loves old cars and is not willing to get rid of his 1980 Pontiac Firebird. Alan decides to make his car into a "Firebird treehouse" that his kids can play in. Alan drains the gasoline from the car so that it won't be a fire hazard, and he rents a forklift so that he can put the car up on concrete blocks that are eight feet off the ground. When Alan's son was young, he played in the Firebird treehouse all the time. But about a decade later, Alan's son gets into drugs. He begins dealing the drugs out of the backyard of Alan's home and storing his stash in the Firebird treehouse. Alan's son arranges to sell drugs to an undercover officer and brings him into the backyard next to the Firebird treehouse. Alan's son gets the drugs out of the treehouse and brings them down to the undercover officer. Rather than buy the drugs, though, the officer climbs up onto the Firebird treehouse. The officer discovers a large stash of drugs. How should the court rule on the admissibility of the drugs recovered from the Firebird treehouse?

A) The court should admit the evidence because the officer had probable cause and could conduct a warrantless search under the automobile exception.

B) The court should suppress the evidence because even though the Firebird is a vehicle it was not readily capable of being used and thus cannot fall under the automobile exception.

ANSWERS TO MULTIPLE-CHOICE QUESTIONS

Answer to Question 56

Answer A is incorrect. The police do not need a warrant because they are searching a vehicle. The police only need probable cause, which they have from their surveillance.

Answer B is incorrect. The automobile exception permits officers to open containers so long as the item they have probable cause to search for could fit in the container. Because the police are searching for drugs and drugs could fit in a "small box the size of a coffee mug," the police can search there.

Answer C is correct. Because police have probable cause to search for drugs and because the automobile exception can substitute for a warrant, the search of the small container under the spare tire is permissible.

Answer D is incorrect. The police probably could have arrested Arnold. However, as explained in Chapter 11, the search of a vehicle incident to arrest doctrine does not authorize a search of the trunk.

Answer to Question 57

Answer A is incorrect. It is true that the search incident to arrest doctrine does not extend to the gas tank (see Chapter 11). However, the cocaine bags can still be admissible under the automobile exception.

Answer B is incorrect. If police have probable cause to search a vehicle under the automobile exception, they can do so on the scene where they find the vehicle, or they can tow the vehicle to a safer location to conduct the search.

Answer C is incorrect. The search incident to arrest doctrine extends to the passenger compartment of the vehicle, but not the gas tank.

Answer D is correct. The police surveillance of the cocaine deal and Mary standing near the vehicle creates probable cause to believe drugs could be found in the vehicle. Further, the plastic bag sticking out of the gas tank is suspicious. It is highly unusual to see a plastic bag sticking out of a gas tank. Accordingly, there is probable cause to believe one or more cocaine bags are in the gas tank. Because we are dealing with a car and have probable cause, the police can search without a warrant. The search can extend to any location where the evidence might be located. The police are permitted to break into or disassemble the area if it is necessary to search for the evidence.

Answer to Question 58

Answer A is incorrect. While there is an abandonment exception to the warrant requirement, the question tells us that the vehicle is lawfully parked. It therefore is not abandoned.

Answer B is correct. Even though the car is turned off and the driver does not appear to be in the vicinity, they could return at any moment and move the vehicle. As long as there is probable cause, the automobile exception allows a warrantless search of a potentially movable vehicle.

Answer C is incorrect. Even if it would be practicable to obtain a warrant, that would not make the evidence inadmissible. The automobile exception does not turn on whether it is possible to obtain a warrant. If there is probable cause and a potentially movable vehicle, the automobile exception excuses the need for a warrant.

Answer D is incorrect. The automobile exception does not turn on whether the driver appears to be close by. It would be too difficult for police to determine which drivers are about to return and move their vehicles and which drivers are unlikely to return soon.

Answer E is incorrect. The automobile exception allows a search anywhere in the vehicle for which there is probable cause. This may include the trunk if there is probable cause to believe evidence could be found in the trunk. Answer choice E states the rule for the search of a vehicle incident to arrest, which does not allow a search of the trunk. The automobile exception (a different exception) can apply even when the search incident to arrest exception does not.

Answer to Question 59

Answer A is correct. The officers saw the license plate, clothing, and ski mask that matched the descriptions given by witnesses, which gives them probable cause to search the vehicle. Because the vehicle is parked on the street, it falls under the automobile exception.

Answer B is incorrect. If the officers have probable cause to search a vehicle that is located in public, they do not need a search warrant.

Answer C is incorrect. The officers do not need a search warrant to look in a car window. Because windows are clear, the contents inside are exposed to public view. Because the police officers were lawfully present when looking in the window, they did not conduct a search.

Answer D is incorrect. The automobile exception does not require that a search be conducted at the scene where the vehicle is found, nor does it require that the search be conducted contemporaneously. Police may search the vehicle hours (or even days) later under the automobile exception.

Answer to Question 60

Answer A is incorrect. Even if the officer had probable cause (which seems doubtful), the officer may not trespass onto the curtilage of the property in order to access an automobile.

Answer B is incorrect. Even if the vehicle was stolen, Karen still has an expectation of privacy in her own home. The driveway is within the curtilage of the home and is protected by the Fourth Amendment. The automobile exception does not extend beyond the automobile itself to authorize entry onto property.

Answer C is correct. The automobile exception allows police to conduct a warrantless search based on probable cause. But the automobile exception does not authorize an officer to trespass on private property to gain access to the vehicle.

Answer D is incorrect. Of course, Karen could not drive the vehicle with the tarp on it. But the automobile exception applies to vehicles that could be moved quickly. Because the tarp could be removed in a matter of moments and the vehicle could then be driven away, it could have fallen under the automobile exception if the officer were lawfully permitted to reach it.

Answer to Question 61

Answer A is incorrect. Although the motor home could be used as a home, it is nevertheless still a vehicle capable of being driven away. Because it is readily mobile, it falls under the automobile exception.

Answer B is incorrect. The police observed multiple hand-to-hand drug sales and they also observed Bailey replenish her drug supply from inside the motor home. Thus, there is probable cause to believe there are drugs inside the motor home.

Answer C is incorrect. The keys do not have to be nearby for police to search a vehicle under the automobile exception.

Answer D is correct. The police have probable cause to believe that there are drugs in a movable vehicle. They can therefore search it without a warrant under the automobile exception.

Answer E is incorrect. If the police had arrested Bailey outside of the motor home they would have a credible argument for invoking the exception for searching a vehicle incident to arrest (see Chapter 11). But here, the police searched the motor home first and then later arrested Bailey at a different location "a few hours later." The search is not contemporaneous with arrest and Bailey likely does not qualify as a recent occupant of the vehicle. Therefore this cannot be characterized as a search incident to arrest.

Answer to Question 62

Answer A is incorrect. To fall under the automobile exception the vehicle does not have to be drivable at that moment. However, it does have to be readily capable of being driven away. Here, the vehicle is up on blocks, has no gasoline, and has not been driven in at least a decade. It could not plausibly be driven away.

Answer B is correct. A car that is not readily capable of being driven cannot fall under the automobile exception.

CHAPTER 11
Searches of Vehicles Incident to Arrest

THE RULE: When police conduct a lawful arrest of a motorist or recent occupant of a vehicle, they can search the passenger compartment of the vehicle (but not the trunk) if: (1) the arrestee is unsecured and within reaching distance of the vehicle; or (2) the officers have a reasonable belief that evidence relevant to the crime of arrest might be found in the vehicle.

Critical Points

- The search of a vehicle incident to arrest exception is an exception to the warrant requirement.
- Because police almost always secure arrestees, the search of a vehicle incident to arrest exception still requires suspicion in most cases. While probable cause is not required, the police must have a reasonable belief that evidence relevant to the crime of arrest might be found in the vehicle.
- The police can search the passenger compartment of the vehicle, but not the trunk. They can search anything inside the passenger compartment, except the contents of a cell phone.
- Because the search of the vehicle is incident to the arrest, it must be contemporaneous with the arrest.
- Different from the regular automobile exception: The search of a vehicle incident to arrest exception is a different exception from the automobile exception (discussed in Chapter 10). Sometimes these two exceptions overlap, but not always.

OVERVIEW OF THE BLACKLETTER LAW

To understand the exception for searches of vehicles incident to arrest it is important to understand that it is a *different* exception than the regular automobile exception. As discussed in Chapter 10, the automobile exception allows the warrantless search of a vehicle based on probable cause. Under the regular automobile exception, police can search where they have probable cause (possibly including the trunk), and the officers can move the vehicle to a safer location and search it hours later.

The exception authorizing a search of a vehicle incident to arrest is different because it is tied to the arrest of the motorist. The search of a vehicle incident to arrest does not apply unless a motorist (almost always the driver) is arrested. Not all arrests allow a search of the vehicle incident to arrest, however. To search a vehicle incident to arrest:

1. The arrestee must be unsecured and within reaching distance of the vehicle; *or*
2. The officers must have a reasonable belief that evidence relevant to the crime of arrest might be found in the vehicle.

Police almost never leave arrestees unsecured because it is dangerous to do so. As such, most searches of vehicles incident to arrest involve officers claiming a reasonable belief that the evidence relevant to the crime of arrest might be found in the vehicle. In many cases, an arrest will give rise to a reasonable belief that the vehicle contains evidence relevant to the arrest. Consider this example of a valid search:

> ***Valid*** *Search of a Vehicle Incident to Arrest*: Imagine that police receive an alert that there has been a bank robbery and the getaway car is a blue Toyota Prius with license plate "ABC-123." The police spot the car, pull it over, and arrest the driver (who is still wearing a ski mask) for bank robbery. Would a reasonable person believe that there could be evidence of the bank robbery in the Prius? Given that the car has just left the scene of the crime and that any stolen money would likely be in the vehicle, the answer is "yes." The police can therefore conclude that there is reason to believe evidence relevant to the crime of arrest might be found in the vehicle.

Now consider an example where police would not have reason to believe evidence of the crime of arrest would be found in the vehicle.

> ***Invalid*** *Search of a Vehicle Incident to Arrest*: Imagine that police are patrolling late on a Saturday night in an area with many bars and restaurants. Police see a man stumble out of a bar and drive away in his car. The driver crosses the yellow line in the center of the road multiple times and speeds right through a stop sign. The officers pull over the car and arrest the driver for drunk driving and running the stop sign. Can the officers search the vehicle incident to arrest? The

answer is "no." The officers do not have reason to believe evidence relevant to the crime of arrest might be found in the vehicle. There is no possible evidence of running the stop sign that could be in the vehicle. And while there sometimes can be reason to believe DWI evidence can be found in a vehicle, there is no such reason in this case because the suspect appears to have gotten drunk in a bar. Therefore officers cannot search the vehicle incident to arrest.

Whether it is reasonable to believe evidence related to the crime of arrest will be found in the vehicle depends on the facts. Consider this modified drunk-driving hypothetical, which would authorize an automobile search incident to arrest.

> ***Valid** Search of a Vehicle Incident to Arrest*: Imagine a different drunk-driving case from the one above. Instead of seeing the driver exit a bar, imagine that the police see a person leave a liquor store with a 12-pack of beer. The person immediately pops open one of the beers and begins drinking it. The officers see the person walk through the parking lot and get into his vehicle, but they do not see where he puts the beer. A few minutes later the officers see the driver cross the yellow line multiple times and run a stop sign. They pull over the car and arrest the driver for drunk driving. Now the officers can search the vehicle incident to arrest because there is reason to believe evidence of the crime of arrest—the beer he bought and began to drink—would be found in the vehicle.

If the police are permitted to search a vehicle incident to arrest, the next question is: *where* can they search? The answer is that police can search the passenger compartment of the vehicle, but not the trunk. This rule dates back to a time when drivers had to insert a key into the trunk in order to open it. The rule makes little sense today, where drivers can open the trunk with a key fob or even with their cell phones. But the Supreme Court has not changed the rule to keep pace with modern technology.

Another limitation is that police cannot search the contents of a cell phone or other electronic device incident to arrest.

Ordinarily the search of an automobile incident to arrest comes into play when police stop a vehicle, arrest the driver, and then search the vehicle. The Supreme Court has also expanded the doctrine to *recent occupants* of a vehicle. For example, imagine that police have grounds to arrest Dave and have been following him. Before they pull him over, Dave parks his car, gets out, and starts to walk away. If police approach Dave—even on the other side of the parking lot—and arrest him, they can subsequently search his vehicle incident to arrest because he was a recent occupant of the vehicle.

Whether police arrest a motorist who is still in the vehicle or someone who was recently the occupant of a vehicle, the subsequent search of the vehicle must be contemporaneous with the arrest.

EXAM TRAPS TO AVOID

- *Not the Trunk*: The search of a vehicle incident to arrest only allows a search of the passenger compartment. The officer cannot rely on this exception to search the trunk.
- *Not for Traffic Offenses*: The search of a vehicle incident to arrest will probably not apply if the suspect is arrested for a traffic offense. The reason is that evidence related to the crime of arrest is unlikely to be found in the vehicle.
- *Unlawful Arrests*: Be sure that there is a *lawful* arrest. Do not assume that just because the question says a person was arrested that a subsequent search is valid. In order for the search of a vehicle incident to arrest to be valid, the arrest must be valid.
- *Noncustodial Situations*: Be sure that the individual has actually been subjected to a *custodial* arrest. If the police asked a person to sit in the police car while they wrote her a ticket, she is not necessarily under arrest and therefore a search would not fall under the search incident to arrest doctrine.
- *Lack of Contemporaneousness*: Be sure that the search is *contemporaneous* with the arrest. If the police are searching moments before or after an arrest it is likely contemporaneous. If hours have gone by since the arrest, the search is probably not contemporaneous.

MULTIPLE-CHOICE QUESTIONS

Question 63

An informant told the police that she saw Billy pick up a new smartphone in an electronics store and run out the front door with it and get into his car. Police procure an arrest warrant for Billy and sit outside of the place where he works. The informant told the police that Billy always gets ice cream immediately after he finishes work for the day. After Billy leaves work, the officers follow him with the goal of arresting him. Billy drives fast, though, and as he is driving through downtown the officers lose sight of him. A minute later, the officers see Billy's car parked across from an ice cream shop. The officers enter the ice cream shop where they find Billy ordering a hot-fudge sundae. The officers arrest Billy, take his car keys, walk across the street, and unlock his car. They search inside the car, including in the glove compartment. The officers take the owner's manual out of the glove compartment. Inside of the manual they find a small bag that contains heroin. Billy moves to suppress the heroin. The prosecution contends the drugs are admissible under the search of a vehicle incident to arrest exception. How should the court rule?

A) The court should suppress the drugs because Billy was not in his car when he was arrested.

B) The court should suppress the drugs because the crime of arrest involved theft of an smartphone and it is not reasonable to search for drugs.

C) The court should admit the drugs because Billy was a recent occupant of the vehicle and the drugs were found during a lawful search of the passenger compartment incident to arrest.

D) The court should admit the drugs because the smartphone could be located anywhere in the vehicle and thus the exception for a search of an automobile incident to arrest authorizes a complete search of the entire vehicle irrespective of how recently the arrestee has been in the vehicle.

Question 64

Nancy is a member of a drug gang. Police have been tracking her for weeks, waiting to catch her in the middle of a drug drop. The officers receive a tip that Nancy will be making a drug delivery on Wednesday morning and that the drugs will be in a red bag. Sure enough, police see Nancy exit her home carrying a red bag and see her place the red bag into the back seat of her car. The officers pull over Nancy, arrest her, and then search her car. The officers find the red bag in the back seat, open it, and discover a kilogram of cocaine inside. The officers then search the rest of the passenger compartment. In the glove box, the officers find an illegal handgun. Nancy has filed a motion to suppress. The prosecution claims that the evidence is admissible under the search of a vehicle incident to arrest. How should the court rule?

A) The court should suppress the cocaine and the gun because the officers had ample time to get a search warrant but did not do so.

B) The court should suppress the cocaine because once the officers found the red bag they should have obtained a warrant before opening it.

C) The court should suppress the gun because once the officers found the red bag they had no reason to continue searching.

D) The court should admit the cocaine and the gun because they were found during a valid search of a vehicle incident to arrest.

Question 65

The police pull over Stan for speeding and ask for his license and registration. After running some checks, the officers discover that there is a warrant out for Stan's arrest on reckless driving charges, and that the automobile he is driving is the subject of forfeiture proceedings because it is known that the vehicle has been involved in narcotics trafficking. The officers arrest Stan, handcuff him, and later have a tow truck take Stan's car to the impoundment lot. At the impoundment lot, multiple officers look through Stan's car. Because most of the officers are new to the police force and because the Department does not have any guidelines on where and what to do with an impounded car, the officers become confused and it takes them five hours to look through the car. At the end of the fifth hour, the police find drugs taped to the bottom of the spare tire in the trunk. Stan moves to suppress the drugs as the result of an invalid search. The prosecutor contends the drugs are admissible as a search incident to arrest. How should the Court rule?

I. The court should grant Stan's suppression motion because the search occurred too long after arrest to be a valid search incident to arrest.

II. The court should grant Stan's suppression motion because there is no reason to believe evidence relevant to reckless driving will be found in the vehicle.

III. The court should grant Stan's suppression motion because the officers exceeded the scope of a valid search of a vehicle incident to arrest.

IV. The court should deny Stan's suppression motion because the search was incident to a lawful arrest.

A) IV

B) I and II

C) I, II, and III

D) I and III

E) II and III

Question 66

Police see a car weaving all over the road just after midnight on a Saturday night. The officers pull over the car and see (and smell) immediately that Danica is drunk. They can also see that Danica is trying to hide something under her seat. The officers ask Danica what she is trying to put under her seat. Danica responds by holding up the item and saying with slurred speech, "You caught me, this is a huge bag of heroin." The officers take the bag of heroin from Danica's hands and they arrest her for both drunk driving and possession of a controlled substance. The officers then tow Danica's vehicle to the police station. At the police station the officers complete the paperwork for Danica's arrest as well as for impounding her car. The officers then get sent out for an emergency 911 call and do not return to the station until 5:00 a.m. when their shift is just about over. At 9:30 a.m., a different officer who is starting her shift for the day looks carefully through Danica's car at the police station. Under the floor mat on the passenger's side, the officer finds a diamond bracelet, which turns out to be stolen. Danica moves to suppress the diamond bracelet. How should the court rule?

A) The court should suppress the bracelet because the search of the vehicle occurred nine hours after arrest and therefore is not contemporaneous and cannot be admissible under any circumstances.

B) The court should suppress the bracelet because the arrest was for drugs and the officers had no reason to believe there would be a stolen bracelet in the car.

C) The court should admit the bracelet because the officers had a valid reason for the delay in conducting a search of the vehicle incident to arrest.

D) The court should admit the bracelet if the officer's careful look through the car complies with the department's inventory policy.

Question 67

Police have been investigating Serena for a few weeks. The officers have a feeling that Serena is a big-time drug supplier responsible for the entire western half of town. Unfortunately for the police, Serena is very careful and the officers have not observed anything that they can definitely point to as probable cause for an arrest warrant. After a week of surveillance, the officers lose their patience and wait for Serena to make a left turn without signaling. At that point, the officers pull over Serena, arrest her for the traffic violation, handcuff her, and take her into custody. The officers then search Serena's car and find a huge quantity of cocaine in the glove compartment. Is the cocaine admissible?

A) No, because there was no reason to believe evidence of the traffic violation would be found in the vehicle.

B) No, because the arrest for a traffic infraction was pretextual in violation of due process.

C) Yes, because police can automatically search the entire passenger compartment of an arrestee's vehicle incident to arrest, including the glove compartment.

D) Yes, because the search was permissible under the automobile exception.

Question 68

Police pull over Evan, who was driving a brand-new Tesla, for going 82 mph in a 70-mph zone. Under state law, it is reckless driving if a person is traveling at more than 80 mph. Different officers handle this criminal offense differently, though. Some officers just give the driver a traffic ticket, while others arrest the driver and take him into custody. The officer says to Evan, "Look, I'm just going to give you a ticket rather than arresting you, but I'm going to look at the dashboard because I know the computer dashboard on Tesla cars displays the top speed the car was driving before it stopped." (Assume that the officer's understanding of what the computer dashboard would show was correct.) The officer then ordered Evan out of the car and looked at the car's computer dashboard and sees that Evan had actually been traveling at 90 mph in the minutes before the officer stopped him. The officer provided the 90 mph information to the prosecutor, who plans to use it in the reckless driving prosecution. Evan moves to suppress the 90 mph information from the search of the Tesla computer. How should the court rule?

A) The information from the Tesla computer should be admitted because reckless driving is an arrestable offense.

B) The information from the Tesla computer should be admitted because there is reason to believe evidence of the crime of arrest could be found in the vehicle.

C) The information from the Tesla computer should be suppressed because there is no reason to believe evidence of the crime of arrest could be found in the vehicle.

D) The information from the Tesla computer should be suppressed because police are not permitted to search incident to a noncustodial citation.

Question 69

Police receive a 911 call about a bank robbery in progress. Officers immediately proceed to the bank and arrive just as three people are getting into a car and quickly driving away. The officers chase the car and eventually force it to stop. The officers arrest all three people in the vehicle. The officers then search the passenger compartment of the vehicle, find nothing, and then search the trunk. Inside the trunk, the officers find a bag with the label "First State Bank," which has $50,000 in cash inside. The prosecutor brings bank robbery charges and wants to introduce the bag and the $50,000 in cash as a valid search incident to arrest. The defendants move to suppress the bag and the cash. How should the court rule?

A) The bag and the cash are admissible as a valid search incident to arrest.

B) The bag and the cash are not admissible because the police did not conduct a valid search incident to arrest.

ANSWERS TO MULTIPLE-CHOICE QUESTIONS

Answer to Question 63

Answer A is incorrect. Police can search a vehicle incident to arrest when they arrest a driver who was a recent occupant of a vehicle. Here the officers had been following Billy and they only lost sight of him for a "minute." Billy is therefore a recent occupant of the vehicle.

Answer B is incorrect. It is true that the crime of arrest was theft of a smartphone, not drugs. But that does not render the search invalid. Police have reason to believe evidence of the crime of arrest (theft of a smartphone) could be found in the vehicle. The officers can look in the glove compartment and containers found inside of the glove compartment when searching a vehicle incident to arrest.

Answer C is correct. The officers only lost sight of Billy for a "minute." And he is just starting to order a hot fudge sundae. Both of these facts suggest that Billy has only recently left his vehicle. Police can conduct a search of a vehicle incident to arrest if they arrest a "recent occupant" of the vehicle.

Answer D is incorrect. While the answer choice correctly indicates that police can search the automobile incident to arrest, it misstates the law. The police cannot search a vehicle incident to arrest "irrespective of how recently the arrestee has been in the vehicle." The law requires that the arrestee be removed from the vehicle or at least be a "recent occupant" of the vehicle.

Answer to Question 64

Answer A is incorrect. Police can conduct a warrantless arrest in public. Once they have conducted a lawful arrest, police can search the vehicle incident to arrest without obtaining a search warrant as long as they have reason to believe evidence relevant to the crime of arrest could be found in the vehicle.

Answer B is incorrect. If the police are conducting a valid search of a vehicle incident to arrest, they can open any items in the passenger compartment. The police do not need a warrant to open a container.

Answer C is incorrect. Police can search the entire passenger compartment of the vehicle when searching incident to arrest as long as there is reason to believe evidence relevant to the crime of arrest could be found. They are not limited to looking for a particular piece of evidence. They can open all containers.

Answer D is correct. The police conducted a lawful arrest and can search the passenger compartment of the vehicle incident to arrest because it is reasonable to believe evidence of the crime of arrest could be found in the vehicle. Because the cocaine and gun were found in the passenger compartment, they are admissible.

Answer to Question 65

Choice I is correct. A search incident to arrest conducted five hours after the arrest is not likely contemporaneous with the arrest.

Choice II is also correct. To search a vehicle incident to arrest, the arrestee must either be unsecured and within reaching distance of the vehicle or there must be reason to believe evidence relevant to the crime of arrest might be found in the vehicle. The question tells us that Stan is handcuffed so he is not unsecured. The crime of arrest is reckless driving. While the vehicle is known to be involved in drug trafficking, that is not the crime of arrest. There is no reason to believe evidence of reckless driving might be found in the vehicle.

Choice III is also correct. A search of a vehicle incident to arrest is limited to the passenger compartment of the vehicle, not the trunk. Here the officers found drugs in the trunk.

Choice IV is incorrect. As noted above, there are multiple reasons why this cannot be a valid search of a vehicle incident to arrest.

Answer Choice C is therefore correct.

Answer to Question 66

Answer A is incorrect. The contemporaneousness requirement—and the nine-hour delay—means that this cannot be a search of an automobile incident to arrest. But a nine-hour delay would not be invalid under the automobile exception or the inventory exception.

Answer B is incorrect. It is true that the officers had no reason to believe a bracelet would be found in the vehicle. However, in arresting Danica for drugs, the officers could reasonably believe there might be other evidence of drug activity in the vehicle. That they found a bracelet instead of drugs does not render the bracelet inadmissible.

Answer C is incorrect. The officers may have had a valid reason for the delay in searching Danica's car. But that does not excuse the contemporaneousness requirement of the search incident to arrest doctrine.

Answer D is correct. While this could not be a valid search incident to arrest, it is possible that it could fall under the inventory exception if the officer followed the department's policy in conducting the inventory (for a discussion of the inventory doctrine, see Chapter 12). Although the answer choices do not specify this, it is also possible that this search would be valid under the automobile exception if the police had probable cause to believe there was evidence in the vehicle.

> *Note*: This question is here to remind you that there are multiple justifications for warrantless car searches. Just because the question involves an arrest does not mean you should focus exclusively on the search of a vehicle incident to arrest doctrine and ignore the other exceptions.

Answer to Question 67

Answer A is correct. Police cannot search a vehicle after all arrests. To search a vehicle incident to arrest, the arrestee must be unsecured and within reach of the vehicle or it must be reasonable to believe evidence related to the crime of arrest will be found in the vehicle. The question says that Serena was handcuffed, so she has been secured. Thus, the prosecution must turn to the other justification for a search of a vehicle incident to arrest. But it is not reasonable to believe evidence of the traffic violation might be found in the vehicle.

Answer B is incorrect. The Supreme Court has held that courts should not consider the subjective belief of the officer when determining the legality of a stop or an arrest. As long as there was a legitimate basis for the stop—and here turning left without signaling is such a basis—then the stop and arrest would be valid.

Answer C is incorrect. The police cannot automatically search the passenger compartment of a vehicle incident to arrest. To conduct a valid search incident to arrest, the arrestee must be unsecured and within reach of the vehicle or it must be reasonable to believe that evidence related to the crime of arrest will be found in the vehicle.

Answer D is incorrect. While police can conduct a warrantless search of a vehicle under the automobile exception, they must have probable cause to do so. The question tells us that the officers only have a "feeling" and that they "have not observed anything that they can definitely point to as probable cause for an arrest warrant."

Answer to Question 68

Answer A is incorrect. It is true that reckless driving is an arrestable offense. However, the officer did not make a custodial arrest in this case. Police cannot conduct a search incident to citation.

Answer B is incorrect. The factual premise in this answer choice is correct. There is reason to believe that the car's dashboard would show evidence of the crime of reckless driving. However, the officer had not placed Evan under arrest for reckless driving. Without a custodial arrest, the police cannot conduct a search incident to arrest.

Answer C is incorrect. The factual premise of this answer choice appears to be incorrect. The question tells us that there is reason to believe evidence of reckless driving (which is defined to include speeding at more than 80 mph) would be found in the vehicle.

Answer D is correct. The police officer never made a custodial arrest of Evan. To conduct a valid search incident to arrest, there must actually be an arrest. In this case, the officer only issued a traffic ticket, and the police are not permitted to search incident to citation.

Answer to Question 69

Answer B is correct. Police can search the passenger compartment of a vehicle when they have reason to believe evidence of the crime of arrest will be found in the vehicle. In this case, it seems reasonable to believe evidence of the bank robbery will be found in the vehicle. It is therefore tempting to choose Answer A. But the evidence was not found in the passenger compartment of the vehicle. After finding no evidence in the passenger compartment, the police searched the trunk. The search incident to arrest doctrine does not allow a search of the trunk. The prosecution might argue that the evidence should be admissible under the automobile exception on the theory that there was probable cause to search the trunk. But that is not what the question asks. The question asks whether the police conducted a valid search incident to arrest. The answer to that question must be "no" because the police cannot search the trunk incident to arrest.

CHAPTER 12
The Inventory Exception

THE RULE: When police impound a vehicle they can inventory the contents of the automobile pursuant to their department's policy. This is an administrative action and therefore the police do not need probable cause or a warrant. If the officers come across evidence during the inventory they can seize it under the plain view doctrine.

Critical Points

- *Exception to Probable Cause and the Warrant Requirement*: The inventory exception is an exception to both probable cause and the warrant requirement.
- *Must Follow Department Policy*: To conduct a lawful inventory, the officers must follow department policy.
- *Container Searches Are Permissible*: When conducting the inventory, police can open containers and log the items inside.
- *No General Rummaging*: Police have to follow the department's policy rather than using the inventory as a subterfuge to engage in rummaging for evidence.
- *Owner's Wishes Don't Matter*: Police are not required to defer to the owner's wishes. If a driver wants to call someone else to pick up his vehicle rather than having it impounded, the police do not have to follow the owner's request.
- *Applies to Items on the Person*: Although most inventory disputes involve automobiles, the police also inventory the items on a person when they book them into jail.

OVERVIEW OF THE BLACKLETTER LAW

The inventory exception is not part of the criminal investigation process. It is an administrative procedure that police departments use to protect the owner's property and to protect the department from dangerous items and false claims of theft. Nevertheless, it would be naïve to conclude that the inventory doctrine has no role in the criminal investigative process. Police know that they can discover evidence during the inventory process and they therefore use it in the hopes of finding evidence.

The most common scenario in which an inventory comes into play is when police are dealing with automobiles. Police regularly come across vehicles that are abandoned, in violation of parking rules, or damaged by accidents. Officers also regularly arrest drivers (such as for drunk driving) and cannot leave the vehicles on the side of the road. In these cases and others, police impound the vehicles and have them towed.

After impounding the vehicle, the police may be able to inventory it. Because the inventory doctrine is an administrative procedure, it does not require probable cause or a warrant. Instead, the officers are required to follow their department's policy on how to conduct the inventory. If the officers come across contraband or other evidence while conducting the inventory, those items are now in plain view and the officers can seize them and use them in a criminal prosecution.

In conducting an inventory, the officers can only take the steps authorized by their department's inventory policy. But if that policy is itself broad, then the officers can look broadly. Police officers can log the items in the passenger compartment and the trunk. They can open containers and log the contents of what is inside the containers.

There are two main limitations on the scope of an inventory. First, police cannot rip or destroy items in the car (for instance, they cannot tear the upholstery to see if contraband is hidden in secret compartments). Second, most courts hold that while officers can open notebooks and pieces of paper to look for loose objects, the officers cannot read documents.

A final point of importance is that the inventory doctrine does not only apply to automobiles. After arresting a suspect, police have to check that person into jail. The officers will inventory the suspect's personal effects (e.g., clothing, jewelry, purse). In doing so, if the officers come across contraband or evidence, they can seize it under the plain view doctrine.

EXAM TRAPS TO AVOID

- *No Valid Reason to Impound*: If a vehicle is lawfully parked, the police have no reason to impound and inventory it. Be sure there is a lawful reason to impound and inventory the vehicle.

- *Police Do Not Follow the Department Policy*: Evidence from an inventory can only be admissible if the police followed their department's policy. If the police search beyond what is permitted in the policy or if it appears they are generally rummaging, the evidence should not be admissible.
- *Do Not Focus on the Driver's Wishes*: An impoundment and inventory is still valid even if the driver proposed a different way (such as calling a friend) to relocate the vehicle.

MULTIPLE-CHOICE QUESTIONS

The following facts apply to Questions 70–73

Late at night, police see a car and they have a hunch that it is transporting drugs, though they lack any specific information. The officers follow the vehicle and see the driver (Chelsea) run through a stop sign. The officers pull over the vehicle and ask Chelsea for her license and registration. The officers soon discover that Chelsea's license is suspended because she was convicted of drunk driving last month. Driving with a suspended license is not an arrestable offense in this jurisdiction, so the officers give Chelsea a ticket. Chelsea asks to get going afterward, but the officers tell her they cannot allow her to drive with a suspended license. Chelsea asks to call a friend to drive her home, but the officers say no. The officers call a tow truck and impound Chelsea's car. At the police impound lot, the officers inventory Chelsea's car.

Question 70

Following the department's policy, the officers begin with the passenger compartment and open the glove compartment. Inside the glove compartment, the officers find a bag of heroin. Is the heroin admissible?

A) The heroin is not admissible because the police engaged in a pretextual stop.

B) The heroin is not admissible because it was not necessary to impound the car since Chelsea could have called a friend to drive the vehicle to Chelsea's home.

C) The heroin is admissible because the officers found it in plain view during a valid inventory.

D) The heroin is admissible because the police had suspicion of criminal activity and can tow the vehicle and search it under the automobile exception.

Question 71

Imagine the same facts as Question 70. In this case, however, police find nothing in the passenger compartment of the vehicle. They next open the trunk. Inside the trunk, the officers see a black toolbox that is closed and latched shut. The officers open the latch, open the toolbox, and look inside. The officers find some tools—a hammer, a screwdriver, multiple wrenches, and a small red box that looks like it would also contain smaller tools. The officers open the red box and inside they find a bag of cocaine. Assuming the officers followed the department's inventory policy, is the cocaine admissible?

A) The cocaine is admissible because this was a valid inventory search.

B) The cocaine is admissible because finding a red box inside of another box creates reasonable suspicion to investigate further.

C) The cocaine is not admissible because (regardless of what the department's policy says) police cannot look through the trunk under the inventory exception.

D) The cocaine is not admissible because (regardless of what the department's policy says) the police cannot open a container that is closed and latched shut under the inventory exception.

E) Both C and D.

Question 72

Assume that after the police impounded Chelsea's car they proceeded to inventory it. The officers consulted the police department's written policy, which says to begin with the passenger compartment. The officers carefully logged each item in the passenger compartment and they opened the glove compartment. Inside the glove compartment, they found a notebook labeled "Chelsea's Deliveries." The officers wondered whether they could open the book and read the contents. They consulted the police department's inventory policy, which says that it is permissible to read documents. The officers read the notebook and discovered incriminating information about drug deliveries. Which of the following is correct?

A) The officers acted unlawfully because it is improper to read a notebook while conducting an inventory.

B) The officers acted unlawfully because it is improper to read a notebook while conducting an inventory; but because the police department's policy said otherwise the evidence is admissible under the good faith exception.

C) The officers acted lawfully because the police department's policy specifically authorized the officers to read the notebook.

D) The officers acted lawfully because, regardless of what the police department's policy authorized, the officers' actions did not violate the Fourth Amendment.

Question 73

Assume for purposes of this question that it was lawful for police to arrest Chelsea for driving with a suspended license and that the officers did arrest her. At the police station, the officers had Chelsea change out of her regular clothes and into the clothes provided by the jail. The officers handed Chelsea a bag in which to place all of her personal items. Chelsea put her clothes, jewelry, and purse into the bag. Two hours after Chelsea was booked and taken to her cell, an officer inventoried Chelsea's personal items. In doing so, the officer opened Chelsea's purse and took out everything inside. The officer came across a package of cigarettes. The officer turned the cigarette package upside down so that the cigarettes would fall out and they could be counted. But instead of cigarettes, a stolen diamond fell out. Chelsea moves to suppress the diamond. What result?

A) The diamond is admissible because Chelsea had no reasonable expectation of privacy in the cigarette package.

B) The diamond is admissible under the inventory exception as long as the officer was following the police department's policy.

C) The diamond is not admissible because it is not permissible to conduct a detailed inventory of items in an arrestee's purse.

D) The diamond is not admissible because it is not permissible to open containers when inventorying an arrestee's personal effects.

Question 74

Police are called to the scene of an accident and find an abandoned vehicle that has been badly damaged in a car crash. There are no people nearby. The police believe that the driver was probably drunk, crashed into a tree, and fled the scene. The officers call a tow truck and impound the vehicle. At the impound lot, the officers are just about to follow the police department's inventory policy, which requires them to begin by logging all items in the passenger compartment and to thereafter log items in the trunk. The officers have a weird feeling, though, and start to look around the impound lot. They quickly notice that there is a man staring at them through the fence that surrounds the lot. The officers go over to the man and ask who he is. The man identifies himself as Carl and says he owns the vehicle. Carl smells very strongly of alcohol. The officers ask him whether he was driving drunk and he responds, "Well yah, I was driving the car, but I only had a little." The officers arrest Carl. Thereafter, Carl stares very strangely at the trunk and starts to mutter words that sound a little like "trunk." The officers are not sure what to make of Carl's behavior, especially because he is obviously drunk. The officers discuss it and decide to look in the trunk. The officers take out the spare tire and underneath it they find a bag of stolen jewelry. Which of the following is correct?

A) The jewelry is admissible as a search incident to arrest.

B) The jewelry is admissible under the inventory doctrine.

C) The jewelry is admissible because even though the search was unconstitutional Carl lacked standing since he abandoned the vehicle at the time of the accident.

D) None of the above.

ANSWERS TO MULTIPLE-CHOICE QUESTIONS

Answer to Question 70

Answer A is incorrect. While the officers might have been drawn to the vehicle because of their hunch of drug activity, the pretextual nature of the stop does not invalidate it. When Chelsea ran the stop sign that created a basis to stop the vehicle.

Answer B is incorrect. While Chelsea might have been able to get a friend to come pick her up and drive her home "late at night," the police were under no obligation to wait around. Chelsea cannot lawfully drive the vehicle because of her suspended license, and the vehicle cannot remain on the side of the road.

Answer C is correct. The officers conducted an inventory that complied with department policy and saw the heroin in plain view, so it is admissible.

Answer D is incorrect. The police had a hunch, but that is not sufficient to search a vehicle under the automobile exception. They would need probable cause to do so. They do not have probable cause because they "lack any specific information."

Answer to Question 71

Answer A is correct. So long as they follow the police department's policy, the officers can search the trunk during an inventory, and they can open closed containers.

Answer B is incorrect. Finding a box inside of another box is not by itself suspicious. Even if it did create reasonable suspicion, that would not authorize the police to search further.

Answer C is incorrect. The police can look through the trunk under the inventory exception if the police department's policy authorizes it.

Answer D is incorrect. The police can open a closed container under the inventory exception if the police department's policy authorizes it.

Answer E is incorrect. As noted above, both C and D are incorrect statements of the law.

Answer to Question 72

Answer A is correct. The inventory exception allows officers to log items and seize any contraband or evidence that is in plain view. By reading the documents, the officers are conducting a search not covered by the inventory exception and not authorized by the Fourth Amendment.

Answer B is incorrect. The good faith exception is not applicable to a warrantless inventory search. Except in rare circumstances, the good faith exception only applies when police are searching pursuant to a warrant (see Chapter 22).

Answer C is incorrect. The police department's policy can only authorize actions that comply with the Constitution. Because reading documents exceeds the scope of a constitutionally permissible inventory search, the officers' actions are unconstitutional and cannot be saved by the unconstitutional police department policy.

Answer D is incorrect. The officers can only conduct an inventory pursuant to the police department's policy. So to the extent that this answer suggests the police department's policy is irrelevant, that is wrong. Additionally, the Fourth Amendment does not allow police to read documents during an inventory.

Answer to Question 73

Answer A is incorrect. Chelsea does have a reasonable expectation of privacy in her belongings—including cigarettes. The inventory may still be permissible, but that does not mean Chelsea has no reasonable expectation of privacy.

Answer B is correct. As long as the officer was following the police department's policy it is permissible to inventory the personal effects of an arrestee.

Answer C is incorrect. In order to protect an arrestee's valuables and to prevent false claims of theft, police officers can inventory the personal items of an arrestee.

Answer D is incorrect. As long as the police department's inventory policy authorizes officers to open containers, the officers may do so when inventorying an arrestee's personal items.

Answer to Question 74

Answer A is incorrect. Although the police have arrested Carl, there is no reason to believe evidence of drunk driving might be found in the vehicle. Additionally, police cannot search the trunk incident to arrest.

Answer B is incorrect. Although police initially planned to conduct an inventory search, the police department's policy requires that they start with the passenger compartment. Because the police started in the trunk and immediately began removing the spare tire to look underneath it, this appears to be general rummaging that is not permitted under the inventory exception.

Answer C is incorrect. Carl has indicated that he owns the vehicle and the police have no reason to think otherwise. As such, he has a reasonable expectation of privacy and thus standing.

Answer D is correct. The search is not justifiable under any of the scenarios in answers A, B or C.

CHAPTER 13
The Plain View Exception

THE RULE: When the police are lawfully present and see an immediately incriminating item in plain view, they may seize that item without a warrant.

Critical Points

- *For Seizures Only*: The plain view exception is for seizures only. It does not authorize warrantless searches.
- *Moving Things Is Not Permitted*: If the officers need to move an item, even by a few inches, the item is not in plain view.
- *Exception to the Warrant Requirement Only*: Because the officers have to know an item is immediately incriminating, they must have probable cause to believe that the item is immediately incriminating. The officers do not need a warrant, though.
- *Need Not Be Inadvertent Discovery*: Courts no longer require the police to discover the item inadvertently. Even if police hoped to find contraband, the evidence can still be in plain view.
- *Plain Touch Doctrine*: A cousin of the plain view doctrine is the "plain touch" doctrine, which allows police (often during a *Terry* frisk) to seize any items that they immediately recognize as incriminating when they feel the item.

OVERVIEW OF THE BLACKLETTER LAW

The first—and most important—thing to understand about the plain view doctrine is that it allows police to conduct a warrantless *seizure* of evidence. The plain view doctrine *never* authorizes a warrantless *search*. When police are conducting a lawful search—whether it is pursuant to a search warrant or it is pursuant to an exception to the warrant requirement—they are allowed to seize any item that they see in plain view and that they immediately recognize to be incriminating. The core elements of the plain view doctrine are therefore: (1) the officers must be lawfully present; (2) the item they are seizing must be in plain view; and (3) the item must be immediately incriminating.

To be lawfully present, the officers must be in a location where they are legally entitled to be. Take three examples—curtilage, house, and car—where the officers might violate the lawfully present prong. (A) If officers trespass onto a suspect's back porch and see illegal drugs, they cannot seize the drugs because they were not lawfully present. (B) If police are executing a warrant for a stolen flat-screen television in the suspect's home, they cannot seize a stolen cell phone they find in a drawer because the warrant did not authorize them to search in the drawer. (C) If police are searching an automobile incident to arrest and search in the trunk, they cannot seize contraband because the search of an automobile incident to arrest exception does not allow a search of the trunk.

For an item to be in plain view, it has to be in a position where the officers can see its incriminating nature without having to conduct further searches. This means that officers cannot turn over items, because doing so would amount to a search. At the same time, if officers use technology that is in general use—for example, a flashlight—to better see the item, that does not prevent a court from saying it was in plain view.

For an item to be immediately incriminating, the officers do not have to know for certain that it is contraband. To be immediately incriminating, the officers simply need probable cause to believe that the item is incriminating.

Finally, courts do not require a finding that the officer came upon the item inadvertently. While courts in the past tried to divine the intent of the officer for being in a particular location, today courts do not focus on the subjective intent of the officer. As such, it is irrelevant whether an officer was hoping to find particular evidence that might have been beyond that listed in a search warrant. What matters is whether the officer is lawfully present when she found the evidence. If the officer is correctly executing an arrest or search warrant, or if she is correctly searching pursuant to an exception to the warrant requirement, then any evidence that is in plain view and immediately incriminating will be admissible.

EXAM TRAPS TO AVOID

- *Searching Beyond the Warrant or Warrant Exception*: If the fact pattern tells you the items the warrant authorizes the police to search for, make sure the officers are not going beyond the scope of that warrant. Similarly, make sure the police are not conducting a warrantless search that goes beyond where they are supposed to be looking.

- *Trespassing Officers*: If an officer finds contraband in plain view, but he entered the house illegally or otherwise trespassed to get onto the curtilage, the plain view exception cannot apply.
- *Slight Movements*: It is human instinct to say that moving an item a small amount is not a search. But the Supreme Court has held otherwise. If the officer moves an item even a few inches to determine that it is contraband, the item was not in plain view.
- *Standard for Immediately Incriminating*: Police often seize items that they do not know for certain to be contraband. Upon looking at a plastic bag that contains white powder, no one can say for certain that the white powder is drugs. But it probably is. If there is probable cause to believe an item is contraband, then it can be seized under the plain view doctrine.

MULTIPLE-CHOICE QUESTIONS

Question 75

Police receive a call about a noise violation on Rugby Road on a Saturday night. The police receive many complaints each month about loud noise on Rugby Road on the weekends because many college students live there and parties are frequently held there. When the police arrive they don't see or hear anything loud or unusual. But the officers know that college students in the front of the neighborhood often alert friends throughout the neighborhood when the police are driving through. So the officers believe it's possible that whoever was having a house party was tipped off and quieted down until the police finished their drive through the neighborhood. The officers stop at 123 Rugby Road—which has been the location of numerous parties this year—and walk into the backyard behind the house. Initially, the officers do not see anything, but as they round the corner of the house and reach the back porch they see more than a dozen young people take off running. Another dozen people are standing on the porch in a haze of smoke. The officers are not sure whether the smoke is from a controlled fire pit, a dangerous out-of-control fire, or just a lot of marijuana smoke. The officers immediately walk up to the porch to figure out the source of the smoke and see a large amount of marijuana on a table on the porch. Marijuana is illegal in this state and the officers arrest multiple people on the back porch for possession of a controlled substance. The defendants move to suppress the marijuana. How should the court rule?

A) The marijuana should be suppressed because it was not found in plain view.

B) The marijuana should be suppressed because the officers were not sure if the smoke was from a dangerous situation and thus there could not be exigent circumstances.

C) The marijuana should be admissible because the smoke created exigent circumstances to go onto the porch and the marijuana was then in plain view.

D) The marijuana should be admissible because it falls under the plain smell doctrine.

Question 76

Police executed a warrant to arrest Rylan for car theft and to seize a bright-red Mercedes that she allegedly stole. After impounding the Mercedes, the officers inventoried its contents pursuant to the police department's policy. In the middle of the trunk, they found a plastic bag with white powder in it. The officers looked at the bag carefully because they had not suspected that Rylan was involved in drug possession or drug distribution. The officers seized the bag of white powder anyway. Subsequently, the state crime lab tested the powder and found that it was cocaine, albeit a very low purity of cocaine. Prosecutors charged Rylan with auto theft and cocaine possession. Rylan has moved to suppress the cocaine. Which of the following is correct?

A) The cocaine is not admissible because police were not authorized to search the trunk, thus it was not in plain view.

B) The cocaine is not admissible because it was not immediately incriminating. The police did not suspect Rylan to be involved in drug activity and they "looked at the bag carefully," thus showing it was not immediately incriminating.

C) The cocaine is admissible because the officers conducted a lawful inventory and found the cocaine in plain view.

D) The cocaine is admissible because the police had a valid search warrant.

Question 77

The police department has been investigating Patrick for selling stolen smart watches. Based on the testimony of an informant, officers get a warrant to search Patrick's house for the smart watches. The officers turn the house upside down. They don't find the smart watches, but they do find something interesting in one of Patrick's filing cabinets. Police discover an old leather-bound book that looks like a ledger. When the officers open the book they learn that it is in fact a ledger. Upon reading the first page, the officers conclude that the ledger documents years of drug sales. In particular, the ledger shows that Patrick has been selling huge quantities of cocaine to his cousin Abigail. The police are never able to find any evidence of the stolen smart watches, but the government prosecutes Patrick for the drugs. If Patrick moves to suppress the ledger, what result?

A) The ledger is admissible against Patrick because the police had a valid warrant.

B) The ledger is not admissible against Patrick because the police lacked authority to read documents.

Question 78

Police arrived at an apartment complex a few moments after receiving a report of gunfire. The officers spoke to a person who lives on the first floor and said that a bullet came through her ceiling and lodged in her floor. Based on the trajectory of the bullet, the officers concluded the shot was fired from directly upstairs in apartment 2D. The officers then entered apartment 2D without a warrant to search for the shooter and to ensure that no further shots would be fired that could injure anyone. On the floor of the living room, the police saw four tablet computers in a pile next to some wrapping paper. Earlier in the day, the officers had been investigating the theft of a dozen tablets from a nearby electronics store that sold used items. The officers had a hunch that the tablets on the floor could possibly be the stolen tablets. The officers pushed the home button on the first tablet and swiped into the settings to read the serial number. The officers then called the electronics store to see if the tablet matched any of the stolen property. The serial numbers matched. Just as the officers were about to leave, Steve walked in the door of the apartment and said, "Hey, what are you doing in my apartment?" Prosecutors concluded that they could not make a case for the shooting, but they charged Steve with stealing the tablets. He has moved to suppress the tablets. What result?

A) The court should admit the tablets under the exigent circumstances exception.

B) The court should admit the tablets because they were found in plain view.

C) The court should suppress the tablets because the police conducted a warrantless search.

D) The court should suppress the tablets as fruit of the poisonous tree resulting from an unlawful entrance into the apartment.

Question 79

Assume the same facts as Question 78, except in this case there was no electricity in the apartment and it was very dark. In searching for the shooter (who was not present) the officers accidentally tripped over the pile of tablet computers. When the officers realized that they had tripped over a pile of tablets they had a hunch that the tablets on the floor were the ones stolen from the used electronics store. This time, however, the tablet on top had piece of tape stuck to the top of it. One officer took out his flashlight and shined it on the tape on top of the tablet. The other officer read the large print, which said "Sammy's tablet. May return to re-purchase." The officers called the electronics store and asked the owner if the writing on the tape made any sense to her. The owner immediately said, "Oh, I wrote that. Sammy sold me the tablet last month and said she might come back and re-buy it. That's why I wrote that." At that moment, Steve walked into the apartment and asked the officers what they were doing in his apartment. Police arrested Steve and he has moved to suppress the tablet evidence before his trial on theft charges. What result?

A) The tablets should be suppressed because the police had to search them in order to determine that they were stolen.

B) The tablets should be suppressed because the tablets were not immediately incriminating when the officers entered the apartment and the officers had to call the electronics store owner to confirm they were stolen.

C) The tablets should be admitted under the plain view doctrine.

D) The tablets should be admitted because even though the officers conducted an improper search of the apartment, they came across the evidence inadvertently.

Question 80

Assume for purposes of this question that when police interviewed the person whose apartment was shot into that the resident told police, "I'm sure it came from directly upstairs. Steve Stevenson lives upstairs. He's always doing dangerous stuff." The officers immediately recognized the name Steve Stevenson because they had been investigating whether he was involved in a recent burglary of Lucky's Used Electronics store. A young man had entered the store last week wearing gloves and a ski mask and had grabbed 10 tablet computers, put them into a shopping bag, and ran out the door. As the officers were walking upstairs to Steve's apartment, one officer said, "This could be our lucky break. I'll keep an eye out for any tablets that Steve might have stolen." The second officer said, "Yah, let's hope we find some good evidence." Once inside, the officers carefully moved from room to room to make sure there was no one armed who might shoot into other apartments. In the living room, the officers found the pile of tablets. When the officers walked over to the tablets they found a pair of gloves, a ski mask, and a shopping bag with the label "Lucky's Used Electronics" right next to the tablets. Just then, Steve entered the apartment and the police arrested him for the burglary of the electronics store. Steve moves to suppress the tablets. What result?

A) The tablets should be admitted because the officers found them in plain view.

B) The tablets should be admitted because Steve has no reasonable expectation of privacy in the apartment given the gunshot through the floor.

C) The tablets should be suppressed because the officers did not locate them inadvertently. The officers entered the apartment hoping to locate stolen evidence, which does not satisfy the plain view doctrine.

D) The tablets should be suppressed because there is not enough evidence to prove they were immediately incriminating.

ANSWERS TO MULTIPLE-CHOICE QUESTIONS

Answer to Question 75

Answer A is correct. To fall under the plain view doctrine, the officers must have been lawfully present. The officers did not have a reason to investigate 123 Rugby

Road in particular, and they also lacked any justification for trespassing into the backyard. Thus, the officers were not lawfully present when they saw the smoke.

Answer B is incorrect. Although the officers were not certain what was causing the smoke on the porch, they did not have to be certain. The officers believed it was possible that there was a dangerous, out-of-control fire on the porch. That possibility creates exigent circumstances that allowed them to look further to protect the occupants of the house and the public. Nevertheless, the officers were not lawfully present when they saw the smoke because they had trespassed in the backyard.

Answer C is incorrect. This answer choice is partly correct. The smoke did create exigent circumstances and the marijuana was in plain view. However, we must take a step further back. The officers only saw the smoke because they had trespassed without individualized suspicion and without a warrant into the backyard. Thus, when the police saw the smoke they were not lawfully present and cannot claim plain view.

Answer D is incorrect. First, the officers never claimed that they smelled marijuana. Second, even if they claimed to smell marijuana, it would only be because they were doing so from a location they were not lawfully permitted to be in.

Answer to Question 76

Answer A is incorrect. Police can inventory the trunk of a vehicle if they are following the department's inventory policy. Here the officers conducted a valid inventory and saw the cocaine in plain view.

Answer B is incorrect. Police officers could not know for certain that the bag contained cocaine. But the lack of certainty and the fact that they looked at the bag "carefully" does not prevent it from being immediately incriminating. Police only need to have probable cause to believe it is incriminating. Courts regularly uphold plain view seizures of bags of drugs because powdered substances in plastic bags are usually illegal drugs rather than, for example, grocery items.

Answer C is correct. The officers conducted a valid inventory, recognized an item in plain view that was immediately incriminating and thus were allowed to seize it.

Answer D is incorrect. The officers had a warrant to seize a vehicle. The warrant did not authorize a search of the trunk for drugs.

Answer to Question 77

Answer A is incorrect. Police exceeded the scope of the warrant because they only had authority to look for smart watches. By reading the ledger, the officers have searched without probable cause and a warrant. The ledger is therefore not in plain view. The evidence should not be admissible against Patrick.

Answer B is correct. Patrick can successfully argue that the ledger exceeded the scope of the warrant and therefore that the contents were not in plain view.

Answer to Question 78

Answer A is incorrect. There were exigent circumstances to enter the apartment, but not exigent circumstances to push the home button on the tablet and swipe into the device.

Answer B is incorrect. The tablets were found in plain view, but their presence alone was not immediately incriminating. Searching the electronic contents of the tablets is not authorized under the plain view doctrine.

Answer C is correct. The police had no warrant to search the contents of the tablets and the search did not fall under any exception to the warrant requirement. The evidence should therefore be suppressed.

Answer D is incorrect. Because there was gunfire and the possibility that someone could get shot, the police had exigent circumstances to enter the apartment without a warrant. The entrance therefore did not create a fruit of the poisonous tree problem.

Answer to Question 79

Answer A is incorrect. The police did not conduct a search before seizing the tablets. The officers were lawfully present. Flashlights are a technology that is widely available to the public. The officers simply read what was on top of the tablet and used other investigative means to conclude that the tablets were stolen.

Answer B is incorrect. Police can use other investigative techniques—such as calling the owner of the electronics store—to piece together whether an item in plain view is immediately incriminating.

Answer C is correct. The officers were lawfully present. The use of a flashlight was not a search. Once the officers spoke to the owner of the electronics store it was immediately apparent that the tablets were stolen.

Answer D is incorrect. If the officers had conducted an improper search, the evidence would not become admissible just because it was found inadvertently.

Answer to Question 80

Answer A is correct. The officers were lawfully present in the apartment and, based on their prior knowledge of the crime and finding the gloves, ski mask, and shopping bag, the tablets on the floor were immediately incriminating.

Answer B is incorrect. Steve did not lose his reasonable expectation of privacy in everything in his apartment simply because the officers had exigent circumstances to look for a shooter.

Answer C is incorrect. In the past, courts held that the plain view doctrine only applied if the evidence was found inadvertently. In those older decisions, the officers' hope to find particular evidence could have been fatal to the admissibility of the tablets. In *Horton v. California* (1990), the Supreme Court held that while evidence will be found inadvertently in most plain view searches, it is not a requirement of the doctrine. This conclusion is consistent with Fourth Amendment law generally, which typically does not give weight to the subjective views or hopes of the officers.

Answer D is incorrect. The police do not need proof beyond a reasonable doubt to meet the immediately incriminating element. Police only need to have probable cause to believe that the item is incriminating. Here the ski mask, gloves, shopping bag, and prior information about the burglary all provide at least probable cause. Thus, the tablets are immediately incriminating.

CHAPTER 14
Terry Stops

THE RULE: Police can detain individuals for a short period when the officers have reasonable suspicion that the person has engaged, is engaged, or is about to engage in criminal activity.

Critical Points

- A *Terry* stop is a limited detention. Because the police need less suspicion to make a *Terry* stop, they can only detain a suspect for a short period.
- *Situations*: A *Terry* stop can happen in a variety of situations.
  - Most common: When police pull over a driver, it is usually a *Terry* stop.
  - Police can also conduct a *Terry* stop of people who are walking down the street.
  - A *Terry* stop can occur when an officer uses physical force to stop a person or when an officer uses a "show of authority" by ordering a person to stop. To be a *Terry* stop, though, the person must actually stop.
  - The *Terry* doctrine applies to objects. An officer can detain an item—such as a suitcase—while conducting a brief investigation into it.
- *Reasonable Suspicion Standard*: To conduct a *Terry* stop, the police need reasonable suspicion—a standard less than probable cause—that criminal activity has happened, is currently happening, or is about to happen.
  - Reasonable suspicion exists if the suspect runs from the police in a high-crime neighborhood without having been provoked.
  - Presence in a high-crime neighborhood, without any other information, is not enough to demonstrate reasonable suspicion.

    - Reasonable suspicion is based on the totality of the circumstances.
    - To find reasonable suspicion, courts look to factors such as shifty movements, presence in a known drug area, pacing back-and-forth in an unusual manner, avoiding eye contact, and running away from the police.
- *How Long Can a* Terry *Stop Take?*
    - Stops of a few minutes are almost certainly constitutional.
    - Stops that take longer for good reasons—for instance, a slow response from the dispatcher in doing a warrant check—are also usually constitutional.
    - Stops that are unnecessarily prolonged—for instance, an officer holding back on giving a ticket while the officer waits for a drug-sniffing dog—are more likely to be unconstitutional.
- *What Can Police Do in a* Terry *Stop?*
    - A *Terry* stop empowers police to prevent people from leaving.
    - Police can also order a driver and passengers out of the vehicle.
    - One officer can walk a drug-sniffing dog around the car while the other officer writes a ticket, as long as the officers do not unnecessarily prolong the stop.
    - A *Terry* stop usually does not allow police to move a person to a new location.
- *Less Than an Arrest*: A *Terry* stop is a limited detention and less than a full-scale arrest.
    - If the police have handcuffed a suspect, the situation has likely escalated beyond a *Terry* stop to a full-blown arrest.
    - If a detention goes on for a long period, or if the police have already finished their limited investigation (such as checking for outstanding warrants), the situation may no longer be a *Terry* stop. Remember that a *Terry* stop is a *limited* detention.
- *More Than a Voluntary Encounter*: A *Terry* stop is not voluntary. A person is being detained against their will.
    - If a reasonable person would feel free to leave, the event does not rise to the level of a *Terry* stop.
    - Police do not need to demonstrate any suspicion if it is a voluntary encounter.

OVERVIEW OF THE BLACKLETTER LAW

To understand the *Terry* doctrine, it helps to situate it between two other goalposts: voluntary encounters and arrests. Think of it as a continuum with voluntary encounters on one end, arrests on the other end, and *Terry* stops in the middle.

Voluntary encounters happen thousands of times a day in the United States. Police talk to people about mundane topics such as the weather, and serious topics such as whether they have information about criminal activity. The police do not need any suspicion to engage in a voluntary encounter, because the people they are talking with are free to leave. Because police do not need any suspicion to conduct a voluntary encounter, it means the police also have no power to detain the person.

On the other end of the spectrum, think about arrests. When police arrest someone they can handcuff them, place them in a police car, and take them to jail. This is a big deal. Arrests are a significant restriction on a person's freedom. And they can last a long time. Accordingly, police need probable cause to conduct a full-scale arrest. Put simply, a major restriction on a person's freedom requires the police to have a considerable amount of suspicion.

Now think of the middle of the continuum between a voluntary encounter and an arrest. The classic example is a traffic stop in which police pull over a car. The driver is not free to leave. No reasonable person who looks in the rearview mirror and sees a police car signaling to them to pull over thinks to themselves "I can ignore that." At the same time, the driver is not handcuffed or locked in the back of a police car. Nor can the traffic stop go on for a long time the way an arrest can. In short, in a traffic stop, the driver's liberty is somewhat restricted—more than in a voluntary encounter, but less than in a full-scale arrest. Traffic stops are detentions, and thus the police need suspicion. But they are limited detentions in which the police can do less. As such, a lower standard of suspicion is required. Traffic stops are not the only type of *Terry* stop. Police can also stop individuals in many other circumstances.

The Supreme Court has decided that reasonable suspicion is the standard for conducting a lawful *Terry* stop. Unfortunately, there is no clear definition of reasonable suspicion. The Court has very few clear rules. For example, in *Illinois v. Wardlow* (2000), the Court held that unprovoked flight upon seeing the police in a high-crime neighborhood amounts to reasonable suspicion. But most *Terry* stops do not involve unprovoked flight. In the typical case, courts assess a host of other factors under a totality of the circumstances test. Courts consider factors like shifty movements, presence in a known drug area, pacing back-and-forth in an unusual manner, avoiding eye contact, and walking away from police, to name just a few. In assessing reasonable suspicion, courts allow officers to draw on their own experience and training.

Reasonable suspicion is a lower standard than probable cause. Police can conduct a *Terry* stop based on less reliable information than they would need to make an arrest. If police get an anonymous tip and confirm some details, that might be enough for reasonable suspicion. However, the police still need to point to articulable facts. And an anonymous tip with no additional information and no confirmation is insufficient by itself.

Because a *Terry* stop gives police the power to detain a person, the officer can restrict their movements. Most obviously, a *Terry* stop means the person cannot leave the scene. At a traffic stop, police have the power to order the driver and passengers out of the vehicle. But officers cannot typically use the power of a *Terry* stop to bring the person to the police station.

The duration of the stop is also a key question in assessing whether a *Terry* stop was constitutional. The Supreme Court has not created a bright-line rule saying how long a *Terry* stop can last. The Court has indicated that the police may not "unnecessarily prolong" the stop. So if the police are checking for outstanding warrants and the dispatcher is slow or busy, a stop that exceeds a few minutes will be constitutional. By contrast, if the officers have already run the warrant check or written a ticket and there is nothing left for them to do, continued detention would exceed the authority under the *Terry* doctrine and be unconstitutional. If a detention goes on for too long to be justified as a *Terry* stop, then the officer has entered arrest territory and must be able to point to probable cause for the arrest to be constitutional.

One situation that often comes up is police using a drug-sniffing dog at a *Terry* stop. For instance, while one officer speaks with the driver or checks for outstanding warrants, another officer walks a drug-sniffing dog around the vehicle. The use of a drug-sniffing dog, by itself, does not turn a *Terry* stop into an arrest. If the officer who is writing a ticket or checking for outstanding warrants does not unnecessarily prolong the stop, the situation continues to be a valid *Terry* stop. If, however, the police prolong the stop to give another officer time to bring a drug-sniffing dog to the scene, then the stop becomes unconstitutional.

Another common exam scenario—based on the Supreme Court case of *California v. Hodari D* (1991)—involves a suspect who is ordered to stop, but instead runs away. The Supreme Court has held that a person is not seized simply because the police officer orders them to stop. Rather, the person must actually stop. This scenario becomes tricky when an officer orders a person to stop but does not have reasonable suspicion to do so. Had the individual stopped moving at that point, there would have been a seizure. But sometimes the person instead runs away and throws away contraband as they are running. Because the person has not yet been seized (because they haven't stopped moving) the property is abandoned. In those unusual situations, the evidence is admissible even though the officer initially lacked reasonable suspicion.

EXAM TRAPS TO AVOID

- Just because an interaction with the police starts as a voluntary encounter or a *Terry* stop does not mean it stays that way. A voluntary encounter can turn into a *Terry* stop if the officer restricts the person's liberty. And a *Terry* stop can turn into an arrest if the officer eventually restricts the person's liberty to an extent consistent with an arrest.
- Watch out for a *Terry* stop that goes on for too long without good reason. That stop may turn into an arrest and require probable cause.
- Do not focus only on running from the police or anonymous informants. Although your professor may focus on major Supreme Court cases about unprovoked flight (*Illinois v. Wardlow* (2000)) or anonymous informants (*Alabama v. White* (1990), *Florida v. J.L.* (2000), or *Navarette v. California* (2014)), remember that there are many other ways for police to have reasonable suspicion.

MULTIPLE-CHOICE QUESTIONS

Question 81

Officer Jackson pulls over Marcus for speeding. While Officer Jackson is asking Marcus for his license and registration, Officer Jackson remembers that he had seen Marcus a few weeks ago hanging out in a known drug area. Officer Jackson takes the license and registration back to his police car and gets on the radio. Officer Jackson calls for Officer Watson to bring his drug-sniffing dog to the scene. Officer Jackson then runs a check to see if there are any outstanding warrants for Marcus's arrest. After a few minutes, it becomes clear that Marcus has a clean record. While Officer Jackson is writing up a speeding ticket, Officer Watson arrives with his drug-sniffing dog. Officer Watson walks the dog around Marcus's car and the dog sits down near the trunk, which is an alert that there are drugs in the trunk. Officer Jackson finishes up writing the ticket, talks with Officer Watson, and they decide to search the trunk. The officers find drugs in the trunk. If Marcus moves to suppress, how should the court rule?

A) The drugs should be suppressed because a valid *Terry* stop does not allow the use of a drug-sniffing dog.

B) The drugs should be suppressed because Officer Jackson had to call in another officer to bring the drug-sniffing dog, thus expanding the *Terry* stop beyond its legal bounds.

C) The drugs should be admitted so long as Officer Jackson did not unnecessarily prolong the traffic stop to wait for the drug-sniffing dog.

D) The drugs should be admitted because the dog sniff is a *Terry* frisk, which requires reasonable suspicion that Marcus is armed and dangerous.

Question 82

Assume the same facts as Question 81. For the purposes of this question, however, assume that when Officer Jackson called for a drug-sniffing dog that Officer Watson responded over the radio "I'm about 15 minutes away." Officer Jackson checked for outstanding warrants and wrote up a speeding ticket. That took about 10 minutes. Officer Jackson then waited the extra few minutes for Officer Watson to arrive. The drug-sniffing dog again alerted to drugs in the trunk. How should the court rule on Marcus's suppression motion?

A) The court should suppress the evidence because Officer Jackson unnecessarily prolonged the traffic stop to wait for the drug-sniffing dog.

B) The court should suppress the evidence because the Supreme Court has held that a traffic stop that is longer than 10 minutes is presumptively unreasonable and requires more than reasonable suspicion.

C) The court should admit the evidence because the extra five minutes that Officer Jackson waited for the drug dog are *de minimis*.

D) The court should admit the evidence because the Supreme Court has held that a traffic stop of less than 20 minutes is presumptively constitutional.

Question 83

It is common for drugs to be sold in the outdoor courtyard of apartment complexes that are located in high-crime areas. Officer Rawls was on patrol and he suspected that dealers would be selling drugs in the courtyard of a high-crime area around noon. Accordingly, Officer Rawls very conspicuously drove his police car right next to the courtyard at noon. When his car pulled up, Officer Rawls saw a man standing in the courtyard. The man looked at Officer Rawls and then turned and ran in the opposite direction. Officer Rawls ran after him, caught him, and put his hand on him to stop him from moving. Just after the man stopped moving, a bag of cocaine fell out of his pocket. The man has moved to suppress the evidence. How should the court rule?

A) The evidence should be suppressed because Officer Rawls lacked reasonable suspicion to stop the man and thus committed an unlawful stop.

B) The evidence should be suppressed because when Officer Rawls put his hands on the man to stop him from running, the event ceased to be a *Terry* stop and became a full-scale arrest for which Officer Rawls lacked probable cause.

C) The evidence should be admitted because the man was present in a high-crime area, thus creating reasonable suspicion.

D) The evidence should be admitted because unprovoked flight from the police in a high-crime area creates reasonable suspicion.

Question 84

Officer Rawls was on patrol in a high-crime area and he had a hunch from having made prior arrests in the outdoor courtyard that dealers would be selling drugs in the courtyard around noon. Accordingly, Officer Rawls very conspicuously drove his police car right next to the courtyard at noon. When his car pulled up, Officer Rawls heard someone yell "5-0," which is a slang term for the police. Officer Rawls then saw a man (Jason) put his hands in and out of his right pocket a few times. Jason then stood there for a minute and looked extremely nervous. Another man who was standing nearby made eye contact with Jason and turned his head to the right as if to signal to Jason to go elsewhere. Jason then walked slowly toward his right toward the front entrance of the apartment complex. Officer Rawls walked up to Jason and said, "Hey, stop before you go inside the building." Jason then said, "Look, you can take the cocaine. I'm just a low-level player in this operation" and handed Officer Rawls a bag of cocaine. Should the evidence be suppressed?

A) The evidence should be suppressed because Officer Rawls only had "a hunch," which is not enough to rise to the level of reasonable suspicion.

B) The evidence should be suppressed because there cannot be reasonable suspicion as Jason "walked slowly" toward the apartment building, which does not demonstrate unprovoked flight.

C) The evidence should be admitted because under the totality of the circumstances there is reasonable suspicion.

D) The evidence should be admitted because Officer Rawls never physically stopped Jason from entering the apartment so he did not seize him.

Question 85

Officer Rawls was on patrol in a wealthy area of New York City. When Officer Rawls walked into the outdoor courtyard of a very fancy apartment building, he saw a man named Banksy dressed in a suit and tie. Based on a hunch that Banksy was not a Wall Street banker but instead a drug courier, Officer Rawls ordered the man to come over to him. Banksy did not comply, though, and instead ran away in the opposite direction. Officer Rawls gave chase and loudly yelled, "Stop. Police. Stop Running!" As Banksy was running, he passed a trash can and threw a small bag in it. Officer Rawls was a marathon runner and kept chasing Banksy. Eventually Banksy got tired and slowed down. Officer Rawls caught up with him and tackled him to the ground. Banksy had nothing incriminating on him, but when the police went back and searched the trash can they found the bag Banksy had thrown away and discovered that it contained heroin. Should the heroin be admissible?

A) The heroin should be suppressed because Officer Rawls ordered Banksy to come over to him based on nothing more than a hunch and thus lacked reasonable suspicion.

B) The heroin should be admitted because even though Officer Rawls ordered Banksy to stop, he did not comply. Thus he had not been seized when he threw away the drugs and thus he abandoned them.

Question 86

Mindy is at the Miami airport, waiting to board a flight to New York City. She has passed through the security checkpoint and is sitting at the gate when two DEA officers approach her. The officers explain that drug couriers often travel from Miami to New York City with hidden cocaine. The officers ask Mindy how long she has been in Miami and whether she lives in New York. The officers continue to ask Mindy questions for a few minutes and finally they ask if they can search her backpack. Mindy pauses for a moment and the officers stand there silently looking at her. Mindy then says "Okay." The officers look through her purse and find a bag of cocaine. Mindy moves to suppress the evidence as the fruit of an illegal stop. How should the court rule?

A) The court should suppress the evidence because the officers engaged in a *Terry* stop without reasonable suspicion.

B) The court should suppress the evidence because the officers pressured Mindy to consent to a search of her backpack.

C) The court should admit the evidence because the officers had reasonable suspicion to stop Mindy and she consented to a search of her backpack.

D) The court should admit the evidence because Mindy voluntarily spoke to the officers and consented to a search of her backpack.

Question 87

Assume again that Mindy is waiting in the airport to board a flight. This time, however, assume that the officers had received an anonymous tip that a tall, blonde woman in her thirties would be taking the 2:00 p.m. flight from Miami to New York and that she was a drug courier. As the officers approached the gate, the only person who matched that description was Mindy. The officers approached Mindy and explained that they were looking into drug smuggling. The officers then told Mindy that she would have to come with them to the DEA office, which was two gates over, so that they could conduct a brief investigation of who she was and whether she was engaged in drug smuggling. When Mindy objected because her flight was leaving soon, the DEA agents said, "That is not a problem. If everything checks out we will bring you back to the gate in time to make your flight to New York. Let's go." It took about two minutes for Mindy and the officers to walk to the DEA office near the next gate. By this point, Mindy appeared extremely nervous. Once inside the DEA office, Mindy saw that the DEA agents had brought her checked suitcase to the office. At this point, Mindy blurted out, "I've got drugs in my suitcase, but it's not my fault."

The officers thereafter searched Mindy's suitcase, and found cocaine. Which of the following is correct?

A) The cocaine should be suppressed because the officers exceeded a *Terry* stop by taking Mindy to the DEA office and they lacked probable cause to do so.

B) The cocaine should be admissible because the officers have engaged in a *Terry* stop supported by reasonable suspicion.

C) The cocaine should be admissible because the anonymous tip gave the officers reasonable suspicion to detain Mindy.

D) The cocaine should be admissible because Mindy voluntarily went to the DEA office and willingly confessed.

Question 88

Police officers have reasonable suspicion to believe that Sally's luggage, which she has taken from an airline baggage check area and is about to carry with her to a waiting taxi, contains drugs. Which of the following accurately describes the police officers' options?

I. The police may seize the luggage before Sally places it in the taxi and allow dogs to sniff it for drugs, so long as the seizure is brief.

II. Police may briefly seize the luggage before Sally places it in the taxi, allow dogs to sniff it for drugs and, if the dog sniff is positive, then secure the luggage while they obtain a search warrant.

III. Police may briefly seize the luggage before Sally places it in the taxi, allow dogs to sniff it for drugs, and if the dog sniff is positive, then search the luggage.

IV. Police may follow Sally out of the baggage claim area, wait until she places the luggage in the taxi, stop the taxi a minute later, seize the luggage, and open the luggage to search for any drugs inside.

A) I and II

B) I, II, and III

C) I, II, and IV

D) I, II, III, and IV

ANSWERS TO MULTIPLE-CHOICE QUESTIONS

Answer to Question 81

Answer A is incorrect. There is no prohibition on police using a drug-sniffing dog during a *Terry* stop. Although the stop was for speeding, the act of walking the dog around the vehicle is permissible.

Answer B is incorrect. The act of calling in another officer with a drug-sniffing dog, by itself, does not transform a *Terry* stop into an arrest. It is true that multiple officers surrounding a suspect could take a valid *Terry* stop and turn it into an unconstitutional arrest. But that did not happen here. Officer Watson simply walked the dog around Marcus's car.

Answer C is correct. It appears that calling Officer Watson and his dog did not unnecessarily prolong the traffic stop. Officer Watson seemingly arrived very quickly while Officer Jackson was still in the process of writing a ticket. Accordingly, this was a lawful *Terry* stop.

Answer D is incorrect. As discussed in Chapter 15, police do need reasonable suspicion that a suspect is armed and dangerous in order to conduct a frisk. However, the act of walking a drug-sniffing dog around a vehicle is not a *Terry* frisk. Indeed, as discussed in Chapter 2, it is not a search at all.

Answer to Question 82

Answer A is correct. Police can use a drug-sniffing dog while conducting a lawful *Terry* stop for a traffic violation. However, the officers cannot unnecessarily prolong the traffic stop in order to wait for a drug-sniffing dog to arrive. Here Officer Jackson had completed all of the steps of the traffic stop and could have given Marcus the ticket and sent him on his way, but he instead delayed giving the ticket so that the drug-sniffing dog would have time to arrive.

Answer B is incorrect. The Supreme Court has never created a presumptive time frame for when a traffic stop has gone on for too long to be a *Terry* stop.

Answer C is incorrect. Five extra minutes does not sound like a long time and it does sound *de minimis*. But that is not the correct test. The test is whether the officer unnecessarily prolonged the traffic stop, which he did here.

Answer D is incorrect. The Supreme Court has never set a time frame in which a traffic stop would be presumptively constitutional.

Answer to Question 83

Answer A is incorrect. As explained in response to Answer D, there is reasonable suspicion to stop the man.

Answer B is incorrect. Police can effect a *Terry* stop by using physical force (and also by using a show of authority, such as ordering a person to stop). An officer's use of force is still consistent with a *Terry* stop as long as it is not so great as to be the equivalent of an arrest. Here, the officer did not draw his weapon or use handcuffs. He simply put his hand on the man, which is permitted under the *Terry* doctrine.

Answer C is incorrect. Presence in a high-crime area—by itself—is not enough to create reasonable suspicion. It can be a piece of evidence that helps to contribute to reasonable suspicion.

Answer D is correct. The Supreme Court held in *Illinois v. Wardlow* (2000) that if a person runs from the police without provocation in a high-crime neighborhood, that creates reasonable suspicion.

Answer to Question 84

Answer A is incorrect. Initially, Officer Rawls only had a hunch. However, other incriminating information developed thereafter, including the person yelling "5-0," the furtive behavior of putting his hand in and out of his pocket, and his nervous appearance.

Answer B is incorrect. The answer correctly notes that walking away slowly is not unprovoked flight. The government therefore cannot rely on flight in a high-crime neighborhood to establish reasonable suspicion. However, as explained below, there is other evidence that creates reasonable suspicion.

Answer C is correct. Officer Rawls knew from his experience that this was a high-crime area and that he had arrested people for selling drugs in the courtyard in the past. Additionally, a person yelling "5-0" furthers the belief that drugs were being sold. The man engaged in the incriminating behavior of repeatedly putting his hands in and out of his pockets. He also acted nervous. Finally, the other man turning his head and seemingly signaling Jason to walk away is also suspicious. Added together, this likely amounts to reasonable suspicion.

Answer D is incorrect. An officer can conduct a *Terry* stop either by using physical force or by engaging in a show of authority such as ordering a person to stop. Because Jason stopped after Officer Rawls ordered him to "stop before entering the building," there has been a *Terry* stop.

Answer to Question 85

Answer A is incorrect. Officer Rawls lacked reasonable suspicion to order Banksy to come to him, but there was no seizure at that moment. Banksy did not comply with Officer Rawls' order to stop. Thus, Banksy was not seized until Officer Rawls caught up with him and tackled him to the ground.

Answer B is correct. Although a police officer can make a seizure by physical force or a show of authority, the Supreme Court has held that a show of authority (such as ordering a person to stop) does not become a seizure until the person complies with the order to stop. Because Banksy did not comply with Officer Rawls' order to stop, the seizure did not occur until Rawls tackled Banksy. When Officer Rawls tackled Banksy he made an illegal *Terry* stop because the officer lacked reasonable suspicion to detain Banksy. But no evidence was discovered as a result of the tackle. The evidence was the bag of heroin that Banksy threw in the trash can while he was running away. Officer Rawls had no reasonable suspicion during that chase, but he did not need any since no seizure occurred until Banksy stopped. Accordingly, even though Officer Rawls lacked reasonable suspicion during the chase, the bag of heroin is admissible because Banksy abandoned it. This answer is sometimes hard for students (and professors!) to wrap their mind around. The facts of this case are drawn from *California v. Hodari D.* (1991). If you are confused by this question, it is worth going back and reading the *Hodari D.* decision in your textbook again.

Answer to Question 86

Answer A is incorrect. The officers did not engage in a *Terry* stop. See *United States v. Mendenhall* (1980). A reasonable person in Mindy's position would have felt free to leave—at least according to the justices on the Supreme Court.

Answer B is incorrect. The officers waited for Mindy to answer and stared at her. This is a subtle pressure tactic, but it is not sufficient to render her consent involuntary.

Answer C is incorrect. The officers did not have reasonable suspicion to stop Mindy. Miami is a known drug city. And drug couriers do in fact transport drugs from Miami to other cities by plane. But reasonable suspicion must be individualized. Every person at the Miami Airport is flying to or from Miami and is therefore in the identical position as Mindy. There was no individualized reasonable suspicion to suggest Mindy is involved in criminal activity.

Answer D is correct. As noted above, there is no reasonable suspicion for the officers to stop Mindy. But they do not need reasonable suspicion if they are just engaged in a voluntary encounter. The police are free to walk up to people and ask them questions. According to the U.S. Supreme Court, a reasonable person in Mindy's situation would have felt free to walk away from the officers or to tell them that she does not wish to speak to them.

Answer to Question 87

Answer A is correct. The facts of this question resemble the Supreme Court's decision in *Florida v. Royer* (1983). Although the officers did not handcuff Mindy or point guns at her, this situation extended beyond a *Terry* stop to be the functional equivalent of an arrest. The key reason was that the officers moved Mindy from the gate to a DEA office. Moving a person is not something typically permitted under the *Terry* doctrine. Taking her checked luggage from another location and moving it also likely exceeded what is permitted under the *Terry* doctrine.

Answer B is incorrect. As explained above, moving Mindy from the gate to the DEA office is more than a *Terry* stop; it is a full-scale seizure akin to an arrest.

Answer C is incorrect. Anonymous tips, by themselves, are typically insufficient to establish reasonable suspicion. Second, even if we concluded that this tip amounted to reasonable suspicion, police would still need a greater level of suspicion because moving Mindy amounted to a full-scale seizure akin to an arrest, which would require probable cause.

Answer D is incorrect. The question indicates that Mindy objected to leaving the gate and that the officers responded by saying she would not miss her flight and then told her "Let's go." This language strongly indicates that Mindy did not go to the DEA office voluntarily, but instead because she was ordered there by the agents. Although she did voluntarily confess once in the office, that confession and the resulting evidence would be inadmissible fruit of the poisonous tree from the illegal arrest. (See Chapter 21 on the Exclusionary Rule and the Fruit of the Poisonous Tree Doctrine.)

Answer to Question 88

Roman numeral I is correct. The police have reasonable suspicion that the luggage contains drugs. The officers can conduct a *Terry* stop of the luggage to briefly detain it to investigate further.

Roman numeral II is correct. The officers can detain the luggage until they procure a warrant. That is particularly true if the officers have not just their original reasonable suspicion, but also probable cause from a positive dog alert.

Roman numeral III is incorrect. While the *Terry* doctrine gives officers the authority to detain an item such as luggage to investigate criminal activity, the *Terry* doctrine does not give the officers authority to search inside the luggage. Indeed, even with probable cause the officers could not search the luggage without a warrant or an exception to the warrant requirement.

Roman numeral IV is incorrect. The officers only have reasonable suspicion. While police could stop a vehicle and search containers inside of it under the automobile exception, that would require probable cause. The facts tell us there is only reasonable suspicion.

Because Roman numerals I and II are correct, Answer A is correct.

CHAPTER 15
Terry Frisks

THE RULE: When police have reasonable suspicion that a person is armed and dangerous, they can conduct a pat-down of the outer layer of the person's clothing. Police can also conduct protective sweeps of an automobile or a home to quickly scan for weapons.

Critical Points

- When police have conducted a valid *Terry* stop of a person they can sometimes—*but not always*—conduct a frisk of that person.
- When police have reasonable suspicion to believe the person is armed and dangerous, they can conduct a limited pat-down—a *Terry* frisk—of the person for weapons.
- The officers must conduct the pat-down with open hands and they can only feel for weapons. The officers cannot use the *Terry* frisk to search for evidence. This means that the police cannot manipulate items with their fingers while conducting a pat-down.
- If an officer feels a weapon during a *Terry* frisk, she can reach into a suspect's clothing and remove it.
- *Interaction with the Plain Touch Doctrine to Find Evidence Besides Weapons*:
    - If an officer is conducting a valid *Terry* frisk for weapons, and she immediately feels an item (for example, a bag of drugs) that she recognizes to be incriminating, the officer can seize the item.
    - But, if an officer is not sure what an item is during a *Terry* frisk, she cannot pull it out of the suspect's clothing to examine it more closely.

- Terry *Sweeps of Cars and Houses*:
  - The Supreme Court has expanded the *Terry* frisk doctrine to also apply to cars and houses. The standard for sweeps is also reasonable suspicion.
  - For cars, police can conduct a *Terry* frisk of the passenger compartment (not the trunk) when they have a reasonable belief that the suspect is dangerous and that he may gain access to a weapon. The officers can take a cursory look in places such as the glove compartment or under the seats to see if there are weapons, but they cannot conduct an in-depth search.
  - For houses, police can make a protective sweep of the whole residence when they are conducting an arrest in the residence. To protect themselves, officers can look around the house to make sure there are no people hiding who could harm the police. The sweep must be quick and cursory and it is limited to the places where a person could be hiding.

OVERVIEW OF THE BLACKLETTER LAW

Recall from Chapter 14 on *Terry* stops that a detention is a less intrusive seizure that falls in between a voluntary encounter and a full-scale arrest. Because a *Terry* stop is a less intrusive seizure, the police need less suspicion than for an arrest, but they can do less.

Terry frisks fit in a similar framework. *Terry* frisks are not a full-scale search requiring probable cause. But neither are they a non-search that the police can conduct with no suspicion whatsoever. Rather, *Terry* frisks are limited searches. The police need less suspicion than they would for a full-scale search, but that lesser suspicion only allows the police to engage in a less intrusive search.

An officer can conduct a *Terry* frisk when she has reasonable suspicion that the suspect is armed and dangerous. In conducting a *Terry* frisk, the officer is typically limited to patting down the outer layer of a suspect's clothing. The officer should use open hands during the pat-down; the officer may not manipulate items between her fingers or otherwise search around through the clothing. The open-handed pat-down is designed to find weapons (because of the reasonable suspicion that the suspect is armed and dangerous), not to search for evidence.

Although the officer cannot conduct a *Terry* frisk in order to gather evidence, if the officer lawfully comes across evidence during the frisk, she can seize it. For example, if an officer is patting down a suspect that she reasonably believes to be armed and dangerous and feels an item that she immediately knows to be incriminating, the officer can reach into the clothing and remove the item. The seizure of the evidence falls under the "plain touch" doctrine, and it often occurs when trained officers say that they felt drugs during an open-handed pat-down.

Police need more suspicion to conduct a *Terry* frisk than they do to conduct a *Terry* stop. A *Terry* stop requires police to have reasonable suspicion of criminal activity. A *Terry* frisk requires reasonable suspicion that a suspect is armed and dangerous. This is a crucial point for the real world and for a law school exam. Just because police can conduct a *Terry* stop does not mean that they can also conduct a *Terry* frisk. In many instances, police will have grounds to stop an individual, but not to frisk him. For example, imagine that a police officer pulls over a driver for running a red light, speeding, or drunk driving. Or imagine that an officer sees a teenager, who is wearing shorts and a tight t-shirt, shoplift a candy bar. In each case, the officer would have reasonable suspicion that criminal activity was afoot. But in none of the situations could an officer credibly say that there was reasonable suspicion that the suspects would be armed and dangerous. Most people who speed are not hiding a gun. And a shoplifter who is wearing a tight t-shirt and shorts is also clearly not hiding a gun. In these situations, and many others, the police can conduct a *Terry* stop, but not a *Terry* frisk.

Determining when police have reasonable suspicion that a suspect is armed and dangerous is not always an easy question. If police stop a suspect because they believe he is involved in a violent crime, we can be nearly certain that the officers have reasonable suspicion the individual is armed and dangerous. An individual who is about to engage in a rape, robbery, or an aggravated assault is quite possibly armed. In these kinds of cases, police are clearly justified in frisking the person they detain. But other cases are much more difficult. Police stop many people and it is not always clear that the suspect has been or is about to engage in a violent crime. For instance, if a man is lurking outside of a store and seems to be casing it, is the individual about to commit a violent robbery or nonviolent shoplifting?

Courts typically have to engage in case-by-case analysis to determine whether a *Terry* frisk was justified. In doing so, courts give a lot of deference to officers who will testify that their training and experience led them to have reasonable suspicion that a suspect was armed and dangerous.

The Supreme Court has expanded the *Terry* frisk doctrine to cars and residences. Once again, however, the court has made matters muddy, rather than clear.

For cars, police can conduct a frisk of the passenger compartment of the vehicle (but not the trunk) if they have a reasonable belief that the suspect is dangerous and that he could gain access to a weapon from the car. In carrying out a frisk of a vehicle, the officer may only conduct a cursory look into the areas where a weapon might be hidden. In practice, this means that police can open the glove compartment, but not look through the pages of a notebook found inside the glove box. An officer can look under the seats, but she cannot open a tiny box that could not possibly contain a weapon.

For residences, officers conducting an arrest can make a protective sweep of the house or apartment if there is reasonable suspicion that there is another person present who could pose a danger. In conducting the sweep, the officer can make a cursory visual inspection in areas of the residence where a person might be hiding. The rationale for the sweep is that the officers have no idea who else could be hiding in the house. The protective sweep enables police to identify a friend or accomplice who might be lying in wait to attack the officers. It bears repeating that the sweep is limited—a cursory examination—and should be conducted quickly so as not to violate any more of the resident's privacy than necessary.

EXAM TRAPS TO AVOID

- Just because the police had reasonable suspicion to stop a person does not mean they also have reasonable suspicion to frisk the person. Think of a traffic stop for a driver who was speeding. The police have reasonable suspicion of criminal activity, but no suspicion that the suspect is armed and dangerous. Always analyze *Terry* stops and *Terry* frisks as two different questions.
- Beware of cases in which an officer removes an object during a *Terry* frisk in order to explore it further. If the officer does not know the object is a weapon or contraband at the moment she touches it, the officer cannot seize the item.
- Beware of cases in which the officer conducts a pat-down but manipulates items. If the officer moves the item with his fingers to determine what it is, the officer has not conducted a valid *Terry* frisk and the item cannot be seized.

MULTIPLE-CHOICE QUESTIONS

Question 89

Officer Miller has been investigating drug activity in a dangerous part of town. After two weeks of work, Officer Miller has learned that a seemingly abandoned house on the corner of First Street is being used to sell drugs. Every day, dozens of people come into the house, stay for only a couple of minutes, and then come back out. Often it is possible to see them holding a small plastic bag when they exit the house. Officer Miller has also observed men with guns under their shirts standing guard around the house. From talking with informants, Officer Miller has learned that Lawrence is the head of the operation, as well as a physical description of Lawrence and what type of clothing he usually wears. While conducting surveillance, Officer Miller sees a man matching Lawrence's description enter the house. Officer Miller really wants to catch Lawrence with drugs, but he knows he doesn't have probable cause to arrest him. Nevertheless, when Lawrence exits the house, Officer Miller stops him, orders him up against a wall, and frisks him. As he is patting down Lawrence, Officer Miller feels a squishy package in his jacket pocket and he immediately recognizes it to be drugs.

Officer Miller pulls the package of drugs out of Lawrence's jacket and thereafter arrests him. Lawrence has moved to suppress the drugs. How should the court rule?

A) The court should suppress the drugs because Miller "really wants to catch Lawrence" and thus engaged in a pretextual search.

B) The court should suppress the drugs because a *Terry* frisk is only for weapons and Officer Miller pulled drugs out of Lawrence's pocket.

C) The court should suppress the drugs because Officer Miller lacked reasonable suspicion to conduct a *Terry* frisk.

D) The court should admit the drugs because Officer Miller had reasonable suspicion to believe Lawrence was armed and dangerous and thus conducted a valid *Terry* frisk.

E) The court should admit the drugs because finding drugs created probable cause to justify a search incident to arrest.

Question 90

Assume the same facts as Question 89 above. This time, however, when Officer Miller patted down Lawrence he did not immediately recognize the squishy package to be drugs. Officer Miller thought it might be drugs, but he was not sure. Officer Miller knew that he could not remove the package without knowing it to be drugs, so he just squeezed it between his index finger and his thumb. The squeeze lasted only two seconds and enabled Officer Miller to be sure that the package was in fact drugs. Thereafter, Officer Miller pulled the package out of Lawrence's pocket and saw that it was in fact drugs. Lawrence has moved to suppress the drugs. How should the court rule?

A) The court should admit the drugs because Officer Miller conducted a lawful *Terry* frisk.

B) The court should admit the drugs because Officer Miller's squeeze of the package lasted only two seconds and was *de minimis*.

C) The court should suppress the drugs because a *Terry* frisk is for weapons and thus cannot be the basis for admitting drugs.

D) The court should suppress the drugs because Officer Miller conducted a search for drugs without a valid basis.

Question 91

Police receive a 911 call from Brandy. She says a man just ran up to her, stuck a gun in her face, and told her to take off her diamond engagement ring and give it to him. Brandy said, "I can't believe he stole the huge ring that my boyfriend just gave me last week when he proposed. The guy who stole it looked really scary. He was pretty short—maybe 5′3″ inches at the most. But he was super muscular." Officers immediately began patrolling the area near where the ring was stolen. A few blocks away, officers saw a short muscular man walking down the street. When the officers ordered him to stop, he took off running, but he was not very fast. The officers stopped him and frisked him. During the frisk, the officer felt a ring with a large stone in the man's front pocket. The officer reached his whole hand deep into the pocket and pulled out a diamond ring. Brandy later identified it as her diamond ring. The man has moved to suppress. What result?

A) The ring should be suppressed because an officer can only seize weapons or items (like drugs) that are illegal to possess. A ring is not an illegal item.

B) The ring should be suppressed because the officer had to reach his whole hand deep into the man's pocket to retrieve the ring.

C) The ring should be suppressed because the officer lacked reasonable suspicion to conduct a frisk.

D) The ring should be admitted because the man's pocket could have contained a weapon.

E) The ring should be admitted because the officer conducted a valid *Terry* frisk and immediately recognized an incriminating item in the man's pocket.

Question 92

The police pull over Todd for speeding, which is not an arrestable offense in this jurisdiction. Although the police do not have any evidence that he has committed a crime, it is well known in the community that Todd has a bad temper and is rumored to carry small knives as weapons. For this reason, the police move Todd away from the car while they write him a ticket, but they do not arrest him. The police conduct a *Terry* frisk of Todd's car to make sure there are no knives Todd can use against the officers. In the trunk, the officer finds a stolen television. Todd is charged with theft of the television. How should the court rule on Todd's motion to suppress the stolen television?

A) The court should deny Todd's motion because the officer had reasonable suspicion to make a *Terry* frisk of Todd's car.

B) The court should deny Todd's motion because police can always move a suspect away from his car and conduct a full-scale search of the automobile.

C) The court should grant Todd's motion to suppress because the police exceeded the scope of a permissible *Terry* search.

D) The court should grant Todd's motion to suppress because once Todd was immobilized it was not permissible for the officers to conduct a *Terry* frisk of the car.

Question 93

Two officers execute an arrest warrant for Stan for the robbery of a gas station. The officers go to Stan's house and knock and announce their presence. No one answers, but they hear a loud commotion inside. The officers push in the door. Inside, near the entrance, they immediately see Stan holding a bag and shoving money into the bag. The first officer grabs Stan and begins to handcuff him. As that is happening, the second officer runs upstairs and begins to look in each room. The second officer moves quickly from room to room and looks only in large spaces such as under the beds and in the shower. The second officer opens a closet on the second floor. The closet is empty, except for an illegal machine gun lying on the floor. In a subsequent prosecution, Stan moves to suppress the illegal machine gun. The court finds that the officers had reasonable suspicion, but not probable cause. How should the court rule?

A) The machine gun is admissible because the officer found it while conducting a valid *Terry* frisk of the house.

B) The machine gun is admissible because the officers were entitled to search the house for contraband since the gas station was robbed.

C) The machine gun is inadmissible. The search incident to arrest doctrine does not permit a search of rooms outside of the arrestee's immediate reach, and the gun was found on a completely different floor.

D) The machine gun is inadmissible because there is no probable cause to believe a gun could be found in the closet.

ANSWERS TO MULTIPLE-CHOICE QUESTIONS

Answer to Question 89

Answer A is incorrect. An officer's hope that he will find incriminating evidence has no effect on whether the search was valid. The subjective intent of an officer is not relevant. If the officer had a valid basis to frisk Lawrence for weapons, then the frisk would be valid, regardless of what the officer hoped to find.

Answer B is incorrect. A *Terry* frisk is only for weapons. However, if in the course of a valid frisk an officer feels something other than a weapon that he immediately recognizes to be incriminating, the officer can seize that item under the plain touch doctrine.

Answer C is incorrect. Officer Miller has learned that Lawrence is the head of a large drug operation. Furthermore, Lawrence has just exited a known drug house that is in a dangerous area and that has armed guards stationed around it. Under these circumstances, an officer could have reasonable suspicion that Lawrence is armed and dangerous.

Answer D is correct. Officer Miller likely has reasonable suspicion that Lawrence is armed and dangerous. Lawrence is the head of a large drug operation. Furthermore, Lawrence has just exited a known drug house that is in a dangerous area and has armed guards stationed around it. Under these circumstances, an officer could have reasonable suspicion that Lawrence is armed and dangerous.

Answer E is incorrect. This answer choice is circular and impermissible. In order to search Lawrence incident to arrest, Officer Miller would first have to have probable cause to arrest him. But here, Officer Miller did not develop probable cause to arrest Lawrence until after searching him. The question tells us that at the moment Officer Miller conducted the search, he lacked probable cause and thus could not have been utilizing the search incident to arrest exception.

Answer to Question 90

Answer A is incorrect. Officer Miller did not conduct a lawful *Terry* frisk. A *Terry* frisk allows an open-handed pat-down for weapons. When conducting a *Terry* frisk, officers cannot manipulate objects between their fingers to determine what the object is.

Answer B is incorrect. Even though Officer Miller only squeezed the package between his fingers for two seconds, he still conducted a search that went beyond a *Terry* frisk and for which he did not have a basis. There is no *de minimis* exception that allows police to conduct a search for drugs with less than probable cause.

Answer C is incorrect. The purpose of the *Terry* frisk doctrine is to allow police to locate dangerous weapons. However, if an officer finds drugs or other contraband during a *Terry* frisk that the officer immediately recognizes to be incriminating, the officer can seize that evidence. The evidence will then be admissible in a prosecution.

Answer D is correct. The *Terry* frisk doctrine allowed Officer Miller to conduct an open-hand pat-down of Lawrence. Officer Miller went further than that, however, when he manipulated the package between his index finger and thumb. That action went beyond a valid *Terry* frisk. Officer Miller lacked a legal basis to conduct such a search.

Answer to Question 91

Answer A is incorrect. Under the plain touch doctrine, an officer can seize an item that is immediately incriminating. Ordinarily a ring is not incriminating. But in this situation, Brandy has told the police that a large diamond ring was stolen by a similar-looking man only a few blocks away. The officer can therefore reasonably conclude that the ring is stolen and therefore contraband.

Answer B is incorrect. It does not matter how far into the pocket the officer has to reach to remove the item. The relevant question is whether the officer immediately recognized the object in the pocket to be incriminating.

Answer C is incorrect. Brandy reported that a man "stuck a gun in her face." This fact provides the officers with reasonable suspicion to believe that the man is armed and dangerous.

Answer D is incorrect. Officers cannot reach into a detainee's pocket and remove small items because the pocket "could have contained a weapon." The *Terry* frisk doctrine only allows a pat-down of the outer layer of clothing to search for weapons.

Answer E is correct. Because Brandy told the police that the perpetrator "stuck a gun in her face," the police had reasonable suspicion that a man matching the description of the perpetrator would be armed and dangerous. The officers could therefore conduct a *Terry* frisk. When the officers felt an object that they immediately recognized to be a ring, they could conclude it was the ring stolen from Brandy only a few blocks away. Accordingly, the item was immediately incriminating.

Answer to Question 92

Answer A is incorrect. The officer did have reasonable suspicion that Todd might be dangerous and able to gain access to a weapon. And officers can conduct a protective sweep of a vehicle. However, the sweep can only be done on the passenger compartment and cannot include a search of the trunk.

Answer B is incorrect. The automobile exception to the warrant requirement only allows the police to conduct a full-scale search of an automobile if they have probable cause.

Answer C is correct. The officers would probably have been justified in conducting a protective sweep of the passenger compartment of the vehicle because they had reasonable suspicion that Todd had knives and was thus armed and dangerous. However, police authority to conduct a protective sweep does not extend to the trunk. Nothing in the question indicates that police had probable cause to search the trunk of the vehicle, thus the evidence should be suppressed.

Answer D is incorrect. Officers can conduct a valid *Terry* frisk even if the person has already been immobilized. Courts want to be sure that the individual does not break free and lunge for a weapon that he has hidden in the vehicle.

Answer to Question 93

Answer A is correct. The Supreme Court expanded the *Terry* frisk doctrine to allow protective sweeps of a house. The officers heard a commotion when they knocked and announced. It is possible that someone besides Stan was hiding in the house while the officers were arresting Stan. That other person—if they existed—could be dangerous to the officers. As such, the officers are permitted to conduct a protective sweep of the house. Moreover, the officers lawfully carried out the sweep. They did not conduct an in-depth search. Rather they only looked in areas (like the closet) where a person could be hiding. The officers found the machine gun in plain view.

Answer B is incorrect. The question says only that the officers have an arrest warrant. They do not have a search warrant. Moreover, nothing in the question indicates that the police have probable cause to believe that evidence from the robbery will be found in the house.

Answer C is incorrect. It is true that the search incident to arrest doctrine does not allow a search of the entire house. However, in this case the officers are not conducting a search incident to arrest. Rather, they are conducting a protective sweep of the house, which is justified under the *Terry* doctrine.

Answer D is incorrect. It is true that the police lack probable cause (and a warrant) to search for evidence of the robbery. However, the officers are conducting a protective sweep, which only requires reasonable suspicion.

CHAPTER 16
Drunk Driving, Drug, and Other Checkpoints

THE RULE: Police cannot set up checkpoints and stop people without suspicion if the primary purpose of the checkpoint is general crime control. Drug checkpoints are therefore unconstitutional. However, if the primary purpose of a checkpoint is for public safety and the level of intrusion is minimal, then the checkpoint can be constitutional. Drunk driving checkpoints—in which a car is stopped with zero suspicion—may be constitutional.

Critical Points

- Drug checkpoints—those where the primary purpose is to discover criminal activity—are unconstitutional.
- DWI checkpoints—those where the primary purpose is to stop people who may currently be drunk and dangerous while driving—may be constitutional if the police set up the checkpoints correctly.
- No individualized suspicion is necessary for DWI checkpoints.
- Police are not allowed much discretion in carrying out DWI checkpoints. Officers cannot decide which particular vehicles they want to stop. Rather, there must be a fixed pattern in which the officers stop every vehicle or, for example, every third vehicle.
- For a DWI checkpoint to be lawful, the stop and traffic backup must be brief. Because the level of intrusiveness is a key factor in the constitutionality of a DWI checkpoint, the driver must only be delayed for a short time.
- The initial interaction between the police officer and the driver at the checkpoint must be brief. The officer can ask a few questions, but the encounter should not ordinarily last more than a minute or two.

- If the officer sees no signs of intoxication, the driver should be allowed to quickly go on her way.
- If the officer sees signs of intoxication or other criminal activity, the officer then has reasonable suspicion to pull the driver over and investigate further.
- If the police publicize the DWI checkpoint in advance—for example, on the radio—then courts will be more likely to find it to be constitutional because drivers will be aware of the checkpoint and can avoid it. An advertised checkpoint is less intrusive.
- The DWI checkpoint must be designed in a way that it will likely be at least somewhat effective. A DWI checkpoint in broad daylight far away from any bars or restaurants is not likely to be effective.
- DWI checkpoints should ordinarily be planned by higher-ups in the police department and implemented by police officers who have limited discretion. If a handful of patrol officers spontaneously decide to create a DWI checkpoint, that makes it less likely to be constitutional.

OVERVIEW OF THE BLACKLETTER LAW

Under the Supreme Court's "special needs" doctrine, police may set up checkpoints that stop vehicles based on no suspicion whatsoever. However, the police cannot simply set up checkpoints for any reason they want. If the primary purpose of the checkpoint is general crime control—in other words, to discover evidence of wrongdoing for purposes of prosecution—then the checkpoint is unconstitutional. By contrast, if the purpose of the checkpoint is to protect public safety, then the checkpoint can be constitutional if it satisfies the rules described below.

The first step is therefore to determine what the primary purpose of the checkpoint is. Drug checkpoints are for the primary purpose of punishing criminal activity and therefore they are unconstitutional. DWI checkpoints, however, are for the primary purpose of getting drunk drivers off the road and therefore have a public safety purpose and are thus potentially constitutional.

For a DWI checkpoint to be constitutional, courts typically put a lot of emphasis on the level of intrusiveness on the driver. If the checkpoint moves quickly and the driver is only delayed for a few minutes, then the level of intrusiveness is minimal.

Because DWI checkpoints are administrative and conducted based on no suspicion, courts expect that they will be designed by supervisors and carried out with little police discretion. Supervisors should therefore decide the time and location of the checkpoint. Officers should not have discretion about which cars to stop. The officers should either stop every car, or they should stick to a pattern (for instance, every third car) and not deviate.

While drunk-driving checkpoints are the most well-known checkpoint used by law enforcement, they are by no means the only type of lawful checkpoint. For example, police have established (and courts have upheld) driver's license checkpoints to ensure that unlicensed, dangerous drivers are not on the roads. (Another example is border checkpoints, which we explore in the next chapter.)

One checkpoint that many people have encountered is the airport checkpoint. Each year, millions of people take off their shoes, walk through metal detectors, and allow their luggage to be x-rayed or even searched by hand. Although the Supreme Court has never clearly addressed the question, there is little doubt that airport security checkpoints are constitutional. One might think that airport checkpoints are legal because people impliedly give their consent to security screening when they buy their airline tickets. The better explanation, however, is that airport security screening falls under the special needs exception. The governmental interest—preventing terrorism and violence on planes—outweighs the invasion of passengers' privacy.

Finally (and especially important for law school exams), it is important to be aware that a checkpoint could have multiple purposes. For example, police could be asking drivers about whether they have had anything to drink, while also using a drug-sniffing dog to look for cars that might be transporting illegal drugs. In "dual purpose" cases, courts try to determine the "primary" purpose of the checkpoint. If the primary purpose is public safety, then the checkpoint will be constitutional even if there is a secondary purpose of general crime control.

EXAM TRAPS TO AVOID

- If a few patrol officers get together and plan their own DWI checkpoint, it is likely to be unconstitutional.
- If the initial interaction between the officer and the driver lasts longer than a few moments, the DWI checkpoint is less likely to be constitutional.
- If the officers set up the checkpoint in the daytime, far away from places where alcohol is served, you should be careful to check that the primary purpose of the checkpoint is public safety (which is permissible), rather than general crime control (which is unconstitutional).
- If the officers ask questions during the checkpoint that are unrelated to drinking and driving, you should be careful to check that the primary purpose of the checkpoint is for legitimate public safety concerns, rather than illegitimate efforts to search for criminal activity.
- If the officers do not follow a fixed pattern (either every vehicle or, for example, every third vehicle) then the checkpoint is likely unconstitutional.

MULTIPLE-CHOICE QUESTIONS

Question 94

On November 27, the New Jersey State Police set up an automobile checkpoint near the Holland Tunnel to catch and deter people who were bringing illegal narcotics from New York City into New Jersey. (The Holland Tunnel connects New York and New Jersey.) The checkpoint was approved by the Superintendent of the New Jersey State Police and was operated by a highly trained group of officers under the supervision of a police captain with 23 years of law enforcement experience. The troopers pulled over every car that came through the Holland Tunnel for a two-hour period. The checkpoint yielded three narcotics arrests and seven drunk-driving arrests. Julie was one of the seven people arrested for drunk driving and she is now appealing her conviction. Which of the following is correct?

A) Julie's conviction should be reversed because the primary purpose of the checkpoint was illegitimate.

B) Julie's conviction should be reversed because the checkpoint was only approved by executive officials and police officers and was not legislatively authorized as required by the Supreme Court.

C) Julie's conviction should be affirmed because even though the primary purpose of the checkpoint was illegitimate, she was arrested and prosecuted for a crime that would have been a legitimate reason to operate a checkpoint.

D) Julie's conviction should be affirmed because the checkpoint was approved by senior officials, it was operated by trained officers, it was conducted for a legitimate purpose in an effective manner, it was carried out in a consistent pattern, and it was effective, thus allowing for a suspicionless detention under the special needs exception.

Question 95

The police department sets up a sobriety checkpoint on South Henry Street at 2:00 a.m. in the hopes of catching people who are driving home drunk. Police pull over every third automobile and ask those drivers a few questions. Tanya is pulled over and police detect alcohol on her breath. Tanya then fails a Breathalyzer test and is arrested. What is Tanya's best argument for challenging her arrest?

A) The sobriety checkpoint was unconstitutional because the police did not stop every single car.

B) The sobriety checkpoint was an unconstitutional seizure because police need at least reasonable suspicion to stop drivers.

C) The sobriety checkpoint was unconstitutional because although the criteria for conducting stops was narrowly tailored, the government cannot demonstrate a compelling justification to support the checkpoint.

D) None of the above.

Question 96

Police set up DWI checkpoint near a bar at 1:00 a.m. on Saturday. The checkpoint was approved by Captain Holt of the Brooklyn Police Department. He picked the location and instructed the officers to stop every car, question each driver for no more than one minute, and "do it completely by the book." The officers followed his instructions exactly. While they were moving cars through the checkpoint, Officer Peralta said to Officer Diaz, "You know how I got an arrest warrant for Doug Judy, the car thief, years ago? Well, I heard a rumor that he drinks at this bar. I hope this checkpoint is what finally lets us capture him." Initially, the checkpoint was operating well. But within an hour it started to back up. A driver complained to the officers that "I've been sitting here for 40 minutes because of your stupid checkpoint." In response, the Sergeant on duty said to the other officers, "You know, he's right. We're getting too backed up. Let's just stop every other car." Accordingly, Officer Peralta skipped the next car in line and began stopping every other car. Two minutes later, the officers stopped Doug Judy. He was completely sober, but Officer Peralta arrested him based on the outstanding arrest warrant for car theft. Judy has moved to dismiss the charges on the grounds that the checkpoint was invalid. Which of the following would be the strongest argument?

A) The decision to change the pattern of stops from every car to every other car was an inappropriate exercise of police discretion.

B) The 40-minute delay was too intrusive and rendered the checkpoint potentially unconstitutional.

C) The sergeant on duty overruling the captain who designed the checkpoint conflicts with the idea that this is an administrative special needs exception.

D) Officer Peralta's comments to Officer Diaz about his motivation to catch Doug Judy demonstrates that the primary purpose of the checkpoint was for general crime control.

Question 97

After attending an office holiday party, Raquel drives home. Raquel lives far out of town; her home is located near Exit 120. It is late in the evening, so the highway is pretty empty. Two miles before she approaches Exit 112, Raquel sees a sign that says "Drug Checkpoint Ahead, Be Prepared To Stop." Raquel wants to go home and is nervous about being stopped at a drug checkpoint. When she reaches Exit 112, Raquel gets off the highway. People normally use Exit 112 to get to the local high school, which of course is closed late in the evening. There is nothing else at Exit 112. When Raquel reaches the bottom of the exit ramp she is surprised to find multiple police officers. (The police actually had not set up a checkpoint on the highway, but instead had arranged themselves at the end of the road at Exit 112.) One officer instructs Raquel to pull over to the side of the road and asks her if she has been drinking alcohol tonight. A second officer runs the license plate on Raquel's car. While that is happening, a third officer walks a drug-sniffing dog around the vehicle. The dog alerts to drugs, which the police quickly find. It turns out there actually was no drug checkpoint on the highway. The sign was a ruse to see who would exit the highway. Raquel is arrested and moves to suppress the drugs on the grounds that she was stopped illegally. Which of the following is correct?

A) The drugs should be suppressed because the sign said that there was a drug checkpoint and the intent of the officers is controlling in determining what kind of checkpoint the police operate.

B) The drugs should be suppressed because by using a drug-sniffing dog the police have converted what would otherwise be a DWI checkpoint into an unlawful drug checkpoint.

C) The drugs should be suppressed because the police have engaged in trickery to get Raquel to exit the highway.

D) If the drugs are admissible it would not be under a checkpoint theory, but instead because the police have arguably demonstrated reasonable suspicion to stop Raquel since she was engaged in incriminating behavior by exiting into an abandoned area to avoid police.

Question 98

Police set up a checkpoint at midnight in a downtown neighborhood known for drug activity. The checkpoint is operated by three officers, one of whom has brought his drug-sniffing dog that he regularly works with in airports. When cars approach, the drivers encounter a sign that says "Driver's License Checkpoint. Be Prepared To Stop." The officers stop each car at the checkpoint and ask the drivers to provide their driver's licenses. One officer takes the license and runs it through a database to make sure it is valid. Another officer stands by the driver's window and asks the drivers basic questions such as whether they have any drugs on them. The third officer walks the drug-sniffing dog around the vehicle. It takes only two minutes to run the license checks and as soon as that is complete the driver is allowed to leave. While the officer was checking Pat's license, the drug dog alerted that there were drugs in the trunk. The officers subsequently searched the trunk and found a kilogram of heroin. How should the court rule on Pat's suppression motion?

A) The court should suppress the heroin because driver's license checkpoints are unconstitutional since they are simply an effort to conduct general crime control.

B) The court should suppress the heroin because the primary purpose of the checkpoint was to search for drugs, and the driver's license check was a secondary purpose.

C) The court should admit the heroin because this was a valid driver's license checkpoint that is constitutional.

D) The court should admit the heroin because the checkpoint was brief and involved a minimal invasion of privacy.

Question 99

Danillo is flying from Washington Dulles Airport to Texas. At Dulles Airport, Danillo goes through the security line. He removes his shoes and places his suitcase on the conveyor belt to be x-rayed. When Danillo walks through the metal detector it rings. The TSA officer asks Danillo to stand to the side and raise his arms so that the officer can run a metal detector wand around his body. The metal detector rings over Danillo's pocket and he remembers that he forgot to remove his keys. When Danillo pulls the keys out of his pocket a bottle of pills falls out and spills all over the floor. The pills were opioids (a Schedule II drug) for which Danillo had no prescription. After being charged with unlawful possession of a controlled substance, Danillo challenges the constitutionality of the airport security process. Which of the following is the best answer?

A) The screening process is constitutional because Danillo impliedly consented to be searched when he purchased an airline ticket.

B) The screening process is constitutional because it falls under the special needs exception and because the government's interest outweighs the level of intrusion.

C) The screening process is constitutional because passengers waive all of their Fourth Amendment rights when they fly.

D) The screening process is unconstitutional because there was no individualized suspicion to search Danillo.

Question 100

On Monday, March 1, at 4:00 p.m., there was a terrible accident at the corner of First and Main Streets. A driver hit a pedestrian who was crossing the street in front of a school. The driver would certainly have known that they hit the pedestrian, but the driver did not stop. Instead, the driver sped away rapidly. The police have spent the whole week investigating, but they have not come up with any leads. Accordingly, exactly one week later, on Monday, March 8, at 4:00 p.m., the police set up a checkpoint at the same intersection. The officers stop every vehicle and ask each person whether they drove through the same location last week (perhaps picking up their kids from the school across the street), and whether they saw the hit-and-run. Trey was stopped at the checkpoint. As the police were asking him whether he saw last week's accident, they realized he was drunk. The officers arrested Trey for drunk driving and he has moved to dismiss the charges on the ground that the checkpoint was unlawful. How should the court rule?

A) The checkpoint is for general crime control and therefore unconstitutional.

B) The checkpoint is only informational and therefore constitutional.

ANSWERS TO MULTIPLE-CHOICE QUESTIONS

Answer to Question 94

Answer A is correct. The question tells us that the primary purpose was to catch people bringing drugs through the tunnel. The fact that the officers actually caught more drunk drivers is irrelevant. To be a lawful checkpoint, the primary purpose must be public safety, not general crime control.

Answer B is incorrect. The Supreme Court has never required that a checkpoint be legislatively authorized in order to be lawful. Here, the checkpoint was approved by a high-ranking official in the police department and operated correctly by an experienced law enforcement officer. Had this been a DWI checkpoint, rather than a drug checkpoint, it would have been constitutional.

Answer C is incorrect. The key question is whether Julie was stopped illegally. Police may not conduct a drug checkpoint because the primary purpose is for general crime control. The fact that Julie was eventually arrested for a crime (DWI) that the police could have set up a checkpoint for is irrelevant. What matters was the type of checkpoint the police actually set up.

Answer D is incorrect. This answer choice is tempting because it describes the factors that would create a valid DWI checkpoint. The officers administered the checkpoint in a proper way by having it approved by a senior official, operated by trained officers, and carried out in a consistent pattern of stopping every car. However, designing and operating the checkpoint correctly is not sufficient. The primary purpose of the checkpoint must still be for a legitimate reason. Here the primary purpose was to search for drugs, which the Supreme Court has said is impermissible.

Answer to Question 95

Answer A is incorrect. The police do not have to stop every single car. It is permissible for the police to follow a pattern. Here the police stopped every third car, which is acceptable.

Answer B is incorrect. Sobriety checkpoints can be conducted without any suspicion. Police do not have to have any individualized suspicion to stop vehicles during a checkpoint.

Answer C is incorrect. The Supreme Court has recognized that keeping drunk drivers off the road is a compelling justification.

Answer D is correct. The officers conducted a valid checkpoint in this question.

Answer to Question 96

Answer A is incorrect. While administrative checkpoints such as DWI checkpoints are supposed to involve very limited police discretion, that does not mean there must be no discretion. In cases like this where traffic is backing up, the decision to stop fewer cars is a reasonable exercise of discretion and is permissible. Moreover, the change from stopping every car to stopping every other car did not in harm the defendant. Had there been no change, he would have been stopped anyway.

Answer B is correct. There is no "magic" time delay that turns a constitutional checkpoint into an unconstitutional one. Forty minutes is a long time, though, and may be long enough to render the checkpoint unconstitutional.

Answer C is incorrect for the reasons explained in response to Answer A. A properly created DWI checkpoint will not give the officers on the scene wide discretion in deciding how to operate the checkpoint. However, here we have a sergeant exercising fairly modest discretion to ensure the checkpoint operates smoothly.

Answer D is incorrect. The subjective motivations of Officer Peralta are irrelevant. Courts determine the primary purpose of a checkpoint from an objective standpoint by looking at how the checkpoint was designed and carried out.

Answer to Question 97

Answer A is incorrect. When assessing the constitutionality of police action, we look at it objectively, not at the subjective intent of the officers. For this to be a drug checkpoint, we would have to conclude—objectively, not subjectively—that the primary purpose was to search for evidence of criminal activity.

Answer B is incorrect. This does not appear to be a DWI checkpoint. The officers are not stopping every vehicle (or a pre-set pattern of vehicles) to briefly assess intoxication. Indeed, this does not look like a checkpoint at all. The police appear to have conducted a traffic stop based on reasonable suspicion. It is permissible to walk a drug-sniffing dog around a vehicle during a valid traffic stop.

Answer C is incorrect. The police have in fact engaged in trickery, but that does not amount to a Fourth Amendment violation.

Answer D is correct. Raquel has exited the highway at the first exit after seeing the sign for the drug checkpoint. Moreover, there is seemingly no legitimate reason for a driver to use that exit in the evening because the school (which is closed) is the only thing at the exit. Some courts would interpret these facts to find reasonable suspicion. Other courts, however, would conclude that Raquel's actions are not incriminating (since it is lawful to exit the highway) and thus there is no reasonable suspicion. [Note: This would make a good essay question.] While courts differ on whether there would be reasonable suspicion, Answer D is the best answer choice because it hedges by saying "If the drugs are admissible. . . ."

Answer to Question 98

Answer A is incorrect. Many courts have upheld driver's license checkpoints. Courts have concluded that license checkpoints—like DWI checkpoints—are for the purpose of ensuring safe roads.

Answer B is correct. Although the officers purport to be operating a driver's license checkpoint, the primary purpose actually appears to be a drug checkpoint. The key factors indicating that it is a drug checkpoint are that: (1) it is being operated late at night; (2) the officer asks about drug possession; (3) it is near a known drug area; and (4) a drug-sniffing dog is on the scene and walking around the vehicle in order to alert when the cars are transporting drugs. The primary purpose is determined not by what a sign says or what an officer believes, but instead by what an objective analysis indicates. Drug checkpoints are unconstitutional.

Answer C is incorrect. For the reasons explained above in response to Answer B, this is not a driver's license checkpoint.

Answer D is incorrect. It is true that the delay was brief and the level of intrusion on the drivers was low. Had this been a valid checkpoint—for drunk driving or driver's license checks—it would likely be constitutional. As explained in response to Answer B, however, the primary purpose of this checkpoint was drug investigation. A checkpoint for an illegitimate purpose cannot be made constitutional because it was carried out in a minimally intrusive manner.

Answer to Question 99

Answer A is incorrect. Most courts have recognized that airport security checkpoints fall under the special needs exception, not some type of implied consent.

Answer B is correct. Although the U.S. Supreme Court has never explicitly held that airport security checkpoints fall under the special needs exception, they have suggested as much in dicta. And lower courts have repeatedly held that airport checkpoints fall under the special needs exception.

Answer C is incorrect. This answer choice is too broad. Even though passengers must submit to security screening, that does not mean they have waived all of their Fourth Amendment rights. For instance, TSA officers could not conduct a body cavity search without a warrant.

Answer D is incorrect. Individualized suspicion is not required for airport security searches to be constitutional. All passengers must submit to screening and courts have not required any type of individualized suspicion.

Answer to Question 100

It would initially appear that Answer A is the correct choice. The police are investigating a criminal offense (hit-and-run from last week). Checkpoints designed for general crime control are unconstitutional. Nevertheless, the Supreme Court unanimously ruled in *Illinois v. Lidster* (2004) that a checkpoint just like this one was constitutional because it was "information seeking." These kinds of stops do not lend themselves to individualized suspicion and are not likely to cause anxiety for drivers. As such, they are constitutional. Answer B is therefore correct.

CHAPTER 17
Border Searches

THE RULE: Most searches at the U.S. border are considered "routine" searches and government officials can conduct them with no individualized suspicion. A small category of more invasive searches (such as drilling into a vehicle to look for drugs) are "non-routine" and government officials must have reasonable suspicion to conduct them.

Critical Points

- Because the government has a significant interest in protecting the U.S. border, government officials have vast authority to conduct warrantless, suspicionless searches at the border.
- The border search doctrine allows government officials to search people, their possessions, and their vehicles.
- Unlike other suspicionless searches (e.g., DWI checkpoints) government officials can take a long time to conduct a border search. A detention and search that takes an hour or longer can still be constitutional.
- "Routine" border searches do not require any suspicion.
- Almost all border searches are classified as "routine." For instance, if border agents spend an hour taking apart a vehicle's gas tank to search for drugs, that is a routine search.
- Nonroutine searches (such as body cavity searches or drilling holes in a vehicle to look for drugs) require reasonable suspicion.
- "Fixed interior checkpoints" are different from true border searches. Border agents are allowed to set up fixed *interior* checkpoints on roads that are near (but not actually at) the border. These interior checkpoints are sometimes set

up 30, 50, or even 70 miles from the actual border. If the interior checkpoints are fixed, the agents can stop vehicles with no suspicion, although they still need probable cause to search the vehicles.

- Roving (i.e., not at a fixed location) border patrols are subject to ordinary search and seizure rules.

OVERVIEW OF THE BLACKLETTER LAW

Hundreds of millions of people pass through border checkpoints in the United States each year. The U.S. government has established constitutional border checkpoints at: (1) the physical borders with Canada and Mexico and (2) international airports (including in cities like Chicago that are in the middle of the country).

Border agents obviously have authority to stop (i.e., seize) people at the border. The agents can also conduct two different types of searches under the border search doctrine. First, government agents can conduct "routine" searches at the border with no suspicion whatsoever. Routine searches include searches of the person, their luggage, and their vehicle. Despite their name, routine searches can be quite invasive. For instance, the Supreme Court has concluded that an hour-long disassembly of a vehicle's gas tank to look for drugs was a routine search that did not require any suspicion.

A second (albeit small) category of border searches is "non-routine" and requires the agents to have reasonable suspicion. Lower courts have found that body cavity searches, strip searches, and drilling holes in vehicles are non-routine. Lower courts are split on the question of whether searches of cell phones at the border are routine or non-routine.

It is important to distinguish between true border searches (at the actual border or at an international airport) from fixed *interior* checkpoints, which are often located dozens of miles from the actual border. For instance, there is a fixed interior border checkpoint on a road in Bangor, Maine, that is 70 miles from the Canadian border. Border agents have less authority at fixed interior checkpoints. The Supreme Court has held that agents may stop vehicles at fixed interior checkpoints and briefly detain individuals for questioning with no suspicion. However, in order to conduct a search of the vehicles at fixed interior checkpoints, the agents must have probable cause.

Finally, beware of roving (i.e., moving, not fixed) border patrols. If a border agent is patrolling near the border and stops and searches a person, the normal Fourth Amendment rules apply. In other words, the government cannot justify a suspicionless stop of a person just because a border agent stopped them near the border. Roving border patrols near the Mexico and Canadian borders are subject to the same Fourth Amendment rules that would apply to a regular police officer pulling over a car in the middle of Kansas.

EXAM TRAPS TO AVOID

- Just because a border stop or search takes a long time, do *not* assume it is invalid or that it is "non-routine" and requires reasonable suspicion.
- Just because border agents conduct a very thorough search (such as combing through a vehicle or even taking apart portions of the vehicle) do *not* assume the agents have exceeded their authority.
- Just because a border search occurs at an international airport (e.g., O'Hare International Airport in Chicago) do *not* assume it is invalid.
- Just because police pulled over a driver near the border, do *not* assume it is covered by the border search exception. The border search exception applies to *fixed* checkpoints, not roving patrols.

MULTIPLE-CHOICE QUESTIONS

Question 101

Winston flew from London, England, to O'Hare Airport in Chicago, Illinois. After picking up his luggage, Winston proceeded to customs. The line moved quickly and the border agent spent only about 15 seconds talking to each of the six people who were in line in front of Winston. When it was his turn, Winston walked up to the desk and the agent asked him where in the United States he was going and how long he planned to stay in the country. Winston answered that he was visiting family in Chicago and would return to London in two weeks. The agent then ordered Winston to open his suitcases for inspection. When Winston asked, "Why me? You let those other people just walk through," the border agent said, "I just have a hunch about you." Winston opened his suitcase and the agent found thousands of dollars that Winston had failed to declare on his customs form and that turned out to be stolen. Winston was arrested and has moved to suppress the money. How should the court rule?

A) The court should suppress the evidence because the agent needed reasonable suspicion to conduct a border search and did not have it.

B) The court should suppress the evidence because Chicago, Illinois, is nowhere near the U.S. border and therefore agents cannot conduct suspicionless border searches.

C) The court should suppress the evidence because the border agent arbitrarily selected Winston for invasive screening while allowing six people in front of him to pass.

D) The court should admit the evidence because the border agent did not need any suspicion to search Winton's suitcase.

E) The court should admit the evidence because Winston consented to a search when he purchased a ticket to fly.

Question 102

Franco is crossing the border from Canada to the United States at Niagara Falls. The agents detect something fishy about Franco's behavior. He seems to be acting weird and is walking very slowly. When Franco reaches the front of the line, the border agents take him aside and pat him down, turn his pockets inside out, and search through his backpack. The agents do not find any drugs, though they do find a piece of paper with the heading "Distribution—123 Calvert Street, 4pm." The agents demand that Franco go into a nearby room and submit to a strip search to determine whether he has drugs taped to his body. A few minutes later, over Franco's loud objections, a trained border agent orders Franco to take off all of his clothes. The agent looks underneath Franco's genitals and finds multiple bags of heroin taped to Franco's body. Franco has moved to suppress the evidence. What result?

A) The evidence should be admitted because the agent does not need reasonable suspicion to search at the border.

B) The evidence should be admitted, but only if the Franco's behavior and the note in his backpack gave rise to reasonable suspicion that he was concealing drugs.

C) The evidence should be admitted, but only if the note in Franco's backpack gave rise to probable cause that he was concealing drugs.

D) The evidence should be suppressed because strip searches require a warrant.

E) The evidence should be suppressed because the agent initially relied on a hunch to look through Franco's backpack and therefore did not have reasonable suspicion to search the backpack.

Question 103

Victoria is returning from a three-week trip to Mexico. She drives to the McAllen Border Station with the intention of driving across the border to her home in Texas. At the border station, agents run Victoria's driver's license and learn that three years ago she had been charged with dealing a large quantity of cocaine. In that case, Victoria was arrested for procuring cocaine in Mexico, storing it in a secret compartment under her car, and then driving across the border so that she could sell the cocaine. For some reason (it's not in the records), the charges against Victoria were dismissed before trial and she has no prior convictions. Based on this information, the agents pull Victoria's car over for additional screening. The agents spend an hour taking apart the muffler of Victoria's car and inside they find numerous packages of cocaine. How should the court rule on Victoria's suppression motion?

A) The cocaine should be admitted because the agents did not need reasonable suspicion to take apart the muffler.

B) The cocaine should be suppressed because it took the agents an hour to take apart the muffler, which exceeds the permissible time for a border detention.

C) The cocaine should be suppressed because Victoria's prior arrest for transporting drugs cannot create reasonable suspicion since the charges were dropped.

D) The cocaine should be suppressed because the agents cannot take apart the car's muffler without reasonable suspicion, which is not present here.

Question 104

Assume the same facts as Question 103. This time, however, assume that the agents did not find any drugs in the muffler. They turned next to the area between the trunk and the passenger compartment because drug couriers often hide drugs there. The agents were unable to see into this area, so they took a crowbar and pried the seats away from the car's frame so they could see into the space behind the seats. In doing so, the agents ripped a six-inch hole in the upholstery of the car. The agents found bags of cocaine behind the seats. Victoria moves to suppress. How should the court rule?

A) The court should suppress the cocaine unless the agents had reasonable suspicion to believe drugs were being smuggled in the car.

B) The court should suppress the cocaine because the officers' failure to find drugs in the muffler eliminated any reasonable suspicion they may have had.

C) The court should admit the cocaine because the agents do not need reasonable suspicion to use a crowbar to look behind the seats.

D) The court should admit the cocaine because Victoria has a reduced expectation of privacy as a result of her prior arrest for drug distribution.

Question 105

Agent Samuels is a border patrol agent. His job is to patrol near the United States-Mexico border and detain people who have crossed the border at locations other than the official border checkpoint. Agent Samuels is patrolling in Brownsville, about 10 miles north of the border checkpoint. He receives a tip from another agent that individuals who evaded the border checkpoint and crossed elsewhere were just seen entering the drive-thru at McDonald's. Agent Samuels immediately proceeds to the McDonald's and pulls over the first car that exited the McDonald's. The driver of the vehicle has a valid Texas driver's license. Agent Samuels searches the trunk of the car, thinking that the individuals who unlawfully crossed the border might be hiding in the trunk. Agent Samuels does not find anyone in the trunk, though he does find an illegal firearm. The driver has moved to suppress. What result?

A) The firearm should be suppressed because the officer randomly pulled over a vehicle at McDonald's and did not have reasonable suspicion for that particular vehicle.

B) The firearm should be suppressed because even though the border patrol agent could stop the vehicle without reasonable suspicion, he could not search without probable cause at an interior location away from the official border checkpoint.

C) The firearm should be admitted because border agents who are on patrol near the border do not need reasonable suspicion to pull over a vehicle.

D) The firearm should be admitted because border agents can conduct a full-scale search of the vehicle when they are near the international border.

Question 106

Agent Tweed is a border patrol officer in Maine. He works about 20 miles from the Canadian border at a fixed interior checkpoint. Agent Tweed's job is fairly boring because most of the people who pass through the checkpoint are tourists who go to Canada for the day and then return to Maine in the evening. To keep himself entertained, Agent Tweed likes to randomly pick out a vehicle and give the driver a hard time. One afternoon, Agent Tweed stops Ralph at the fixed interior checkpoint as he is driving from Canada back to Maine. Agent Tweed asks Ralph where he has been in Canada and whether he is bringing anything back into the United States. Ralph answers that he bought some hockey equipment and has it in the trunk. Agent Tweed orders Ralph to open the trunk. After seeing the hockey equipment, Agent Tweed continues to search through the trunk. Inside of a toolbox, he finds a small amount of marijuana. Federal prosecutors charge Ralph with drug possession and he moves to suppress. What result?

A) The marijuana should be admissible because border patrol officers can conduct warrantless searches of vehicles at all border checkpoints.

B) The marijuana should be admissible because border patrol agents can conduct warrantless searches of vehicles at fixed interior checkpoints that are less than 30 miles from the international border.

C) The marijuana should be suppressed because border agents who are operating away from the actual border must demonstrate reasonable suspicion to stop a vehicle.

D) The marijuana should be suppressed because border agents who are operating away from the actual border can stop a vehicle at a fixed interior checkpoint without reasonable suspicion, but they need probable cause in order to search the vehicle.

ANSWERS TO MULTIPLE-CHOICE QUESTIONS

Answer to Question 101

Answer A is incorrect. A search of a person's belongings at the border is a routine search that does not require any suspicion. The officer did not need reasonable suspicion to search Winston's suitcase.

Answer B is incorrect. The border search exception applies at international airports such as O'Hare. The government has just as compelling of an interest in screening people and items arriving by airplane as it does for screening vehicles at the Canadian and Mexican borders.

Answer C is incorrect. Border agents have broad discretion to determine who to stop and search. There is no requirement (as there is for DWI checkpoints) that agents subject all passengers (or a fixed pattern of passengers) to identical screening.

Answer D is correct. A search of a person's belongings at the border is a routine search that does not require any suspicion.

Answer E is incorrect. The border search exception falls under the special needs doctrine, not a doctrine of implied consent.

Answer to Question 102

Answer A is incorrect. Strip searches are non-routine and therefore require reasonable suspicion.

Answer B is correct. Because strip searches are non-routine, the agents need reasonable suspicion to believe they would find drugs. The facts here are thin. Franco is acting strangely according to the officers and the note could be interpreted to relate to drugs. But of course the note might be for something completely unrelated to drug activity. Furthermore, we have no reason to believe that Franco has been involved in prior drug activity. A court might very well conclude there is no reasonable suspicion here. However, the answer choice is phrased to account for a different outcome because it says the strip search could occur "if" the evidence gave rise to reasonable suspicion.

Answer C is incorrect. Non-routine searches can be conducted if the officers have reasonable suspicion. They do not need probable cause.

Answer D is incorrect. Border agents can conduct strip searches without a warrant, but they need reasonable suspicion.

Answer E is incorrect. While the officers need reasonable suspicion to conduct the strip search, they do not need reasonable suspicion to detain Franco and search his backpack. An ordinary search of a person and their belongings at the border is routine and does not require any suspicion.

Answer to Question 103

Answer A is correct. Border agents can conduct an in-depth search of a vehicle, including taking apart things like the muffler or gas tank, without first having reasonable suspicion. Because the agents can disassemble the muffler without cutting holes in it or otherwise destroying it, the search is "routine" and they do not need reasonable suspicion.

Answer B is incorrect. Courts have upheld delays of an hour or more at the border while the police conduct searches or investigations. Because of the need to protect the border, officers have more discretion and can take longer in their investigations than they would at a DWI checkpoint or traffic stop.

Answer C is incorrect. The agents do not need reasonable suspicion to search the muffler of Victoria's car. If they did need reasonable suspicion, Victoria's prior criminal charges could create that suspicion, however.

Answer D is incorrect. Border agents can conduct routine searches without having reasonable suspicion. Courts have held that in-depth searches of vehicles—including taking apart pieces of the car—are routine searches.

Answer to Question 104

Answer A is correct. This appears to be a more invasive search that should be classified as a non-routine search requiring reasonable suspicion. Lower courts have held that drilling a hole in the gas tank of a vehicle is non-routine. This fact pattern is similar in that the officers' use of a crowbar breaks the seats away from their attachment to the frame of the car and rips the upholstery. When officers break or destroy part of a vehicle, the search is typically non-routine and it requires reasonable suspicion.

Answer B is incorrect. Drug couriers hide drugs in many locations in the car. Drugs are stored in gas tanks, mufflers, secret compartments under the vehicle, behind the seats, and other locations. The fact that the officers come up empty in the first location they search does not mean that reasonable suspicion (if it existed here) would have been eliminated.

Answer C is incorrect. As explained in response to Answer A, the use of a crowbar to pry the seats away from the frame is akin to drilling a hole in the gas tank. This is an invasive and non-routine search, particularly because the officers have broken the seat and torn the upholstery. Accordingly, the agents do need reasonable suspicion.

Answer D is incorrect. Probationers and parolees have a reduced expectation of privacy. However, Victoria has not been convicted of any crime and does not fall in either of those categories. Accordingly, she has the same expectation of privacy as any other driver crossing the border.

Answer to Question 105

Answer A is correct. While border agents can pull over vehicles with no suspicion at border checkpoints, they cannot do so in roving patrols. Agent Samuels did not pull over the vehicle at the border. The stop is therefore subject to ordinary Fourth Amendment rules about *Terry* stops.

Answer B is incorrect. When a border agent is engaged in a roving patrol away from the border checkpoint (as opposed to a fixed interior checkpoint), the agent must have reasonable suspicion to stop the vehicle.

Answer C is incorrect. As noted above, a border agent engaged in a roving patrol away from the border checkpoint must have reasonable suspicion to stop the vehicle.

Answer D is incorrect. When a border agent conducts a roving patrol, the agent is subject to the normal Fourth Amendment rules for automobile searches. In this case, the agent would have needed probable cause to invoke the automobile exception to the warrant requirement to search the vehicle.

Answer to Question 106

Answer A is incorrect. Agent Tweed is working at a fixed interior checkpoint, not a checkpoint at the actual border. Agents can stop vehicles without suspicion at a fixed interior checkpoint, but they cannot conduct warrantless searches.

Answer B is incorrect. Regardless of whether a fixed interior checkpoint is 29 miles or 31 miles from the border, agents cannot conduct warrantless searches.

Answer C is incorrect. Border agents at fixed interior checkpoints can stop vehicles and conduct limited questioning of drivers without reasonable suspicion.

Answer D is correct. Border agents at fixed interior checkpoints can stop vehicles and conduct limited questioning of drivers without reasonable suspicion. However, to search the vehicle, the agents need either probable cause or consent. Agent Samuels had neither when he searched through Ralph's trunk.

CHAPTER 18
School Searches

THE RULE: Public school children have Fourth Amendment rights. However, because school children have a reduced expectation of privacy, administrators and teachers can conduct searches without a warrant or probable cause as long as they act reasonably.

Critical Points

- School officials do not need a warrant or probable cause to search a student or their effects. While students maintain some Fourth Amendment protection, they have a reduced expectation of privacy, and thus officials need less suspicion to search.
- School officials do need some individualized suspicion to search particular students. The officials must point to reasonable grounds to search.
- School officials can point to potential violations of the criminal law *or* potential violations of school policy as a basis to conduct a search.
- In conducting searches, school officials must ensure that the search is not excessively intrusive. Officials cannot conduct strip searches in order to find evidence of minor violations of school rules.
- School officials can conduct randomized drug testing of students who opt to participate in extracurricular activities. The school officials do not need to have suspicion to set up drug testing, but they must carry out the testing in a way that does not overly compromise the privacy interests of the students.

OVERVIEW OF THE BLACKLETTER LAW

There are two types of school searches: (1) searches of particular students based on some suspicion that they have broken the criminal law or a school rule; and (2) suspicionless drug testing of students participating in extracurricular activities.

At the outset, it is important to recognize that public school students do have Fourth Amendment rights. However they have less Fourth Amendment protection because they are being supervised by school officials and thus have a reduced expectation of privacy.

When a school official receives information that a particular student is engaged in misconduct, the official can conduct a search without probable cause and without a warrant. The misconduct can either be a violation of the criminal law, or a violation of a noncriminal school policy. For instance, possession of acetaminophen or ibuprofen is not illegal, but a public school might prohibit students from possessing painkillers on school grounds. The level of suspicion does not have to be high. The school official needs only "reasonable grounds," which is roughly the same as reasonable suspicion.

Once a school official has information that a student is violating a law or a school policy, the official may search the student, her locker, and her belongings. The key restriction however is that the search must not be "excessively intrusive" in light of the circumstances. For example, the Supreme Court has held that a strip search of a student to find over-the-counter pain medication is excessively intrusive. While possessing such medication might be in violation of school policy, forcing students to disrobe and be subjected to a strip search is too intrusive in light of the low-level nature of the infraction.

In addition to searching particular students based on suspicion, school officials also sometimes order random drug testing of groups of students. The Supreme Court initially upheld such testing of student athletes and later expanded it to allow drug testing of all students involved in extracurricular activities. The Court has reasoned that students opt into extracurricular activities. For that reason, the Court has never authorized random drug testing of all students enrolled in the school. In assessing whether random drug testing is constitutional, courts weigh the government's need for testing (e.g., rumors of drug activity at the school) along with the level of intrusion imposed on the students. Courts would therefore be more likely to uphold random drug testing if the students retain some degree of privacy in giving their samples (as opposed to being viewed unclothed by school officials while giving a urine sample).

EXAM TRAPS TO AVOID

- Just because school officials need only limited suspicion to search a student does not mean that they can conduct searches based on no suspicion.
- Just because school officials suspect that a student has violated the law or school policy does not mean the school officials can search everywhere. If school officials have reason to believe a student has drugs in his locker, that does not authorize a strip search of the student.
- Strip searches will typically be unlawful, especially if the law or policy the student is accused of breaking is minor. However, if the school officials suspect the student of serious misconduct, a strip search may be permissible.
- The Supreme Court has upheld random drug testing for students involved in extracurricular activities, but it has never upheld random drug testing of all students simply because they are enrolled in the school.

MULTIPLE-CHOICE QUESTIONS

Question 107

Samantha is a tenth-grade student at Herbert Hoover High School. Samantha is on the school's cheerleading squad and has generally received good grades. She has no disciplinary record. Like many other schools in the country, Herbert Hoover High School has a problem with students buying and selling drugs on school property. To tackle the drug problem, the school's principal began interrogating students who already had been caught committing a disciplinary infraction. After being caught for any offense, those students are asked which of their peers had drugs. Trevor was caught bringing a knife to school. The principal took Trevor into her office and told him point-blank that he faced expulsion unless he turned over the name of at least one student who was in possession of drugs. The principal made clear that Trevor would still be suspended for a week for possessing the knife but that if he cooperated he would not be expelled permanently. Not wanting to be expelled, Trevor told the principal that "Samantha has opioids that have been crushed into a powder. She keeps it in her bra so that no one will see it. She goes to the bathroom every day before gym class and snorts it." The following day, the principal watched Samantha go into the bathroom before gym class. The principal then followed Samantha into the bathroom and told her to take off her shirt and turn her underwear inside out. The principal found OxyContin in Samantha's bra and turned the evidence over to the police. Is the OxyContin admissible against Samantha?

A) Possibly yes. The principal had reasonable suspicion that Samantha had a dangerous drug and specific information that she kept it in her undergarments. Accordingly, a strip search for illegal drugs may be permissible.

B) Possibly yes. Although strip searches are invasive, students have very limited Fourth Amendment protections in schools and can only challenge strip searches if they were conducted in a manner that shows "an egregious and callous disregard for individual privacy."

C) No. Although strip searches are permitted based on reasonable suspicion in middle schools, the state must demonstrate probable cause to conduct such searches in high school students who are closer to adulthood.

D) No. Although strip searches are permissible in schools, the Court has held that such searches require probable cause that the student has drugs and a warrant, unless it would be "impractical" to get a warrant.

Question 108

Assume the same facts as Question 107, except this time Trevor told the principal that Samantha kept acetaminophen in her bra. Trevor explained that every student thinks third-period math is stressful and that some students take acetaminophen before class because it helps them mellow out and make it through the class. Possession of acetaminophen by children under the age of 18 is not a crime, but it does violate school policy. Once again, the principal followed Samantha into the bathroom and ordered her to lift her shirt and turn her underwear inside out. Pills fell out of Samantha's bra, but they were OxyContin, not acetaminophen. How should the court rule on Samantha's motion to suppress?

A) The court should suppress the OxyContin because school officials only suspected Samantha of violating school policy (not a criminal law) and they cannot conduct a warrantless search of any kind.

B) The court should suppress the OxyContin because school officials cannot conduct an invasive strip search when they only have reason to believe Samantha has committed a relatively minor violation.

C) The court should admit the OxyContin because, while the school officials should not have conducted a strip search for a minor infraction, they in fact found evidence of a serious violation of the criminal law.

D) The court should admit the OxyContin because the principal had reasonable suspicion to believe Samantha had violated school policy.

Question 109

Drug use is rampant at Herbert Hoover High School. In recent months there have been rumors of student athletes using steroids to improve their strength. In particular, there have been a lot of rumors about members of the football team using steroids. The school principal decides to implement random drug testing. She orders every student athlete, including the members of the darts team, to submit to drug testing over a two-week period. A member of the darts team—Quincy—tests positive for steroids and is arrested. Quincy has moved to dismiss the charges on the ground that the random drug test was unconstitutional. What result?

A) The drug test was unconstitutional because darts is a sport that has nothing to do with strength (just precision) and there was no reason for darts players to take steroids and thus no reason to subject them to drug testing.

B) The drug test was unconstitutional because students retain some (albeit limited) Fourth Amendment protections and cannot be subjected to suspicionless searches.

C) The drug test was constitutional because student athletes signed up for their extracurricular activities and can therefore be subjected to random drug tests if school officials have an important reason to conduct the test and minimize the degree of privacy intrusion.

D) The drug test was constitutional because school officials act *in loco parentis* and students therefore lack Fourth Amendment protections.

Question 110

Assume the same facts as Question 109. This time, however, the principal orders random drug testing of all students engaged in extracurricular activities, not just student athletes. D'Angelo, who is a member of the Chess Club, tests positive for illegal steroids and is prosecuted. If D'Angelo challenges the random drug testing, how should the court rule?

A) The court should uphold the drug-testing program because Supreme Court precedent allows random drug testing of all students who participate in extracurricular activities if there is some evidence of a drug problem in the school.

B) The court should strike down the drug-testing program because students in the Chess Club are not athletes and thus are completely disconnected from the initial rationale for testing students for steroids.

Question 111

Assume the same facts as Questions 109 and 110. For purposes of this question, assume that the principal ordered random drug testing of all students in the entire school, regardless of whether they were involved in extracurricular activities. A student who was not involved in extracurricular activities tested positive and has challenged the constitutionality of the random drug test. How should the court rule?

A) The court should probably uphold the random drug testing because there is no meaningful difference between students who participate in extracurricular activities and those who do not.

B) The court should probably strike down the random drug testing because the Supreme Court has only upheld random drug testing for students engaged in extracurricular activities and it has signaled that schools cannot test all students simply because they are enrolled in the school.

ANSWERS TO MULTIPLE-CHOICE QUESTIONS

Answer to Question 107

Answer A is correct. Although the Supreme Court held a particular strip search unconstitutional in *Safford v. Unified School District #1 v. Redding* (2009), the Court did not indicate that all strip searches would be unconstitutional. Rather, the Court found the strip search invalid in *Safford* because the degree of intrusion was out of proportion to the severity of the offense (possessing over-the-counter pain medicine). The facts in this question are quite different. Opioids are far more dangerous than over-the-counter medication and they have resulted in thousands upon thousands of deaths when crushed and snorted in the way described in the question. Accordingly, it is possible that a court would find the strip search of Samantha to be constitutional.

Answer B is incorrect. The relevant test is not "egregious and callous disregard for individual privacy."

Answer C is incorrect. The Supreme Court has never stated that strip searches would be subjected to different standards depending on whether school officials were searching middle school as opposed to high school students. Courts are supposed to focus on the degree of privacy intrusion. Arguably, high school students might suffer greater privacy intrusions from a strip search because their bodies have developed more and are closer to maturity. However, probable cause is not the correct standard.

Answer D is incorrect. School officials do not have to point to probable cause to conduct strip searches. Rather, they may conduct searches if they are reasonable under a balancing analysis that weighs the government interest and the degree of privacy intrusion on the individual.

Answer to Question 108

Answer A is incorrect. School officials can conduct some warrantless searches when they have grounds to believe that a student is violating either a criminal law or a school policy.

Answer B is correct. The Supreme Court's decision in *Safford v. Unified School District #1 v. Redding* (2009) indicated that an invasive strip search to look for evidence of only minimally dangerous over-the-counter painkillers was out of proportion to the rule violation. While school officials can sometimes conduct strip searches, the Court made clear that they cannot do so just to look for acetaminophen.

Answer C is incorrect. The school officials were searching for acetaminophen but found OxyContin. In assessing the legality of the search, what matters is what the officials were searching for, not what they ultimately found. Accordingly, the strip search to look for acetaminophen was unconstitutional.

Answer D is incorrect. While the principal may have had reasonable suspicion, that is not the only analysis a court should conduct when assessing whether a strip search was constitutional. Courts must consider the nature of the violation and the degree of intrusion on the child.

Answer to Question 109

Answer A is incorrect. The Supreme Court has upheld random drug testing of student athletes based on their participation in extracurricular activities. The Court did not require school officials to assess and justify which types of student athletes are most likely to use a particular drug. Because members of the darts team are extracurricular student athletes, they can be subjected to random drug testing.

Answer B is incorrect. Random drug testing is a suspicionless search. The Court has upheld random drug testing of student athletes. While the answer choice correctly states that students retain some Fourth Amendment protections, it is incorrect to suggest that students can never be subjected to suspicionless searches.

Answer C is correct. The Supreme Court has upheld random drug testing of student athletes. Courts are supposed to weigh the intrusion on the students' privacy against the importance and efficacy of the testing. In this question, it is clear that the school has a drug problem among student athletes and drug testing is likely to reduce that problem. The answer choice indicates that the school officials will have to minimize the degree of intrusion while conducting the test (e.g., by not forcing students to fully undress and be viewed while giving the sample).

Answer D is incorrect. Students in school are committed to the temporary custody of the school officials. This does not mean, however, that students have no Fourth Amendment privacy guarantees. The Supreme Court has rejected the argument that students have no Fourth Amendment protection, although it has recognized that students have a lesser expectation of privacy than adults.

Answer to Question 110

Answer A is correct. In *Board of Education v. Earls* (2002), the Supreme Court expanded its precedent to approve random drug testing of all middle school and high school students engaged in competitive extracurricular activities.

Answer B is incorrect. The Supreme Court has not required school officials to limit random drug testing to the group that precipitated the initial concern.

Answer to Question 111

Answer A is incorrect. The Supreme Court's jurisprudence in this area has put a lot of emphasis on the fact that students voluntarily participate in extracurricular activities. The Court has thus drawn a distinction between students who volunteered for extracurricular activities and those students who are in school for basic educational purposes.

Answer B is correct. Although the Court has never explicitly decided a case on this issue, the logic of the Court's earlier rulings, as well as comments in a concurring opinion, strongly signal that the Court believes drug testing all students simply because they are enrolled in the school would be unconstitutional.

CHAPTER 19
DNA Swabs and Routine Booking Procedures

THE RULE: When police make an arrest with probable cause for a serious offense and they bring the suspect to the station to be detained in custody, it is reasonable to take and analyze a cheek swab of the arrestee's DNA as a routine booking procedure.

Critical Points

- The Supreme Court has upheld warrantless DNA swabs as constitutional, although the only major opinion on the issue seems to limit it to cases involving serious offenses.
- Warrantless DNA swabs are only permissible if they are not invasive. If police were to take DNA from a blood draw, rather than a cheek swab, it would not be permissible.
- Warrantless DNA swabs are a search, but they are constitutional even without a warrant because they are a reasonable routine booking procedure that can occur as part of an arrest.

OVERVIEW OF THE BLACKLETTER LAW

The Supreme Court has long authorized police to take certain administrative steps after they have made an arrest and brought a suspect to the police station. Police may fingerprint and photograph arrestees without a warrant. The police may engage in routine booking procedures like this because it is reasonable.

As DNA technology has improved, states and the federal government have created DNA databases in an effort to solve crimes. States have their own statutes that impose restrictions on what can be done with DNA samples. The state statutes are not our concern for a course on constitutional criminal procedure. We are concerned with what the Fourth Amendment permits.

In reviewing a Maryland statute, the Supreme Court has held that it is constitutional for police who have arrested a suspect based on probable cause and brought him to the police station to take a cheek swab for his DNA. Consistent with the Maryland statute, the Court held that warrantless cheek swabs are permissible for "serious offenses." Maryland's statutory definition of "serious offenses" does not tell us what the Fourth Amendment's definition of "serious offenses" should be. And, unfortunately, the Supreme Court has not defined what "serious offenses" means for Fourth Amendment purposes. Moreover, it is not clear whether or not the Court will expand the constitutionality of DNA swabs to nonserious offenses in future cases.

EXAM TRAPS TO AVOID

- Beware of officers conducting a warrantless DNA swab for offenses that do not seem "serious." Although the Supreme Court has not defined what it means for an offense to be "serious" for DNA swab purposes, a misdemeanor crime should raise red flags. It is possible that the Court will uphold DNA swabs for misdemeanor crimes in the future, but at present such swabs might not be constitutional.
- Be sure that the officers are extracting the DNA through a noninvasive DNA swab, rather than a more invasive procedure. The Supreme Court found the cheek swab to be reasonable because it was minimally invasive.
- Be sure that the suspect has been subjected to a custodial arrest and been taken to the police station.

MULTIPLE-CHOICE QUESTIONS

Question 112

Police have arrested Tara for armed robbery. They caught her exiting a bank with an overflowing bag of money. The officers handcuffed Tara and brought her to the police station. At the station, the officers acted pursuant to a state law that required them to take the DNA of any person arrested for a serious crime. The officers drew a small amount of blood from Tara's index finger with a pin prick. (The officers simply pricked Tara's finger with a tiny needle and when a drop of blood came out they directly applied a testing strip to catch it and then gave Tara a bandage.) When the officers added Tara's blood sample to the DNA database it matched an unsolved murder. Prosecutors later charged Tara with murder and she has moved to suppress the DNA match. How should the court rule?

A) The court should probably reject the suppression motion because the officers acted pursuant to state law.

B) The court should probably reject the suppression motion because Tara was arrested for a "serious offense."

C) The court should probably grant the suppression motion because the DNA test was more than minimally invasive.

D) The court should probably grant the suppression motion because police cannot take DNA samples from arrestees without a warrant.

Question 113

Police are called because Max was waving a shotgun at a group of people. Witnesses told the police that Max was "acting crazy" and that he would not put the gun down. After 20 minutes of negotiation, the police were eventually able to get Max to place the gun on the ground. The officers immediately arrested Max for the crime of felony assault by menacing. The officers brought Max to the police station where, in addition to fingerprinting him, they also swabbed the inside of his mouth to scrape some DNA off of the inside of his cheek. The cheek swab lasted only a few seconds and did not hurt. A grand jury subsequently indicted Max for the assault by menacing charge. A few weeks later, however, prosecutors dropped the case when they learned that Max had used the shotgun to fend off an intruder and that he refused to put the gun down because he reasonably believed the intruder was still nearby. Max, who is a privacy advocate, has asked you whether it was permissible for the police to use a cheek swab to take his DNA. Which of the following is correct?

A) The DNA cheek swab was constitutional, but only because Max was actually indicted for the assault by menacing.

B) The DNA cheek swab was constitutional because Max was arrested for a serious crime and the cheek swab was part of the booking procedure.

C) The DNA cheek swab was unconstitutional because Max was not charged with one of the "serious" offenses for which DNA cheek swabs are permitted.

D) The DNA cheek swab would have been constitutional if Max had eventually been convicted, but because the charges were dropped and no conviction was eventually obtained, it violated the Fourth Amendment.

E) The DNA cheek swab was unconstitutional—regardless of the result of Max's case—because DNA cheek swabs can only be conducted *after* conviction.

Question 114

Police observe Tenley sneaking out of Target, walking to her car, and then pulling a small package out of her pants as she is about to get into her car. The officers walk up to her and say, "Hey, what's going on?" Tenley, who was extremely nervous about getting caught, just blurts out, "You got me, I shouldn't have done it. I shoplifted a package of batteries." The officers arrest her for misdemeanor shoplifting and bring her to the station. While at the police station they act pursuant to state law and swab the inside of her cheek for DNA. Tenley has asked you whether the police complied with the Fourth Amendment in taking her DNA. What should you tell her?

A) There is a strong argument that the officers did not comply with the Fourth Amendment because current Supreme Court jurisprudence has only approved warrantless DNA cheek swabs for "serious offenses."

B) There is a strong argument that the officers did not comply with the Fourth Amendment because they had no arrest warrant and there was no basis to conduct a warrantless arrest.

C) There is a strong argument that the officers did comply with the Fourth Amendment because taking DNA is always reasonable.

D) There is a strong argument that the officers did comply with the Fourth Amendment because the officers only needed reasonable suspicion to take a DNA cheek swab.

Question 115

Officers have a hunch that Kim committed a cold-blooded murder. They have tried to interview Kim and to get her to give hair and blood samples, but she has declined to cooperate. In the course of surveilling Kim, they see her hit a man with what looks like a metal pole. The officers immediately stop Kim, place her in handcuffs, and swab the inside of her cheek for her DNA. In this jurisdiction, however, the officers must clear all arrests with the prosecutor's office before booking people into jail. The prosecutor asks the officers, "Do you want to charge her with aggravated assault?" and the officers reply "Yes." The prosecutor then said, "Well, then, you have to have evidence that she hit him with a deadly weapon. What did she hit him with?" The officers said, "Hold on," and then went to find the weapon. The officers quickly discovered that Kim had hit the man with her umbrella. Moreover, they learned that the man was her ex-boyfriend and he acknowledged that he had said something rude to Kim and started the altercation, and that he did not want to press charges. The officers got back on the phone and explained this to the prosecutor. The prosecutor said, "This is such a weak case, you have to cut her loose." The officers took off the handcuffs and let Kim go home. Nevertheless, the officers retained Kim's DNA sample and were subsequently able to use it to link Kim to other offenses. What result if Kim moves to suppress evidence resulting from the DNA sample?

A) The police captured the DNA evidence unconstitutionally because they were trying to look for evidence of another crime (the murder) and thus were not taking the DNA evidence as a result of the aggravated assault arrest.

B) The police captured the DNA evidence unconstitutionally because the officers took the sample at the scene rather than when the suspect would be booked at the station.

C) The police captured the DNA evidence constitutionally because aggravated assault is a serious offense and the officers reasonably believed that they had effectuated a valid arrest.

D) The police captured the DNA evidence constitutionally because the officers had reasonable suspicion that Kim was involved in criminal activity.

ANSWERS TO MULTIPLE-CHOICE QUESTIONS

Answer to Question 112

Answer A is incorrect. The officers did comply with state law, but that does not mean they have complied with the Fourth Amendment. In this case, unlike *Maryland v. King* (2013), the officers took the DNA through a blood sample that required breaking the skin and extracting fluids from inside the body. It was probably not minimally invasive.

Answer B is incorrect. Armed robbery is a serious offense. However, being arrested for a serious offense is not the only consideration. The Supreme Court has signaled that warrantless DNA testing of arrestees is permissible if the test is done in a minimally invasive way. As explained above, breaking the skin to extract bodily fluids probably does not satisfy that standard.

Answer C is correct. The Supreme Court has upheld warrantless DNA cheek swabs for serious offenses because cheek swabs are minimally invasive. Drawing blood, even if only with a pin prick, is not minimally invasive.

Answer D is incorrect. The Supreme Court has upheld warrantless DNA cheek swabs for serious offenses. While more invasive DNA extraction is likely unconstitutional, this answer choice is too broad because it suggests all warrantless DNA extraction is unconstitutional.

Answer to Question 113

Answer A is incorrect. The legality of a warrantless DNA cheek swab does not turn on whether the suspect is eventually indicted. The question is whether he was brought to the police station for booking following a lawful arrest.

Answer B is correct. The Supreme Court has upheld warrantless DNA cheek swabs as a routine booking procedure when a suspect is lawfully arrested and brought to the police station.

Answer C is incorrect. Assault by menacing is almost certainly a serious offense. It is a violent offense.

Answer D is incorrect. The legality of a warrantless DNA cheek swab does not turn on whether the defendant was eventually convicted. As noted above, the key question is whether the suspect was lawfully arrested and brought to the police station for routine booking.

Answer E is incorrect. The Supreme Court has allowed warrantless DNA cheek swabs during the routine booking process following arrest. They can therefore be taken before conviction.

Answer to Question 114

Answer A is correct. In *Maryland v. King* (2013), the Supreme Court held that warrantless DNA cheek swabs are constitutional for "serious offenses." It is possible that in the future the Court will also specifically approve warrantless DNA cheek swabs for nonserious offenses—such as shoplifting—but that has not occurred yet.

Answer B is incorrect. The police had probable cause to arrest Tenley because of her confession (not to mention the other suspicious activity they observed). When police have probable cause, they can arrest in public without a warrant. The arrest was therefore lawful.

Answer C is incorrect. Taking DNA is not always reasonable. For example, if the officers had held Tenley down and drawn her blood against her will, that would not be a reasonable taking of DNA.

Answer D is incorrect. To take a DNA cheek swab, the police do not need reasonable suspicion. However, they do need to conduct a valid arrest, which requires probable cause. The reference to reasonable suspicion in this choice is incorrect.

Answer to Question 115

Answer A is incorrect. The subjective intent of the officer is not relevant in most Fourth Amendment questions, including this one. What matters is whether the officers conducted a lawful DNA cheek swab, not whether they had the intent to use it for one prosecution as opposed to another.

Answer B is correct. The Supreme Court has upheld warrantless DNA cheek swabs at the police station as part of the routine booking exception. While the Court referenced some search incident to arrest precedent (and some special needs precedent) in its decision, the Court indicated that the DNA swab was in the same category as fingerprints and photographs that happen at the station, not at the scene of the arrest. Accordingly, here the police overstepped their bounds by conducting the cheek swab on the street rather than at the police station.

Answer C is incorrect. Aggravated assault is a serious offense and the officers reasonably believed that they had effectuated a valid arrest. Nevertheless, as explained above, Answer B is correct because DNA cheek swabs, like fingerprints and photographs, are part of the routine booking exception that must occur at the station.

Answer D is incorrect. The officers did not have reasonable suspicion that Kim was involved in a murder. The question tells us that they only had a hunch. Regardless, the reasonable suspicion standard is irrelevant here. The officers need probable cause for an arrest. Only at that point can the officers conduct a warrantless DNA cheek swab at the police station.

STEP 6
Is There Standing to Challenge the Search or Seizure?

Chapter 20: Standing

If police conduct an unlawful search or seizure, that does not necessarily mean that evidence will be suppressed. To challenge a search or seizure, the defendant must have standing. This means that the police must have violated the defendant's personal Fourth Amendment rights.

CHAPTER 20
Standing

The Rule: To bring a successful suppression motion, a defendant must show more than that a Fourth Amendment violation occurred. The defendant must show that that her *own personal* Fourth Amendment rights were violated.

Critical Points

- Courts do not decide whether to suppress evidence in general. Rather, courts look to see if evidence should be suppressed as to a particular person.
- To have standing, a defendant must demonstrate that law enforcement officers invaded her own reasonable expectation of privacy.
- *Homes Generally*: A person will almost always have standing to challenge an illegal entry or search of their own home.
- *Overnight Guests*: Overnight houseguests typically have standing to challenge an illegal entry into the home or an illegal search of a common area or the bedroom where the guest is staying.
- *Commercial Guests and Short Social Visits*: People who are present only for commercial purposes or short social visits typically do not have standing.
- *Drivers*: A driver will almost always have standing to challenge the stop or search of his car.
- *Passengers and Stops*: Passengers will typically have standing to challenge an illegal stop of the vehicle.
- *Passengers and Searches*: If the stop of a vehicle was lawful, but the police illegally searched the vehicle, the passenger will usually not have standing to challenge the search of the vehicle.

OVERVIEW OF THE BLACKLETTER LAW

To have standing, a person must have had a reasonable expectation of privacy in the area that the police searched. The inquiry focuses on where the police searched, not whether the evidence is incriminating to a particular defendant. For instance, imagine that police illegally search a house to look for evidence of a bank robbery and they find the stolen money and the guns used in the robbery. Defendant A lives in the house, but Defendant B does not live there. Defendant A has standing because she has a reasonable expectation of privacy in her own house. Defendant B is out of luck, though. Even though the police searched illegally and found evidence that could be used against both defendants, Defendant B has no standing to challenge a search of someone else's house. The stolen money and guns will be admissible against Defendant B, but not against Defendant A.

For home searches, it is important to distinguish between residents, roommates, overnight guests, and commercial guests. First, residents obviously have standing to challenge an illegal search of their own home. This is true whether you own or rent a home. Whether you are paying the mortgage or writing a rent check to the landlord, you have a reasonable expectation of privacy in the place where you live and you therefore have standing to object to an illegal entry or an illegal search of that location.

Things are slightly more complicated with roommates. Imagine two law students—Adam and Zeus—who share a two-bedroom apartment (each with their own bedroom). If the police break into the apartment without a warrant, both Adam and Zeus would have standing to challenge the illegal entry. Now imagine a more complicated situation. The officer knocks on the door and Adam and Zeus let him in, though they do not consent to a search of the apartment and the officer has no lawful grounds to search. If the officer illegally searches in the common areas (e.g., the kitchen or living room), Adam and Zeus both have standing to challenge the illegal search. Adam and Zeus both have a reasonable expectation of privacy in their kitchen and their living room. Things get more complicated, though, if the officer illegally searched only one of their bedrooms. For example, imagine that the officer knocked on the door and Adam and Zeus let the officer in. The officer asked for consent to search the bedrooms and both Adam and Zeus said "No." The officer then searched Adam's bedroom anyway and found drugs that were linked to both Adam and Zeus. Adam can obviously object to the search of his own bedroom. But can Zeus challenge the search of Adam's bedroom? In most cases, the answer is probably "no." Zeus does not have a reasonable expectation of privacy in Adam's bedroom. After all, Zeus has his own bedroom where he sleeps and keeps his personal property.

The same sets of rules apply to overnight guests. The Supreme Court has held that overnight guests can have standing given that they have a reasonable expectation of privacy in the area where they are staying. As a result, an overnight guest can challenge an illegal entry by the police. The overnight guest can also challenge an illegal search of a common area or in the area where the guest is sleeping overnight. The guest has a reasonable expectation of privacy in these areas. However, if the overnight guest is crashing on a couch in the living room, she probably does not have standing to challenge a search of the homeowner's bedroom. The reason is that the guest does not have a reasonable expectation of privacy in a bedroom she is not staying in.

Commercial guests are the least likely to have standing. The Supreme Court has taken the position that commercial guests—those who are present for business purposes—do not have a reasonable expectation of privacy. For instance, imagine that officers break into an apartment without a warrant and find multiple people standing at the kitchen table bagging drugs. None of the individuals lives in the apartment. They are only there to bag drugs. None of the commercial guests would have standing to challenge the illegal police entry.

Illegal Car Stops → Standing for Passengers and Drivers: Imagine that police illegally stop a vehicle for no reason whatsoever. The driver and the passenger of the vehicle both have standing to challenge the illegal stop of the vehicle. For purposes of the stop, there is no difference between the rights of the driver and the passenger. Both of them are being detained by the police officer in violation of the Fourth Amendment. Because their liberty is being restricted, they can both point to a violation of their Fourth Amendment rights. So if police find evidence as a result of the illegal stop, the driver and passenger can both successfully move to suppress the evidence.

Legal Car Stops, but Illegal Searches → Standing for Drivers, but Not Passengers: Sometimes police will have legal authority to stop a vehicle, but not to search it. For example, imagine that police stop a vehicle that is traveling at 10 mph over the speed limit and then search the trunk of the car and find cocaine. The stop was perfectly legal (the driver was speeding), but the search was illegal (there was no probable cause to believe drugs were in the trunk). This situation leads to different results for the driver and the passenger. The driver has standing to challenge the search of the trunk because it is his car and he has a reasonable expectation of privacy in the trunk. Accordingly, the court will suppress the drugs as to the driver. But the passenger is in a worse position. Sure, the passenger has standing to challenge the initial stop of the vehicle, but that does her no good given that the initial stop was perfectly lawful (Police are certainly allowed to stop speeding vehicles.) The search of the trunk was still illegal (the officer did not have probable cause), but the passenger has no standing for the trunk because she does not have a reasonable expectation of privacy in the trunk of someone else's car.

EXAM TRAPS TO AVOID

- Just because the police conduct was outrageous does not mean there is standing.
- Just because the police seized the defendant's property does not mean the defendant has standing. The question is not whether the defendant owned

the property, but rather whether the person had a reasonable expectation of privacy in the area searched.

- Just because the defendant was lawfully present does not mean she has standing. A person can be lawfully present in a house or a car, yet have no standing to challenge a search of the house or car because she has no reasonable expectation of privacy in those locations.

MULTIPLE-CHOICE QUESTIONS

Question 116

Acting on a tip, Officer Small went to Stella's apartment, broke in, and searched it. Under Stella's bed, Officer Small found a small bag containing diamonds and a note that said: "Here are the goods from the Nordstrom heist.—Elliot." It is well known in the community that Elliot is Stella's friend and that he is a jewel thief. Officer Small also knew that Nordstrom had been burglarized last week. Based on the evidence found in Stella's home, Officer Small procured a search warrant for Elliot's apartment. The search of Elliot's apartment yielded burglar tools from the Nordstrom burglary. The prosecutor wants to use the diamonds, the note, and the burglar tools as evidence against Elliott. Elliot moves to suppress the diamonds, the note, and the burglar tools. How should the court rule?

A) The court should suppress all of the evidence because it was procured illegally.

B) The court should suppress the diamonds and the note because the search of Stella's apartment was unlawful, but the court should admit the burglar tools located in Elliott's apartment.

C) The court should not suppress any of the evidence because they would have discovered it all inevitably anyway.

D) The court should not suppress the diamonds or the note because Elliot had no standing to challenge the search of Stella's apartment, and the court should not suppress the burglar tools because the police had a warrant to search Elliot's apartment.

Question 117

Lisa and her friend, Dana, were driving down the road. Lisa owned the car and was driving it in compliance with all traffic laws. Dana was sitting in the front passenger seat. A police officer recognized Dana because another officer had been talking about his hunch that Dana was involved in a dangerous drug gang. The officer stopped the vehicle and ordered everyone out of the vehicle. A few minutes later, the officer heard Lisa and Dana arguing. Lisa said something that sounded like "You ran drugs from Florida to New York? Are you crazy?" The officer searched the trunk of the car and found a stolen, unregistered firearm. The officer arrested both

Lisa and Dana for possession of a stolen weapon. Lisa and Dana move to suppress the gun. What result?

A) Both Lisa and Dana have standing because they were unlawfully stopped.

B) Lisa has standing because it is her vehicle. Dana lacks standing to challenge the search of Lisa's vehicle.

C) Dana lacks standing because she confessed to selling drugs. Lisa still maintains standing because she never waived her rights.

D) Neither Lisa nor Dana has standing because the stop was lawful.

Question 118

Assume the same facts as Question 117, except in this case the officer pulls the vehicle over because it was exceeding the speed limit by 10 mph. The officer then orders Lisa and Dana out of the car and searches the trunk. The officer says he is looking for drugs, but has no probable cause to believe there are drugs in the trunk (or anywhere in the car, for that matter). While searching in the trunk, the officer looks under the spare tire and finds a ledger. The ledger—which includes a list of drug transactions—implicates both Lisa and Dana in drug dealing. Dana moves to suppress the ledger as the product of an illegal car search. How should the court rule?

A) Dana has standing because she was lawfully present in the vehicle when the illegal search occurred.

B) Dana has standing because the ledger implicates her in criminal activity; thus, she is directly affected by the illegal search.

C) Dana does not have standing because as a passenger in the vehicle she lacks a reasonable expectation of privacy.

D) Dana does not have standing because a person cannot have a legitimate expectation of privacy when the evidence is incriminating.

Question 119

Assume the same facts as Question 118, except in this case the officer pulls the vehicle over for speeding and then unlawfully searches the passenger compartment of the vehicle. The officer comes across a suitcase that has Dana's name in large print on the luggage tag. Dana calls out to the officer, "Hey, that's my suitcase. You can't look in there." The officer ignores Dana, opens the suitcase, and finds an illegal weapon that has Dana's fingerprints on it and that she later conceded belonged to her. Does Dana have standing to suppress the weapon?

A) Yes, Dana has standing because she was an occupant of the car that was stopped.

B) Yes, Dana has standing because she has a reasonable expectation of privacy in what is clearly her own suitcase.

C) Yes, Dana has standing because the officer found a gun that belongs to her.

D) No, Dana has no standing because she is not the driver of the vehicle.

The following facts apply to Questions 120–123.

Police have been surveilling 123 Main Street for weeks because they believe that it is being used as a stash house for a drug-dealing operation. The officers have seen known drug dealers coming in and out of the house, and they have received tips from reliable informants confirming that it is a drug house. On Sunday, the officers knocked and announced their presence and then pushed in the front door of 123 Main Street. The officers immediately saw a kilogram of drugs on the kitchen table. Four men were standing around the kitchen table and appeared to be placing the drugs into small plastic bags. The officers seized the drugs and arrested the three men.

Question 120

The first person arrested by the police was Enrique. Enrique was renting the house at 123 Main Street. He lived there and was on the lease, but he did not own the house. Enrique moves to suppress the drugs found on the kitchen table. What result?

A) The court should suppress the drugs because Enrique has standing and the search was unlawful.

B) The court should not suppress the drugs because the police conducted a lawful search.

C) The court should not suppress the drugs because Enrique had no standing since he did not own the house.

D) The court should not suppress the drugs because the police properly knocked and announced before entering.

Question 121

The second person the police arrested at 123 Main Street on Sunday was Frank. Frank did not live there and he was not on the lease. Frank was dating Enrique, though, and he was staying at 123 Main Street for the weekend, including sleeping there on Saturday night. Can Frank successfully challenge the admission of the drugs?

A) Yes, Frank has standing because he was an overnight guest.

B) Yes, Frank had standing because Enrique had invited him to be in the apartment that afternoon.

C) No, Frank does not have standing because he is not on the lease at 123 Main Street.

D) No, Frank does not have standing because he does not live at 123 Main Street and is not a long-term visitor.

Question 122

The third person arrested on Sunday at 123 Main Street was Harry. Enrique needed help to bag the drugs, so he paid Harry $100 to assist with the bagging. Harry had never been to 123 Main Street before that day. About two hours after Harry arrived at 123 Main Street and began bagging drugs, the police unlawfully entered the house without a warrant and seized the drugs and arrested everyone. Harry has moved to suppress. Does Harry have standing?

A) Harry has standing because he has been in the house for two hours and thus has a meaningful connection to the property.

B) Harry has standing because he is there pursuant to a commercial arrangement that gives him a reasonable expectation of privacy.

C) Harry does not have standing because he is a commercial guest.

D) Harry does not have standing because he had never been to the property before that day.

Question 123

The fourth person arrested on Sunday at 123 Main Street was Gary. Gary is the brother of Enrique (who lives at 123 Main Street). Gary lives on the other side of the country and is in town for one week to visit his brother. Enrique gave Gary a key to 123 Main Street and he set Gary up in the guest bedroom so that he would be comfortable for the week. For purposes of this question only, assume that the officers learned from three very reliable informants that the drug dealers working out of 123 Main Street were aware that the police were investigating them and that they had already cleared out all the drugs and moved them to a new location. The informants also explained that there were still many illegal firearms in the house and that the occupants would be moving the guns out of the house later that day. Rather than wait for a warrant and risk the guns being moved, the officers entered pursuant to the exigent circumstances exception to seize the illegal firearms. Once inside, the officers searched the kitchen and found nothing. They then looked in Enrique's bedroom. Inside of a small handheld jewelry box (the kind you would keep a watch or a ring in) the officers found a small bag of cocaine and a note saying: "belongs to Gary, so he can sell it when he finishes visiting." Gary has moved to suppress the bag of cocaine. How should the court rule?

A) The court should conclude that Gary has standing because he has a key to the house.

B) The court should conclude that Gary has standing because the cocaine clearly belongs to him and thus he has an expectation of privacy in the bag.

C) The court should conclude that Gary does not have standing because, while he could have challenged the officers' entry into the house, he lacks a reasonable expectation of privacy in boxes found in Enrique's bedroom.

D) The court should conclude that Gary does not have standing because the police had exigent circumstances.

Question 124

Will and Skyler are walking down the street when they see a police officer staring at them. They duck into a store and Will says to Skyler, "Quick, put my bag of methamphetamine in your purse. The cops would never search you. They think only people who look like me have meth." Skyler takes Will's methamphetamine and puts it in her purse. Right after they leave the store, the police officer approaches them and says "Have you been dealing drugs? You look all sweet and innocent, but I get the feeling you are up to something sketchy." Skyler says, "No, we're just out shopping." The officer doesn't believe her though and grabs her purse. The officer rummages through the purse and finds the bag of methamphetamine. Will says, "Hey, that's mine," and the prosecutor subsequently charges Will with possession of a controlled substance. How should the court rule on Will's motion to suppress the drugs?

A) Will has no standing because he has no reasonable expectation of privacy in Skyler's purse.

B) Will has standing, but only if he and Skyler are dating.

C) Will has standing because he had only put the drugs in Skyler's purse a moment earlier.

D) Will has standing because he was the only person besides Skyler who had anything in the purse and thus he had a significant connection to the purse.

ANSWERS TO MULTIPLE-CHOICE QUESTIONS

Answer to Question 116

Answer A is incorrect. The police did conduct an illegal search of Stella's apartment (they had no warrant), but the fact pattern gives no indication that Elliot has standing to challenge a search of Stella's apartment. Moreover, the police lawfully searched Elliot's apartment with a valid warrant.

Answer B is incorrect. Remember that it is Elliot who is moving to suppress the evidence. Elliot has no standing to challenge the search of Stella's apartment. So even though the search of Stella's apartment violated the Fourth Amendment, Elliot is out of luck.

Answer C is incorrect. The inevitable discovery exception (see Chapter 23) only applies to cases in which the police would have found the evidence lawfully anyway.

Nothing in this question indicates the police would have eventually found the evidence in a lawful manner.

Answer D is correct. Elliot lacks standing to challenge the search of Stella's apartment and thus the diamonds and note are admissible against him. Elliot has standing to challenge the search of his own apartment, but the police had a warrant for that search and thus the evidence was lawfully seized from Elliot's apartment.

Answer to Question 117

Answer A is correct. The officer did not have a valid reason to stop the vehicle. And the officer's hunch that Dana was involved in a drug ring is not sufficient to effectuate a valid traffic stop. Dana has therefore been seized unlawfully. This gives her standing to challenge the unlawful stop and any evidence that is found thereafter.

Answer B is incorrect. It is true that Dana would normally lack standing to challenge the search of Lisa's vehicle. However, Dana has standing to challenge the initial unlawful stop and to utilize the fruit of the poisonous tree doctrine to move to suppress evidence found as a result of the unlawful stop.

Answer C is incorrect. First, we do not know that Dana has confessed to selling drugs. Lisa has made a comment that could be construed as inculpatory evidence against Dana. But Dana might deny having run the drugs. Second, Lisa's comment does not break the causal chain from the initial unlawful stop. Accordingly, Dana still has standing based on the initial unlawful stop and the evidence found in the trunk is fruit of the poisonous tree.

Answer D is incorrect. The stop was not lawful because the officer did not have a valid reason to stop the vehicle. Additionally, the officer's hunch about Dana being in a drug ring does not create reasonable suspicion to stop the vehicle.

Answer to Question 118

Answer A is incorrect. At one point—many decades ago—the Supreme Court recognized a doctrine of automatic standing for people who were lawfully present when the police engaged in a Fourth Amendment violation. The Court overruled that doctrine, however, and now requires that each individual show that they have personally had their Fourth Amendment rights violated. Dana must therefore show more than that she is lawfully present. She must instead demonstrate that the officer invaded her reasonable expectation of privacy.

Answer B is incorrect. A person does not have standing just because the police found incriminating evidence. The test is not whether a person is affected by evidence being found. Rather, the individual must demonstrate that the police searched an area in which she had a reasonable expectation of privacy.

Answer C is correct. Ordinarily, passengers in vehicles do not have a reasonable expectation of privacy in the vehicle and thus lack standing. This would seem to be particularly true of the area underneath the spare tire in the trunk.

Answer D is incorrect. Individuals can (and often do) have standing to challenge a search that turns up incriminating evidence. For example, if police find contraband after barging into a home without probable cause and a warrant, the owner of the home surely has standing to challenge the unlawful entry. The police finding incriminating evidence does not eliminate standing.

Answer to Question 119

Answer A is incorrect. Dana has standing to challenge an illegal stop of the vehicle because she is being detained. However, here the officer *lawfully* stopped the vehicle for speeding.

Answer B is correct. It states the rule that standing turns on whether the police searched an area for which the individual had a reasonable expectation of privacy.

Answer C is incorrect. A person does not have standing simply because the police find contraband belonging to them. A person has standing only if the police searched an area for which they have a reasonable expectation of privacy.

Answer D is incorrect. In most cases, passengers do not have a reasonable expectation of privacy in the vehicle. Drivers control the vehicle and can make the decision to include certain passengers and exclude others. However, in some instances, a passenger can have a reasonable expectation of privacy in containers within a vehicle. Here, even though Dana is a passenger, it is clear that the suitcase belongs to her and that she has a reasonable expectation of privacy in the suitcase.

Answer to Question 120

Answer A is correct. As resident living at 123 Main Street, Enrique has standing. The police entered without a warrant and had no apparent exigent circumstances. Thus, the police entered unlawfully and cannot claim the plain view doctrine. The drugs were therefore seized unlawfully. Enrique has standing to challenge the unlawful entry.

Answer B is incorrect. As explained above, the police did not have a warrant or exigent circumstances. The search was therefore unlawful.

Answer C is incorrect. A person can have standing without owning the property. Renters have standing because they have a reasonable expectation of privacy in the property they reside in.

Answer D is incorrect. The police did knock and announce, but the question does not say there was a warrant. The police entry was therefore unlawful.

Answer to Question 121

Answer A is correct. The Supreme Court has indicated that overnight guests have standing to challenge an illegal police entry into the premises where they are staying.

Answer B is incorrect. Frank does not have standing to challenge police entry simply because Enrique had invited him into the apartment. Frank needs a greater connection to the apartment than simply being a temporary invitee in order to have a reasonable expectation of privacy.

Answer C is incorrect. Frank does not have to be on the lease in order to have standing. A person can have a reasonable expectation of privacy in a home even if they are not on the lease or the deed. For example (though this is not the only example), people regularly move into homes of other people after they get married. The new resident will have the ability to use the entire house and to exclude others, even if they are never added to the lease.

Answer D is incorrect. A person does not have to be a long-term visitor to have standing to challenge an illegal police entry. The Supreme Court has indicated that being an overnight guest is sufficient.

Answer to Question 122

Answer A is incorrect because a guest does not acquire standing simply because they have been inside the premises for two hours. This is particularly true when the person is present solely for a commercial transaction.

Answer B is incorrect. The Supreme Court has reached the opposite conclusion. When someone is present solely for a commercial transaction they are very unlikely to be able to demonstrate the reasonable expectation of privacy necessary to confer standing.

Answer C is correct. People who are present solely for commercial purposes do not have standing.

Answer D is incorrect. Often it will be true that a person who has never been to the property before will not have standing. But that will not always be true. For instance, if a person flew across the country to visit their friend or relative and stayed overnight, they would have standing even if they had never previously been to the property before. Accordingly, this answer choice is not completely correct. Given that the Supreme Court has clearly indicated that commercial guests do not have standing, Answer C is a much better choice.

Answer to Question 123

Answer A is incorrect. That Gary has a key to the house and is staying in the guest bedroom strongly indicates that he has standing to challenge an unlawful entry into the house. It also suggests that Gary would have standing if the police entered lawfully and then searched unlawfully in a common area or in the guest bedroom where Gary was staying. But here the police entered lawfully and then searched Enrique's bedroom. The police did not behave unlawfully until they searched small boxes in Enrique's bedroom. (The search was unlawful because firearms—which is what the officers were supposed to be looking for—cannot fit in small jewelry boxes). Although the police searched illegally when they looked in the small jewelry box, Gary lacks standing to challenge that search. No facts suggest that a temporary guest who is staying in the spare bedroom has a reasonable expectation of privacy in small boxes located in the private bedroom of the person who lives in the house full-time. Gary therefore lacks standing to challenge an illegal search of the small box found in Enrique's room.

Answer B is incorrect. It is true that the bag of cocaine literally has Gary's name on it. However, ownership of an item is not sufficient to confer standing. The question is whether the person had a reasonable expectation of privacy in the area searched by the police. Gary had no such reasonable expectation of privacy in the small jewelry box in Enrique's room.

Answer C is correct. Gary probably had standing to challenge the police entry. However, the police had exigent circumstances and thus the entry was lawful. The police exceeded the scope of their probable cause, however, when they looked in a small box that could not possibly have held a gun. That search was illegal. But because Gary has no standing in the bedroom of the house's primary resident, he cannot challenge the search of the jewelry box.

Answer D is incorrect. Exigent circumstances allow the police to enter and search without a warrant. But the exigent circumstances doctrine does not allow police to search in areas for which they do not have probable cause. The officers had no reason to look in small jewelry boxes because they only had probable cause to search for guns, which are much larger.

Answer to Question 124

Answer A is correct. People rarely have a reasonable expectation of privacy in the containers of other individuals. In *Rawlings v. Kentucky* (1980), a case with similar facts to this question, the Supreme Court rejected the defendant's contention that he had a reasonable expectation of privacy in another's purse.

Answer B is incorrect. Just because two people are dating does not mean that one has a reasonable expectation of privacy in another person's purse.

Answer C is incorrect. A person does not gain a reasonable expectation of privacy in a container (here a purse) simply because they recently deposited items into that container. While Will recently placed his meth into Skyler's purse, that does not mean he has control over the purse or that he could stop Skyler from allowing other people to place items in the purse.

Answer D is incorrect. A person does not have a reasonable expectation of privacy simply because they are the only one (besides the owner) who is storing an item in the purse. There is no indication that Will could stop Skyler from putting other people's items in her purse. Indeed, there is nothing to stop Skyler from opening her purse and showing the officer the contents of the purse (including the methamphetamine).

STEP 7
Does the Exclusionary Rule Apply?

Chapter 21: The Exclusionary Rule and the Fruit of the Poisonous Tree Doctrine

The Supreme Court has created an exclusionary rule that requires courts to suppress illegally seized evidence. The Court has also recognized a fruit of the poisonous tree doctrine. If police conduct an illegal search or seizure and then later find evidence, that evidence will also be suppressed because it is fruit of the initial illegal search or seizure. This step therefore requires that you trace the evidence back and see if it was found as a result of an illegal search or seizure.

CHAPTER 21

The Exclusionary Rule and the Fruit of the Poisonous Tree Doctrine

THE RULE: Subject to a number of exceptions, evidence found as a result of a Fourth Amendment violation will be suppressed and not admissible against the defendant whose rights were violated.

Critical Points

- The text of the Fourth Amendment does not include any instructions on what to do about illegally seized evidence. Nevertheless, the Supreme Court created the exclusionary rule to deter the police.
- The exclusionary rule requires suppression of evidence found as a direct result of a Fourth Amendment violation.
- The "fruit of the poisonous tree" doctrine also requires suppression of evidence found "down the road" after a Fourth Amendment violation has occurred. For instance, imagine that the police illegally search the trunk of a car, find a key to a safe deposit box, and then subsequently search the safe deposit box and find incriminating evidence. The evidence in the safe deposit box is fruit of the poisonous tree (the illegal trunk search) and thus inadmissible.

OVERVIEW OF THE BLACKLETTER LAW

The Fourth Amendment forbids unreasonable searches and seizures, but it does not actually say what courts should do if the police commit a violation. The Supreme Court has created a judicial remedy—the exclusionary rule—requiring that illegally seized evidence be suppressed. The premise of the exclusionary rule is that suppressing the evidence is supposed to deter the police from committing future violations.

Usually, the application of the exclusionary rule is simple. If the police search the trunk of your car in violation of the Fourth Amendment and find drugs, those drugs should be excluded. This is what we might think of as a one-step problem.

Fruit of the poisonous tree situations are what we might think of as multi-step problems. The fruit of the poisonous tree doctrine provides that when police search illegally and as a result later find evidence "down the road," the later-discovered evidence should be suppressed. For example, imagine again that the police illegally search the trunk of your car. Instead of finding drugs, this time they find an envelope labeled "Drug Stash—123 Main Street" and inside the envelope they find a key. The officers go to 123 Main Street and discover that it is an abandoned house where no one lives. They use the key, go inside, and find a huge stash of illegal drugs. The driver of the vehicle does not live at 123 Main Street and would seemingly lack the ability to challenge the warrantless entry into that building (see Chapter 20 discussing standing). However, the driver can challenge the evidence under the fruit of the poisonous tree doctrine. The poisonous tree is the illegal search of the trunk. The fruit is both the key found in the trunk and, more importantly, the illegal drugs discovered at 123 Main Street. In short, the fruit of the poisonous tree doctrine allows the defendant to move to suppress the evidence found later. Thus, even if the defendant lacks standing to challenge a later search (e.g., the entrance into 123 Main Street) the defendant can still successfully move to suppress the evidence by pointing to the earlier illegal search (e.g., the illegal search of his trunk) in which his rights were violated.

The Supreme Court has recognized multiple exceptions to the exclusionary rule and the fruit of the poisonous tree doctrine. In theory, all of these exceptions exist because they are situations in which suppressing the evidence is unlikely to deter the police from future misconduct. We explore these exceptions—which you are very likely to see on an exam—in Chapters 22–24.

EXAM TRAPS TO AVOID

- If police do not initially find any evidence from an illegal search or seizure, do not stop there. Look forward to see if the police later discover incriminating evidence that can be linked back to the illegal police conduct. In other words, don't forget about the fruit of the poisonous tree doctrine.
- Law school exams are filled with police illegally searching and seizing. Before concluding that evidence should be suppressed, though, you have to determine whether any of the exceptions to the exclusionary rule apply. Look at the exceptions described in Chapters 22–24: good faith, inevitable discovery, independent source, and attenuation.

MULTIPLE-CHOICE QUESTIONS

Question 125

After a thorough investigation, the police have probable cause to believe that Janet was involved in a recent diamond robbery that carries a 20-year prison sentence. The police know that Janet is home on Wednesday mornings and, after knocking and announcing their presence, wait for 30 seconds before pushing in the front door and arresting Janet in her kitchen. After placing Janet under arrest, the police search her person and find diamonds in her jacket pocket. The police later confirm that the diamonds are from the diamond robbery they have been investigating. Janet moves to suppress the diamonds. How should the court rule?

A) The suppression motion should be granted because the diamonds are the fruit of an unlawful arrest.

B) The suppression motion should be granted because police cannot reach inside pockets when they search incident to arrest. They can only pat down the outer layer of the suspect's garment.

C) The suppression motion should be denied because the diamonds were discovered incident to a lawful arrest.

D) The suppression motion should be denied because the police were entitled to search anywhere in the house that the diamonds could have been hidden.

Question 126

The police stop Dustin for speeding. After writing him a ticket, the officer asks to search Dustin's trunk, but Dustin refuses. The officer then decides to search Dustin's trunk anyway. In the trunk, the officer finds a shopping bag from a Walgreens pharmacy and inside the bag are 20 boxes of cold medicine. The active ingredient in the cold medicine is pseudoephedrine, which is used to make methamphetamine. Because cold medicine can be turned into methamphetamine, stores are required to record the identification of any person who buys it. No store following those rules would sell 20 boxes to the same person. The officer therefore has a hunch that Dustin must have stolen the cold medicine so that he could cook it into methamphetamine. The officer has no proof of that, though, and so he lets Dustin go. A few minutes later, the officer goes to the town's only Walgreens and asks the manager if he can view the store's security footage. The security tape clearly shows Dustin grabbing boxes of cold medicine off the shelf, covertly putting them in a bag, and then walking out the front door of the store with without paying for them. The officer thereafter finds Dustin and arrests him. After Dustin is arrested, he moves to suppress the incriminating video. How should the court rule?

A) The video should be suppressed because it is fruit of the poisonous tree.

B) The video should be admitted because the manager voluntarily consented to turn over the video to the police officer.

C) The video should be admitted because time passed between the illegal search of the trunk and the officer asking to review the tape at the Walgreens.

D) The video should be admitted because the officer did nothing illegal by asking the Walgreens manager to see the videotape.

ANSWERS TO MULTIPLE-CHOICE QUESTIONS

Answer to Question 125

Answer A is correct. When police conduct a lawful arrest, they can search incident to arrest. The question says that the police had probable cause to believe Janet was involved in the diamond robbery. So initially it looks like the evidence should be admissible. But we have to look back further. The police did not have a warrant to enter Janet's house. They have thus entered illegally. The diamonds are thus fruit of the poisonous tree.

Answer B is incorrect. When police conduct a search incident to arrest they can reach into the arrestee's pockets and open everything on her person. (See Chapter 9.)

Answer C is incorrect. The officers lacked a warrant to enter Janet's house. Because there were no exigent circumstances to justify the warrantless entry, the evidence was not found incident to a lawful arrest.

Answer D is incorrect. The search incident to arrest doctrine is limited to the area within the arrestee's immediate reach, not "anywhere in the house."

Answer to Question 126

Answer A is correct. The search of Dustin's trunk was illegal and it led to the officer finding the Walgreens bag with the boxes of cold medicine. As a result of that illegal search, the officer went to the Walgreens and viewed the security video. The security video is thus the fruit of the poisonous tree and not admissible.

Answer B is incorrect. It is true that the manager voluntarily consented to the officer viewing the security video. But we must look not just at that event, but also backward in time. The officer asked for the security footage as a direct result of finding the Walgreens bag and Sudafed boxes from the illegal trunk search. Accordingly, the security video is fruit of the poisonous tree.

Answer C is incorrect. As we will see in Chapter 24, there is an attenuation exception to the fruit of the poisonous tree doctrine. If intervening events occur that break the chain between the illegal police action and the discovery of evidence, courts will find that the discovery of evidence was attenuated and the evidence is therefore admissible. The question therefore is whether there is attenuation between the illegal trunk search and the officer viewing the videotape. In this case there is no attenuation to break the chain. Only a "few minutes" has passed since the illegal trunk search. More importantly, no event has occurred that breaks the causal chain. For example, if the Walgreens manager had called the police and said someone had stolen from the store, that might constitute an intervening event.

Answer D is incorrect. This answer choice is wrong for the same reason as Answer B. It is true that the officer did nothing illegal when he asked the manager to view the security video. But we need to look beyond that moment. By looking backward we can see that the officer only asked to view the security video because he had a hunch that came from the illegal search of the trunk. That illegal search was a poisonous tree. And the security video is the fruit of that poisonous tree. The fact that the officer did not do anything illegal when he asked the manager to view the security video does not eliminate the fruit of the poisonous tree problem.

STEP 8
Does an Exception to the Exclusionary Rule Apply?

The final step of a search and seizure analysis is to determine whether an exception to the exclusionary rule should apply. If the police executed an invalid warrant, the evidence may be admissible if the officers objectively acted in good faith. Regardless of whether there was a warrant, you should also consider the inevitable discovery, independent source, and attenuation exceptions. The inevitable discovery exception applies when the police would have found the evidence if they had acted lawfully. The independent source exception applies if the police found the evidence in two separate searches, one lawful and the other unlawful. And the attenuation exception can apply if the police found the evidence long after the illegal conduct, particularly if there were intervening events.

CHAPTER 22

The Good Faith Exception

THE RULE: When police officers act in good faith reliance on a warrant (or in a few other situations) courts will not suppress evidence found during a search or seizure that was conducted in violation of the Fourth Amendment.

Critical Points

- The most common good faith situation is when police rely in good faith on a warrant that was not actually supported by probable cause.
- Good faith is determined objectively. Courts do not ask whether the officers who executed the warrant believed it was valid. Rather, they ask whether a *reasonable* officer would have believed the warrant was valid.
- The good faith exception can also apply in other types of warrantless searches, such as:
  - The police rely on a database that incorrectly said there was an arrest warrant for the defendant.
  - The police conducted a search or seizure based on binding judicial precedent that was overruled after the search or seizure occurred.
- The good faith exception cannot apply if:
  - The warrant was procured by a police officer who knowingly gave the magistrate false information;
  - The magistrate wholly abandoned her role (e.g., rubber-stamping the warrant application without reviewing it);
  - The officer relied on an affidavit that was so bare-bones that no reasonable officer could believe it created probable cause; or

- The officer relied on a warrant that was so facially deficient that no reasonable officer could have believed it to be valid.

OVERVIEW OF THE BLACKLETTER LAW

The key to understanding the good faith exception is to think about why the Supreme Court created the exclusionary rule. The Court believed that excluding unlawfully seized evidence would deter police officers from committing misconduct in the future. In some situations, however, excluding evidence is not likely to deter police officers. Enter the good faith exception, which allows courts to admit evidence when a reasonable officer would have thought she was doing the right thing. An officer cannot be deterred when she didn't realize she was doing something wrong.

The first—and most significant—good faith situation is the one in which police go to the trouble of applying for a warrant, convince a magistrate to issue the warrant, execute the warrant, only to later discover that the warrant was invalid. In this scenario, the police officer did everything right, it just turned out that the magistrate never should have signed the warrant, or that magistrate filled out the warrant incorrectly. Because the police did everything right, excluding the evidence would not likely deter the officers in the future. Therefore, even though the police action violated the Fourth Amendment (because they searched or seized pursuant to a defective warrant), the good faith exception saves the evidence from being excluded. This situation often plays out when the magistrate issued the warrant, but a court later concludes there was insufficient evidence to establish probable cause and thus the magistrate never should have issued the warrant. Another classic good faith situation occurs when the magistrate issues the warrant but fails to sufficiently describe the places to be searched or the items to be seized. The warrant is defective, but the police acted in good faith and thus the evidence is not excluded.

There are two other common good faith situations, but before discussing those it is helpful to understand when the good faith exception does *not* apply. The Supreme Court has been reluctant to allow the good faith exception to apply to *warrantless* searches and seizures that the officers executed in good faith. For instance, imagine that the police search a car without a warrant. Perhaps the police believed they had consent. Or perhaps the police believed that they had probable cause and the search fell under the automobile exception to the warrant requirement. But in both instances, the police were wrong. There was no consent and there was no probable cause for the automobile exception to apply. The Supreme Court has *not* extended the good faith exception to such warrantless searches. This is an important point, so let's repeat it: for the most part, warrantless searches cannot give rise to the good faith exception—even if reasonable officers would have believed the warrantless search or seizure complied with the Fourth Amendment.

Of course, most rules have exceptions and there are two exceptions to the general proposition that warrantless searches and seizures cannot give rise to the good faith exception. The first exception is when the police rely on existing judicial precedent to conduct a warrantless search or seizure, but that precedent is later overruled. Imagine that police conduct a warrantless search of an arrestee's cell phone incident to arrest because the state supreme court has clearly stated that such searches comply with the Fourth Amendment. However, after the police conduct the cell phone search, the U.S. Supreme Court holds that police cannot search cell phones incident to arrest. Our defendant would of course point to the new U.S. Supreme Court decision as a reason why his conviction should be reversed. The defendant's argument will fail, however, because the officers relied on an existing judicial precedent (the state supreme court decision) in good faith when they conducted the search.

The second situation in which the good faith exception will apply to a warrantless search or seizure is when a clerical or database error has occurred. For instance, imagine that an officer detains a driver for a traffic violation and learns that there is an outstanding arrest warrant for the driver. The officer makes the arrest, but we later learn that there actually was no outstanding arrest warrant. The database was wrong and thus the officer made an improper warrantless arrest. The Supreme Court has held that the good faith exception applies to this type of warrantless search or seizure.

For all of the situations described above, we need to focus on whose good faith matters. When applying the good faith exception it is important to review the case from an objective (rather than subjective) standpoint. Courts do not focus on what the police officer who conducted the search or seizure personally thought. The subjective view of the officer on the scene is not relevant. Rather, when determining whether the good faith exception applies, we must determine what an objectively reasonable officer would have thought. For example, imagine that Officer Olivia executed a search warrant that was later determined not to be based on probable cause. We do not ask what Officer Olivia was thinking when she executed the warrant. Rather, we should examine whether a reasonable officer in Officer Olivia's situation would have thought the warrant was valid.

Finally, the Supreme Court has been clear that there are a few situations in which the good faith exception will not apply. These are all variations on the theme that a reasonable police officer would not have believed she was executing a lawful warrant. The specific scenarios that cannot give rise to a good faith exception occur when: (1) the warrant was procured by a police officer who knowingly gave the magistrate false information; (2) the magistrate wholly abandoned her role (e.g., rubber-stamping the warrant application without reviewing it); (3) the officer relied on an affidavit that was so bare-bones that no reasonable officer could believe it created probable cause; or (4) the officer relied on a warrant that was so facially deficient that no reasonable officer could have believed it to be valid.

EXAM TRAPS TO AVOID

- Do not be fooled into applying the good faith exception for run-of-the-mill *warrantless* searches and seizures. When the police illegally search without a warrant, the good faith doctrine usually does *not* apply.
- While the good faith exception usually does not apply to warrantless searches and seizures, there are two situations in which warrantless searches can fall under the good faith exception: (1) clerical (database) errors; and (2) police relying on existing judicial precedent that is overruled after the search occurred.
- In analyzing good faith claims, do not pay attention to what a particular officer personally believed. Rather, focus on what an objectively reasonable officer would have thought.
- Informants sometimes lie, and police sometimes have bad information. The good faith exception can still apply if the officer *unintentionally* gave the magistrate false information in a warrant application.

MULTIPLE-CHOICE QUESTIONS

Question 127

Officer Hart works undercover in the narcotics unit and has been surveilling what he thinks is a drug operation. Officer Hart sat in his unmarked car at the end of the block. Using binoculars, he watched a man (Marcus) who had been standing on the corner for about two hours. Over those two hours, 15 different people came up to Marcus, talked to him for a moment, and then shook his hand. After the handshake, Marcus would put something in his pocket and the other people would also put something in their pockets and quickly walk away. Based on his experience in the narcotics unit, Officer Hart knew this behavior was consistent with drug purchases. After each drug purchase, Marcus would then lean against a car parked on the corner. Officer Hart never saw Marcus enter the car; he only saw Marcus leaning against the car. After watching two hours of drug sales, Officer Hart arrested Marcus. Officer Hart then walked up to the car Marcus had been leaning against and searched it as well. Under the floor mat in the front passenger seat, Officer Hart found 20 small bags of heroin. Subsequent investigation determined that the car was registered to Marcus's girlfriend and that he was using it with her permission. At Marcus's trial, the prosecutor sought to introduce the heroin found under the car's floor mat. Marcus argued, however, that there was no probable cause to search the car given that Officer Hart only saw Marcus leaning against the vehicle and never saw him enter the vehicle. The trial judge said that it was a close call, but she ultimately concluded that Officer Hart lacked probable cause to search the vehicle. How should the trial judge rule on Marcus's suppression motion?

A) The judge should deny the suppression motion because Officer Hart relied on his expertise as a narcotics expert and truly believed that he had probable cause to search the vehicle.

B) The judge should probably deny the suppression motion because Officer Hart acted in objectively reasonable good faith that he had probable cause to search the vehicle.

C) The judge should grant the suppression motion because Officer Hart searched the car in violation of the Fourth Amendment.

D) The judge should grant the suppression motion because Officer Hart searched the car before learning that it was registered to Marcus's girlfriend.

Question 128

A police officer has frequently used an informant named Max to gather information. Recently Max told the officer that a man named Brent was selling drugs out of Apartment 1D at 123 Main Street. The officer surveilled the location and saw that an unusually large number of people were going in and out of Apartment 1D during the day. The officer applied to a magistrate for a search warrant for Apartment 1D. In the affidavit, the officer recounted Max's tip, that Max has been correct in the past, and the surveillance indicating that many people were coming in and out of the apartment. The magistrate issued the search warrant. The officer then executed the search warrant and found drugs inside. The police arrested Brent, and he moved to suppress the evidence on the grounds that there was insufficient probable cause. The trial judge rejected the suppression motion and Brent was convicted. A few months later, however, an appellate court agreed with Brent that there was insufficient probable cause and that the magistrate should not have issued the warrant. Brent is now seeking to have his conviction thrown out. How should the court rule?

A) Brent's conviction should be reversed because the warrant was clearly invalid and thus the evidence is fruit of the poisonous tree.

B) Brent's conviction should be reversed because the officer who applied for the defective warrant is the one who ultimately executed it and conducted the search.

C) Brent's conviction should be upheld as long as a reasonable officer would have believed the warrant was valid.

D) Brent's conviction should be upheld because the officer believed he was executing a valid warrant.

Question 129

Assume the same facts as Question 128. For purposes of this question, though, assume that the informant, Max, had lied to the officer. Max did not have any knowledge of Brent selling drugs out of Apartment 1D. Max and his girlfriend had recently broken up, and now Max's ex-girlfriend was dating Brent. Max made up the drug story in an effort to harm Brent. The officer recounted Max's tip in her affidavit accompanying the warrant application. The magistrate issued the search warrant for Apartment 1D, which the officer then executed. The officer found drugs on the kitchen table. Eventually, all of the facts come out and Brent moves to suppress the drugs. How should the court rule?

A) The court should suppress the drugs because the officer made materially false statements in his affidavit.

B) The court should admit the drugs because the officer did not knowingly lie to the court to obtain the warrant.

Question 130

Police arrested Jacob for robbery. While taking Jacob into custody, the officers discovered a cell phone in his pocket. The cell phone had no password on it, so the officers began to look at it. Jacob vocally objected to the officers looking through his phone, but the first officer said, "I think the law allows us to search your phone incident to arrest." The officers therefore ignored Jacob's objection and looked through his text messages. The third message from the top was from someone the police had also been investigating and the message included the address of a store that had recently been robbed. Jacob moved to suppress the incriminating text message, but the trial judge denied the motion because the state supreme court had previously issued a ruling upholding searches of cell phones incident to arrest. The prosecutor introduced the incriminating text message at trial and Jacob was convicted. While his appeal was pending, the U.S. Supreme Court decided *Riley v. California* and held that the Fourth Amendment does *not* allow police to search cell phones incident to arrest. Should Jacob's conviction be reversed?

A) Yes, because illegally seized evidence was admitted at Jacob's trial.

B) Yes, because even though the officers acted in good faith, the good faith exception only applies to searches carried out with warrants.

C) No, because the good faith exception applies since an objectively reasonable officer would have relied on the state supreme court decision.

D) No, because the officers who searched Jacob's phone believed they were allowed to search the phone.

Question 131

A police officer pulled over a vehicle for speeding and asked the driver (Amy Fadams) for her license. The officer ran a driver's license check, but because of static on the radio the clerk misunderstood the officer and ran a check for Amy Badams. There was an outstanding warrant for Amy Badams for money laundering and the clerk told the officer, "There is a warrant out for her arrest. You should take her into custody." The officer proceeded to arrest Amy Fadams. The officer searched Fadams incident to the arrest and found cocaine in her pocket. A few days after arrest, Fadams' defense attorney pointed out that the initial arrest had been incorrect because there was no outstanding warrant for Fadams. The defense attorney argued that the cocaine charges should therefore be dismissed. Should the prosecutor have to dismiss the charges?

A) The prosecutor can continue with the case because the good faith exception only applies to invalid searches, not an unlawful arrest.

B) The prosecutor can continue with the case because the officer acted in good faith when she arrested Fadams.

C) The prosecutor should dismiss the case because this was a warrantless arrest and the good faith exception never applies to warrantless arrests.

D) The prosecutor should dismiss the case because the officer made a mistake in communicating with the clerk and thus the good faith exception does not apply.

ANSWERS TO MULTIPLE-CHOICE QUESTIONS

Answer to Question 127

Answer A is incorrect. The fact that Officer Hart "truly believed" there was probable cause is irrelevant. The subjective view of the officer does not determine whether there is probable cause. Even if the good faith exception applied (which it didn't because this was a warrantless search), good faith would have to be determined from an objective standpoint, not from the subjective view of Officer Hart.

Answer B is incorrect. The good faith exception does not usually apply to warrantless searches. Thus, even though this answer choice correctly mentions that the good faith exception should be analyzed from the view of an objectively reasonable officer, it is an incorrect choice because the good faith exception does not apply in this case.

Answer C is correct. The good faith exception to the exclusionary rule typically applies when police search with a warrant in good faith but it is later determined that there was insufficient probable cause for the warrant. The good faith exception applies in rare situations without a warrant, such as reliance on existing precedent that is later overruled or errors in a database, but those situations are not present here. Because Officer Hart conducted a warrantless search that violated the Fourth Amendment, the evidence should be suppressed.

Answer D is incorrect. The information about the car being registered to Marcus's girlfriend does not do much to improve the case for probable cause to search the vehicle. It is not clear that the judge's ruling would be any different had Officer Hart possessed this information.

Answer to Question 128

Answer A is incorrect. The search was illegal, but it does not appear that it was "clearly invalid." The officer had a tip from an informant who had been correct in the past, as well as confirming surveillance. The magistrate issued a warrant based on that information. A reasonable officer could therefore have believed the warrant was valid and thus executed it in good faith. As such, the evidence should not have been suppressed.

Answer B is incorrect. This choice is incorrect for the same reason that Answer A is incorrect. There appeared to be probable cause and the magistrate issued what appeared to be a valid search warrant. It was only later that the officer learned there was insufficient probable cause. Under these circumstances, an objectively reasonable officer could have believed there was probable cause and thus the good faith exception should apply.

Answer C is correct. For the reasons stated above, the officer believed there was probable cause based on the tip and the surveillance. A magistrate issued what appeared to be a valid warrant that was only later found to be supported by insufficient probable cause. Under these circumstances—even though the search was invalid—an objectively reasonable officer could have believed that the warrant was valid when he executed it. Accordingly, the good faith exception should apply.

Answer D is incorrect because the subjective view of the officer is irrelevant.

Answer to Question 129

Answer A is incorrect. This answer choice is tempting because the officer did include a false statement in the warrant application. However, the officer did not know that he was including a dishonest statement. For the good faith exception to be inapplicable, the officer had to knowingly give false information to the magistrate in an effort to procure a warrant. There is no evidence that that happened here, however.

Answer B is correct. The good faith exception does not apply if the officer knowingly gave false information to the magistrate in an effort to procure a warrant. Here, however, the officer unintentionally used false information because he did not know that the informant was lying. Accordingly, the good faith exception still applies.

Answer to Question 130

Answer A is incorrect. The officers relied on valid, existing judicial precedent when they searched Jacob's phone incident to arrest. Accordingly, the incriminating text message is admissible under the good faith exception and should not be suppressed.

Answer B is incorrect. In the vast majority of cases the good faith exception only applies when the police have searched pursuant to a warrant. But there are exceptions. One of those exceptions is when the police conduct a warrantless search or seizure pursuant to existing judicial precedent that is later overturned.

Answer C is correct. Although we now know the search of Jacob's cell phone was unconstitutional under *Riley v. California*, at the time the officers conducted the search it was valid under state law. Accordingly, the officers acted in objectively reasonable good faith in conducting the search of Jacob's cell phone incident to arrest. The incriminating text message is therefore admissible under the good faith exception.

Answer D is incorrect. The subjective views of the officers are irrelevant in determining whether the good faith exception applies. Rather, we have to assess whether an objectively reasonable officer would have believed that the search complied with existing precedent.

Answer to Question 131

Answer A is incorrect. The good faith exception applies to both searches and seizures.

Answer B is correct. This was a clerical error. A reasonable officer in this situation would have effectuated the arrest. Suppressing the evidence therefore would not deter the police from future misconduct. Thus, this is one of the unusual cases in which the good faith exception applies in the absence of a warrant.

Answer C is incorrect. The good faith exception usually applies in cases where there was a defective warrant. There are some cases, however, in which the good faith exception applies to warrantless searches and seizures. Clerical errors like this one fall into that category.

Answer D is incorrect. The fact that the officer made a mistake is what makes the good faith exception applicable. This answer choice therefore has the rule backward.

CHAPTER 23

The Inevitable Discovery and Independent Source Exceptions

THE RULE: INEVITABLE DISCOVERY: When police find evidence as a result of an illegal search or seizure, the evidence will still be admissible if the police inevitably *would have found* the evidence anyway through a lawful search.

THE RULE: INDEPENDENT SOURCE: When police find evidence as a result of an illegal search or seizure, the evidence will still be admissible if police officers also *actually found* the same evidence as a result of a lawful separate search.

Critical Points

- The inevitable discovery exception applies when the police: (1) find the evidence illegally, but (2) would have eventually found the evidence lawfully.
- Because the evidence was illegally seized and would normally be suppressed under the exclusionary rule, the government bears the burden of demonstrating by a preponderance of the evidence that the evidence would inevitably have been found legally.

OVERVIEW OF THE BLACKLETTER LAW

The inevitable discovery and independent source exceptions sound similar, but they are two different exceptions. It is not possible for both of them to apply at the same time.

The inevitable discovery exception applies when the police found evidence through an unlawful search or seizure. Put simply, the first search was illegal. However, if the illegal search had never happened, the police would have eventually found the evidence in a lawful way. For example, imagine that one set of officers illegally searched a house and found incriminating evidence. At the same time, another set of officers was in the process of obtaining a search warrant from a magistrate that would have enabled them to search the same house and find the same evidence. The evidence should be admissible because the second set of officers *would have* found the evidence lawfully. In short, the inevitable discovery exception is for situations in which the police would have found the evidence anyway.

The independent source exception applies when the police actually found the evidence lawfully the second time they searched. Imagine that police illegally enter a house without a warrant, find evidence, but do not seize it. Then the officers (either the same ones or different ones) apply for a warrant to search that house and do not mention anything they saw in the first (illegal) search. The magistrate issues the warrant and the officers then search the house legally, find evidence, and this time they seize it. The evidence is admissible under the independent source exception. In short, the independent source exception is for situations in which the police *actually found* the evidence lawfully, albeit after there had been an earlier illegal search.

The inevitable discovery doctrine and the independent source exception are exceptions to the exclusionary rule. Because the police violated the Fourth Amendment and the evidence would normally be suppressed under the exclusionary rule, the burden is on the government to demonstrate that the exclusionary rule should not apply.

EXAM TRAPS TO AVOID

- The inevitable discovery and independent source doctrines are two different exceptions that apply in different circumstances.
- The key concept for inevitable discovery is that the police eventually would have found the evidence through a lawful search in the future. If the case does not involve a "would have found the evidence anyway" situation, then it is not an inevitable discovery question.
- The government bears the burden of proving inevitable discovery by a preponderance of the evidence. If it is unclear whether the police would eventually have found the evidence lawfully, do not apply the inevitable discovery exception.
- The independent source doctrine is for cases in which the police searched twice—once illegally and once legally. If the police found the evidence through a second search that was done completely lawfully, the evidence may be admissible.

- For the independent source doctrine, be sure that the officers have not used evidence from the first illegal search as a basis for conducting the second search. If police used any of the evidence from the first illegal search in their warrant application for the second search, then the independent source doctrine does not apply.
- If it is unclear whether the second search was conducted lawfully and without evidence found during the first illegal search, then the independent source exception does not apply. The government bears the burden of proving an independent source.

MULTIPLE-CHOICE QUESTIONS

Question 132

There is a rivalry between the 33rd and 34th Police Precincts in New York City. When there is a case that involves both Police Precincts—often large-scale drug gangs—the Precincts compete to see who can take credit for the arrests. Both Precincts have discovered that gang leaders are working out of a house at 123 State Street. The officers from the 33rd Precinct enter the house without a warrant and seize a huge amount of cocaine. After the officers from the 33rd Precinct have bagged up all the evidence and are about to leave the scene, the officers from the 34th Precinct arrive with a warrant in hand to search 123 State Street. As the officers from the 33rd precinct are driving away with the evidence, they yell out the window, "You lose again—34th Precinct losers." The prosecutor is annoyed with the officers from the 33rd Precinct for unlawfully entering 123 State Street without a warrant. Which of the following is the prosecutor's best argument for admitting the cocaine evidence anyway?

A) The cocaine falls under the independent source doctrine.

B) The cocaine falls under the inevitable discovery doctrine.

C) The cocaine falls under the good faith exception.

D) The cocaine falls under the attenuation exception.

Question 133

Police observe Zelda driving alone in her car at 1:00 a.m. on a Saturday night. Zelda is weaving all over the road. The officers pull her over and immediately notice that she smells of alcohol. The officers administer the field sobriety tests and Zelda fails all of them. The officers place her under arrest for drunk driving. One of the officers then searches the trunk of Zelda's car and finds evidence from a recent robbery. The police then impound Zelda's car and inventory the contents just as the department's inventory policy instructs them to. Zelda later moves to suppress the evidence. How should the court rule?

A) The court should admit the evidence because the search was conducted incident to arrest.

B) The court should admit the evidence because the search was permissible under the automobile exception.

C) The court should admit the evidence if the police department inventory policy extends to the trunk.

D) The court should admit the evidence pursuant to the attenuation exception.

Question 134

Max was running a chop shop in Brooklyn, New York. Max would buy stolen cars, chop them up for parts, and then sell the parts on the black market. A Brooklyn police officer from the 99th Precinct was investigating a car theft and had received a tip from an informant that the car was being taken to the chop shop at 101 Fury Road. The officer did not have a warrant, but entered the premises anyway and discovered 10 stolen cars. It turns out that Max was running one of the largest illegal chop shops in the entire state. The operation was so big that the NYPD Special Crimes unit had an active investigation with considerable evidence and was close to applying for a search warrant for 101 Fury Road. How should the court rule on Max's suppression motion?

A) The court should suppress the evidence because the officer conducted an illegal warrantless search.

B) The court should suppress the evidence because the inevitable discovery exception only applies when the police have already applied for a warrant.

C) The court should admit the evidence because the inevitable discovery exception applies whenever there is a chance that the police would have found the evidence lawfully.

D) The court should probably admit the evidence under the inevitable discovery exception because the Special Crimes unit would have found the evidence anyway.

Question 135

Officer Beverly has been surveilling Keith for weeks based on allegations that he has been selling stolen property out of a magic shop. One night, Officer Beverly sneaks into the magic shop, which Keith had left unlocked. Inside, Officer Beverly sees stolen property on the table. She does not touch the evidence, but instead sneaks back out and closes the door behind her. The next day, Officer Beverly applies for a search warrant for the magic shop. Officer Beverly's affidavit does not mention that she saw stolen property in the magic shop the night before. Instead, she recounts her weeks of surveillance and the tip of an anonymous informant who has given reliable information in the past. The magistrate issues the warrant and Officer Beverly searches the magic shop and once again finds the stolen property sitting in the same place on the table. Keith later discovers from his security surveillance footage that Officer Beverly had entered the magic shop illegally before procuring the warrant and he moves to suppress the evidence. How should the court rule?

A) The evidence should be admissible under the independent source doctrine.

B) The evidence should be admissible because Keith left the door to the magic shop unlocked and thus Officer Beverly's entry did not violate the Fourth Amendment.

C) The evidence should be inadmissible because Officer Beverly failed to disclose her earlier entry into the magic shop to the magistrate and thus she cannot invoke the independent source doctrine.

D) The evidence should be inadmissible because Officer Beverly's initial entry into the magic shop was not done in good faith and thus the independent source exception cannot apply.

ANSWERS TO MULTIPLE-CHOICE QUESTIONS

Answer to Question 132

Answer A is incorrect. The officers from the 34th Precinct did not end up searching lawfully pursuant to the warrant they procured. Therefore, they did not find the evidence lawfully.

Answer B is correct. The officers from the 34th Precinct had a properly issued search warrant and were about to execute it. Had the officers from the 33rd Precinct not searched illegally, the officers from the 34th Precinct would have found the evidence lawfully. This situation falls under the inevitable discovery doctrine.

Answer C is incorrect. For the good faith exception to apply, the officers from the 33rd Precinct would have had to search 123 State Street pursuant to a defective warrant that a reasonable officer would have believed to be valid. The officers from the 33rd Precinct had no such warrant.

Answer D is incorrect. There is no attenuation between the illegal search by the officers from the 33rd Precinct and the discovery of the cocaine. To the contrary, the cocaine was found as a direct and immediate result of the illegal search.

Answer to Question 133

Answer A is incorrect. The search of a vehicle incident to arrest exception does not allow a search of the trunk.

Answer B is incorrect. There was no probable cause for the police to believe evidence would be found in the trunk. Thus, the automobile exception does not apply.

Answer C is correct. The police found the evidence through an illegal search. However, because they were arresting Zelda for drunk driving, the police would have had to impound the vehicle. Following impoundment, the police would have inventoried the vehicle and looked in the trunk if the police department's inventory policy extends to the trunk. As such, the officers would inevitably have found the robbery evidence after they impounded the vehicle and inventoried its contents. Thus, even though the officers initially found the evidence illegally, they inevitably would have found it lawfully.

Answer D is incorrect. For evidence to be attenuated from an initial illegal search, there must have been intervening events or a considerable amount of time must have passed. Neither are present here. The officers immediately found the evidence during an illegal search. There was no attenuation.

Answer to Question 134

Answer A is incorrect. The police officer did search illegally by entering without a warrant. However, the police department would have found the evidence lawfully when the Special Crimes unit procured a warrant and searched lawfully.

Answer B is incorrect. The inevitable discovery exception is not limited to cases in which the police have already procured a search warrant.

Answer C is incorrect. This answer choice recognizes the inevitable discovery exception, but it misstates the test. The government bears the burden of proving the inevitable discovery exception and it cannot do so by showing only a "chance" that the government would have found the evidence later in a lawful way.

Answer D is correct. The inevitable discovery exception can apply in this situation if the government can prove the Special Crimes unit would have found the evidence lawfully as a result of a warrant.

Answer to Question 135

Answer A is correct. Officer Beverly's second entrance into the magic shop was lawful. Because she did not rely on any of the information she found from her first illegal entry, the second search is an independent source and the evidence should be admissible.

Answer B is incorrect. Officer Beverly entered the magic shop illegally. The fact that she did not have to break down the door or pick the lock does not mean she did not violate the Fourth Amendment.

Answer C is incorrect. There is no requirement that Officer Beverly disclose her earlier entry into the apartment. The only restriction is that Officer Beverly cannot rely on what she saw inside the magic shop when she submits her affidavit to the magistrate. Because Officer Beverly only included her surveillance evidence and the informant's tip, her warrant application was acceptable.

Answer D is incorrect. The good faith exception is a distraction in this question. Officer Beverly's initial illegal entry into the magic shop did not have to be in good faith for the independent source exception to apply.

CHAPTER 24
The Attenuation Exception

THE RULE: When police find evidence a long time after an illegal search or seizure, or after intervening events, the discovery of the evidence may be attenuated from the police misconduct and thus admissible.

Critical Points

- The longer the time lapse between the Fourth Amendment violation and the discovery of the evidence, the more likely it is that the attenuation exception will apply.
- The more intervening events that occur between the Fourth Amendment violation and the discovery of the evidence, the more likely it is that the attenuation exception will apply.
- The less flagrant the Fourth Amendment violation, the more likely the attenuation exception will apply.
- Actions freely taken by the defendant himself are likely to break the chain of causation and allow the attenuation exception to apply. For example, if the defendant freely returned to the police station after being illegally arrested and released, the act of freely returning would break the causal chain and allow for the attenuation exception to apply.
- The attenuation exception applies if an illegal search or seizure leads to the police discovering the identity of a witness.
- Giving a suspect *Miranda* warnings—by itself—does *not* break the causal chain and amount to attenuation.
- The attenuation exception applies in two circumstances that don't really seem like they should fall under the attenuation doctrine:

- If the police have a valid warrant, but fail to knock and announce their presence when executing the warrant, the evidence will not be excluded.
- If the police stop a person without reasonable suspicion, but it turns out that there is an outstanding warrant for the person, any evidence found during a search incident to arrest will still be admissible.

OVERVIEW OF THE BLACKLETTER LAW

Let's start by discussing when the attenuation doctrine does not apply. If police commit a Fourth Amendment violation that immediately leads to the discovery of incriminating evidence, courts will not invoke the attenuation doctrine. Rather, the attenuation doctrine is for situations in which something happens between the Fourth Amendment violation and the police finding the evidence. The best way to think of the problem is to imagine a straight line with the Fourth Amendment violation on one end and the discovery of the evidence on the other end. Are the two points on the line very close together with nothing happening in between? If yes, then there is no attenuation. By contrast, if the two events on the line are far apart, or if you can point to something notable that happened in between, then there may be attenuation.

A long stretch of time between the Fourth Amendment violation and discovery of the evidence can amount to attenuation. The Supreme Court has not adopted a bright-line rule here, however, so it is hard to say how long is long enough. Most courts would likely find a few hours to be insufficient, while several days might be enough for attenuation. But again, there is no bright-line rule or magic number.

An intervening event (especially if it is freely taken by the defendant) between the constitutional violation and discovering the evidence can amount to attenuation. For example, imagine that police illegally arrest a suspect. The officers try to interrogate the suspect after the arrest, but he refuses to cooperate. The suspect posts bail and goes home. The next day, however, the suspect *voluntarily* returns to the police station to try to explain to the police why he has done nothing wrong. In the course of talking with the police, the suspect incriminates himself. The confession is fruit of the poisonous tree because the illegal arrest led to him eventually confessing. However, courts would say that the attenuation exception to the exclusionary rule should apply. There was an intervening event—the defendant freely choosing to return to the police station—that broke the causal chain. Put differently, the confession is attenuated from the illegal arrest and thus admissible.

The attenuation doctrine often calls on courts (and students) to determine whether enough time has passed or a significant enough intervening event has occurred to break the causal chain. These situations are grey areas that are susceptible to multiple interpretations. They are classic topics for essay questions.

There are two bright-line rules for the attenuation doctrine. First, the Court has held that giving a suspect *Miranda* warnings—by itself—is not enough to break the causal chain. Thus, if police violate the Fourth Amendment, give the suspect *Miranda* warnings, and she then confesses, we know that the *Miranda* warnings alone are not enough to create attenuation. Second, if the police find the existence of witnesses as a result of a Fourth Amendment violation, we know that the testimony of those witnesses will fall under the attenuation doctrine. In other words, courts are unwilling to suppress the testimony of a witness who was discovered as a result of a Fourth Amendment violation.

Finally, there are two situations that the Supreme Court has grouped under the attenuation doctrine, but that do not really seem to fit under that heading. First, when officers are executing a valid warrant, but they fail to adequately knock and announce their presence, the evidence will not be suppressed. Second, if the police stop a person without reasonable suspicion, but it turns out that there is an outstanding warrant for the person, any evidence found during a search incident to arrest will still be admissible. For example, imagine that police stop Ray on the street for no reason. While one officer questions Ray, the other officer radios into headquarters to find out if he has any outstanding warrants. The officers then learn—for the first time—that there is an existing warrant for Ray's arrest. The officers then arrest Ray and search him incident to arrest and find drugs in his pocket. Ray would argue that the drugs should be suppressed as the result of an illegal detention (because there was no valid reason to stop him in the first place). The Supreme Court has held (partly on attenuation grounds) that the initial illegal detention is overcome by the fact that there was an existing warrant for Ray's arrest.

EXAM TRAPS TO AVOID

- Do not use the attenuation doctrine if no time has passed or nothing of consequence has occurred between the Fourth Amendment violation and the discovery of the evidence.
- Do not give a bright-line answer to a grey question. If some (but not a lot of) time passed between the Fourth Amendment violation and finding the evidence, you should analyze both sides of the attenuation argument. Similarly, if the intervening event is of debatable significance, be sure to examine both sides of the issue rather than automatically invoking or rejecting the attenuation exception.
- Do not conclude that the *Miranda* warnings, by themselves, are enough for the attenuation exception.
- Do not suppress the testimony of witnesses because they were discovered as a result of a Fourth Amendment violation. The identity of witnesses is attenuated from the police misconduct.

MULTIPLE-CHOICE QUESTIONS

Question 136

Every cop in town knows Finley, who has gotten into trouble more times than you can count. Following a burglary, the police have no leads, so they pick up the usual suspects, starting with Finley. The officers arrest Finley, read him his *Miranda* rights, take him to the police station and begin to interrogate him. Before they get very far, there is a knock on the door and the officers are told that Finley's sister has posted bail for him. Finley is released and spends the night sleeping on his sister's couch. The next day, Finley's sister tells him, "You've got to clean up your life. I can't keep bailing you out." Finley responded, "Yah, I know. I shouldn't have done that burglary." His sister shook her head and then left for work. Finley meditated for an hour to think hard about his life. Thereafter, Finley drove to the police station and confessed to the burglary. While he was locked up pending trial, though, Finley had second thoughts and moved to suppress his confession. How should the court rule?

A) The confession should be admissible under the attenuation doctrine because the officers read Finley his *Miranda* rights, which broke the causal chain.

B) The confession should be admissible under the attenuation doctrine because there was a break in custody and Finley voluntarily returned to the police station and confessed thereafter.

C) The confession should be admissible under the independent source doctrine because Finley confessed to his sister.

D) The confession should be admissible under the inevitable discovery doctrine because the police would inevitably have learned about Finley's confession from his sister.

E) The confession should be inadmissible because it was the fruit of an illegal arrest.

Question 137

Assume the same facts as Question 136, except for this question imagine that when there was a knock on the door of the interrogation room, the officers were told "Finley's girlfriend posted bail for him." Finley then jumped up and said, "Ha, I'm going home, suckers. And my girlfriend is the only one who knows about —" Finley realized he'd made a mistake and immediately stopped talking. After Finley left the jail, the officers walked back to the records department and saw that someone named Maya was the person who had posted bail for Finley. Police did a little digging and learned where Maya lived. The next day, they went to Maya's house and asked her some questions about what Finley had been up to. After a few minutes, Maya indicated that Finley had committed the burglary. Before trial, Finley moves to suppress the incriminating statements made by Maya. What result?

A) The statements should be suppressed because they are fruit of the poisonous tree resulting from the illegal arrest of Finley.

B) The statements should not be suppressed because the attenuation doctrine renders them admissible.

Question 138

The police have been surveilling a known drug house and are about to raid the house. Moments before the raid, Willy walks past the drug house on his way to work and the police stop him. The officer asks Willy for his name and when Willy responds the officer radios into headquarters to see if there are any warrants out for Willy's arrest. In fact, a court had issued an arrest warrant for Willy a few months ago because he had failed to pay some overdue parking tickets. The officer thereafter places Willy under arrest and searches him. In Willy's front pocket the officer feels a squishy substance, pulls it out, and sees that it is a small bag of cocaine. Prosecutors eventually drop the parking ticket cases, but they do file charges for cocaine possession. Willy moves to suppress the cocaine as the product of an illegal stop. What result?

A) The cocaine is admissible because under the attenuation doctrine the police would have found it anyway when they raided the drug house.

B) The cocaine is admissible because the valid arrest warrant creates attenuation from the unlawful stop.

C) The cocaine is inadmissible because there was no reasonable suspicion to stop Willy and there is no attenuation between the illegal stop and finding the cocaine.

D) The cocaine is inadmissible because the officer did not immediately recognize the squishy substance in the pocket to be contraband and there was no attenuation between feeling the substance and pulling it out of Willy's pocket.

ANSWERS TO MULTIPLE-CHOICE QUESTIONS

Answer to Question 136

Answer A is incorrect. Giving the *Miranda* warnings, by itself, is not enough to break the causal chain and create attenuation.

Answer B is correct. The causal chain is broken because of Finley's intervening act when he voluntarily returns to the police station. His confession is therefore attenuated from the illegal arrest.

Answer C is incorrect. The question seems to be suggesting that Finley's confession is an independent source. This is not the right concept, though. The independent source exception applies when the police find evidence illegally and then—completely separately—find evidence lawfully. Here, the officers only found the evidence one time. Attenuation, not independent source, is the more appropriate legal doctrine to consider.

Answer D is incorrect. This answer is tempting. If the police were on the verge of getting Finley's sister to recount his incriminating confession, then the inevitable discovery exception could apply. But the government bears the burden of proving the inevitable discovery exception and there is nothing in the fact pattern to suggest that they are close to finding Finley's sister or that she would give up information against her brother.

Answer E is incorrect. Finley's confession is fruit of the poisonous tree. But for his illegal arrest, he would not have confessed. However, the attenuation exception applies because of the break in custody and Finley's decision to voluntarily return to the station and confess. Accordingly, his confession is admissible and this answer choice is incorrect.

Answer to Question 137

Answer A is incorrect. The police were able to get Maya's statements as a result of the illegal arrest of Finley. However, as explained below, the statement is still admissible under the attenuation doctrine.

Answer B is correct. The Supreme Court has indicated that if police learn the identity of a witness as a result of a Fourth Amendment violation, the witness's testimony will not be suppressed. Here, discovering Maya's identity and subsequently getting her to provide incriminating information is sufficiently attenuated from the illegal arrest.

Answer to Question 138

Answer A is incorrect. This choice is wrong for multiple reasons. First, if the police would have found the evidence anyway, then it would fall under the inevitable discovery exception, not the attenuation exception. Second, there is no reason to believe the police would have found the evidence anyway in a lawful manner. By the time the police would have conducted the raid, Willy would have been gone from the area.

Answer B is correct. The facts of this question are drawn from the Supreme Court's decision in *Utah v. Strieff* (2016). In that case the Court acknowledged that the stop of the individual was unlawful, but concluded that it was not a flagrant violation. Moreover, the existence of a valid arrest warrant—even if the original officers did not know about it—strongly supported finding attenuation. According to the Court, the valid warrant pre-dated the stop and the officer was obligated to arrest the individual.

Answer C is incorrect. This answer choice would have been correct prior to the Supreme Court's decision in *Utah v. Strieff* (2016). However, as explained in response to Answer B, the Court decided that the existence of a valid arrest warrant prior to the stop allowed a finding of attenuation.

Answer D is incorrect. Given the Supreme Court's decision in *Utah v. Strieff* (2016), the arrest was valid. Accordingly, when the officer felt the squishy substance in Willy's pocket, the officer was conducting a search incident to arrest, not just a *Terry* frisk. Because it was a search incident to arrest, the officer was not limited to seizing items the officer immediately recognized as incriminating. Rather, a search incident to arrest allows the officer to remove items from the pocket and examine them. Accordingly, the officer's actions in removing the squishy substance from Willy's pocket were permissible.

Roadmap for Interrogation Problems

If you are presented with a confession, your first instinct might be to jump into a *Miranda* analysis. While *Miranda* is a big part of the law of interrogations, there are other Fifth Amendment rules that you must understand and apply. Most importantly, you should consider whether a confession is coerced. Below are seven steps you should think through every time you are presented with an incriminating statement.

1. Is the evidence **non-testimonial** or does the suspect have **immunity**, such that there can be no Fifth Amendment problem?
   - *Testimonial versus Non-testimonial*: The Fifth Amendment's protection against self-incrimination only applies if the evidence is testimonial.
   - Verbal or written statements are usually testimonial (and covered by the Fifth Amendment), while blood samples, handwriting samples, standing in a line-up, and some other actions are non-testimonial (and not protected by the Fifth Amendment).
   - *Immunity*: If a prosecutor has immunized a person they can no longer invoke their Fifth Amendment right to remain silent.
2. Analyze whether this was a **coerced confession** or a voluntary confession.
   - Confessions are involuntary when the police use force, the threat of force, or extreme psychological trickery.
   - A confession cannot be coerced unless the officer has taken some action. A suspect who confesses because he hears voices is not coerced for Fifth Amendment purposes.

- To determine whether a confession was coerced, you should look at the totality of the circumstances and consider factors such as the length of the interrogation, whether it occurred late at night, how long it took, whether the suspect remained handcuffed, the suspect's age, level of education, and prior experience with law enforcement.

3. Determine whether the police engaged in a **custodial interrogation** such that the *Miranda* doctrine applies.
    - *Miranda* applies only when the suspect is in custody and subject to interrogation.
    - Custody usually means the suspect is under arrest, although there can be custody when there is a functional equivalent of arrest.
    - To determine custody, you should consider factors such as the number of officers, tone of voice of the officers, whether weapons were drawn, the length of the interaction, the time of day (e.g., late at night), and whether other people were around.
    - Interrogation usually occurs when the police ask questions, but police can also engage in interrogation when they make statements or take actions that are reasonably likely to elicit an incriminating response.

4. Determine whether the **public safety, routine booking question, or covert operative** exceptions to *Miranda* apply.
    - *Public Safety*: When an officer reasonably believes there is an immediate need to protect the police or the public from an immediate danger, they can question a suspect without first giving the *Miranda* warnings.
    - *Routine Booking Questions*: At the police station, officers can ask "routine booking questions" such as name, address, and date of birth without having to give the *Miranda* warnings.
    - *Covert Operations*: If police use undercover agents or informants to get incriminating information from a suspect, the *Miranda* doctrine does not apply because the suspect does not know he is being questioned by a police agent.

5. If the *Miranda* doctrine applies and the police provided the proper warnings, determine whether the officers obtained a **valid waiver**.
    - The suspect does not have to explicitly say "I waive."
    - Waiver can be inferred from the circumstances, such as the suspect immediately beginning to answer questions.
    - Waiver can occur when a suspect sits silently for a long time (potentially hours) after receiving the warnings and then eventually talks.

6. If a suspect invoked her *Miranda* rights, determine which right she invoked to figure out what the rules are for **reinitiation** by the police.
   - If a suspect invokes her *right to counsel*, police must permanently cease questioning. The officers cannot reapproach the suspect later to try to seek a waiver.
   - If a suspect invokes her *right to silence*, police must cease questioning. However, the officers can later reapproach the suspect if they have waited long enough.
   - If the suspect reinitiates communication with the officers after having invoked her *Miranda* rights, the police can seek a waiver and if the suspect waives, the police can question her.

7. If the confession is coerced or there was a *Miranda* violation, assess whether subsequently discovered evidence should also be suppressed as **fruit of the poisonous tree**.
   - If a coerced confession leads police to find other evidence, that additional evidence will also be suppressed under the fruit of the poisonous tree doctrine.
   - If a *Miranda* violation leads police to find physical evidence, that evidence will be admissible because the fruit of the poisonous tree doctrine does not ordinarily apply to *Miranda* violations.
   - *Two-Step Interrogations and Multiple Confessions*: If police get a confession without reading the *Miranda* warnings, but then comply with *Miranda* and get a second confession, that second confession may be admissible. The second confession in a "two-step interrogation" can be admissible if the police forgot to give the warnings initially and took curative measures (such as telling the suspect that the first confession is inadmissible).

STEP 1
Are You Dealing with a Fifth Amendment Problem?

The Fifth Amendment protects against compelled self-incrimination. As we will see, the big Fifth Amendment issues are whether a confession is coerced or whether it violates the *Miranda* doctrine. But before analyzing those questions, you should first assess whether the suspect is even at risk of incriminating himself under the Fifth Amendment in the first place. If the evidence is non-testimonial—meaning it does not reveal a suspect's thoughts—then there can be no Fifth Amendment violation. Similarly, if the suspect has been granted immunity by the prosecutor, then her statements cannot be used against her. Before analyzing whether the prosecution's evidence comes from coercion or a *Miranda* violation, you should first ask whether the evidence is testimonial (Chapter 25) and whether the suspect has been granted immunity (Chapter 26).

CHAPTER 25
Testimonial versus Non-testimonial Situations

THE RULE: The Fifth Amendment only applies to testimonial evidence, which is evidence that reveals a person's thoughts.

Critical Points

- The Fifth Amendment protects individuals from having to reveal testimonial evidence. Evidence is testimonial if it conveys a person's thoughts or beliefs.
- If the evidence is testimonial, we must check to make sure the police complied with the Fifth Amendment (including *Miranda*). If the evidence is non-testimonial, the Fifth Amendment does not apply and we do not have to consider whether the police complied with *Miranda* and other Fifth Amendment requirements.
- *Statements Are Usually Testimonial:* Most statements from a witness—whether oral or written—are testimonial. When people make statements they are usually conveying information from their minds that reveals their thoughts.
- *But Some Statements Can Be Non-testimonial*: For example, having a person speak in a lineup is non-testimonial because it only reveals the sound of the individual's voice, not their thoughts. Similarly, having a person write random words on a page is non-testimonial because it only reveals the appearance of their handwriting, not their thoughts.
- *Most Actions Are Non-testimonial*: Sometimes police want a person to do an action that will produce incriminating evidence. Although the evidence is damaging to the suspect, that does not mean it is testimonial. Blood draws,

a suspect's movements are non-testimonial because they do not require a suspect to convey her thoughts.

- *But Some Actions Can Be Testimonial:* If I ask you if you are happy to read this book and you nod your head from side to side without speaking, I know what you are thinking. You are conveying your thoughts without words. Your response is an action, but it is testimonial.

OVERVIEW OF THE BLACKLETTER LAW

The Fifth Amendment protects a person from being compelled to be a witness against himself. That raises the question of what it means to be a "witness." The Supreme Court has adopted a somewhat broad understanding of "witness." Importantly, a person's out-of-court statements to the police qualify, even though the person is not under oath and sitting in a courtroom. But the word "witness" is not all-encompassing. Some incriminating evidence that police gather from a person's words or actions is not covered by the Fifth Amendment because it is not testimonial. In short, testimonial communications are covered by the Fifth Amendment, while non-testimonial evidence is not.

A communication is testimonial if it reveals information from a person's thoughts. If a person has to think about something and then reveal information based on those thoughts, the response will be testimonial.

Verbal or written communications are usually testimonial. If a police officer asks you a question and you answer, your response is testimonial. There are exceptions, however. If police arrange a lineup and have everyone in the lineup say the same words so that a witness can hear the sound of their voices, the verbal statements are non-testimonial. The answers do not reflect the thoughts of the people in the lineup. The words only show the timbre of their voices. Similarly, if police have a suspect give a handwriting sample, that is non-testimonial. Even though the suspect wrote words on the page, the words are there to show what his handwriting looks like, not what the suspect thinks about anything.

Physical actions or displays are usually non-testimonial. This issue often comes up in drunk-driving cases. If police ask a person to walk in a line heel-to-toe or to touch their finger to their nose with their eyes closed, these actions are non-testimonial. The suspect's actions reveal their level of intoxication, not any particular thoughts. Similarly, asking a person to stand in a lineup, try on a piece of clothing before the jury, or walk to show a limp are all non-testimonial actions. They reveal physical evidence, not thoughts. There are exceptions to the general proposition that actions are non-testimonial, though. If I ask you a question and you respond by nodding your head up-and-down or side-to-side, you have conveyed your thoughts, even though you did not use any words.

EXAM TRAPS TO AVOID

- Just because a person is compelled to do something (e.g., stand in a lineup) does not mean the evidence is testimonial. Whether something is testimonial turns on whether it reveals a person's thoughts, not whether they were compelled.
- Just because a blood draw is non-testimonial and is not covered by the Fifth Amendment does not mean that the Fourth Amendment does not apply. To draw bodily fluids, the police need a warrant or an exception to the warrant requirement.

MULTIPLE-CHOICE QUESTIONS

Question 139

Police arrest Sam for drunk driving, take him to the police station, and place him in a locked interview room where he is left alone for 15 minutes. When the officers return, they ask Sam to take 10 heel-to-toe steps in one direction and to then turn around and take 10 heel-to-toe steps to walk back to where he started. Sam fails this test. Shortly thereafter, a nurse comes into the room and takes a sample of Sam's blood to test his blood-alcohol level. Sam vigorously objects, but the officers tell him he has no choice. The blood test demonstrates that Sam has a blood-alcohol level of .21, well over the legal limit. Which of the following best states the law?

A) The heel-to-toe test is inadmissible because Sam was not read his *Miranda* rights before being asked to do it, and the blood test is inadmissible because Sam refused to consent to it.

B) The heel-to-toe test is inadmissible because Sam was not read his *Miranda* rights before being asked to do it, but the blood test is admissible so long as the police had a warrant for the blood draw.

C) The heel-to-toe test is admissible because Sam's movements are non-testimonial, and the blood test is inadmissible because Sam must consent in writing.

D) The heel-to-toe test is admissible because Sam's movements are non-testimonial, and the blood test is admissible so long as the police had a warrant for the blood draw.

Question 140

Assume the same facts as Question 139, except this time the officer arrested Sam for drunk driving, brought him to the police station, and then instructed him to state his name and date of birth. Sam answered correctly, but slurred his words. Would Sam's answer be testimonial or non-testimonial?

A) Testimonial because Sam had to reveal factual information from his thoughts.

B) Non-testimonial because Sam's answers reveal his level of intoxication, not his thoughts.

Question 141

Assume the same facts as Question 140, in which the officer asks Sam his name and date of birth and Sam replied correctly with slurred speech. This time the officer asks one more question: "When you turned six years old, do you remember what date that was?" Sam responded, "No, I don't." Sam now claims that the sixth birthday question was testimonial. Is he correct?

A) Yes, because the question effectively forced him to respond with information about his thoughts—namely that he was admitting he was too intoxicated to figure out the date of his sixth birthday.

B) No, because the question and answer are only revealing that Sam is intoxicated, which is a physical manifestation.

Question 142

Police arrest Benicio for a bank robbery. Shortly after arrest, the officers put Benicio in a lineup against his will so that the bank employees can try to identify him. One employee tells the police, "I think that's him, but I'm not sure. I would recognize his voice, though. He told us to 'put the money in the bag,' so you should make him say that." The officers then order Benicio to step forward and loudly say "Put the money in the bag." Thereafter, two bank employees say that Benicio was the robber. Which of the following is correct?

A) Forcing Benicio to be in the lineup violates the Fifth Amendment. Forcing Benicio to say "Put the money in the bag" also violates the Fifth Amendment.

B) Forcing Benicio to be in the lineup violates the Fifth Amendment, but forcing him to say "Put the money in the bag" is not a Fifth Amendment violation.

C) Forcing Benicio to be in the lineup is constitutional, but forcing him to say "Put the money in the bag" is testimonial and violates the Fifth Amendment.

D) There is no Fifth Amendment violation in forcing Benicio into the lineup, nor is there a Fifth Amendment violation in forcing him to say "Put the money in the bag."

ANSWERS TO MULTIPLE-CHOICE QUESTIONS

Answer to Question 139

Answer A is incorrect. Half of the answer is correct. Police cannot draw Sam's blood without a warrant or an exception (such as consent). However, the first part of the answer is wrong. Police do not need to read suspects their *Miranda* rights before asking them to take sobriety tests like the heel-to-toe test because such tests do not reveal a person's thoughts. The heel-to-toe test is non-testimonial and thus outside of the Fifth Amendment's protection.

Answer B is incorrect. Half of this answer is correct as well. The blood draw would be permissible if the police had a warrant. However, for the reasons described in response to Answer A, the police do not need to read a suspect his *Miranda* rights before asking him to perform a sobriety test. The heel-to-toe test is non-testimonial and thus outside of the Fifth Amendment's protection.

Answer C is incorrect. As noted above, the heel-to-toe test is non-testimonial. This portion of the answer is correct. A person can consent to a blood draw without doing so in writing. While it might be wise for the police department to get the consent in writing so that there will be no dispute later, the Fourth Amendment does not require it.

Answer D is correct. As noted above, the heel-to-toe test is non-testimonial because it does not reveal a person's thoughts and is therefore outside of the Fifth Amendment's protection. A blood draw is permissible if the police have a warrant.

Answer to Question 140

Answer B is correct. The Supreme Court concluded in *Pennsylvania v. Muniz* (1990) that providing his name and date of birth were akin to standing in a lineup and saying his name aloud. They did not reveal his thoughts and instead just showed his slurred speech. Sam's answer was therefore non-testimonial.

Answer to Question 141

Answer A is correct. This question also comes from *Pennsylvania v. Muniz* (1990). The Supreme Court held that the answer to the sixth birthday question was not revealing a physical attribute, such as slurred speech or bodily movement. Rather, the answer revealed Sam's thoughts. He stated to the officer that he could not identify the date of his sixth birthday. This information about his thoughts is testimonial and thus covered by the Fifth Amendment.

Answer to Question 142

Answer D is correct. Forcing a person to be in a lineup is not testimonial. A lineup reveals a person's physical appearance, not their thoughts. Forcing Benicio to say "Put the money in the bag" is also not testimonial. Although Benicio is saying the same words that the perpetrator uttered during the crime, the words do not reveal Benicio's thoughts. Benicio's statement "Put the money in the bag" serves only to allow witnesses to hear the timbre of his voice. This is a physical manifestation, not a revelation of Benicio's thoughts. Accordingly, it is non-testimonial.

CHAPTER 26
Immunity

The Rule: If the prosecutor gives a person immunity, that will eliminate the Fifth Amendment protection and require the person to answer questions.

Critical Points

- There are two types of immunity: (1) transactional immunity; and (2) use and derivative use immunity. Both types of immunity protect a person's statement from being used against them and thus eliminate their ability to invoke the Fifth Amendment as a reason not to answer questions.
- Transactional immunity is the broader type of immunity. If a prosecutor gives a person transactional immunity, the person cannot later be prosecuted for offenses related to the testimony. Transactional immunity is broader than the Fifth Amendment because it not only forbids the statement from being used against the suspect, but also forbids the person from even being prosecuted. Because it is so valuable, prosecutors typically only give transactional immunity when a person is pleading guilty.
- Use and derivative use immunity is coterminous with the Fifth Amendment. In other words, use and derivative use immunity exactly overlap the protection afforded by the Fifth Amendment. If a person is given use and derivative use immunity, the prosecutor cannot use their statement or any evidence found as a result of their statement against them. It is theoretically possible that prosecutors could still bring charges against a person who was given use and derivative use immunity (though it does not happen often).

- Prosecutors have near-total power to give (or refuse to give) immunity. A person cannot turn down immunity. If the prosecutor confers immunity, the person must accept it.
- When prosecutors want to compel a statement, they only need to give use and derivative use immunity. Prosecutors do not have to give transactional immunity if they don't want to. And a suspect cannot refuse to give a statement on the grounds that they "only" got use and derivative use immunity rather than transactional immunity.
- If a person is given immunity and still refuses to testify, she can be held in contempt of court and jailed.

OVERVIEW OF THE BLACKLETTER LAW

In building a case, prosecutors often want information from a witness who does not want to give it up. Imagine a drug gang with a kingpin at the top who employs dealers, lookouts, and bodyguards to make the drug conspiracy work successfully. Then imagine that police arrest a low-level player, such as one of the dealers who is selling $10 bags of drugs on the corner. The low-level dealer is not a significant player in the operation and the prosecutor is much more interested in prosecuting the kingpin. The low-level dealer does not want to incriminate himself, so he refuses to give a statement about himself or the kingpin. The prosecutor can get around this situation by conferring immunity on the low-level dealer. Once the dealer has immunity, his Fifth Amendment privilege is eliminated, because nothing he says can be used against him. Immunity thus requires the dealer to testify.

There are two types of immunity: (1) transactional immunity and (2) use and derivative use immunity. Transactional immunity is much broader. Transactional immunity prevents a person's statement from being used against them and it also prevents them from being prosecuted for any of the topics they testified about. Transactional immunity is broader than the Fifth Amendment, which only protects against compelled incriminating statements. Because transactional immunity is so broad, prosecutors do not typically give it unless a person is pleading guilty.

Use and derivative use immunity is coterminous with the Fifth Amendment. That means the prosecution cannot use any statement made by the person, nor can they use any evidence derived from that statement. Imagine that a prosecutor confers use and derivative immunity on Barry and he then says, "I was involved in the robbery with Charles and we buried the gun behind a tree." The police later find the gun buried behind the tree. The prosecution cannot use Barry's statement against him, nor can the prosecution use the gun the police found as a result of Barry's confession. This does not mean the prosecutor cannot bring bank robbery charges against Barry.

If there is completely separate evidence of the crime—for instance, security camera footage showing Barry at the crime scene—the prosecution could bring charges based on the other evidence. Use and derivative use immunity does not forbid prosecution—it only forbids use of the compelled testimony and evidence found from the compelled testimony. (Of course, prosecutors often choose not to bring a prosecution even if they are allowed to.)

As noted, use and derivative use immunity is coterminous with the Fifth Amendment. This means that the two concepts completely overlap. As a result, when a person has use and derivative use immunity, they have the same protection as the Fifth Amendment. (And when a person has transactional immunity, they have greater protection than the Fifth Amendment.) Because immunity provides at least as much protection as the Fifth Amendment, a person's ability to rely on the Fifth Amendment is eliminated. The person must answer police questions and testify in court. They cannot rely on the Fifth Amendment's self-incrimination clause as a reason to refuse to testify because their statements are immunized and they therefore cannot incriminate themselves. In our drug gang example above, the low-level dealer may not want to turn on the drug kingpin and incriminate him. (Drug kingpins are known to kill people who provide evidence against them.) But the low-level dealer will not have any Fifth Amendment privilege to rely on. The low-level dealer will have two choices: (1) testify or (2) be held in contempt.

A final important point is that a person cannot refuse immunity. The low-level dealer cannot say "I don't want immunity, because it would be dangerous for me to testify against the kingpin." Nor can a person say "You're only offering me use and derivative use immunity and I will only testify if you give me transactional immunity." Because the Fifth Amendment is coterminous with use and derivative use immunity, the person must accept it and cannot hold out for the broader transactional immunity.

EXAM TRAPS TO AVOID

- A person cannot refuse immunity.
- A person who has been provided with use and derivative use immunity cannot hold out for transactional immunity.
- Look beyond the statement itself. The reason the doctrine is called *use and derivative use* immunity is that it applies not just to statements, but also to evidence found as a result of immunized statements. If police find additional evidence as a result of an immunized confession, that evidence is not admissible.

MULTIPLE-CHOICE QUESTIONS

Question 143

Oliver receives a subpoena instructing him to testify before a grand jury investigating a plot to kill a U.S. senator. The prosecutor grants Oliver use and derivative use immunity and demands that he testify about all that he knows. Oliver resists, stating that he does not want to talk, but the prosecutor says he has no choice. Oliver eventually tells the grand jury that he was involved in the plot and the location where the conspirators meet. The police follow up on Oliver's statements, find the meeting location, and discover evidence that Oliver has built a bomb that was to be used to blow up the senator's car. Which of the following correctly describes the prosecutor's options?

A) The prosecutor cannot use Oliver's statements to the grand jury or the bomb as evidence against Oliver because he has immunity.

B) The prosecutor cannot prosecute Oliver because he was not read his *Miranda* rights and all of the evidence is fruit of the poisonous tree.

C) The prosecutor can use the bomb as evidence in a conspiracy prosecution against Oliver, but he cannot use Oliver's testimony to the grand jury.

D) The prosecutor can use Oliver's testimony because, even though he was granted immunity, it is trumped by the public safety exception.

Question 144

Assume the same facts as Question 143. For purposes of this question, though, imagine that Oliver told the prosecutor, "I don't want your immunity. If I gave up information on the other conspirators they would surely kill me. There's no way I'm saying anything." Which of the following is correct?

A) The prosecutor cannot force a person to accept immunity.

B) Normally, the prosecutor can force a person to accept immunity, although not in situations like this where the person has raised a claim of personal safety.

C) The prosecutor can force a person to accept immunity.

D) In cases where the prosecutor wants to confer immunity but the recipient wants to reject it, the judge must make a final determination whether the testimony is necessary.

Question 145

Assume the same facts as Questions 143 and 144. For purposes of this question, though, assume that Oliver said, "Use and derivative use immunity is not sufficient. I will testify, but I have to be granted transactional immunity first. Otherwise, I'm sticking with my Fifth Amendment right not to incriminate myself." Can Oliver do this?

A) Yes. The Fifth Amendment protection against self-incrimination is coterminous with transactional immunity. He cannot be forced to accept a lesser level of immunity that would cause him to lose his Fifth Amendment rights.

B) No. The Fifth Amendment protection against self-incrimination is coterminous with use and derivative use immunity. Although the prosecutor has the option to confer greater protection, she does not have to.

Question 146

Cal was apprehended for a bank robbery. Cal admitted to being a minor player in the operation but would not say anything else. The prosecutor gave Cal transactional immunity and demanded his statement. Cal confessed to the bank robbery, identified his coconspirators, and told the police where they hid the weapons and the money. The police tracked down the evidence. The next day, a witness showed up at the police station. The witness said that she was about to enter the bank when she saw three men walking in with guns. She hid behind a tree while they walked in and stayed there until they walked out. The witness said that when the three men came out that one of them pulled off his mask as he was getting into the getaway vehicle. The witness was sure that the man was Cal because she had been his high school math teacher just two years earlier. The prosecutor decides to charge Cal with bank robbery. Which of the following is correct?

A) The prosecutor can bring bank robbery charges against Cal as long as the prosecutor does not try to introduce into evidence Cal's confession, the guns, or the money.

B) The prosecutor can bring bank robbery charges against Cal and introduce any evidence because Cal was not a minor player.

C) The prosecutor cannot bring bank robbery charges because Cal has immunity from prosecution.

D) The prosecutor cannot bring bank robbery charges because the witness's identification is derivative evidence.

ANSWERS TO MULTIPLE-CHOICE QUESTIONS

Answer to Question 143

Answer A is correct. Because Oliver has use and derivative use immunity, the prosecutor cannot use any incriminating statements Oliver made after being granted immunity. The prosecutor also cannot use any evidence derived from Oliver's statements, which includes the bomb found as a result of Oliver's statements.

Answer B is incorrect. Because Oliver had use and derivative use immunity, he was not at risk of self-incrimination. Accordingly, his Fifth Amendment rights have effectively been eliminated and it is therefore not possible for there to be a *Miranda* violation. In any event, as described in Chapter 34, the fruit of the poisonous tree doctrine ordinarily does not apply to *Miranda* violations.

Answer C is incorrect. Oliver has use and *derivative* use immunity. This means that prosecutors cannot use his statement to the grand jury and they also cannot use any evidence found as a result of that statement. Therefore the bomb is not admissible.

Answer D is incorrect. There is a public safety exception to the *Miranda* doctrine (See Chapter 31.) The public safety doctrine does not override a grant of immunity, however. Once a prosecutor has conferred immunity and procured an incriminating statement, the prosecutor cannot reverse the immunity grant and use the statement against the individual.

Answer to Question 144

Answer A is incorrect. The prosecutor can in fact force a person to accept immunity.

Answer B is incorrect. A person cannot reject immunity by claiming that their personal safety would be compromised.

Answer C is correct. Prosecutors have unilateral power to confer immunity. They can force a person to accept immunity.

Answer D is incorrect. Prosecutors have unilateral power to confer immunity. The judge cannot overrule the prosecutor's decision by concluding that the witness's testimony is not necessary.

Answer to Question 145

Answer B is correct. The Fifth Amendment protection against self-incrimination is coterminous with use and derivative use immunity. Use and derivative use immunity provides the same protection as the Fifth Amendment's self-incrimination clause. That means if a prosecutor confers use and derivative use immunity, a witness is not losing any Fifth Amendment protection. While Oliver would surely like to have transactional immunity (which is broader and affords protection against prosecution), the prosecutor is under no obligation to give more protection than what is afforded by the Fifth Amendment.

Answer to Question 146

Answer A is incorrect. This answer choice describes what would be correct if the prosecutor had given Cal use and derivative use immunity. But in this question Cal was given transactional immunity, which means he cannot be prosecuted for crimes related to the statements he gave.

Answer B is incorrect. Cal has transactional immunity. The fact that a witness claims Cal might have been more than just a "minor player" does not provide a basis for retracting the transactional immunity.

Answer C is correct. Cal has transactional immunity. As such, he cannot be prosecuted for any crime he gave statements about under that immunity grant. Because Cal made incriminating statements about the bank robbery pursuant to his grant of transactional immunity, he cannot be prosecuted for the bank robbery.

Answer D is incorrect. This answer is factually inaccurate. The witness came forward separately from Cal's incriminating statements. Therefore the evidence is not derivative. In any event, Cal does not have use and derivative use immunity. He has transactional immunity.

STEP 2
Was the Confession Voluntary or Coerced?

Chapter 27: Voluntariness of Confessions

The Fifth Amendment protects against coerced confessions. We are often so focused on the *Miranda* doctrine that we forget to stop and consider whether the confession violated the Fifth Amendment because it was coerced. You should always look at the police conduct and ask, under the totality of the circumstances, whether the officers used physical force, threat of force, or extreme psychological trickery to improperly extract a confession.

CHAPTER 27
Voluntariness of Confessions

THE RULE: If a court concludes, under a totality of the circumstances test, that police coerced a confession, it is not admissible.

Critical Points

- *The Test*: In determining whether a confession was coerced, courts look at the totality of the circumstances to determine whether a suspect's will was overborne.
- *The Factors to Consider*: Courts consider the actions of the officers and the circumstances of the interrogation. For instance, courts might consider the length of the interrogation, whether it occurred late at night, and whether the suspect remained handcuffed. Courts also consider the characteristics of the suspect who confessed. Many factors are relevant, such as the suspect's age, his level of education, and prior experience with law enforcement.
- *Three Typical Scenarios*: The three main situations in which courts find coerced confessions are:
    - The officers used physical force or deprivation of basic necessities (such as food or water);
    - The officers threatened physical force or deprivation of basic necessities; or
    - The officers used extreme psychological pressure.
- *Not Sufficient to Demonstrate Coercion*: Some police tactics—such as promising leniency or lying about the strength of the evidence—almost never amount to coercion. Police regularly promise that they will put in a good word with the prosecutor if the suspect confesses. Police also regularly en-

gage in deception, such as claiming that they have more evidence than they actually do. These tactics might encourage a suspect to confess, but except in unusual cases this is not enough to render a confession involuntary.

- *State Action Is Required*: There cannot be a coerced confession without state action, usually by a police officer. If a person is delusional and believes God or Satan is forcing them to confess, the confession is not coerced because there was no state action.
- *Fruit of the Poisonous Tree Doctrine*: If a coerced confession leads police to other evidence, that additional evidence will be suppressed under the fruit of the poisonous tree doctrine. Both the confession and any evidence the confession led to will be suppressed.
- *No Impeachment Exception*: A coerced confession is not admissible in the prosecutor's case-in-chief and it is also not admissible as impeachment evidence.

OVERVIEW OF THE BLACKLETTER LAW

The Fifth Amendment forbids coerced confessions. Courts sometimes call these involuntary confessions. The terms "coerced confession" and "involuntary confession" mean the same thing.

The Supreme Court has set out very few bright-line rules for what amounts to coercion. Instead, courts consider involuntariness claims under a totality of the circumstances test. When trying to figure out whether a confession was coerced, the first thing to look at is the actions of the police. Very aggressive police tactics can render a confession involuntary. Most obviously, hitting a suspect can be coercive. Depriving a suspect of food or water for a long period may also be sufficient to render a suspect's confession involuntary. Interrogating a person for a very long time in the middle of the night might also be coercive. Also consider whether a suspect was handcuffed or otherwise in a very uncomfortable situation while being interrogated. In short, physical force and certain conditions during an interrogation can render it unconstitutionally coercive. There is no bright-line rule, though. You must consider each case under its own facts and under a totality of the circumstances test.

In addition to physical force, the *threat* of physical force can render a confession involuntary. Even if a suspect is in a comfortable chair and the officer never touches him, the confession can be involuntary if the officer threatened to beat him up unless he confessed. A threat can be coercive if it involves physical harm or if it involves other types of harm. In one case, the Supreme Court said a threat to wrongfully arrest a suspect's wife rendered his confession involuntary. While we know the outcome in cases where the Supreme Court has already analyzed a detailed set of facts, it is hard to know in other cases whether a threat renders the confession involuntary. Once again, you must consider the totality of the circumstances.

A third way in which a confession can be involuntary is if the police utilize extreme psychological pressure. For instance, if police lied to a suspect and said the government would take away his children for refusing to cooperate, this kind of deception *could* be too much. They key word in the previous sentence is "could." Police deception or even outright lying does not automatically make a confession involuntary. To the contrary, police often lie to suspects, and courts regularly permit this tactic. Thus, if police lie to a suspect and say his fingerprints were at the crime scene, or that a witness saw him shoot the victim, or that they had recovered the murder weapon, those lies are probably not enough to make a confession involuntary. I say "probably not" because the involuntariness test is a totality of the circumstances test. That means we do not just look at the lie the police told, but the entire context of the interrogation.

In considering the full context under a totality of the circumstances test, courts must consider not just the police action but also the relevant characteristics of the suspect. If the police tell an elaborate lie to a young, mentally disabled suspect, there is some (small) prospect that the confession could be involuntary. By contrast, if the suspect is a well-educated, middle-aged lawyer, there is practically zero chance that the lie could render the confession involuntary. In short, when assessing the totality of the circumstances test it is important to consider the characteristics of the suspect. Characteristics like age, education, IQ, and prior experience with the criminal justice system are all relevant.

Although a totality of the circumstances inquiry could go either way, it is common for courts to reject claims that confessions were involuntary. Put differently, the police conduct usually needs to be pretty bad for a confession to be deemed involuntary.

When courts find a confession to be involuntary the repercussions are serious, though. The confession itself will be excluded. Moreover, exceptions that apply in the Fourth Amendment context and in the *Miranda* context will be inapplicable. For example, evidence seized in violation of the Fourth Amendment can usually be used to impeach a defendant when they take the witness stand. But a coerced confession cannot be used to impeach the defendant. Similarly, if police violate the *Miranda* doctrine (see Chapter 34) physical evidence they find as a result of the un-Mirandized confession will be admissible. But physical evidence found as a result of a coerced confession will be excluded.

One final issue that sometimes comes up with coerced confessions is state action. In order for a defendant to argue that his confession was involuntary and should be suppressed, he must point to some state action. In other words, the police officer must have done something to coerce the confession. If a person confesses because they believe God ordered them to confess, they might later think that the confession was involuntary. After all, a person might believe they had no choice but to confess when God told them to do so. That argument will fail in court, though, because there was no state action since the police officer did not do anything to coerce the confession.

EXAM TRAPS TO AVOID

- It is difficult for professors to write multiple-choice questions about coerced confessions because there are very few bright-line rules. Each case is very fact-specific. Accordingly, the correct answer is often "it depends." Be on the lookout for answer choices that are not all or nothing.
- Lying to a suspect is usually not enough to render a confession involuntary.
- A police officer's promise that prosecutors will go easier on a suspect who confesses is usually not enough to render a confession involuntary.

MULTIPLE-CHOICE QUESTIONS

Question 147

The police are investigating a bank robbery and they have probable cause to believe that Bill was one of the robbers. The officers arrest Bill on Tuesday afternoon and bring him to the police station. After booking him, the officers move him to an interrogation room. The officers read Bill his *Miranda* rights, and he waives his right to counsel and right to silence. The officers tell Bill, "Look, we know you robbed the bank. Two eyewitnesses have already identified you. We just need to know who you were working with. If you tell us who else was in on the robbery, the prosecutor will probably go much easier on you." Within 15 minutes of the interrogation starting, Bill confesses and implicates the other robbers. It turns out that no eyewitness had identified Bill as the robber. The police simply lied to Bill to get him to confess. Which of the following is correct?

A) Bill's confession is involuntary because the police engaged in deception.

B) Bill's confession is involuntary because the police lied to Bill and also told him that the prosecutor would go easier on him if he confessed.

C) Bill's confession cannot be coerced because the officers read him his *Miranda* rights and he waived them.

D) Bill's confession was not coerced because under the totality of the circumstances the police did not overbear his will.

Question 148

For purposes of this question, assume that Bill sits in the interrogation room for a few minutes waiting for the officers to come in, and during that time Bill hears a voice. Bill believes it was the voice of God telling him that he must confess. Bill shakes his head and says to himself that he doesn't want to confess and that he didn't commit the crime. Bill hears the voice again, though, and the voice says, "You have no choice, you must confess or you will be taken by Satan to spend eternity in hell." The officers enter a few minutes later and introduce themselves. The officers ask Bill if he robbed the bank and he says, "I don't think I should have to tell you." One of the officers says, "You know, a lot of people feel like that. But let me tell you, people always feel better when they get things off their chest. People who tell the truth have a clean conscience and they can be at one with God." Upon hearing the word "God," Bill immediately confesses. The entire interrogation lasts less than three minutes. Bill subsequently moves to suppress his confession, saying it was coerced. How should the court rule?

A) The confession was coerced because the police unfairly manipulated the fact that Bill was hearing the voice of God tell him to confess.

B) The confession was coerced because Bill's delusions about hearing the voice of God tell him he "must" confess rendered his confession involuntary.

C) The confession was not coerced because the officers did not know about the voices in Bill's head and thus did nothing to manipulate his religious beliefs in a way that rendered the confession involuntary.

D) The confession was not coerced because it is impossible for a three-minute interrogation to be coercive.

Question 149

Assume for purposes of this question that police know that Bill was extremely religious. The officers find the minister from the church that Bill attended when he was a child. The officers bring the minister to the station to help them interrogate Bill. After the officers enter the interrogation room, they say they found someone who they think Bill should talk to. The minister then enters the room, sits down in front of Bill, and says, "God knows what you've done. You should confess your crimes so that you can be saved." A few minutes later, Bill confesses. Which of the following is correct?

A) In considering whether Bill's confession was involuntary, the court should consider that the police knew Bill was extremely religious.

B) In considering whether Bill's confession was involuntary, the court should only focus on the police questioning and not the minister's statements because he is a private non-state actor.

C) The court should reject Bill's attempt to suppress the confession because he was not subjected to force or threat of force.

D) The court should reject Bill's attempt to suppress the confession because the police have not said anything that is provably false.

Question 150

Police went to Jasmine's home to question her about her involvement in a recent jewel theft. When Jasmine answered the door and saw the officers, she let them in. Jasmine invited the officers to sit down at her kitchen table and she made coffee for all of them to drink. After a few minutes of discussion, one of the officers said, "Enough of all this fake hospitality. We know you did it." The officer grabbed Jasmine's hand and bent her fingers backward toward her forearm. At first the officer applied mild pressure and Jasmine said nothing. Then the officer pulled her fingers back even more forcefully and said, "You're wasting our time." Jasmine yelled out, "Stop, that hurts! Okay, I was in on it." Is Jasmine's confession admissible?

A) Yes, because she was not in custody and thus the Fifth Amendment does not apply.

B) Yes, because she invited the officers into her home and she was free to ask them to leave at any time.

C) Yes, because even though the officer applied physical force, there is nothing to indicate Jasmine confessed only because of the force.

D) No, because the officer procured the confession through physical force, rendering it involuntary.

E) No, because the police never read Jasmine her *Miranda* warnings.

Question 151

Assume the same facts as Question 150. In confessing, Jasmine not only said "I was in on it" but also provided a lot of details about the jewel theft. After getting Jasmine's detailed confession, the police investigated three new witnesses who they had found independent of their interrogation of Jasmine. The three new witnesses all clearly linked Jasmine to the jewel theft. The evidence therefore indicates that Jasmine's confession was 100% accurate. If we presume that Jasmine's confession was involuntary, but that it was 100% accurate, what should the court do?

A) Admit the confession because it is accurate evidence.

B) Suppress the confession because a confession can be involuntary even if it is 100% true.

Question 152

After Maynard was shot and killed, police arrested Kevin for the murder. During an interrogation, Kevin repeatedly denied being anywhere near the scene of the crime. Eventually, one of the detectives got frustrated by Kevin's unwillingness to confess and started hitting and kicking Kevin. The detective continued to hurt Kevin until he confessed to being near the scene of the crime, killing Maynard, and hiding the gun in a dumpster behind the Starbucks on Main Street. Police thereafter went to the Starbucks and located the gun, which had Kevin's fingerprints on it and matched the bullets removed from Maynard's body. In response to Kevin's motion to suppress, the judge forbid prosecutors from introducing Kevin's confession in their case-in-chief because it had been coerced. The judge did allow the prosecutors to introduce the gun. Additionally, when Kevin testified at trial and said he was never near the crime scene, the judge allowed the prosecutors to introduce Kevin's confession as impeachment evidence. How should the trial judge have ruled?

I. The gun should be admissible because the fruit of the poisonous tree doctrine does not apply to coerced confessions.
II. The gun should not be admissible because it is fruit of the coerced confession.
III. The confession should be admissible as impeachment evidence.
IV. The confession should not be admissible because coerced confessions cannot be admitted even as impeachment evidence.

A) I and III
B) I and IV
C) II and III
D) II and IV

ANSWERS TO MULTIPLE-CHOICE QUESTIONS

Answer to Question 147

Answer A is incorrect. The police did lie to Bill about the eyewitness identification. However, ordinary police deception (including lying about the strength of the evidence against a suspect) is not enough to render a confession involuntary.

Answer B is incorrect. This is a closer case than Answer A, but still is not enough to render a confession involuntary. Lying to a suspect about the evidence and telling him that the prosecutor will probably go easier on him if he confesses are standard police tactics. Courts regularly uphold interrogations that are far more manipulative than this.

Answer C is incorrect. *Miranda* is a separate obligation that police must satisfy. The fact that the officers follow their *Miranda* obligations does not mean that the confession cannot be involuntary. For example, if police read a suspect his *Miranda* rights and got a proper waiver, but then proceeded to beat the suspect until he confessed, the confession would be coerced, even if it did not violate *Miranda*.

Answer D is correct. The voluntariness of confessions is governed by a totality of the circumstances test. Although there are no bright-line rules, it would be exceedingly unlikely that the facts of this case would be sufficient to render the confession involuntary.

Answer to Question 148

Answer A is incorrect. The officers did not know about the voices in Bill's head and therefore those voices are not relevant for determining voluntariness. The officers' statements about feeling better by confessing and being at one with God are relevant considerations, but those statements are not so psychologically manipulative as to be coercive.

Answer B is incorrect. God cannot coerce a confession for Fifth Amendment purposes. There must be state action. This answer choice is therefore incorrect because it suggests that Bill's confession could be involuntary simply because he thought God was ordering him to confess.

Answer C is correct. The officers were not engaged in particularly deceptive behavior. While they did use a psychological ploy to tug at Bill's emotions, such techniques do not ordinarily render a confession involuntary.

Answer D is incorrect. A three-minute interrogation could be coercive in some circumstances. For instance, if police physically beat a suspect, his confession would be involuntary even if the entire length of the interrogation was short.

Answer to Question 149

Answer A is correct. The voluntariness of a confession is determined under a totality of the circumstances test. When police engage in deceptive tactics, we do not look only at the police tactics. We must also consider the characteristics of the suspect. Here the police likely brought the minister in to help them because they knew that Bill was extremely religious. In determining whether the psychological manipulation tactics the police used were coercive, we must consider not just the presence of the minister but also that Bill was extremely religious.

Answer B is incorrect. The minister is a private citizen. However, the question makes clear that he is acting at the direction of law enforcement. Accordingly, there is state action.

Answer C is incorrect. A confession can be involuntary even if there is no force or threat of force. Although it does not happen often, a court can find a confession to be involuntary because the police utilized psychological manipulation that was so extreme as to be coercive.

Answer D is incorrect. Extreme psychological manipulation can be coercive even if the police do not say anything that is provably false. The key factor is not whether the police lied, but instead whether they engaged in extreme psychological manipulation.

Answer to Question 150

Answer A is incorrect. For the *Miranda* doctrine to apply, there must be custodial interrogation. But this is not a *Miranda* question. The officer engaged in illegal physical force to procure a confession. As such, the confession is coerced.

Answer B is incorrect. This answer is nearly identical to Answer A and is wrong for the same reason. Jasmine was not in custody. But that inquiry is not relevant here.

The question is whether the police coerced the confession through physical force. They did.

Answer C is incorrect. This answer is factually incorrect. Jasmine had not confessed before the officer forcibly bent her fingers. She confessed immediately after saying "Stop, that hurts."

Answer D is correct. When police use physical force—in this case painfully bending Jasmine's fingers in a way that might break them—the subsequent confession is involuntary.

Answer E is incorrect. The police would not have read Jasmine her *Miranda* warnings in this case because she was probably not in custody. (See Chapter 29). The *Miranda* warnings are not relevant here because even if the police complied with *Miranda*, their use of physical force renders the confession involuntary.

Answer to Question 151

Answer A is incorrect. The involuntariness test focuses on whether the confession is coerced. A confession does not cease to be coerced simply because it turns out to be true.

Answer B is correct. The Fifth Amendment protects against involuntary confessions, regardless of whether they turn out to be accurate or not. Guilty people, just like innocent people, have a Fifth Amendment right not to be compelled by force to provide incriminating information against themselves.

Answer to Question 152

The fruit of the poisonous tree doctrine *does* apply to coerced confessions. And there is no impeachment exception for coerced confessions. Accordingly, the prosecution cannot introduce the gun, nor can it introduce Kevin's statement as impeachment evidence. The reason is that coerced confessions are unacceptable and there should not be exceptions that allow the police to benefit from coercing a confession. Answer D is therefore correct. As we will see, the answer would be different if the police violated the *Miranda* doctrine rather than coercing the confession (see Chapter 34).

STEP 3
Does the *Miranda* Doctrine Apply? Custodial Interrogation

If the confession was voluntary, we must next consider the separate question of whether the police followed the *Miranda* doctrine. The *Miranda* doctrine applies when: (1) the suspect is in custody and (2) the police engage in interrogation.

Custody usually means the suspect is under arrest. But even if there has been no formal arrest, a court can still find that a defendant was in custody. Chapter 29 explores the factors that courts consider in determining custody, including the presence of a large number of officers, aggressive tone of voice by the officers, weapons being drawn, the time of day (e.g., late at night) and other factors.

Interrogation usually means that the police are asking questions. But the Court has recognized that the police can engage in interrogation by their statements or actions, even if they never ask anything in the form of a question. Chapter 30 explores the test for interrogation, which asks if the police conduct was reasonably likely to elicit an incriminating response.

Before digging into custody and interrogation, though, we start with Chapter 28, which provides a big-picture overview of the *Miranda* doctrine.

CHAPTER 28
Miranda: The Basics

THE RULE: For the police to engage in custodial interrogation, they must warn the suspect that he has the right to remain silent and the right to counsel, and they must obtain a valid waiver of those rights.

Critical Points

- *The Miranda Rights*:
  - You have the right to remain silent.
  - Anything you can say can be used against you in a court of law.
  - You have the right to an attorney.
  - If you cannot afford an attorney, one will be appointed prior to any questioning if you so desire.
- *Form of the Warnings*:
  - Many police departments give the warnings both verbally and in writing. But there is no requirement that police do both. Verbal or written warnings are acceptable.
  - The warnings do not have to be given in the exact way that they are listed in the *Miranda* decision. The warnings can be given out of order or paraphrased.
  - In rare cases, the officers will give the warnings so defectively (for example, omitting major portions) that they will not be sufficient.
- *Custodial Interrogation*: The warnings are only required if the suspect is in custody and subject to interrogation (See Chapters 29 and 30). There are a

few types of custodial interrogations where *Miranda* does not apply, though (See Chapter 31).

- *All Crimes*: The *Miranda* doctrine applies to all crimes, not just felonies.
- *Waiver*: In addition to giving the warnings, the police must also obtain a valid waiver of the *Miranda* rights from the suspect (See Chapter 32).
- *Fruit of the Poisonous Tree*: Except in unusual cases, *Miranda* does not have a fruit of the poisonous tree doctrine. This means that statements that violate *Miranda* will be suppressed, but other evidence found as a result of the suspect's confession will not be suppressed. (See Chapter 34).

OVERVIEW OF THE BLACKLETTER LAW

As we discussed in Chapter 27, the Fifth Amendment forbids coerced confessions. Under that rule, the voluntariness of a confession is judged by a totality of the circumstances test. Unfortunately, the Court's coerced confession jurisprudence proved to be hard to apply and offered very little protection to criminal defendants. The voluntariness test provided very few clear rules about what the police could do, and courts rarely found confessions to be coerced under the test. Suspects found themselves in a coercive environment with little legal protection.

To deal with the failures of the involuntariness doctrine, the Supreme Court added an additional layer of protection for suspects who are in the coercive environment of custodial interrogations. The Court's solution was to create a prophylactic rule for all interrogations that required the police to notify suspects of their rights prior to the beginning of any custodial interrogation.

In *Miranda v. Arizona* (1966), the Supreme Court required police to inform suspects that they have the right to remain silent, that anything they say can be used against them in a court of law, that they have the right to an attorney, and that if they cannot afford an attorney, one will be appointed for them prior to any questioning if they so desire.

Many observers predicted that the *Miranda* doctrine would lead to the end of confessions and that it would amount to a get-out-of-jail-free card for guilty defendants. This has not come to pass, however, because the Supreme Court has narrowed the *Miranda* doctrine in the years since it was handed down. A helpful way to understand the scope of the *Miranda* doctrine is to think of a broad protection that the Supreme Court has undercut at nearly every opportunity. Consider the following limitations.

The *Miranda* doctrine requires the police to read the warnings to suspects. However, the Court has repeatedly allowed police to read the warnings out of order, to change the language, or to even skip parts of the warnings without finding them to be defective. The warnings need not be given in writing or in easily accessible forms for suspects who may have difficulty understanding them.

The *Miranda* doctrine applies when the suspect is in custody and is subject to interrogation. Yet, in the years since *Miranda*, the Court has adopted narrow views of custody and interrogation (See Chapters 29 and 30). It has also exempted some categories of police interactions from *Miranda* altogether (See Chapter 31).

The *Miranda* doctrine requires that the police obtain a valid waiver before conducting an interrogation. On the flip side, the police must stop an interrogation if the suspect invokes his right to counsel or silence. The Court has adopted a broad view of waiver, making it easy for police to satisfy the waiver doctrine. And it has adopted a narrow view of invocation, making it hard for suspects to invoke their rights to counsel and silence. (See Chapters 32 and 33).

Confessions that violate *Miranda* will be suppressed, but the Court has decided that the fruit of the poisonous tree doctrine does not apply to *Miranda* violations (See Chapter 34).

EXAM TRAPS TO AVOID

- Be sure that the suspect is actually in custody before finding a *Miranda* violation (See Chapter 29).
- Be sure that the conduct the police are engaged in actually amounts to interrogation (See Chapter 30).
- Do not find a *Miranda* violation just because the warnings were not given in the exact order or because the police did not use the exact language that the Supreme Court used in its *Miranda* decision. Courts show police *a lot* of flexibility in the form of the warnings.
- Be sure to check that: (1) the warnings were given; *and* (2) the suspect actually waived his *Miranda* rights. Professors sometimes write questions in which the warnings were given but the suspect never waived.
- Do not assume that all evidence found as a result of a *Miranda* violation will be suppressed. For the most part, the fruit of the poisonous tree doctrine does not apply to *Miranda* violations. Usually, the incriminating confession will be suppressed, but other evidence found as a result of the confession will be admissible (See Chapter 34).

MULTIPLE-CHOICE QUESTIONS

Question 153

Police arrest Duncan for buying drugs. The officers handcuff him, bring him to the station, and place him in an interrogation room. The officers sit down at the desk across from Duncan and read him his *Miranda* rights: "You have the right to remain silent; anything you say can be used against you in a court of law; you have the right to an attorney; and if you cannot afford an attorney, one will be appointed to you prior to any questioning if you so desire." The officers also show him a piece of paper with the rights listed. Duncan reads the paper and the officers wait patiently for him to finish. After he puts it down, Duncan says, "Pass. I'm not talking." The officers respond, "That's how you want to play it, huh? You know the person you bought drugs from was a prostitute. It would be a shame if your wife and kids found about you hiring prostitutes. It would be terrible if all of your neighbors found out, too." Duncan immediately got upset and said, "It's not like that. I would never try to hire a prostitute. You have to believe me. My wife will be so upset if she thinks I did that." The officers responded, "Well, if you don't tell us what happened we're going to tell her you're paying for sex." Duncan responded, "If I tell you, will you promise not to tell my wife that you suspected me of prostitution?" After the officers nodded at Duncan, he responded, "I was trying to buy drugs. I've bought drugs on that corner before. I must have asked the wrong person this time, though. I swear I wasn't trying to solicit a prostitute." Is Duncan's confession that he had bought drugs before admissible?

A) No, because the police coerced him into waiving his *Miranda* rights by promising not to tell his wife in exchange for the confession.

B) Yes, because the officers never asked Duncan a specific question and thus did not interrogate him.

C) Yes, because he was properly Mirandized and confessed.

D) Yes, because he received the *Miranda* warnings both in writing and verbally.

Question 154

Assume the same facts as in Question 153. For purposes of this question, though, assume that the police never gave Duncan a paper with the warnings written on it. They only told him the warnings verbally. Have the police properly given the *Miranda* warnings?

A) Yes, because there is no specific required method of administering the *Miranda* warnings.

B) No, because the Supreme Court's decision in *Miranda v. Arizona* required the police to provide the warnings both verbally and in writing.

Question 155

Assume the same facts as in Questions 153 and 154. For purposes of this question, assume that the officers gave the *Miranda* warnings as follows:

> You have the right to remain silent. Anything you say can be used against you in court. You have a right to talk to a lawyer for advice before we ask you any questions, and to have him with you during questioning. You have this right to the advice and presence of a lawyer even if you cannot afford to hire one. We

> have no way of giving you a lawyer, but one will be appointed for you, if you wish, if and when you go to court. If you wish to answer questions now without a lawyer present, you have the right to stop answering questions at any time until you've talked to a lawyer.

Duncan's lawyer has moved to suppress the confession on the grounds that the officer's statement that "We have no way of giving you a lawyer, but one will be appointed for you, if you wish, if and when you go to court" undermines the *Miranda* doctrine because it suggests that the right to counsel is only for trial. How should the court rule?

A) The court should suppress the confession because the officers did not adequately convey the *Miranda* warnings and a reasonable person would not have understood their right to counsel during interrogation.

B) The court should admit the confession because the police do not have to state the rights exactly as written in the *Miranda* decision and in this case it was sufficiently clear that the suspect had a right to a lawyer.

Question 156

Assume the same facts as in Questions 153–155. For purposes of this question, assume that the officers gave the *Miranda* warnings as follows:

> We have to give you the *Miranda* warnings so that you understand your rights. You can waive your rights of course, but that's up to you. You have the right to remain silent. You don't have to talk to us. Many people choose to talk, but you don't have to. You should know, though, that anything you say can be used against you in a court of law.

Duncan's lawyer moves to suppress the confession on the grounds that the warnings were improper. How should the court rule?

A) The warnings are inadequate and the confession should be suppressed.

B) The warnings are adequate and the confession should be admissible.

Question 157

Police receive a tip that Diane carried out a burglary at 123 Main Street. The officers investigate and find Diane's fingerprints at the scene, even though she does not live there. The officers obtain an arrest warrant and locate Diane. The officers handcuff her and bring her to the station. At the station, the officers sit Diane down at a desk and tell her they are going to do some paperwork to process her arrest. Diane says, "Can you take these handcuffs off? They're uncomfortable." The officers respond, "Sorry. Department policy requires that you remain in the handcuffs until we finish the paperwork and put you in the cell." Diane, who is very uncomfortable in the handcuffs, says, "Let's just get this over with so I can get these things off. I did it. I broke into 123 Main Street to steal their jewelry." Prior to trial, Diane's lawyer moves to suppress her confession as a violation of *Miranda*. How should the court rule?

A) The confession is admissible because Diane had not yet been put in a jail cell and was therefore not in custody.

B) The confession is admissible because Diane was not interrogated.

C) The confession should be suppressed because the police never read Diane her *Miranda* rights.

D) The confession should be suppressed because it is unconstitutionally coercive to take a confession from someone who is handcuffed.

Question 158

Quinn drives down the road at 70 mph in a 55-mph zone. Officer Taylor is in his police car using a radar gun and sees that Quinn is speeding. Officer Taylor turns on his sirens and pulls Quinn over. When Officer Taylor starts to write Quinn a speeding ticket, Quinn starts to yell that it is not fair because everyone speeds. Officer Taylor ignores her, and Quinn escalates the situation by calling Officer Taylor a bunch of rude names. In response, Officer Taylor rips up the ticket and orders Quinn out of the car. Officer Taylor arrests her for speeding (which is an arrestable offense under the state's criminal code). Officer Taylor handcuffs Quinn and locks her in the back of the police car. Officer Taylor then says, "You're not so tough now, are you? Why don't you just admit that you were speeding?" Quinn just wants to go home and she responds, "Yes, I was speeding." Quinn later moves to suppress her incriminating statement. Which of the following is correct?

A) The confession should be suppressed because Officer Taylor never read the *Miranda* rights and never obtained a valid waiver.

B) The confession should be admitted because the *Miranda* doctrine does not apply to misdemeanors such as the low-level traffic offense of speeding.

C) The confession should be admitted because Quinn was never in custody.

D) The confession should be admitted because Officer Taylor never conducted a custodial interrogation.

ANSWERS TO MULTIPLE-CHOICE QUESTIONS

Answer to Question 153

Answer A is correct. The officers provided the *Miranda* warnings verbally and in writing and Duncan responded to questions. Ordinarily, this would constitute a valid waiver. But here it appears that Duncan was coerced into waiving by threats from the officers to disseminate embarrassing information about him to his family and neighbors. A *Miranda* waiver cannot be valid if it is coerced.

Answer B is incorrect. The police engage in interrogation when they ask express questions or their functional equivalent. As we will explore in more detail in Chapter 30, the functional equivalent of express questioning is a statement or action that is reasonably likely to elicit an incriminating response. Here, the officers' colloquy with Duncan certainly was reasonably likely to elicit an incriminating response. Thus, even though the police did not ask express questions, they have engaged in interrogation.

Answer C is incorrect. The police properly gave Duncan the *Miranda* warnings. However, as explained above, Duncan's waiver was coerced. To comply with *Miranda*, the officers must adequately convey the *Miranda* rights and also obtain a valid waiver. They failed to obtain a valid waiver in this case.

Answer D is incorrect. Receiving the *Miranda* rights both in writing and verbally does not eliminate the obligation that the police obtain a valid waiver.

Answer to Question 154

Answer A is correct. The *Miranda* decision never specified the exact way in which the warnings must be administered. In subsequent decisions, courts have made clear that police are not obligated to provide the warnings both verbally and in writing.

Answer to Question 155

Answer B is correct. The Supreme Court has given the police a lot of leeway in how they convey the *Miranda* warnings. If the officers convey the gist of the *Miranda* protections then they are sufficient.

Answer to Question 156

Answer A is correct. Although the Supreme Court has given police flexibility in the way they read the warnings, the Court still requires that the core *Miranda* rights be conveyed to the suspect. Here the officers have interspersed comments when they have conveyed to Duncan that he has the right to remain silent. That is probably not a big enough problem to render the warnings invalid. However, there is a much bigger problem. The officers left out the *Miranda* warnings about the suspect having "the right to an attorney; and if you cannot afford an attorney, one will be appointed for you prior to any questioning if you so desire." Failure to convey the warning about the existence of the right to counsel is almost certainly fatal. Accordingly, the confession should be suppressed.

Answer to Question 157

Answer A is incorrect. A person can be in custody without being in a jail cell. Diane is handcuffed and has been brought to the police station. She is in custody. (For more detail on what constitutes custody, see Chapter 29.)

Answer B is correct. For the *Miranda* doctrine to apply, a person must be subjected to custodial interrogation. Diane is in custody, but the police have not interrogated her. The police have not asked her any questions, nor have they made any statements that are reasonably likely to call for an incriminating response. Because there is no interrogation, the police did not have to read Diane her *Miranda* warnings. (For more detail on what constitutes interrogation, see Chapter 30.)

Answer C is incorrect. As detailed above, police only have to read the *Miranda* warnings before custodial interrogation. Here, Diane was in custody, but she was not subject to interrogation.

Answer D is incorrect. Coerced confessions are not admissible. However, there is nothing here to suggest that Diane's confession is coerced. Diane was handcuffed in compliance with department policy and to ensure the safety of the officers. That is not unduly coercive.

Answer to Question 158

Answer A is correct. Even though this is an extremely low-level offense, the *Miranda* doctrine still applies. Quinn was in custody (because she was handcuffed and locked in the back of a police vehicle) and Officer Taylor questioned her about the crime (Why don't you just admit that you were speeding?"). The fact that this was a low-level misdemeanor does not excuse the officer's obligation to comply with *Miranda* before conducting a custodial interrogation.

Answer B is incorrect. The *Miranda* doctrine applies to all crimes, even low-level traffic misdemeanors.

Answer C is incorrect. Quinn was in custody when she was handcuffed and locked in the back of the police car.

Answer D is incorrect. This was a custodial interrogation. Officer Taylor questioned Quinn about whether she was speeding while she was handcuffed in the back of the police car. Both interrogation and custody are present.

CHAPTER 29

Is the Suspect in Custody for *Miranda* Purposes?

THE RULE: The *Miranda* doctrine applies only when the suspect is in custody. If the suspect is not in custody, the police can ask as many questions as they want without first having to read the *Miranda* warnings.

Critical Points

- If a suspect is not in custody, the police can question him without giving the *Miranda* warnings.
- Custody is analyzed from an objective standpoint. It does not matter what the officer thought or what the suspect thought. The question is whether the suspect's freedom has been curtailed to a degree consistent with a formal arrest.
- A person who has been formally arrested is always in custody.
- A person who has been handcuffed and locked in the back of a police car is almost always in custody.
- Location is an important factor in determining whether a person is in custody.
  - When a suspect is transported to the stationhouse, it is very likely he is in custody.
  - If the suspect is questioned in his home, he is probably not in custody.
- Location is not always determinative, however.
  - If a suspect voluntarily agrees to go to the stationhouse, he may not be in custody.

  - If a suspect is at home, but it is the middle of the night and four officers surround him with weapons drawn, he is probably in custody even though he is sitting in his own home.
- Courts consider many factors in determining whether a person is in custody. Here are some (but not all) factors that courts consider:
  - Number of officers
  - Tone of voice of the officers
  - Whether weapons are drawn
  - The length of the interaction
  - Time of day (e.g., late at night)
  - Whether other people were present
  - Whether the person was able to get up and move around.
- When police question someone under the age of 18, the juvenile's age is a factor to consider because children likely feel more restrained when interacting with the police than adults.
- Traffic stops (*Terry* stops) are not custodial. A person who is pulled over by the police for a traffic violation is seized under the Fourth Amendment, but she is not in custody for Fifth Amendment purposes. This means that the police can question drivers at most traffic stops without first reading them the *Miranda* rights.

OVERVIEW OF THE BLACKLETTER LAW

As we explored in Chapter 27, the Supreme Court created very few clear rules for determining whether a confession was involuntary. The *Miranda* doctrine was intended to provide suspects with clear guidance about their Fifth Amendment rights. Unfortunately, the *Miranda* doctrine has failed to establish clear, workable rules. The first area where we see this problem is the test for whether a person is in custody. The Supreme Court has adopted a few pretty clear rules for determining custody. In many cases, though, we are forced to look to the totality of the circumstances, which undermines the concept of having clear rules.

First, the clear rules. When a suspect has been placed under arrest, she is in custody. When a suspect has been handcuffed and locked in the back of the police car we can be fairly certain that she is in custody, even if the police never said, "You are under arrest." Similarly, when the police transport a person to the police station, that typically means that the person is in custody. By contrast, when a person is in her own home when she is questioned by the police, it is quite likely that she is not in custody.

Although it is usually the case that an interrogation at the station is custodial and that an interrogation at a person's home is noncustodial, that is not always the case. If a person voluntarily goes to the police station for questioning, it is quite possible that she will not be in custody. And if the police are in a suspect's home, but question her at gunpoint, it is quite likely that she is in custody. In short, we must look at the full set of circumstances.

This leads us to the key point. As soon as we move away from the obvious cases—formal arrests, typical police station interrogations, and typical home interrogations—we must look very carefully at all of the facts of the situation. Custody is determined from a totality of the circumstances test. This means that there will not always be clear answers.

So in the unclear situations, what factors should you look for in determining whether a suspect is in custody? First, start with the number of officers. If a suspect is questioned by one or two officers, that in itself does not tell us much about whether the suspect was in custody. But if a larger group of officers is questioning the suspect, that makes it more likely she is in custody. Second, look at the behavior of the officers. When the police officers raise their voices or demand that a person move to a particular location, that makes custody more likely. If the officers have drawn their weapons, that also makes custody more likely. Similarly, if a suspect is handcuffed, custody is more likely. An interrogation that goes on for a long time, or an interrogation conducted in the middle of the night is more likely to be custodial. Finally, if the suspect is a juvenile, the suspect's young age makes custody more likely because children often feel more restrained when interacting with the police than adults.

The difficulty of a totality of the circumstances test is that it will often be unclear whether the suspect is in custody. Moreover, sometimes the factors described above will point in different directions. For instance, imagine that four officers are closely surrounding the suspect in an abandoned and isolated parking lot in the middle of the day, but none of the officers ever raises their voice or draws their weapon. The suspect is probably not in custody, but the answer is uncertain. If you are faced with a problem like this on an essay question, it is important to point out the countervailing factors and explain which way each one cuts.

Finally, it is important to understand one common scenario in which the suspect is not in custody. Police conduct millions of traffic stops each year. As we learned for the *Terry* doctrine, a person is seized when a reasonable person would not feel free to leave (See Chapter 14). When a police officer turns on her sirens and signals for a driver to pull over, that driver cannot simply ignore the officer and drive away. The driver is seized for Fourth Amendment purposes. But the driver is not in custody for Fifth Amendment purposes. The driver's liberty is somewhat restricted, but she is not restrained to the same degree as would be associated with a formal arrest. For this reason, police can ask the driver questions at a traffic stop without reading her the

Miranda warnings. The driver might be detained under the *Terry* doctrine, but she is not in custody for purposes of the *Miranda* doctrine.

EXAM TRAPS TO AVOID

- Never assume that *Miranda* warnings are required just because the police are questioning a suspect. Always check to make sure that the person is in custody.
- Drivers often make incriminating statements during traffic stops. In most cases, the *Miranda* warnings are not required because the driver (while not free to leave under the Fourth Amendment) is not in custody under the Fifth Amendment.
- Be sure to look at the situation at the time the statement was made. A person may eventually end up under arrest. But the relevant inquiry is not what happened to the person in the end. The question is whether they were in custody when they gave the incriminating statement.
- Usually, a person at the stationhouse is in custody and a person at home is not in custody. But look for unusual situations, such as the person who voluntarily went to the station (and is not in custody) or the person who is surrounded by police at home (and is in custody).

MULTIPLE-CHOICE QUESTIONS

Question 159

Police pull Sam over for weaving on the highway at 2:00 a.m. on Saturday. When Sam rolls down the window, the officers immediately smell alcohol. The officers ask Sam, "Have you been drinking this evening, sir?" Sam responds, "Obviously. It's Saturday, so I start drinking around 1:00 p.m. and go straight through for the next 12 hours." Police ask Sam to do some sobriety tests and take a Breathalyzer test, but Sam says, "I know better than that. I'll never pass." The officers arrest Sam for drunk driving. The only evidence against Sam, therefore, is the officer's observations and Sam's statement. Sam has moved to suppress the statement. What result?

A) The statement is inadmissible because the police engaged in express questioning of Sam without first giving him the *Miranda* warnings.

B) The statement is inadmissible because the police arrested Sam without probable cause before getting the statement, thus rendering it fruit of the poisonous tree.

C) The statement is admissible because Sam responded to valid police questioning.

D) The statement is admissible because even though the police violated the *Miranda* doctrine, any error is harmless since the police saw Sam commit the crime.

Question 160

Three police officers dressed in full uniform and carrying handguns came to Tina's office. The three officers told Tina that they suspected she was selling drugs. The officers questioned Tina about her daily activities, who she interacted with, her criminal history, and where she goes after work. The officers never read Tina her *Miranda* rights. Tina made incriminating statements to the officers and is now moving to suppress those statements. How should the court rule on Tina's motion?

A) Tina's motion should be granted if a reasonable person in Tina's position would have thought that her freedom of action had been curtailed to a degree associated with a formal arrest.

B) Tina's motion should be granted if a reasonable person in Tina's position would not have felt free to leave.

C) Tina's motion should be denied because the police did not conduct "interrogation" since the questioning was on innocuous topics.

D) Tina's motion should be denied because she was not handcuffed and there cannot be custody without handcuffs.

Question 161

Federal agents are investigating Jane, a prominent business leader, for mail and wire fraud. The agents knock on Jane's door and tell her that they have some questions about her recent business dealings. Jane says, "I'm happy to answer your questions. Obviously, I haven't done anything wrong." The agents say, "Well, we can't ask the questions here. We have to go over a lot of documents to show you what we're investigating. It would help if you could come down to the FBI office." Jane was reluctant, but she agreed to talk with the agents at the FBI office. A few minutes after the agents left, Jane drove to the FBI office. The agents directed her to a windowless room and mostly closed the door. For two hours, Jane reviewed documents with the FBI agents as they asked questions. The agents never read Jane the *Miranda* warnings. Jane drove home feeling confident that the FBI agents would drop the case. But a week later, prosecutors indicted her for mail fraud. The indictment included incriminating statements that she had made at the FBI office. Jane's lawyer has moved to suppress her statements at the FBI office. How should the court rule?

A) The court should suppress the statements because Jane was in custody since she was at the police station and was never read the *Miranda* warnings.

B) The court should suppress the statements because Jane was subjected to a coercive environment.

C) The court should admit the statements because the fact that Jane was allowed to leave after the interrogation conclusively demonstrates that she was not in custody.

D) The court should admit the statements because the totality of the circumstances indicates that Jane was not in custody.

Question 162

Assume the same facts as Question 161. For purposes of this question, though, imagine that when Jane answered the door that the FBI agents said in a stern voice, "You are under investigation for mail fraud and wire fraud. We'd like to ask you some questions. You can get whatever you need—medicine, eyeglasses, whatever—and bring it with you." Jane asked, "Am I under arrest?" The agent responded, "I wouldn't call it that." Jane grabbed her glasses and got into the back of the agents' unmarked car for the ride to the FBI office. At the office, the agents took Jane to the same windowless office, closed the door all the way, but did not lock it. The agents never read Jane her *Miranda* warnings, but they only questioned her for about 10 minutes. Which of the following is correct?

A) Jane was not in custody because the agent did not consider her to be under arrest.

B) Jane was not in custody because the door to the interrogation room was not locked.

C) Jane was not in custody because the interrogation only lasted 10 minutes.

D) Jane was likely in custody under the totality of the circumstances.

Question 163

Assume the same facts as in Questions 161 and 162. This time, however, assume that when Jane answered the door that she was holding her purse. In front of Jane were five uniformed police officers. Two of the officers had their hands on their guns. The other three officers had their guns out of their holster and raised toward the door. Jane screamed, "What are you doing?" The officers responded, "We need to ask you some questions. Put down the purse and step away from the door." The officers frisked Jane for weapons and then moved her to a bench near the front door and told her not to move from the bench. The officers lowered their guns, but kept them unholstered in their hands. One of the officers then questioned Jane about her business dealings. None of the officers read Jane her *Miranda* rights. Was Jane in custody in this situation?

A) No, because she was at her home.

B) No, because she was not under arrest.

C) Yes, because this situation was the functional equivalent of arrest.

D) Yes, because a reasonable person would not feel free to leave.

Question 164

The manager of a car dealership specializing in luxury cars reported that someone stole a Porsche from the dealership late on Saturday night. From the surveillance footage it looks like the perpetrator was a young woman, but it is impossible to see her face. Fortunately, all of the luxury vehicles have tracking devices on them. Using the tracking device, the police see that the Porsche is parked at 123 Main Street. The officers proceed to that address and see the Porsche in the driveway. The officers investigate further and learn that three people live in the house—a married couple named Amanda and Daniel, and their 15-year-old daughter named Samantha. The officers do a little digging and learn that Daniel and Amanda left on a flight to Japan seven days ago. The officers figure that Samantha must have been the one who stole the car. The officers knock on the door and Samantha answers. The officers tell her they think the car in her driveway is stolen. They ask Samantha to step outside and answer some questions. The officers walk Samantha over to the Porsche so that her back is near the car. They then stand directly in front of her on her right and left side, so that she cannot go anywhere. With their hands on their holstered firearms, the officers then ask her where she was the previous night. Samantha doesn't answer and tries to walk back to the house. The officers stand in her way, though, and say, "Hang on. We really need to talk about this." Samantha stops moving. A moment later, she confesses to stealing the car. The officers never read Samantha her *Miranda* rights. Which of the following is correct?

A) Samantha is in her own driveway and also in a place where the public can see her so she was probably not in custody.

B) Because Samantha is not handcuffed, she cannot be in custody.

C) Because Samantha is a juvenile it is more likely that she is in custody in this situation.

D) Because Samantha is a juvenile, the police cannot question her without first receiving permission from her parent or guardian.

ANSWERS TO MULTIPLE-CHOICE QUESTIONS

Answer to Question 159

Answer A is incorrect. The police did ask Sam an express question: "Have you been drinking this evening, sir?" However, *Miranda* only applies if Sam was in custody. Here, Sam was not in custody. He was just stopped under the *Terry* doctrine.

Answer B is incorrect. The police did not arrest Sam before he gave his statement. They arrested him after he made an inculpatory statement.

Answer C is correct. The police engaged in interrogation when they asked Sam if he had been drinking. But that interrogation did not violate the *Miranda* doctrine because Sam was not in custody. The officers had conducted a valid *Terry* stop by pulling him over. Sam was not free to leave, but that does not mean he was subject to a custodial arrest. Sam was still sitting behind the wheel of his vehicle when he answered the officers' questions. Accordingly, Sam was not in custody.

Answer D is incorrect. The police did not commit a *Miranda* violation. Because Sam was not in custody, the *Miranda* doctrine did not apply and the police did not have to give him *Miranda* warnings.

Answer to Question 160

Answer A is correct. The *Miranda* doctrine applies when a person is in custody. The question does not say that Tina was placed under arrest. However, a person can be considered in custody even if the officers never specifically said she was under arrest. The test is whether a person's freedom of movement was curtailed to a degree consistent with an arrest.

Answer B is incorrect. This answer choice states the wrong test. To determine if there has been a *Terry* stop, we ask whether a reasonable person would have felt free to leave. That is not the test for custody under the *Miranda* doctrine.

Answer C is incorrect. Beginning a conversation by saying that you suspect a person of selling drugs does not seem innocuous. Regardless, innocuous questions can be interrogation. If the police asked express questions or their functional equivalent (statements reasonably likely to elicit an incriminating response), it amounts to interrogation.

Answer D is incorrect. A person can be in custody for *Miranda* purposes even if they were not handcuffed. Here, the suspect was surrounded by three officers. This might amount to interrogation, even in the absence of handcuffs.

Answer to Question 161

Answer A is incorrect. Under the totality of the circumstances, it appears that Jane was not in custody. She voluntarily went to the FBI office. She drove herself to the station. While she was in a windowless room, the door was not closed entirely and it was not locked. Jane never asked to leave and was never told she could not leave.

Answer B is incorrect. This was not a coercive environment. There were no weapons drawn, no raised voices, and no handcuffs. No interrogation is pleasant. But unpleasantness does not equal the kind of coercion forbidden by the Fifth Amendment.

Answer C is incorrect. The fact that Jane was allowed to leave after the interrogation ended suggests that Jane was not in custody. But that fact alone is not dispositive. Police could conduct a custodial interrogation and release the person from custody afterward.

Answer D is correct. It appears, under all the circumstances, that Jane was not in custody. She voluntarily went to the FBI office. The officers did not transport her to the FBI office. Rather, she drove herself there. While she was in a windowless room, the door was not closed entirely nor was it locked. Jane never asked to leave and was never told she could not leave. Under all the circumstances, it appears that Jane was not in custody.

Answer to Question 162

Answer A is incorrect. The subjective view of the officer as to whether a person is in custody is not controlling. Custody determinations are made from an objective standpoint, not the subjective views of the officer or the suspect.

Answer B is incorrect. Whether a door is locked is a factor that could have an impact on determining whether the suspect is in custody. But it is not dispositive. And under the facts of this case, it is likely not a particularly important factor.

Answer C is incorrect. The length of an interrogation can be a factor in determining whether a person was in custody. Once again, though, it is not a dispositive factor. Here the short length of the interrogation is outweighed by the other factors.

Answer D is correct. It looks from the totality of the circumstances like Jane was in custody. The agents spoke to her sternly and ordered her to the FBI office. She did not drive there on her own, but instead was in the back of the FBI agents' vehicle. Once at the station, she was directed to an interrogation room where the door was completely closed. While there are factors cutting against custody—the unlocked door, the lack of handcuffs, and the short duration—these factors are likely outweighed by the factors suggesting custody.

Answer to Question 163

Answer A is incorrect. While a person who is in their home is rarely in custody, that is not always the case. Here the other factors, specifically the large number of officers with weapons drawn, outweigh the fact that Jane is at home.

Answer B is incorrect. A person can be in custody even if they are not formally under arrest.

Answer C is correct. A person can be in custody if they are under arrest or if their liberty is restrained to a level consistent with an arrest. Here there were a large number of officers. The officers had brandished their weapons and indeed even pointed the guns toward Jane. The officers frisked Jane and ordered her to sit on a bench and not move. Even after lowering their weapons, they did not holster their guns. All of these factors amount to custody.

Answer D is incorrect. This answer states the wrong test. Whether a reasonable person would feel free to leave is the test for determining whether a person has been detained under the *Terry* doctrine. The test for whether a person is in custody is whether their liberty has been restrained to a degree consistent with an arrest.

Answer to Question 164

Answer A is incorrect. When a person is in their own home (or the curtilage of their own home) they are typically not in custody. In this case, though, Samantha's movements have been restrained and the officers have behaved in an intimidating manner by holding their hands on their guns. More importantly, Samantha is a juvenile, which makes the case for custody stronger than if she had been an adult. All things considered, it appears Samantha is in custody.

Answer B is incorrect. While handcuffs are a strong indication that a person is in custody, they are not a requirement. For example, if a suspect were surrounded by numerous officers with their guns drawn, the suspect would be in custody even if not handcuffed.

Answer C is correct. Samantha is only 15 years old. Being a juvenile does not automatically mean that Samantha is in custody when she interacts with the police. However a juvenile's age is a factor to be considered in determining whether she is in custody. Here, the answer is phrased in terms of custody being "more likely" that she is in custody. That is a correct statement of the law.

Answer D is incorrect. Police are not obligated to obtain permission from a juvenile's parents in order to question them. A juvenile's age is a factor in determining whether she was in custody. But lack of parental permission does not automatically mean the juvenile was in custody.

CHAPTER 30

Have the Police Engaged in Interrogation for *Miranda* Purposes?

THE RULE: The police engage in interrogation when they ask express questions or their functional equivalent. The functional equivalent is something reasonably likely to elicit an incriminating response.

Critical Points

- *Express Questioning:* When police engage in express questioning—for example, "Where were you at the time of the crime?"—that amounts to interrogation.
- *Functional Equivalent of Questioning*: It can be interrogation even if the police do not use sentences that end with a question mark.
  - The functional equivalent of questioning can also be interrogation.
  - The test is whether the officer's actions are reasonably likely to elicit an incriminating response.
  - Courts do not look at the subjective intent of the officers and whether they hoped that their tactics would result in a confession. Whether there is interrogation is an objective inquiry.
- *Volunteered Statements*: If a suspect blurts out incriminating information, there is no *Miranda* violation because the officers have not engaged in interrogation.
- *Taking Blood Samples*: When police take a blood sample (or a hair sample or a DNA sample), that is not interrogation.

- *Undercover Agents:* When police use an undercover agent to question a suspect, that does not amount to interrogation. A suspect cannot feel coerced if she does not realize she is speaking with the police.

OVERVIEW OF THE BLACKLETTER LAW

The *Miranda* warnings only apply when the police engage in custodial interrogation. (For a discussion of custody, see Chapter 29.) In most instances, it is obvious when the police have engaged in interrogation. If the officers ask a suspect a question related to the crime, it is interrogation. For example, asking a suspect where he was on the night in question or what he knows about any of the evidence would amount to interrogation.

The harder question for determining interrogation is what happens when the police do not ask an express question. Police engage in all kinds of tactics that do not involve direct questions. For example, what if the police made a declarative statement "We know you committed the crime, but we just need to figure out why you did it." Or what if the police do not say anything, but instead drop the murder weapon on the table in front of a suspect? In both instances, the police have not asked an express question but courts would almost certainly conclude that these tactics amount to interrogation. The reason is that the Supreme Court has said that interrogation includes *both* express questioning and its "functional equivalent." The Court has defined "functional equivalent" to be anything that is reasonably likely to elicit an incriminating response.

Like many other aspects of criminal procedure, determining whether there was an interrogation is done from the viewpoint of a reasonable person. Accordingly, the subjective viewpoint of the officer does not matter. Similarly, a police tactic is not interrogation just because a suspect was fooled or now thinks it should count as interrogation. Courts look objectively. That said, in assessing the situation, courts will consider whether the officers manipulated the personal characteristics and vulnerabilities of the suspect. For instance, if a suspect is very religious and the officers knowingly played on that to extract a confession, a court will consider the suspect's religiosity in determining whether the police engaged in interrogation.

So far, we have explored what qualifies as interrogation. We also know that there are a few situations that do *not* amount to interrogation. When a suspect volunteers a statement—in other words, when a suspect blurts out something—that is not interrogation. A situation does not become an interrogation just because a suspect has confessed. Whether a situation is an interrogation depends on the actions of the police.

Another common situation that does not amount to interrogation is the use of an undercover agent. Police often send undercover officers or informants into a jail cell to try to gather information from a suspect. Even though the suspect is incarcerated and being questioned by the police agent, it is not custodial interrogation. The reason, according to the Supreme Court, is that the *Miranda* doctrine was designed to reduce police coercion, and a suspect cannot feel coerced if he does not know he is dealing with the police.

Finally, suspects often object to blood draws or the taking of other bodily samples (such as hair samples or DNA scrapes under fingernails). Suspects claim that taking such samples (even with a warrant) forces them to incriminate themselves. The suspects are incorrect, however. The Fifth Amendment offers no protection against blood draws or other bodily samples because the information they reveal is non-testimonial. Bodily samples do not reveal a suspect's thoughts and therefore cannot be interrogation.

EXAM TRAPS TO AVOID

- For something to be the functional equivalent of express questioning, it must be *reasonably* likely to elicit an incriminating response. Do not assume that every police ploy or tactic meets this standard. Just because some people will fall for a tactic does not mean that it is reasonably likely that the average person would.
- The fact that an officer hopes that a tactic will lead to a confession does not mean the police tactic is interrogation. The subjective hopes of an officer are not relevant.
- Be on the lookout for vulnerabilities of the suspect that the officer is aware of. If the police exploit a suspect's known vulnerabilities, you should factor that into the determination of whether the situation was reasonably likely to elicit an incriminating response.

MULTIPLE-CHOICE QUESTIONS

Question 165

Police have just arrested Margaret for bank robbery. The officers put her in a holding cell and leave for about 20 minutes. When they return, the officers say, "Look, we know what you've done." The officers then drop a backpack in front of the jail cell. Margaret says, "What is that supposed to prove?" The officers responded, "That's the type of backpack the robber put the money in." Margaret responded, "Big deal. That just shows that you are smart enough to watch the bank's surveillance tape." The officers then opened the backpack and took out a pile of money. The officers threw the money on the floor and said, "We found the backpack in the trunk of a car parked around the corner from your apartment." Margaret was stunned for a moment and then said, "All right, you've got me. I did it." The officers had never read Margaret her *Miranda* warnings. Is Margaret's confession admissible?

A) No, because the police engaged in psychological trickery that renders the confession involuntary.

B) Probably not, because although the police never asked any questions, their actions were reasonably likely to elicit an incriminating response.

C) Yes, because the officers never questioned Margaret and thus there was no interrogation and no *Miranda* violation.

D) Probably yes, because declarative statements can only amount to interrogation if the officers engage in psychological trickery that shocks the conscience.

Question 166

For purposes of this question, assume that the police officers arrested Margaret for bank robbery. The officers intended to interrogate her so they put her in an interrogation room and said they would be back in a couple of minutes with some coffee and donuts. Outside of the room, the officers worked out their plan. The first officer would read Margaret the *Miranda* warnings and be the "good cop." The second officer would be the "bad cop" and would tell Margaret about the huge sentence she would get if she didn't cooperate and confess. The officers then picked up their coffee cups and opened the door to the interrogation room. The moment they walked inside, Margaret said, "Is that coffee for me?" The officer playing "good cop" said "Yes." Margaret took one sip of the coffee and said, "I want to confess. I robbed the bank." Is Margaret's confession admissible?

A) Yes, because Margaret has made a voluntary admission without interrogation.

B) Yes, because Margaret is not in custody since the officers were kindly providing her with coffee and donuts and thus created an atmosphere that is not akin to an arrest.

C) No, because the police intended to interrogate Margaret but never actually read her the *Miranda* warnings.

D) No, because the police interrogated Margaret by bringing her coffee and starting to talk with her.

Question 167

A security guard for an elementary school is found beaten and unconscious at 5:00 a.m. on Tuesday. Police notice that the guard's gun is missing. Around 6:00 a.m., Mark is arrested near the scene of the crime because he had blood all over his shirt. Police read Mark his *Miranda* rights, and Mark says that he wants to talk to a lawyer. On the drive to the station, Mark is sitting in the back of the police car. The officer who is driving is using the police radio to talk with the dispatcher. Over the radio, the dispatcher says that the school day will begin in less than two hours and that a child might find the guard's gun if the police don't find it first. The officer who is driving the car agrees and says that it would be a tragedy if a child were hurt. Mark hears all of this and says, "I did it, and the gun is in the sandbox." Should Mark's statement be suppressed?

A) Yes, because he was in custody and he was interrogated by being subjected to express questioning.

B) Yes, because he was in custody and he was interrogated by being subjected to the functional equivalent of questioning.

C) No, because he was not subjected to questioning.

D) No, because he was properly read his *Miranda* rights.

Question 168

Police have arrested Andre for theft of copper wire from the back of a pickup truck. The officers know that people often steal copper wire so that they can sell it at construction sites and take the quick cash and buy drugs. The officers notice that Andre's hand is shaking, which is a sign of drug withdrawal. Putting all this information together, the officers figure that Andre is probably a heroin user and that he is in withdrawal. The officers sit Andre down in the interrogation room and begin by saying, "Look, you're under arrest for theft. I know you want to get out of here. We both know that it's really easy to score heroin just a few blocks from here. If you give us some information about where you've been selling the copper wire we'll let you walk right out of here. We'll even drop you off a couple of blocks from here where it's easy to get heroin." Two minutes later, Andre tells the officers who he sells the copper wire to after he's stolen it. In determining whether the police engaged in interrogation, is it relevant that the police believed Andre was a heroin user in withdrawal?

A) Andre's individual characteristics are irrelevant in this circumstance.

B) In determining whether a suspect was reasonably likely to make an incriminating statement, the court should consider that the officers thought Andre was a heroin user and in withdrawal.

Question 169

Police pull over Trevor on suspicion of drunk driving. Trevor was slurring his speech and he smelled of alcohol. The officers asked Trevor to blow into a Breathalyzer machine to see if his blood-alcohol level was over the legal limit. Trevor refused. The officers arrested Trevor and took him to the police station. The officer then successfully applied to a magistrate for a search warrant to draw Trevor's blood. At the police station, a nurse came into the holding cell with a needle and told Trevor to sit down so that they could draw his blood. Trevor objected and said, "It's my body. You can't make me incriminate myself with my own blood." Which of the following is correct?

A) Drawing Trevor's blood over his objection is interrogation and violates the Fifth Amendment.

B) Drawing Trevor's blood over his objection is not interrogation and there is no Fifth Amendment violation.

Question 170

Police arrested Lance yesterday for the aggravated assault of Walter. Unfortunately, Walter was beaten so badly that he does not remember the assault. Police have tried to interrogate Lance, but all he would say is, "I acted in self-defense. Walter attacked me and I just defended myself. I'm really tired. I don't want to talk anymore right now." The officers returned Lance to his cell. A few hours later, after Lance had woken up from his nap, the police sent an undercover officer into Lance's jail cell. The undercover officer pretended that he had been arrested for burglary. Later that night, the undercover officer told Lance about the crime that he had supposedly committed. The undercover officer was very convincing and Lance reciprocated by saying what he was arrested for. The undercover officer then asked Lance, "Did you hit Walter first? Or did Walter start it?" Lance replied, "I told the cops that Walter started it, but that was a lie. I punched him in the face first. Walter never actually put a hand on me!" Prosecutors want to use this incriminating statement against Lance, but Lance's attorney has moved to suppress it as a *Miranda* violation. Which of the following is correct?

A) Lance's testimony is not admissible because the undercover agent never gave Lance the *Miranda* warnings.

B) Lance's testimony is not admissible because Lance had already invoked his right to a lawyer and thus there can be no further questioning by the police.

C) Lance's testimony is admissible because Lance did not know he was dealing with a police agent.

D) Lance's testimony is admissible because the *Miranda* doctrine cannot be the basis for suppressing such a plainly incriminating statement.

ANSWERS TO MULTIPLE-CHOICE QUESTIONS

Answer to Question 165

Answer A is incorrect. The officers here did not engage in the kind of extreme psychological tactics that would render a confession involuntary. Assuming the bag is actually from Margaret's trunk (and you should assume the facts in the question are true unless directed otherwise), the officers have merely presented Margaret with incriminating evidence. This tactic does not render the confession involuntary.

Answer B is correct. Interrogation can take the form of questions, statements, or actions that are reasonably likely to elicit an incriminating response. In this instance, the police tactics are the functional equivalent of an interrogation because a reasonable person in Margaret's position might very well respond to the backpack and money on the floor by confessing.

Answer C is incorrect. This answer choice suggests that there can never be an interrogation unless the officers ask questions. The rule is otherwise. If police engage in conduct that is reasonably likely to elicit an incriminating response, that can amount to interrogation, even if the police do not ask any questions.

Answer D is incorrect. This answer does not correctly state the legal test. A declarative statement by the police can amount to interrogation if the police do something that is reasonably likely to elicit an incriminating response. The police conduct does not need to "shock the conscience."

Answer to Question 166

Answer A is correct. In this case, the police did not question her. Nor did they do anything that was reasonably likely to elicit an incriminating response. The officers simply brought Margaret coffee. Margaret has made a spontaneous incriminating statement. Just because an incriminating statement is made does not mean there was an interrogation.

Answer B is incorrect. Margaret was placed under arrest, taken to the police station, and placed in an interrogation room. This amounts to custody.

Answer C is incorrect. This answer correctly states the facts as they occurred in the question, but it is wrong as a matter of law. The subjective intent of the officers is not relevant. What is relevant is whether the facts as they occurred would cause a reasonable observer to believe that the officers conducted an interrogation.

Answer D is incorrect. Simply bringing a suspect a drink and answering "Yes" to indicate it is coffee is not something that is reasonably likely to elicit an incriminating response.

Answer to Question 167

Answer A is incorrect. Mark was in custody, but this situation does not amount to interrogation. The officers did not ask an express question.

Answer B is incorrect. Interrogation occurs if there is express questioning or its functional equivalent. To be the functional equivalent of questioning, the situation must be reasonably likely to elicit an incriminating response. The facts of this case are very similar to *Rhode Island v. Innis* (1980), in which the Supreme Court held that the officers' discussion was not reasonably likely to elicit an incriminating response.

Answer C is correct. As noted above, the Supreme Court's decision in *Rhode Island v. Innis* (1980) held that this type of situation was not reasonably likely to elicit an incriminating response. Accordingly, it is not the functional equivalent of questioning and therefore does not amount to interrogation.

Answer D is incorrect. Mark was properly read his *Miranda* rights, but he invoked the right to counsel. The giving of the *Miranda* rights therefore cannot be the basis for refusing to suppress the statement. If the statements are admissible, it must be because this situation did not amount to interrogation.

Answer to Question 168

Answer B is correct. If officers know that a suspect has particular vulnerabilities that would make him more likely to make incriminating statements, that must be taken into consideration. To be clear, the determining factor is not what the particular officers subjectively believed. Rather, we must focus on what a reasonable officer with the same information would think. A reasonable officer who knew that a suspect was a heroin user and suffering from withdrawal would think that the comments about immediately releasing the suspect in an area where he could buy heroin is likely to elicit an incriminating response.

Answer to Question 169

The Supreme Court has held that drawing blood (or other bodily samples) is not a Fifth Amendment event. Although Trevor's blood might convey incriminating information, it is non-testimonial because it does not convey his thoughts. Accordingly, Answer B is correct.

Answer to Question 170

Answer A is incorrect. Undercover agents are not obligated to provide *Miranda* warnings. The *Miranda* doctrine was designed to eliminate the coercive environment that comes with custodial interrogation. The Supreme Court has recognized that suspects are not in a coercive environment when they do not realize they are speaking with a police officer. Accordingly, the *Miranda* warnings are not required in this situation.

Answer B is incorrect. Lance did not invoke his right to counsel. Rather, Lance said, "I'm really tired. I don't want to talk anymore right now." Because Lance has only invoked his right to silence, it is possible for the police to re-approach him. Moreover, Lance believes he is speaking with another arrestee. No *Miranda* warnings are necessary when a suspect does not realize he is speaking with the police.

Answer C is correct. Undercover agents do not have to give the *Miranda* warnings. The *Miranda* doctrine was designed to eliminate coerciveness that comes from custodial interrogation. When a suspect does not realize he is talking with a police officer, it is not possible for the suspect to feel coerced by a government agent. Therefore, the *Miranda* warnings are not necessary.

Answer D is incorrect. Police must comply with the *Miranda* doctrine. If the officers fail to comply with Miranda, their misconduct is not washed away simply because the suspect's statement is incriminating. Here, there was no *Miranda* violation. But had there been a *Miranda* violation, the explanation in this answer choice would be incorrect.

STEP 4
Does an Exception to the *Miranda* Doctrine Apply?

Chapter 31: The Public Safety, Routine Booking, and Covert Operatives Exceptions to Miranda

If the suspect is in custody and the police are engaged in an interrogation, the police are usually obligated to comply with the *Miranda* doctrine. There are three situations in which the Court has decided the *Miranda* doctrine does not apply: public safety emergencies, routine booking questions, and the use of undercover agents or informants.

Under the public safety exception, the police can ignore the *Miranda* doctrine when an officer reasonably believes there is a need to protect the police or the public from an immediate danger.

The routine booking questions exception applies to information such as name, address, and date of birth that the officers record at the police station.

The covert operations exception applies when police use undercover agents or informants to obtain incriminating information from a suspect. Because the suspect does not realize that she is dealing with the police, the *Miranda* doctrine does not apply.

CHAPTER 31

The Public Safety, Routine Booking, and Covert Operatives Exceptions to *Miranda*

THE RULE: Although police must give the *Miranda* warnings and obtain proper waivers when they engage in custodial interrogation, there are exceptions for public safety, routine booking, and covert operatives that do not require the warnings to be given.

Critical Points

- *Public Safety Exception*:
  - When an officer reasonably believes there is an immediate need to protect the police or the public from an immediate danger, the officer can question a suspect without first giving the *Miranda* warnings. Any incriminating statements will be admissible.
  - For questions to fall under the public safety exception, the officers must ask questions necessary to secure their own safety or the safety of the public. If the officers go further and ask questions that are solely to gather incriminating evidence, the responses to those questions will not be admissible.
  - Courts should not try to discern the subjective motivations of the officer. The key question is whether there was an immediate need to protect the police or the public, not what an individual officer personally believed.
- *Routine Booking Questions*: At the police station, the police ask "routine booking questions," such as name, address, and date of birth. Technically, this is custodial interrogation, but the *Miranda* doctrine does not apply.

- *Covert Operatives*: Police sometimes use undercover agents or informants in jails to get incriminating information from a suspect. This would seem to be custodial interrogation because the suspect is in jail and is being questioned. The Court has held that *Miranda* does not apply, though, because even though the suspect is incarcerated and is being questioned, the questioning is not coercive because he does not know he is being questioned by a police agent.

OVERVIEW OF THE BLACKLETTER LAW

As we learned in Chapters 29 and 30, the *Miranda* doctrine applies to custodial interrogations. If a suspect is in custody and being subjected to interrogation, the police must first have given the *Miranda* warnings and obtained a proper waiver. There are three significant exceptions, however, in which *Miranda* does not apply: public safety, routine booking questions, and covert operations.

The public safety exception is the most heavily tested of the three exceptions. When police are in a situation where they reasonably believe it is necessary to protect themselves or the public, they may ask questions to eliminate the danger. In *New York v. Quarles* (1991), a woman told the police late at night that she had just been raped and that the perpetrator was inside a nearby grocery store. The officers entered the store and found the suspect, but he then ran away. After the officers found and handcuffed the suspect, they discovered an empty gun holster on his body. Without reading the *Miranda* warnings, the officer asked where the gun was and the suspect told them. Although the suspect was interrogated while in custody, the Supreme Court held that *Miranda* warnings were not required because of the public safety emergency. The Court explained that when an officer objectively believes that it is necessary to protect the police or the public from an immediate danger, she can skip the *Miranda* warnings and question the suspect. The questions, however, must be for public safety purposes, not solely to gather incriminating testimonial information for a future prosecution.

In assessing whether the public safety exception applies, courts should look from the perspective of an *objectively reasonable* officer, not the personal *subjective* view of the officer asking the question. Moreover, the public safety exception should be assessed based on the facts known to the officer when she asked the questions, not what was later discovered. If the officer reasonably believed that there was a public safety emergency, then the un-Mirandized question is acceptable, even if it we later learn that there was in fact no such emergency.

The second exception to the *Miranda* doctrine is for routine booking questions. When police arrest a person and bring them to the station, the officers need certain basic information to process the arrest. The necessary information includes name, address, date of birth, and other basic information including weight and eye color.

Even though asking for this information is interrogation and the suspect is in custody, the Supreme Court has held that police need not read the suspect the *Miranda* warnings and obtain a waiver. In short, there is a "routine booking questions" exception to *Miranda*. If any of the information the suspect gives in response to the routine booking questions is incriminating, it will be admissible.

The third exception to the *Miranda* doctrine is for covert operations. Police departments regularly use undercover agents or informants to try to gather information directly from suspects. They sometimes use this tactic after a suspect has been arrested and is sitting in jail. When the suspect is incarcerated, he is obviously in custody. And when an undercover agent or an informant acting at the direction of law enforcement asks questions—such as "What are you in for?"—the police are interrogating the suspect. Nevertheless, the Supreme Court has held that the *Miranda* doctrine does not apply because the suspect does not know he is dealing with law enforcement. Indeed, it would be very strange for an undercover agent to say to his cellmate, "Hey, I'm just another arrestee and I'm definitely not an under-cover cop. But if I were an undercover cop, you would have the right to remain silent and the right to an attorney . . ." The undercover agent exception eliminates what would be a very strange discussion.

EXAM TRAPS TO AVOID

- Just because an officer initially asks a question that would fall under the public safety exception does not mean that all of the officer's subsequent questions fall under the exception. Beware of situations in which there is a public safety exception to the Miranda warnings for the initial question, but not for subsequent follow-up questions that are not necessary to protect public safety.
- As in most other areas of criminal procedure, you should assess the public safety exception from the standpoint of a reasonable officer. Do not focus on the subjective, personal views of the officer.
- In assessing whether the public safety exception should apply, consider the facts as the police knew them at the moment they questioned the suspect. Just because it turns out there was no real emergency does not mean a reasonable officer would not have thought there was an emergency at the time.

MULTIPLE-CHOICE QUESTIONS

Question 171

Police arrested Tom for a burglary on Saturday night and left him in a jail cell until he could have his first court hearing on Monday morning. On Sunday, officers lead a man named Ian to Tom's jail cell and say, "Tom, this is your bunkmate. No fighting." In fact, Ian is an undercover officer who is seeking to get a confession from Tom. Ian says he was arrested for drunk driving, but that it's his fourth offense and that he's probably not going to make bail. Ian then asks Tom what he's in for. When Tom says, "I didn't do anything," Ian responds, "Yah, sure. What did you do?" Over the next hour, Tom tells Ian about the house he had broken into and the items he had stolen. At trial, Tom seeks to prevent Ian from testifying on the grounds that it violated the *Miranda* doctrine. Which of the following is correct?

A) Ian's testimony is not admissible because Ian never gave Tom the *Miranda* warnings.

B) Ian's testimony is not admissible because there was no emergency justifying the use of an undercover agent and the failure to give *Miranda* warnings.

C) Ian's testimony is admissible because Tom did not know he was dealing with a police agent.

D) Ian's testimony is not admissible because there was no public safety justification for the police ruse.

Question 172

The owner of a jewelry store called the police saying that he caught Juanita trying to steal a garnet ring out of the display case. The officers came to investigate and found it strange that Juanita would try to take the garnet ring, which is far less valuable than the diamond rings that were in the same display case. Nevertheless, the owner of the store was emphatic that he saw Juanita try to walk out with the ring. Although the evidence was a little thin, the police arrested Juanita for theft and brought her to the police station. At the station, the officers did not read Juanita the *Miranda* warnings but they required her to provide biographical information, including her name, age, date of birth, and address. Juanita answered all of the questions, including stating that she was born on January 11. The prosecutor, who was interested in gemstones, immediately recognized something interesting. Garnet is the birthstone for people born in January. At trial, the prosecutor argued to the jury that the store owner would have had no way of knowing that Juanita was born in January and thus his story that Juanita was trying to steal the garnet stone as opposed to the diamonds was more compelling. Juanita objected, but the judge overruled the objection and the jury convicted her. She is now appealing. Which of the following is correct?

A) The officers violated *Miranda* by questioning Juanita about her date of birth without first reading her the warnings and obtaining a waiver.

B) The officers did not violate *Miranda* because the biographical questions were routine booking questions.

C) The officers did not violate *Miranda* because they never interrogated Juanita since they told her to provide biographical information rather than asking her.

D) The officers did not violate *Miranda* because Juanita was not yet in custody when they gathered her biographical information.

Question 173

Police have been furiously searching for a kidnapped child. An informant reported that Victor Villain dragged the child into a grey Honda Accord with license plate "ABC-123." While on patrol, an officer sees that vehicle parked in a driveway and alerts the rest of the department. Officers descend on the address and immediately break down the front door. Inside, Victor Villain is sitting there smiling and says, "Took you long enough." The child is not inside the house, however. The officers say, "Where is the child?" Victor just laughs but doesn't say anything. One officer walks over to Victor and handcuffs him. After Victor is handcuffed, a different officer begins to punch him. As he is punching Victor, the officer asks, "Where is the child?" Victor holds out for a minute, but the officer is strong and eventually Victor tells the police where the child is. The police go to that location and find the child in fine health. They also find a packet of papers—including background information about the child—that has Victor's fingerprints all over them. Victor has moved to suppress his statement identifying the location of the child and the papers with his fingerprints. How should the court rule?

A) The court should suppress the confession, but not the papers.

B) The court should suppress the papers, but not the confession.

C) The court should suppress both the papers and the confession.

D) The court should not suppress either the papers or the confession.

Question 174

Assume the same facts as Question 173 above. This time, however, assume that when police entered Victor's house that he was not smiling and that he was instead very surprised to see the police. The officers immediately grabbed him and handcuffed him. The officers yelled, "Where is the child?" Victor said, "The abandoned house across the street. I'm sorry." The police find the child, unharmed, in the house across the street. Prosecutors later seek to use Victor's statement at trial against him (because the statement indicates he knew where the child was and "I'm sorry" shows wrongful intent). How should the court rule on Victor's suppression motion?

A) The court should suppress the statements because the police conducted custodial interrogation without giving the *Miranda* warnings.

B) The court should admit the statements because the public safety exception to the *Miranda* doctrine should probably apply.

C) The court should suppress the statements because it turned out that the child was not in any actual danger.

D) The court should suppress the statements because the police lacked authority to break into Victor's home and thus the statements are fruit of the poisonous tree from the illegal entrance.

Question 175

Assume the same facts as Question 174. Once again, the police asked Victor where the child was without giving the *Miranda* warnings and Victor responded, "The child is in the abandoned house across the street. He's a great kid. I'm sorry." The officer then asked, "How do you know he's a great kid?" Victor responded, "I used to coach his soccer team and he helped me cash in on the vending machines." The officer said, "What? I don't understand. Cash in on what?" Victor then responded, "After soccer practice he would help me steal money from the vending machines behind the middle school." Is Victor's statement about stealing from the vending machines admissible?

A) Yes, it falls under the public safety exception.

B) Yes, because Victor voluntarily confessed.

C) No, because there was no public safety concern that required asking the follow-up questions.

D) No, because Victor was coerced into making the incriminating statement about the vending machines.

Question 176

Assume the same facts as Questions 173–175. This time, however, imagine that when the police asked where the child was that Victor responded, "He's playing with my son in the backyard. Are you here because I let the kids ride home without seat belts so that they could stand up in the back seat of the car and stick their heads out of the sunroof? Look, I'm sorry about that." The police go into the backyard and speak to the child who tells them that Victor did not kidnap him at all. The child explains that his parents had arranged for him to have a playdate with his friend (Victor's son) and that they had arranged for Victor to pick the kids up after school. The child also confirms that Victor let them stand up in the back seat and drive home with their heads sticking out of the sunroof. The officers issue Victor a traffic citation for failure to seat belt the children. Victor moves to dismiss that charge as resulting from a *Miranda* violation. What result?

A) Victor's incriminating statement about the seat belt violation is not admissible because there was no kidnapping and thus there was no public safety concern.

B) Victor's incriminating statement about the seat belt violation is not admissible because the police lacked a justification to question the child.

C) Victor's incriminating statement about the seat belt is admissible because the *Miranda* doctrine is only for serious crimes and does not cover traffic offenses.

D) Victor's incriminating statement about the seat belt is admissible because the public safety exception applies.

ANSWERS TO MULTIPLE-CHOICE QUESTIONS

Answer to Question 171

Answer A is incorrect. Undercover police are not obligated to give *Miranda* warnings. When a person does not know they are dealing with the police, the interaction is not coercive and thus the *Miranda* doctrine does not apply.

Answer B is incorrect. There does not have to be an emergency to justify the use of an undercover informant. While the public safety exception does excuse the giving of the *Miranda* warnings, that exception does not apply in situations involving undercover agents.

Answer C is correct. The *Miranda* doctrine is designed to reduce the coerciveness of custodial interrogations. When a suspect does not know he is dealing with an officer, the situation is not coercive. Accordingly, the Supreme Court has held that undercover police and police informants need not give *Miranda* warnings before questioning a suspect.

Answer D is incorrect. The police do not have to demonstrate a public safety reason for placing an undercover agent in a jail cell.

Answer to Question 172

Answer A is incorrect. Biographical questions, such as name and date of birth fall under the routine booking exception to *Miranda*. Thus, police do not have to first read the warnings and obtain a valid waiver.

Answer B is correct. Biographical information such as name, address, eye color, and, most importantly here, date of birth fall under the routine booking questions exception to *Miranda*. Thus, police do not have to first read the warnings and obtain a valid waiver.

Answer C is incorrect. If there were no routine booking questions exception, the officers' actions would constitute interrogation. As explained in Chapter 30, interrogation is not limited to direct questions. The functional equivalent of a question also constitutes interrogation.

Answer D is incorrect. Juanita had been arrested and transported to the police station. She was in custody for *Miranda* purposes.

Answer to Question 173

This question does not really belong in this chapter and is here to trick you. This case involves a *Miranda* violation because Victor is in custody and being interrogated without having been read the warnings and provided a valid waiver. The public safety exception could very well apply to this *Miranda* violation. But the bigger problem is not the *Miranda* violation, but instead that the officer beat the information out of Victor. Accordingly, Victor's statement is coerced. There is no public safety exception to the prohibition on coerced confessions. Accordingly, Victor's confession identifying the location of the child is not admissible. Because the fruit of the poisonous tree doctrine applies to coerced confessions (see Chapter 34), the papers with his fingerprints are also inadmissible. This question is here to remind you that you should not focus exclusively on *Miranda* violations. It is possible for an interrogation question to turn on the coerced confession doctrine. Answer C is correct.

Answer to Question 174

Answer A is incorrect. This is a custodial interrogation because Victor is handcuffed and being questioned. However, a kidnapped child who might be in danger would certainly qualify as a public safety emergency that would excuse the reading of the *Miranda* warnings.

Answer B is correct. Ordinarily, when a swarm of police officers enter a house, handcuff a suspect, and immediately question him, that would amount to custodial interrogation requiring the *Miranda* warnings. However, here there is a public safety situation. The kidnapped child may be in grave danger and the public safety exception to the *Miranda* doctrine therefore should apply.

Answer C is incorrect. We do not judge the public safety exception from what eventually happened, but instead from what a reasonable officer on the scene would have perceived. Here, the officers reasonably thought that the child was in danger.

Answer D is incorrect. If the police had entered unlawfully, that would have violated the Fourth Amendment; and subsequently discovered evidence would have been suppressed under the fruit of the poisonous tree doctrine. However, the police entry here was lawful under the exigency doctrine. Police had probable cause to believe that Victor had kidnapped a child and was inside with the child. That creates probable cause to enter and triggers the exigent circumstances exception to the warrant requirement.

Answer to Question 175

Answer A is incorrect. The initial question about the location of the child falls under the public safety exception. But that doctrine does not permit questions that are not reasonably prompted by a concern for public safety. It is difficult to see why the officers need to inquire "How do you know he's a great kid?" There is even less justification for the officers to ask follow-up questions about the vending machine theft. These questions are designed to gather incriminating information, not to protect public safety.

Answer B is incorrect. Victor's confession might not have been coerced, but that does not mean it is admissible. If there is no public safety justification for the follow-up questions, then the *Miranda* warnings are required. Because the police failed to do so here, the subsequent incriminating statements would not be admissible.

Answer C is correct. The public safety doctrine does not permit questions that are not reasonably prompted by a concern for public safety. In this case, it is hard to see why the officers need to inquire "How do you know he's a great kid?"

There is even less justification for the officers to ask follow-up questions about the vending machine theft. These questions are designed to gather incriminating information, not to protect public safety. Accordingly, the public safety exception should not apply, and the statements should be suppressed as a *Miranda* violation.

Answer D is incorrect. Victor was not coerced into making the incriminating follow-up questions. His statement is inadmissible because of the *Miranda* violation, not because it was coerced.

Answer to Question 176

Answer A is incorrect. Whether the public safety exception applies is not assessed from hindsight. At the time the police asked the question, they reasonably believed Victor had kidnapped the child. The fact that it turned out that Victor had not kidnapped the child does not retroactively eliminate the applicability of the public safety exception.

Answer B is incorrect. The police still had a justification to question the child because they did not know whether Victor was lying. Nevertheless, the question is not asking about the child's statement but instead about whether Victor's statement (which was given before the police questioned the child) is admissible.

Answer C is incorrect. The *Miranda* doctrine applies to all criminal offenses, including traffic offenses.

Answer D is correct. When the officers asked Victor where the child was, they reasonably believed that there was a kidnapped child who was in danger. The question "Where is the child?" therefore falls under the public safety exception to the *Miranda* doctrine. Victor's incriminating statement about the seat belt came in response to the police question "Where is the child?" That Victor gave an incriminating response that was related to a totally different crime does not render the police action a *Miranda* violation. Rather, the police acted pursuant to the public safety exception.

STEP 5
If the *Miranda* Doctrine Applies, Did the Police Obtain a Valid Waiver?

Chapter 32: Miranda *Waiver*

If the *Miranda* doctrine applies, it is not sufficient that the police correctly gave the warnings. The officers also need to obtain a valid waiver. Often police have a suspect sign a document indicating that she waives her *Miranda* rights. In other cases, a suspect will explicitly say aloud "I agree to talk." But the *Miranda* doctrine does not require a signed document or an explicit statement for the waiver to be valid. Waiver can be inferred from the circumstances and the actions of the suspect.

CHAPTER 32
Miranda Waiver

THE RULE: The government must prove not only that a suspect was given the *Miranda* warnings, but also that the suspect voluntarily waived her rights. Waiver does not have to be explicit or in writing. Waiver can be demonstrated through the actions of the suspect.

Critical Points

- The government must prove by a preponderance of the evidence that the suspect waived his *Miranda* rights.
- Waiver can be inferred from the circumstances. The suspect does not have to say "Yes, I waive." Nor does the suspect have to sign or initial anything for there to be a valid waiver.
- Waiver is determined based on a totality of the circumstances test.
- Waiver can occur when a suspect sits silently for a long time (potentially hours) after receiving the warnings and then eventually starts talking.
- The police cannot threaten a suspect to get him to waive.

OVERVIEW OF THE BLACKLETTER LAW

Police departments typically have *Miranda* waiver forms for suspects to initial or sign. One part of the form shows that the suspect was given the warnings. The next part of the form indicates that the suspect waives the *Miranda* rights. While most *Miranda* waivers are in writing, they do not have to be. The Supreme Court has made clear that there can be a valid *Miranda* waiver without it being in writing and without the suspect making an explicit statement that she waives her rights. Instead, suspects can waive their *Miranda* rights by a "course of conduct." Put differently, we can infer a valid waiver from the actions and behavior of the suspect.

Waiver is determined by a totality of the circumstances test. Courts thus consider the words uttered by the suspect, his body language, whether he proceeded to answer questions after being read his rights, and a variety of other factors.

The government bears the burden of proving waiver by a preponderance of the evidence. Of course, the police cannot threaten a suspect to get him to waive his *Miranda* rights. But that does not mean it is particularly difficult for police to secure a waiver. The vast majority of defendants waive their *Miranda* rights. Indeed, in the decades since *Miranda* was decided, the Supreme Court has made it easier for the government to establish a valid waiver. For example, in a 2010 case the police read a suspect his rights and the suspect thereafter said nothing for almost three hours. The officers continued to ask the suspect questions and eventually the suspect responded and made incriminating statements. The Court concluded that this series of events amounted to a valid waiver.

EXAM TRAPS TO AVOID

- Do not be tricked into thinking the police complied with *Miranda* just because they read the warnings. The government must also demonstrate that the suspect waived his rights.
- There is no requirement that a suspect waive in writing or that the suspect explicitly say "I waive" or "I agree to answer questions." A suspect's behavior can indicate that she waived her rights to silence and counsel.

MULTIPLE-CHOICE QUESTIONS

Question 177

The police arrested Xavier for armed bank robbery and read him his *Miranda* rights. Xavier said, "Go ahead and try to ask me questions, you'll get nothing because I'm too smart to say anything that will incriminate me." The interrogating officer then told Xavier, "We know you robbed the bank; your fingerprints are all over the place. So why don't you just tell us and get it over with." (In fact, there were no such fingerprints.) Xavier just sat quietly for about 45 seconds, at which point the interrogating officer said, "We can sit here too if that's the game you want to play." The officers waited another 90 seconds in silence. Xavier then said, "So what if I did it, you'll never be able to prove it." Can the prosecution use this statement against Xavier at trial?

A) Yes, because the officers read Xavier his *Miranda* rights and conducted a proper interrogation.

B) Yes, because Xavier cannot benefit from his *Miranda* rights unless he requests a lawyer.

C) No, because Xavier invoked his right to silence and police violated that right by continuing to question him.

D) No, because the interrogation was unconstitutionally coercive.

Question 178

Police arrested Eric on suspicion of money laundering. Police believed that Eric and his coconspirators were running an illegal drug business and putting the profits into a local restaurant to make it look as though the restaurant was earning huge (and legal) sums of money, when in fact the restaurant earned no money and was just a front for the drug business. Officer Miller arrested Eric on Tuesday afternoon while he was sitting in the empty restaurant. The officer read Eric the *Miranda* warnings and asked him if he understood. Eric immediately began to cry. Eric nodded his head up and down and tried to say something but he was crying so hard that no words came out. (Officer Miller later told her supervisor that she thought Eric was crying because he was scared.) After handing Eric a tissue, Officer Miller began speaking. She said, "Look, we know you're involved. Let me just set out all the evidence we have against you and your money laundering operation." After a few minutes of Officer Miller laying out the evidence, Eric began to cry even harder. Officer Smith handed Eric another tissue and while he was wiping his eyes, Officer Miller picked up a big box and placed it on the table. When Eric looked up, Officer Miller said, "All of this is evidence. We've got surveillance of drug deals, we've got bank records, and we've even got receipts from your food supplier showing that you haven't purchased enough food to even run a restaurant." When Eric stopped crying about 10 minutes later, he said, "Okay, you're right, we're laundering the drug money through the restaurant." Which of the following is correct?

A) Eric's confession is inadmissible because he never waived his *Miranda* rights.

B) Eric's confession is inadmissible because Officer Miller thought Eric was scared and his waiver therefore is involuntary.

C) Eric's confession is admissible because Eric waived his rights to counsel and silence.

D) Eric's confession is admissible because even though the officers violated *Miranda* by continuing to press him while he was crying, *Miranda* is a prophylactic rule that does not require suppression in the face of a corroborated confession.

Question 179

Police arrested Fran for accounting fraud. The officers put her in an interrogation room and read her the *Miranda* warnings. The officers then placed a piece of paper in front of her and asked her to initial at the top to indicate that she had received the warnings and at the bottom if she agreed to waive her *Miranda* rights. Fran read the paper, looked up, and said the following: "Do you think I'm dumb? I'm not signing anything. I'll tell you what you need to know so that you'll understand I haven't committed any accounting fraud. But there's no way I'm signing anything. Do you understand?" The officers said, "We understand. Why don't you explain to us why we were wrong to arrest you?" Fran then told the officers what the entries in her accounting books meant and why they were perfectly legitimate. After consulting with an expert in forensic accounting, the officers learned that Fran's statements about the entries in her accounting books were actually incriminating. Can the prosecutor use those statements at trial?

A) No, because Fran refused to sign a written waiver.

B) No, because Fran made clear she was only willing to talk to correct the officers' misunderstandings, and that she was unwilling to make any incriminating statements.

C) Yes, because Fran was read and then knowingly waived her *Miranda* rights and confessed.

D) Yes, because Fran was read her *Miranda* rights.

Question 180

Police arrested Bailey for stealing pills from a pharmacy. The officers suspected that Bailey planned to sell the pills rather than consume them, and they wanted to know who she was working with. The officers read Bailey her *Miranda* rights and she just stared at them afterward. The officers knew she could speak because an hour earlier they had gotten her to spell her name, give her date of birth, and state her address. But after receiving the warnings, Bailey just sat quietly and stared out the window of the jail cell. The officers asked her some questions about why she chose that particular pharmacy and why she grabbed particular drugs instead of others. But Bailey never answered. So the officers just sat there with her and filled out paperwork. More than an hour later, the officers said, "So, Bailey, do you want to be the one who takes all the heat for this crime? Or do you want to give us something so that we can get your sentence knocked down for cooperation?" At that point, Bailey said, "Fine, I'll tell you about the OxyContin distribution operation I was working with." Is Bailey's confession admissible?

A) Yes, because Bailey waived her *Miranda* rights by responding to questions.

B) No, because Bailey never waived her *Miranda* rights and the officers continued to question her.

ANSWERS TO MULTIPLE-CHOICE QUESTIONS

Answer to Question 177

Answer A is correct. Although Xavier has not explicitly said "I waive my *Miranda* rights," that is not required for a valid waiver. Instead, we can infer waiver from Xavier's behavior. Here, Xavier has made a statement that suggests waiver—"Go ahead and try to ask me questions." Additionally, his behavior indicates he is willing to answer questions without counsel.

Answer B is incorrect. The *Miranda* rights include not just the right to counsel, but also the right to remain silent. Xavier has waived both rights. This answer choice is incorrect because it suggests *Miranda* only provides a right to counsel.

Answer C is incorrect. Xavier did not invoke his right to silence. He immediately began answering questions. And even after the police (falsely) told him about fingerprints, Xavier only sat quietly for a few minutes before again making statements.

Answer D is incorrect. The facts in this question do not amount to an unconstitutionally coercive interrogation. Police lied to Xavier about his fingerprints being present at the crime scene, but lying about the evidence, by itself, is not sufficient to render a confession involuntary.

Answer to Question 178

Answer A is incorrect. Eric understood his *Miranda* rights (because he nodded his head up and down) and thereafter answered police questions. The officer showed Eric a box that apparently contained incriminating evidence. This does not render his waiver involuntary, however. Under the totality of the circumstances, Eric has freely, knowingly, and voluntarily waived his right to counsel and silence.

Answer B is incorrect. The subjective views of Officer Miller are not relevant. Moreover, the fact that Eric might have been scared does not render a *Miranda* waiver involuntary. Many criminal suspects are scared when they are taken into custody. Being scared does not render a *Miranda* waiver involuntary.

Answer C is correct. The officer read Eric his *Miranda* rights. Eric indicated that he understood the rights. Thereafter, Eric answered questions. This amounts to a valid waiver.

Answer D is incorrect. Both parts of this answer choice misstate the law. Asking a suspect to waive his *Miranda* rights while the suspect is crying does not render the waiver invalid. Moreover, if the police had committed a *Miranda* violation, the confession would not be admissible simply because it had later been corroborated. A confession obtained in violation of the *Miranda* doctrine should be suppressed.

Answer to Question 179

Answer A is incorrect. A suspect does not have to sign anything in order to validly waive her *Miranda* rights. A suspect can waive by a course of conduct. Here, Fran made clear that she would answer questions, which is a valid *Miranda* waiver.

Answer B is incorrect. When a suspect waives her *Miranda* rights, she does not do so solely for the purpose of making only exculpatory statements. If a suspect waives her right to counsel and her right to remain silent, then *any* statement she makes can be used against her. The fact that a suspect believes she is only making exculpatory statements does not stop the statements from being used against her if they actually contain incriminating material.

Answer C is correct. The police read Fran her *Miranda* rights and she waived them. Fran does not have to waive her rights in writing for the waiver to be valid. There is also no requirement that Fran explicitly say "Yes, I waive" in order for the waiver to be valid. Here, Fran's course of conduct indicates a valid waiver.

Answer D is incorrect. Fran was read her *Miranda* warnings. But simply reading the *Miranda* warnings is not sufficient. The police must obtain a valid waiver. This answer choice says nothing about waiver and incorrectly suggests a confession can be admissible simply because the police read the rights.

Answer to Question 180

Answer A is correct. The Supreme Court has held that if a suspect is read her *Miranda* warnings, sits quietly for hours, and then begins answering questions, that constitutes waiver. You might (logically) think that a suspect who refuses to say anything after being read her *Miranda* rights has invoked her right to silence, but the Supreme Court has held the opposite.

STEP 6
If the Suspect Invoked His *Miranda* Rights, Can the Police Reinitiate Interrogation?

Chapter 33: Invocation and Reapproaching a Suspect Who Has Invoked

If a suspect invokes his *Miranda* rights, the police must stop the interrogation. What happens next depends on whether the suspect invoked the right to counsel or the right to silence.

If a suspect invokes his right to *counsel*, police must permanently halt questioning. The officers cannot reapproach the suspect later to try to seek a waiver.

If a suspect invokes his right to *silence*, police must cease questioning. However, the officers can later reapproach the suspect as long as they have waited long enough.

Finally, regardless of which right was invoked, police can begin a new interrogation if the suspect reinitiates communication and the police read the *Miranda* rights again and obtain a valid waiver.

Chapter 33 reviews the rules for reinitiating interrogation after invocation.

CHAPTER 33
Invocation and Reapproaching a Suspect Who Has Invoked

THE RULE: When a suspect invokes his right to counsel, all interrogation must cease permanently. When a suspect invokes his right to silence, all interrogation must cease for the time being, although the police can later reapproach the suspect and seek a waiver.

Critical Points

- Most suspects do not invoke their *Miranda* rights. But when they do invoke, it is usually at the beginning of an interrogation, right after the police have read the rights.
- A suspect can also invoke her *Miranda* rights in the middle of an interrogation. In other words, even if a suspect initially waived her rights, she can invoke them later and stop an interrogation.
- *Invocation Must Be Unambiguous*:
  - To invoke the right to counsel, the suspect must do so unambiguously. Saying "*Maybe* I should have a lawyer" is not sufficient.
  - To invoke the right to silence, the suspect must do more than simply sit quietly. Similarly, it is not sufficient for a suspect to use ambiguous language like "I might not want to say any more." To invoke the right to silence, the suspect must do so unambiguously.
- *Consequences of Invocation*: If a suspect has invoked her *Miranda* rights, it is important to understand which right—the right to counsel or the right to silence—has been invoked because the Supreme Court treats the rights differently.

- If a suspect invokes his right to *counsel*, police must permanently cease questioning. The officers cannot reapproach the suspect later to try to seek a waiver.
- If a suspect invokes his right to counsel and he is afforded an opportunity to speak with a lawyer, the police still cannot reapproach him later and seek a waiver. Once a suspect has invoked his right to counsel, the police cannot conduct any interrogation in the absence of counsel.
- If the suspect invokes his right to counsel and is released from custody, the police can reapproach him and seek a waiver if 14 days have passed since the release from custody, even if the suspect was never given a lawyer.
- If a suspect invokes his right to *silence*, police must cease questioning. However, the officers can later reapproach the suspect as long as they have "scrupulously honored" his request for silence. In other words, when a suspect says "I don't want to talk anymore" police can later come back to him and say "Do you want to talk now?" as long as they have waited long enough.
- *Miranda* is not offense-specific. That means that once a suspect has invoked her right to counsel, police cannot try to question her about *any* crime unless the suspect is the one who reinitiated communications.

• *Reinitiation by the Suspect*
  - If the suspect reinitiates communication with the officers after having invoked his *Miranda* rights, the police can seek a waiver, and if the suspect waives the police can question him.
  - If the suspect says something like "What is going to happen to me now?" that is sufficient to constitute reinitiation because it relates to the investigation.
  - If the suspect says something like "I'm thirsty, can I get some water?" that is not sufficient to constitute reinitiation.
  - If a suspect reinitiates communication with the police, the officers must first read the suspect his *Miranda* warnings and obtain a waiver before they begin to question him.

OVERVIEW OF THE BLACKLETTER LAW

Recall from Chapter 32 that the government bears the burden of proving that a suspect validly waived her *Miranda* rights. Most suspects waive their rights at the very beginning of an interrogation, either by signing a written form or by engaging in behavior—a course of conduct—that indicates they are willing to waive their rights. In a small percentage of cases, a suspect will very clearly invoke her *Miranda* rights at the beginning of an interrogation. In an even smaller percentage of cases, a suspect will waive her *Miranda* rights at the beginning of an interrogation, but later invoke the right to counsel or silence in the middle of an interrogation. Waiver and invocation are overlapping concepts. A few issues come up, however, that are typically addressed under the label of invocation.

First, we need to understand that for a suspect to invoke his right to counsel, he must do so unambiguously. In the well-known case of *Davis v. United States* (1994), a suspect initially waived his *Miranda* rights. More than an hour into the interrogation, though, the suspect said, "Maybe I should have a lawyer." The Supreme Court held that the suspect's statement did not amount to invocation because it was ambiguous. Moreover, the Court indicated that officers are under no obligation to clarify ambiguous requests for counsel. The officers can simply continue the interrogation as if nothing has happened.

The same rule requiring unambiguous invocation applies to the right to silence. If a suspect says something like "Maybe I shouldn't talk anymore" the police can ignore it and continue the interrogation. Or if a suspect sits silently for a long period, the officers can ignore that as well. In *Berghuis v. Thompkins* (2010), the officers read the suspect the *Miranda* rights but the suspect refused to sign a waiver. Thereafter the police asked the suspect questions for almost three hours while the suspect just sat there. The suspect never said he wanted to invoke his right to remain silent, he just sat mostly silently for hours. Eventually, the suspect made incriminating statements. The Court concluded that sitting mostly silently was *not* an unambiguous invocation. Rather, to be unambiguous, the suspect would have had to actually say he wanted to remain silent or that he did not want to talk with the police. In short, the suspect needs to clearly say that he wants to invoke his right to silence or counsel.

Most suspects do not invoke their *Miranda* rights. But if they do invoke, what happens next? The answer depends on which right the suspect has invoked. If a suspect invokes the right to counsel, the interrogation must permanently cease. If a suspect invokes the right to silence, the interrogation must temporarily cease, but the officers can reapproach the suspect to later seek a waiver of the *Miranda* rights. Finally, if the suspect reinitiates discussion, the police may be able to seek a waiver and restart the interrogation. Let's take each of those three scenarios in turn.

Invoking the Right to Counsel: The Supreme Court treats the invocation of the right to counsel very seriously. Once a suspect has unambiguously invoked, all interrogation must cease. The police cannot reapproach the suspect later to try to get her to waive her *Miranda* rights. Even if the suspect meets with a lawyer, the police still cannot approach the suspect and ask for a *Miranda* waiver after the lawyer has left. Moreover, the *Miranda* right to counsel is not offense-specific, i.e., not just for the offense the suspect was arrested for. Once a suspect has invoked her right to counsel, no officer can question her about *any* crime without her lawyer. In short, invocation of the right to counsel means the police can only deal with the suspect through her lawyer. The Court has recognized one minor exception to the rule that police cannot approach a suspect who has invoked her right to counsel: If a suspect invoked her right to counsel but was released from custody for at least 14 days, the police can reapproach and seek a waiver, even if the suspect was never given a lawyer.

Invoking the Right to Silence: The Supreme Court treats the invocation of the right to silence less seriously than invocation of the right to counsel. If a suspect unambiguously invokes the right to silence, the police must halt the interrogation. But they do not have to halt the interrogation forever. If the officers "scrupulously honor" the suspect's request for silence, they can reapproach the suspect and ask him again to waive his *Miranda* rights. The idea here is that when a person indicates they do not want to talk to the police they may not be saying they don't *ever* want to talk. The suspect may basically be saying "I don't want to talk *right now*." Accordingly, the Court allows the police to reapproach a suspect who has invoked the right to silence because, after waiting a reasonable period, the suspect might then be willing to talk. Unfortunately, the Court has not given clear guidance on how long the police must wait before reapproaching the suspect.

Reinitiating: Although the police cannot reapproach a suspect who has invoked the right to counsel (or too quickly reapproach a suspect who has invoked the right to silence), that does not stop the suspect from reinitiating contact with the police. If a suspect who has invoked his *Miranda* rights reinitiates discussion, the officers may seek a new *Miranda* waiver and (if the suspect waives) then start interrogating the suspect. The tricky question here is: what amounts to reinitiation by the suspect? The Court has indicated that when the suspect brings up the criminal case or the investigation, that amounts to reinitiation. For instance, if a suspect asks the officers an open-ended question—such as "What is going to happen to me now?"— that amounts to reinitiation. By contrast, if the suspect only asks the officers for a basic necessity—such as "Can I have some food or a drink of water?"—that does not amount to reinitiation.

EXAM TRAPS TO AVOID

- Do not be too quick to find invocation of the right to counsel. To invoke, the suspect must do it unambiguously. If there is hedging language like "might" or "maybe," that is probably not sufficient for invocation.
- Do not be too quick to find invocation of the right to silence. If the suspect uses words like "might" or "maybe" that is probably not enough for invocation. And if the suspect just sits quietly without saying anything, that does not amount to unambiguous invocation either.
- If a suspect is unclear—i.e., ambiguous—when she requests counsel or silence, the police can ignore it. The officers are not obligated to clarify whether the suspect wants to invoke his rights.

- Remember that the right to counsel and the right to silence are treated differently. It is much easier for the police to reapproach a suspect who has invoked only the right to silence.

MULTIPLE-CHOICE QUESTIONS

Question 181

Police have arrested Jamey for attempted murder. The officers know that Jamey shot Marilynn but they do not know why. They assume Jamey will claim she acted in self-defense, so they want to find out the details. The officers read Jamey her *Miranda* rights and Jamey waives both verbally and in writing. After an hour of discussion, Jamey senses things are not going well. She says to the officers, "I'm done. I want a lawyer." Which of the following is correct?

A) The interrogation must permanently cease because Jamey has invoked her right to counsel.

B) The officers must scrupulously honor Jamey's request and thus the interrogation must cease for a reasonable period.

C) The officers can continue to question Jamey because she has made a valid waiver of her *Miranda* rights.

D) The officers can continue to question Jamey because her invocation of the right to counsel was ambiguous.

Question 182

Assume the same facts as Question 181, except for purposes of this question assume that Jamey told the officers, "I'm not sure it's a good idea for me to be talking. Maybe I should talk to a lawyer." Now, which of the following is correct?

A) The police must halt the interrogation and clarify with Jamey whether she actually wants a lawyer.

B) The police must cease the interrogation because Jamey has invoked her right to counsel.

C) The police can ignore Jamey's statement because it is an ambiguous invocation.

D) The police must allow Jamey to consult with an attorney and after the lawyer departs the officers can resume the interrogation.

Question 183

Police have arrested Chuck for murder. The officers read Chuck his *Miranda* rights and Chuck says, "No, I don't want to talk now." The officers return Chuck to his jail cell at noon and leave him alone. Seven hours later, the officers go back to Chuck's jail cell and say, "It's been a while. We just wanted to see if you've changed your mind and want to talk with us." Chuck nods his head up and down. Which of the following is correct?

A) The police can immediately begin asking Chuck questions because they have scrupulously honored his right to remain silent.

B) The police can begin asking Chuck questions, but only if they first read him his *Miranda* warnings again and Chuck waives his rights.

C) The police cannot ask Chuck questions because he invoked his right to silence and the police cannot reapproach him to ask him to waive.

D) The police cannot ask Chuck questions because they must wait at least 48 hours before reapproaching a suspect who has invoked his right to silence.

Question 184

Assume the same fact as Question 183. For purposes of this question, though, imagine that after the police read Chuck his *Miranda* rights that he says, "I'm not saying anything. I want a lawyer." The officers return Chuck to his jail cell. The next day the officers come to Chuck's cell and say, "We just wanted to see if you've changed your mind and want to talk with us." Chuck says, "Fine. I guess I'll talk." The officers read Chuck his *Miranda* rights and he signs a written waiver. An hour later, Chuck confesses to the murder. Which of the following is correct?

A) Chuck's confession is admissible because the police obtained a valid waiver.

B) Chuck's confession is inadmissible because the police were not permitted to reapproach a suspect who invoked his right to counsel.

Question 185

For purposes of this question, assume the same facts as Question 184 with the following variation. After Chuck said, "I'm not saying anything. I want a lawyer" the police returned Chuck to his jail cell. The next day the police brought Chuck to a private room where he met with the public defender for more than an hour. At the end of the meeting, the public defender went back to the courthouse and Chuck went back to his jail cell. Later that day, the police officers came to Chuck's jail cell and said, "Well, now you've had a chance to speak to your lawyer, are you willing to speak to us now?" Chuck was hesitant and said "Well—" The officers said, "Look, no pressure. Let us just read you the *Miranda* warnings and then you can decide. Obviously, it's up to you." The officers read Chuck the *Miranda* warnings and handed him a written copy of the warnings. The officers then left Chuck alone for 20 minutes. When the officers returned, Chuck had signed the *Miranda* waiver. Subsequently, the officers questioned Chuck about the murder and he confessed. Is Chuck's confession admissible?

A) Yes, because the officers gave Chuck ample time to consider whether to waive his right to counsel.

B) Yes, because Chuck had an opportunity to meet with counsel and thereafter signed a valid waiver of his *Miranda* rights.

C) No, because Chuck invoked his right to counsel and he cannot later reverse that decision.

D) No, because Chuck invoked his right to counsel and the police improperly reapproached him and questioned him without his lawyer present.

Question 186

Police have arrested Howard for auto theft. The officers read Howard his *Miranda* warnings and were hoping he would waive his rights so that they could ask him who else he was working with. But Howard immediately said, "I won't say a word without speaking to my lawyer." The officers returned Howard to his jail cell and did not say another word to him. Four hours later the officers heard a clamor from Howard's jail cell. When the officers arrived at the cell, Howard immediately said, "I need a cup of coffee. What do I have to do to get a cup of coffee?" The officers brought Howard some coffee and then asked him if he had changed his mind and was willing to talk about the auto theft charge. Howard agreed to talk and the officers provided Howard with a new set of *Miranda* warnings and obtained a waiver. Howard subsequently confessed. Is his confession admissible?

A) Yes, because Howard reinitiated contact with the officers and thus they can seek a valid waiver.

B) No, because Howard's statements to the officers did not constitute reinitiation.

Question 187

Assume the same facts as Question 186 above. For purposes of this question, however, imagine that when police went to Howard's cell that Howard said, "So, I've got to know. What's going to happen to me now?" The officers then explained that Howard did not have to talk to the officers and Howard said he understood. The officers further explained that the case was being referred to the prosecutor and that Howard was likely going to be criminally charged with murder. Howard again said he understood. The officer read Howard his *Miranda* rights and Howard waived. An hour later, Howard made an incriminating statement. Is Howard's statement admissible?

A) Yes, because he reinitiated discussion of the criminal investigation with the officers.

B) No, because Howard never indicated a desire to forgo the right to counsel he had invoked and thus the police reapproached him in violation of *Miranda*.

Question 188

Police officers from Smith County arrested Erin for money laundering and read her the *Miranda* rights. Erin responded by saying, "I want a lawyer." The officers ceased interrogation and took Erin from the interrogation room to her jail cell. Two days later, police from a neighboring county—James County—learned that Erin had been incarcerated in Smith County. The James County officers had been looking for Erin because they suspected she was involved in an armed robbery that had recently happened in James County. The James County officers drove to the Smith County jail and went to Erin's cell. The James County officers told Erin they suspected her of being involved in the armed robbery and that they wanted to talk to her about it. The James County officers read Erin her *Miranda* rights and got Erin to give a signed waiver. In less than an hour, Erin confessed to involvement in the James County armed robbery. Is Erin's confession admissible?

A) Erin's confession to the James County officers is admissible because she waived her *Miranda* rights in response to interrogation by officers from a completely different county for a different crime.

B) Erin's confession to the James County officers is admissible because her interrogation occurred 48 hours after her invocation of the right to counsel.

C) Erin's confession to the James County officers is inadmissible because her request for a lawyer to Smith County officials is imputed to James County officers and therefore no valid waiver could have occurred when the James County officers questioned her.

D) Erin's confession to the James County officers is inadmissible because it is fruit of the poisonous tree from the Smith County officers' failure to provide Erin with counsel after she invoked.

Question 189

Ari is an inmate in the Los Angeles Detention Center, serving a multiyear sentence for mail fraud. A police detective went to the detention center to interview Ari about unrelated assault allegations. Shortly after the detective began his questioning, Ari invoked his *Miranda* rights and said he refused to speak to the detective without an attorney being present. The detective ended the interview, left the detention center, and never returned. Two years later, Los Angeles police reopened the assault case against Ari. By this time, Ari had finished serving his sentence for mail fraud and had been living in a city near Los Angeles for more than six months. The new detective found Ari and read him his *Miranda* rights. Ari expressed surprise at the renewed questioning because he thought the assault investigation had been closed years ago. Ari did not request an attorney, and he subsequently confessed to the detective. Ari's lawyer has moved to suppress his confession. Which of the following is correct?

A) Ari's confession should be excluded because he requested a lawyer during his interview at the Los Angeles Detention Center and the police thus violated his *Miranda* rights by later questioning him without a lawyer present.

B) Ari's confession should be admissible because while he was entitled to a lawyer when he requested one at the Los Angeles Detention Center, more than 14 days have passed since he was released from custody and thus there was no *Miranda* violation in approaching him and seeking a waiver.

C) Ari's confession should be admissible because while he was entitled to a lawyer when he requested one at the Los Angeles Detention Center, failure to provide a lawyer is only error if the police reapproach the suspect within a "reasonably close period" and two years is too long.

D) Ari's confession should be admissible because he was not entitled to a lawyer because he was already incarcerated on other charges and thus the limited rationale for the *Miranda* doctrine (to prevent coercive interrogations) was not present.

ANSWERS TO MULTIPLE-CHOICE QUESTIONS

Answer to Question 181

Answer A is correct. A suspect who has already waived her right to counsel can invoke her rights in the middle of an interrogation. When that happens, the interrogation must cease.

Answer B is incorrect. The "scrupulously honor" language and the rule that police must cease an interrogation for a period of time (but not permanently) is for invocation of the right to silence. Here, Jamey has invoked her right to counsel. Invocation of the right to counsel requires an interrogation to cease immediately and permanently unless the suspect reinitiates.

Answer C is incorrect. Jamey's initial waiver was valid. However, a suspect is permitted to invoke the right to counsel or silence in the middle of an interrogation.

Answer D is incorrect. Jamey's invocation was not ambiguous. She specifically said "I want a lawyer."

Answer to Question 182

Answer A is incorrect. Jamey's request for counsel is ambiguous. But the officers do not have to halt the interrogation or clarify whether she actually wants a lawyer. Because the request for counsel is ambiguous, the officers can ignore it.

Answer B is incorrect. Because Jamey's request for counsel is ambiguous the police can ignore it.

Answer C is correct. The Supreme Court has held that when a suspect is ambiguous as to whether they are requesting counsel, the police need not halt the interrogation or clarify what the suspect wants. The Court has specifically considered the phrase "Maybe I should have a lawyer" and concluded that such a statement is ambiguous and thus does not require police to halt the interrogation and provide counsel.

Answer D is incorrect. This answer is wrong for multiple reasons. First, Jamey has made an ambiguous request for counsel because "Maybe I should have a lawyer" is ambiguous. Second, if Jamey had made an unambiguous request for counsel that would require the police to permanently halt the interrogation, police could not resume the interrogation after the lawyer left.

Answer to Question 183

Answer A is not the best choice. This answer choice is very tempting, but notice that after the police reapproached Chuck that they did not again read him the *Miranda* warnings. Police can reapproach a suspect who has invoked his right to silence as long as they "scrupulously honor" his request for silence. Here, it appears the police have done so because they left Chuck alone for seven hours. However, before beginning another interrogation the police must reread Chuck the *Miranda* warnings and obtain a valid waiver. This answer choice does not say that the officers did that.

Answer B is the best choice. As noted above, police can reapproach a suspect who has invoked his right to silence if they scrupulously honor his request for silence. If the suspect then indicates that he is willing to talk, the police must still read him his *Miranda* rights and obtain a valid waiver.

Answer C is incorrect. Police can reapproach a suspect who has invoked his right to silence. The officers must "scrupulously honor" his original request to remain silent, but the officers can, at a reasonable point, go back to the suspect and ask if he is willing to waive his *Miranda* rights.

Answer D is incorrect. There is no specific 48-hour period that the police must wait. Rather than adopt a bright-line rule like 48 hours, the Supreme Court has adopted a grey rule that police must "scrupulously honor" the suspect's original invocation of his right to silence.

Answer to Question 184

Answer B is correct. Chuck has unambiguously invoked his right to counsel by saying "I want a lawyer." When a suspect invokes his right to counsel, all interrogation must cease and the police cannot reapproach a suspect and seek a waiver. Because Chuck has requested counsel, the police can only deal with him through counsel.

Answer to Question 185

Answer A is incorrect. The officers did give Chuck 20 minutes, which seems like plenty of time. But that is not the relevant issue. Chuck had invoked his right to counsel. The police are not permitted to reapproach Chuck and ask him to reverse his decision, no matter how long they give him to consider it.

Answer B is incorrect. This answer choice is tempting, but it is incorrect. While Chuck had an opportunity to meet with his lawyer, that does not mean the police can re-approach Chuck and ask him to waive his *Miranda* rights after the lawyer leaves. Once a suspect has invoked his right to counsel, the police may not attempt to question the suspect outside the presence of his lawyer.

Answer C is incorrect. This answer choice is overbroad. Police cannot reapproach a suspect who has waived his right to counsel and seek to have him reverse his decision. But that does not mean Chuck can never change his mind. If Chuck himself decides to reinitiate discussion of the crime with the officers, Chuck can choose of his own accord to reverse his decision to invoke the right to counsel or silence.

Answer D is correct. After Chuck invoked his right to counsel, the police properly halted the interrogation and allowed him to meet with a lawyer. However, it was impermissible for the police to then reapproach Chuck and seek a *Miranda* waiver after the public defender left. Once a suspect has invoked his right to counsel, the police may not reapproach the suspect to seek a waiver. The police must not try to question the suspect outside the presence of his lawyer.

Answer to Question 186

Answer B is correct. Howard invoked his right to counsel, which means police cannot reapproach him to ask for a *Miranda* waiver unless Howard reinitiates. Howard did start the conversation with the officers when he asked for coffee, but this does not amount to reinitiation. Howard did not indicate a willingness to discuss the crime or his criminal case. Rather, he was seeking a drink. The Supreme Court recognized in *Oregon v. Bradshaw* (1983) that "[t]here are some inquiries, such as a request for a drink of water or a request to use a telephone that are so routine that they cannot be fairly said to represent a desire on the part of an accused to open up a more generalized discussion relating directly or indirectly to the investigation." Because Howard did not reinitiate, the police have improperly sought a *Miranda* waiver from a suspect who had invoked his right to counsel, and Howard's confession must be suppressed.

Answer to Question 187

Answer A is correct. Although Howard never said, "I want to talk about the murder charge I was arrested for," such a blunt statement is not necessary for reinitiation. The Supreme Court has held that language like "What's going to happen to me now?" relates to the investigation (rather than basic human needs such as food or water) and thus opens the door for police to seek a new waiver. In short, Howard's statement "What is going to happen to me now?" amounts to Howard reinitiating discussion with the police and invites the police to seek a *Miranda* waiver. Since the officers thereafter obtained a waiver, Howard's confession should be admissible.

Answer to Question 188

Answer A is incorrect. This answer would be correct if the *Miranda* doctrine were offense-specific. But the *Miranda* doctrine is not offense-specific. If a suspect invokes her right to counsel under *Miranda* for one offense, it prevents any officer from questioning her—even for other offenses—in the absence of counsel.

Answer B is incorrect. An invocation of the right to counsel does not expire after 48 hours. To the contrary, if a suspect remains in custody, the invocation of the right to counsel never expires. Police cannot approach a suspect who has already invoked his right to counsel to seek a *Miranda* waiver.

Answer C is correct. When a suspect invokes her right to counsel, that invocation applies to all officers and all offenses. No officer is permitted to seek a waiver from a suspect who has already invoked her right to counsel.

Answer D is incorrect. Erin's confession is not admissible because the James County officers have violated the *Miranda* doctrine by seeking a waiver from a suspect who has already invoked her right to counsel. This is not a fruit of the poisonous tree violation. (As discussed in Chapter 34, the fruit of the poisonous tree doctrine does not ordinarily apply to the *Miranda* doctrine.) Erin's confession will not be suppressed because it is fruit of the poisonous tree from the Smith County officers' actions. Rather, the confession is inadmissible because the James County officers—at the time they seek a waiver—are violating *Miranda*.

Answer to Question 189

Answer A is incorrect. This answer would ordinarily be correct. However, in this case Ari has been released from custody for more than 14 days since initially invoking his right to counsel. The Supreme Court decided in *Maryland v. Shatzer* (2010) that when a person has been released from custody for at least two weeks, he has had time to re-center himself and seek legal advice if necessary. Therefore, once it has been more than two weeks since the suspect has been released from custody, it is permissible for the police to reapproach the suspect and seek a new waiver.

Answer B is correct. As noted above, the Supreme Court addressed this situation in *Maryland v. Shatzer* (2010). The Court concluded that a person who has been released from custody for at least two weeks has had an opportunity to readjust themselves and assess their legal options. Accordingly, once it has been more than two weeks since the suspect has been released from custody, police may reapproach the suspect and seek a new waiver.

Answer C is incorrect. The Supreme Court has never suggested that an invocation of the right to counsel expires after a "reasonably close period." There is no such test.

Answer D is incorrect. Police must always provide a suspect with *Miranda* warnings before engaging in custodial interrogation. This is true for suspects who are already incarcerated and serving prison time for another crime.

STEP 7
Is Evidence Found from an Unlawful Confession Fruit of the Poisonous Tree?

Chapter 34: Fruit of the Poisonous Tree for Miranda *and Involuntary Confessions*

If the police coerced a confession or committed a *Miranda* violation, the confession will be suppressed. But your analysis does not end there. Sometimes an unlawful confession leads police to physical evidence. And in rare cases police extract a second confession after initially getting a first confession from a *Miranda* violation. Chapter 34 explains that the Supreme Court rigorously applies the fruit of the poisonous tree doctrine to coerced confessions, but not to *Miranda* violations.

CHAPTER 34

Fruit of the Poisonous Tree for *Miranda* and Involuntary Confessions

THE RULE: Evidence found as a result of a coerced confession is not admissible, but evidence found as a result of a *Miranda* violation usually is admissible.

Critical Points

- If a coerced confession leads police to find other evidence, both the confession and any evidence that the confession led to will be suppressed.
- If a *Miranda* violation leads police to find physical evidence, the incriminating statement procured in violation of *Miranda* will be suppressed, but the physical evidence found as a result of the *Miranda* violation will be admissible.
- If a *Miranda* violation leads to police learning a witness's name, the testimony of that witness will typically be permissible.
- *Two-Step Interrogations and Multiple Confessions*: Sometimes police obtain a confession after a *Miranda* violation, then give the proper *Miranda* warnings and get a second confession. This is called a two-step interrogation. When it is clear that the officers have intentionally undertaken a two-step interrogation and that they have not engaged in curative measures (such as telling the suspect that the first confession is inadmissible), both confessions will be inadmissible.

OVERVIEW OF THE BLACKLETTER LAW

The Supreme Court has vigorously applied the fruit of the poisonous tree doctrine to coerced confessions. If police coerce a suspect into confessing, the confession will be excluded and any evidence that the police find as a result will also be excluded. For example, imagine that police physically assault a suspect during an interrogation and the suspect confesses to a murder and tells the police where the murder weapon is hidden. The confession will be excluded because it was coerced; the murder weapon will be excluded as it is fruit of the poisonous tree because it was found as a result of a coerced confession.

The Supreme Court does *not* vigorously apply the fruit of the poisonous tree doctrine to confessions obtained in violation of *Miranda*. Indeed, the Court has signaled that the fruit of the poisonous tree doctrine applies to *Miranda* violations in only the rarest of cases. Imagine the same hypothetical as in the paragraph above, except this time the police fail to give the *Miranda* warnings, rather than physically hitting the suspect. The suspect's confession will be inadmissible because of the *Miranda* violation. But the murder weapon will be admissible because the fruit of the poisonous tree doctrine does not apply to physical evidence found as a result of a *Miranda* violation. Similarly, if police locate a witness as a result of a *Miranda* violation, the testimony of that witness will be available.

One of the most difficult fruit of the poisonous tree problems is the so-called two-step interrogation. The police sometimes interrogate a suspect in violation of *Miranda*, get a confession, and then say "Oops, we forgot to give you the *Miranda* warnings." The officers then give the *Miranda* warnings and get a waiver, and then the suspect confesses again. The first confession is always inadmissible because it stemmed directly from a *Miranda* violation. How to handle the second confession is a tricky question, though. On the one hand, as explained above, there is generally no fruit of the poisonous tree doctrine for *Miranda* violations. On the other hand, the two-step interrogation completely undermines the *Miranda* doctrine and allows the police to do an end-run around *Miranda*'s requirements. The Supreme Court addressed this problem, but unfortunately the Court was deeply fractured and did not offer a clear answer. The Court seemed to indicate that if police *intentionally* engaged in a two-step interrogation, both confessions would be inadmissible unless the Court took curative measures after the *Miranda* violation. For example, if police officers failed to give the *Miranda* warnings and got a confession, the problem could be rectified if the police told the suspect, "Hey, we forgot to give you the *Miranda* warnings. Your first confession isn't admissible." Then, if the police properly Mirandized the suspect and got a valid waiver, the second confession would be admissible.

EXAM TRAPS TO AVOID

- Do not treat coerced confessions and *Miranda* violations the same for fruit of the poisonous tree doctrine purposes. The fruit of the poisonous tree doctrine always applies to coerced confessions, but almost never to *Miranda* violations.
- If the police conducted a two-step interrogation, look closely for facts that suggest whether they did so intentionally or accidentally. If the police intentionally engaged in a two-step ploy, it is likely that both confessions (the one before the *Miranda* warnings and the one after the warnings) will be inadmissible.

MULTIPLE-CHOICE QUESTIONS

Question 190

Police arrest Jeff without probable cause and quickly take him to the police station for questioning. The police read Jeff his *Miranda* rights and Jeff says that he understands those rights and does not need a lawyer because he has done nothing wrong. Police ask Jeff a couple of questions and after only five minutes Jeff confesses to having committed a burglary. At trial, Jeff moves to suppress his confession. How should the court rule?

A) Jeff's motion should be granted because his confession is the fruit of an illegal arrest.

B) Jeff's motion should be granted because the police did not give him a sufficient amount of time to consider his decision to decline counsel before they began questioning him.

C) Jeff's motion should be denied because his confession was given voluntarily and intelligently.

D) Jeff's motion should be denied because he was read his *Miranda* rights.

Question 191

Ryan is under arrest for the kidnapping of a young child. Officer Cable is eager to see Ryan convicted. During interrogation, Officer Cable "softened Ryan up a little" by punching him in the stomach a couple of times and scaring him with a German Shepherd police dog. After a few hours with Officer Cable, Ryan said, "I kidnapped her, she's alive, and I can tell you where she is if you leave me alone." As a result of the interrogation, the child was safely returned to her family and the police discovered physical evidence linking Ryan to the crime. Ryan has moved to suppress his confession and the physical evidence. How should the court rule?

A) The court should admit the confession and the physical evidence because the officer's actions were justified under the public safety exception.

B) The court should exclude the confession because it was coerced, but it should admit the physical evidence because the fruit of the poisonous tree doctrine does not apply.

C) The court should admit the confession under the ongoing crime doctrine, but it should exclude the physical evidence under the fruit of the poisonous tree doctrine.

D) The court should exclude the confession because it was coerced and exclude the physical evidence under the fruit of the poisonous tree doctrine.

Question 192

In which of the following situations is the subjective belief of a government actor, as opposed to the objective view, potentially relevant?

A) Whether there is a public safety situation that justifies police questioning before the officer gives any *Miranda* warnings.

B) Whether an officer engaged in a two-step process of not giving the *Miranda* warnings, securing a confession, and then providing the *Miranda* warnings.

C) Whether the officer acted in good faith in believing that the suspect had waived his *Miranda* rights.

D) Whether the officer believed that the deception used during an interrogation did not amount to extreme psychological manipulation.

E) None of the above.

Question 193

Police arrested Will for the armed robbery of a gas station. The officers read Will his *Miranda* rights, and Will responded by saying, "Lawyer. I want my lawyer." The officers said, "Look, calm down. This doesn't have to be hard. We just want to talk." Will then responded, "I don't want it to be difficult either. I just want to go home. It's not fair." The officers asked, "What do you mean? What's not fair?" Will then said, "It wasn't even my idea. It was Mike's idea. I can prove he was the leader, too. That's why the money is buried behind a tree in his backyard." The officers went to Mike's house but found that he had already fled the state. In Mike's backyard, behind a tree, they found the stolen money. The prosecutor wants to charge Will. Although Will never specifically said, "I robbed the gas station," the prosecutor is confident that his statements amount to a confession and that the jury would convict. Which of the following is a correct statement about the admissibility of the evidence against Will?

A) Will's statement is inadmissible because there was a *Miranda* violation, but the physical evidence is admissible.

B) Will's statement is admissible because there was no *Miranda* violation, and the physical evidence is also admissible.

C) Will's statement is inadmissible because there was a *Miranda* violation, and the physical evidence is also inadmissible.

D) Will's statement is inadmissible because there was a *Miranda* violation, and the physical evidence is inadmissible because the police searched the backyard without a warrant.

Question 194

Anderson is under arrest for aggravated assault of Chris. There is no video of the incident and no eyewitnesses. Officers Roberts and Stevens are investigating the case and they believe that Anderson is guilty, but they are concerned that he will try to claim it is a case of mistaken identity. Officers Roberts and Stevens therefore decide to interrogate Anderson in the hopes of getting him to give a story that is inconsistent with the "someone else did it" theory. When the officers enter the interrogation room, they immediately take a sympathetic tone and tell Anderson, "Look, we know you hit him and we don't blame him. He's a loudmouth and he probably started it. We bet you acted in self-defense. We just need to figure out what happened." Anderson trusts the officers and tells them, "Yah, I hit him. But you're right, he started it." The officers whisper something to each other and then say, "Okay, okay" and read Anderson his *Miranda* rights. Anderson waives his rights, and then the officers say, "Okay, just tell us once more about you hitting Chris is self-defense." Anderson responded by saying, "I hit him with a bat, but he started it." Is Anderson's statement "I hit him with a bat" admissible?

A) Yes, it is admissible because Anderson was properly Mirandized and he waived.

B) No, it is not admissible because the police violated *Miranda*.

Question 195

Assume the same facts as Question 194. This time, however, assume that after Anderson made his first statement that the officers said, "Okay, let's get you to write that down." Officer Roberts opened a desk drawer and took out the police department's standard confession form. When Officer Roberts looked at the front of the document (which was the section about receiving and waiving *Miranda* rights), he turned to Officer Stevens and said, "Oh crap, we forgot to read him his *Miranda* rights." Officer Stevens said, "I thought you were going to do it. This is your fault." Anderson then asked, "What's going on?" Officer Roberts replied, "We made a mistake. We were supposed to read you the *Miranda* rights before we asked you any questions. The statements you just made are not admissible." The officers then left the room for 15 minutes to go ask a supervisor what to do. When they returned, the officers said, "Okay, let's try this again. We've got to do a proper *Miranda* waiver before we can get any binding statements from you." Officer Roberts then read Anderson the *Miranda* warnings and handed him the standard confession form and asked him to initial that he had received the warnings and then to initial if he was willing to waive his *Miranda* rights. Anderson signed the document and again said, "Like I said, I hit him with a bat, but he started it." Which of the following is correct?

A) Anderson's confession "Like I said, I hit him with a bat" is admissible because the police cured the defect from the first interrogation.

B) Anderson's confession "Like I said, I hit him with a bat" is admissible because there is never a fruit of the poisonous tree problem resulting from violations of *Miranda*.

C) Anderson's confession "Like I said, I hit him with a bat" is not admissible because it included the phrase "Like I said" and referenced the earlier inadmissible confession.

D) Anderson's confession "Like I said, I hit him with a bat" is not admissible because this was a two-step interrogation.

ANSWERS TO MULTIPLE-CHOICE QUESTIONS

Answer to Question 190

Answer A is correct. This is a trick question. As we learned, the fruit of the poisonous tree doctrine typically does not apply to *Miranda* violations. But this question does not involve a *Miranda* violation (though it does involve *Miranda* warnings). The violation here is the unlawful arrest without probable cause. There is a fruit of the poisonous tree doctrine for illegal arrests in violation of the Fourth Amendment. And a *Miranda* waiver after arrest, by itself, does not break the chain for fruit of the poisonous tree purposes. Accordingly, the confession should be suppressed because it stemmed from the illegal arrest.

Answer B is incorrect. Police do not have to wait a particular amount of time for a suspect to consider his *Miranda* rights before obtaining a valid waiver.

Answer C is incorrect. Jeff's confession was not coerced. But that is not the issue in this case. There was an unlawful arrest that raised a fruit of the poisonous tree problem.

Answer D is incorrect. As explained in response to Answer A, the reading of the *Miranda* rights, by itself, is not enough to break the chain stemming from an illegal arrest. There is a fruit of the poisonous tree problem that is not remedied solely by giving *Miranda* warnings.

Answer to Question 191

Answer A is incorrect. There is a public safety exception for the *Miranda* doctrine, but the Court has never recognized a comparable exception for coerced confessions.

Ryan's confession is coerced because the officer used physical force to obtain it. Accordingly, the confession is inadmissible and the fruit of the poisonous tree doctrine renders the subsequently discovered physical evidence inadmissible as well.

Answer B is incorrect. The fruit of the poisonous tree doctrine applies to coerced confessions. Accordingly, the physical evidence is inadmissible.

Answer C is incorrect. The Supreme Court has never recognized an "ongoing crime exception" to the Fifth Amendment.

Answer D is correct. The confession is coerced because the officer punched Ryan in the stomach and threatened him with a police dog. Coerced confessions are not admissible. Moreover, because the coerced confession led to the physical evidence, that evidence is also inadmissible under the fruit of the poisonous tree doctrine.

Answer to Question 192

As you learned through your criminal procedure course and this book, the subjective intent of the officer is almost never relevant for Fourth or Fifth Amendment purposes. It is not applicable to determining whether there is a public safety exception to *Miranda*, whether the suspect waived his *Miranda* rights, or whether the police deception was too coercive. The subjective intent of the officer is potentially relevant, however, in the two-step interrogation process where the suspect confesses without having received *Miranda* warnings, and then the officer reads the warnings for the first time and the suspect confesses again. The Supreme Court—in a fractured decision—seemed to suggest that the admissibility of the second confession may turn on whether the officers intentionally failed to read the *Miranda* warnings at first in the hope of tricking the suspect into believing the "cat was out of the bag" so that he would not invoke his *Miranda* rights after later being warned. Because the test turns in part on whether the officers intentionally engaged in this ploy, the subjective intent of the officers would be relevant. Answer B is therefore correct.

Answer to Question 193

Answer A is correct. The police violated *Miranda* by continuing to question Will after he had invoked his right to counsel. As a result, Will's incriminating statements are not admissible. However, the fruit of the poisonous tree doctrine does not apply to physical evidence found as a result of a *Miranda* violation. Thus the physical evidence is admissible.

Answer B is incorrect. There was a *Miranda* violation in this case. The police properly read Will his *Miranda* rights, but he did not waive them. To the contrary, he specifically said he wanted a lawyer. At that point, all questioning should have ceased. The officers continued to question Will, though, and therefore his incriminating statements cannot be admitted.

Answer C is incorrect. While Will's statements did violate *Miranda* and should therefore be suppressed, physical evidence found as a result of a *Miranda* violation will not be excluded. The fruit of the poisonous tree doctrine does not apply to physical evidence found as a result of a *Miranda* violation.

Answer D is incorrect. While Will's statements did violate *Miranda* and therefore should be excluded, the physical evidence found thereafter should be admitted. Assuming that the police did search Mike's backyard illegally, Will lacks standing to object to a search of Mike's property.

Answer to Question 194

Answer A is incorrect. Anderson was not properly Mirandized. The police initially questioned him without giving him the *Miranda* warnings and obtaining a proper waiver.

Answer B is correct. This appears to be a two-step interrogation. The officers interrogated Anderson without first giving him the *Miranda* warnings and obtaining a proper waiver. After Anderson made incriminating statements, the officers only then gave the *Miranda* warnings and obtained a proper waiver. Anderson's second confession is therefore potentially inadmissible under the Supreme Court's decision in *Missouri v. Seibert* (2004). Although the Court's decision was fractured, the key factor appears to be whether the officers conducted a two-step interrogation on purpose and without curative measures before obtaining the second confession. Here it looks like the police acted intentionally. The officers made a plan before entering the interrogation room. After Anderson's first confession, the officers immediately whispered to themselves and then immediately gave Anderson the *Miranda* warnings. Moreover, the officers took no curative steps. For instance, they could have told Anderson that the first confession would not be admissible before seeking a *Miranda* waiver and interrogating him further. They did not do so. As such, it looks like the police conducted a deliberate two-step interrogation and that Anderson's confession should not be admissible.

Answer to Question 195

Answer A is correct. This question involves a two-step interrogation problem. However, unlike in Question 194, it does not appear that the officers intentionally utilized a two-step interrogation to get around *Miranda*. Moreover, they engaged in curative measures by: (1) telling Anderson that the first confession would not be admissible; and (2) taking 15 minutes in between the two interrogations.

Answer B is incorrect. There is *almost* never a fruit of the poisonous tree doctrine for *Miranda*. However, the doctrine does apply to intentional two-step interrogations. Answer B is therefore too broad.

Answer C is incorrect. The fact that a second confession obtained in compliance with *Miranda* references an earlier confession that was obtained in violation of *Miranda* does not automatically render the second confession inadmissible.

Answer D is incorrect. This answer choice is too broad. Not all two-step interrogations are unconstitutional. If the police accidentally failed to read the warnings but then cured their error (as they did here by saying that the first confession would not be admissible) the second confession can be admissible.

Rules Governing Other Investigative Techniques

Although searches, seizures, and confessions will make up the bulk of your criminal procedure course, two other investigative tactics are also important.

Police sometimes try to extract confessions after formal judicial proceedings have begun. Although this might seem like it would be covered by the *Miranda* doctrine, police officers' attempts to elicit confessions are governed by the Sixth Amendment (not *Miranda*) if formal judicial proceedings have already begun. The distinction between the Sixth Amendment right to counsel and *Miranda* is important, because the Sixth Amendment gives defendants greater protections than *Miranda*. Chapter 35 describes the Sixth Amendment right to counsel.

Police also use lineups and other identification procedures to identify suspects and to build a criminal case against them. Suspects have a due process right that the identification procedure not be unnecessarily suggestive. And suspects also have a Sixth Amendment right to counsel, but only if the police use a live identification procedure (rather than photos), and only after formal adversary proceedings have begun. Chapter 36 reviews the limited circumstances when the Sixth Amendment right to counsel applies at identifications and the types of due process claims that suspects can raise.

CHAPTER 35

Interrogations Under the Sixth Amendment

THE RULE: Police may not deliberately elicit information from a defendant after adversary criminal proceedings have begun. Unlike in the *Miranda* context, the suspect need not be in custody for the Sixth Amendment right to counsel to apply.

Critical Points

- The Sixth Amendment right to counsel applies when police try to deliberately elicit information from a defendant after adversary criminal proceedings have begun.
- There is unfortunately no clear guidance on what "deliberate elicitation" means. The concept operates much like interrogation under the *Miranda* doctrine. Arguably, deliberate elicitation is broader than interrogation, though, because it considers the officer's intent, rather than only what a reasonable person would have perceived.
- The Sixth Amendment right to counsel applies when adversary criminal proceedings have begun. This includes situations after indictment, information, arraignment, or a preliminary hearing.
- Defendants can waive the Sixth Amendment right to counsel and consent to questioning by the police.
- The Sixth Amendment right to counsel is offense-specific. If a defendant has been indicted for murder, the police cannot deliberately elicit information about the murder charge. But the officers can approach the same defendant and attempt to question him about another crime that he has not yet been charged with.

- The Sixth Amendment right to counsel is broader than the *Miranda* right to counsel in a few important ways:
  - Unlike *Miranda*, the Sixth Amendment right to counsel applies even when the defendant is not in custody.
  - Unlike *Miranda*, the Sixth Amendment right to counsel can apply when the police use undercover agents or informants.
  - Unlike *Miranda*, the fruit of the poisonous tree doctrine applies to the Sixth Amendment right to counsel.
  - Deliberate elicitation under the Sixth Amendment is broader than interrogation under *Miranda* because "deliberate" means courts take into consideration the officer's intent.

OVERVIEW OF THE BLACKLETTER LAW

As we learned in Chapters 29 and 30, a *suspect* who is subject to custodial interrogation has a Fifth Amendment right to counsel under the *Miranda* doctrine. The Sixth Amendment right to counsel—the so-called *Massiah* right, named after the Supreme Court's decision in *Massiah v. United States* (1964)—is different. It applies not to suspects, but to *defendants* for whom adversary criminal proceedings have already begun. Although the purpose of both the *Miranda* and *Massiah* rights is the same—to protect individuals' right to counsel when interacting with the police—there are important differences.

The first important thing to understand is that the Sixth Amendment right to counsel only applies after adversary criminal proceedings have begun. If police are questioning someone at the crime scene, or at the police station, we are in the *Miranda* world, not the Sixth Amendment world. A custodial arrest might be unpleasant for a suspect, but it does not amount to adversary criminal proceedings. Rather, you should be on the lookout for things like an indictment, an information, an arraignment, or a preliminary hearing. In those situations, the wheels of the judicial process have begun. The suspect has become a defendant, and adversary criminal proceedings are underway. So, when a question tells you that a person has been indicted or arraigned, or that the prosecutor has filed an information, or that judge has conducted a preliminary hearing, you should apply the Sixth Amendment right to counsel, not the *Miranda* doctrine.

The second thing to know about the Sixth Amendment right to counsel is that it utilizes slightly different terminology. Whereas *Miranda* focuses on whether the police have conducted an interrogation, the Sixth Amendment focuses on whether the officers have "deliberately elicited" a statement from the individual. In most cases, there is no practical difference in analysis between interrogation and deliberate elicitation. In addition, be aware that the word "deliberate" suggests that the intent of the officers may matter for Sixth Amendment purposes. Throughout your criminal procedure course and this book, we have regularly ignored the police officers' subjective views and we did so for determining whether an interrogation occurred under the *Miranda* doctrine. For the Sixth Amendment deliberate elicitation standard, though, courts may well look to what the police officers intended or hoped would happen as a result of their tactics.

The third significant point about the Sixth Amendment right to counsel is that it applies in situations where *Miranda* does not. Recall that police do not need to read the *Miranda* warnings or seek a waiver if they use an informant or an undercover officer to question the suspect. Police can send an undercover agent into the suspect's jail cell to seek out incriminating statements. And the police can send an informant to meet a suspect in a bar and tape record their conversation. *Miranda* does not apply in those situations because the suspect does not know she is dealing with the police and therefore could not be coerced. By contrast, the police would have violated the Sixth Amendment if they used those tactics on a defendant who is already subject to adversary criminal proceedings. Once there has been an indictment, information, arraignment, preliminary hearing, or a later-stage process, the defendant is fully enmeshed in the criminal justice system. The police must approach the suspect through her lawyer. Trying to trick the defendant at that later stage into confessing without counsel present violates the Sixth Amendment.

The Sixth Amendment right to counsel also differs from the *Miranda* doctrine because Sixth Amendment violations have a fruit of the poisonous tree doctrine. If adversary proceedings have begun and the police deliberately elicit an incriminating statement in violation of the Sixth Amendment, the statement *and* any evidence found as a result of it will be excluded. By contrast, if the police procure an incriminating statement from a *Miranda* violation, only the statement will be excluded, not any additional evidence found as a result.

Finally, there is one way in which the Sixth Amendment right to counsel is narrower than the *Miranda* doctrine. Under *Miranda*, if a suspect invokes his right to counsel, the police cannot question him about *any* crimes. By contrast, the Sixth Amendment right to counsel is offense-specific. If adversary criminal proceedings have begun, police cannot seek to question a defendant about the crime for which he is charged. But officers can try to question the individual about other crimes.

EXAM TRAPS TO AVOID

- Professors will rarely say "This is a Sixth Amendment question" or "This is a *Miranda* question." So you should be sure to read the question carefully to figure out whether adversary criminal proceedings have begun (such that you apply the Sixth Amendment rules from this chapter) or whether it is before adversary criminal proceedings have begun (such that you apply the *Miranda* rules).

- The Sixth Amendment right to counsel is more protective than the *Miranda* right to counsel. Most notably, there is no custody requirement for the Sixth Amendment right counsel. Be on the lookout for situations in which *Miranda* would not apply—undercover informants, jail interrogations, discussions with government agents in public places—but the Sixth Amendment right to counsel might be violated.
- It is not a Sixth Amendment violation simply because a defendant gave incriminating information to an officer or undercover agent. If the government agent just sat quietly, there cannot be a Sixth Amendment violation. The government agent must deliberately elicit incriminating information for it to violate the Sixth Amendment.

MULTIPLE-CHOICE QUESTIONS

Question 196

Juan has been indicted for possession with intent to distribute cocaine. At his arraignment, Juan requested a lawyer and said that he would like to post bail. The judge set bail at $20,000, but Juan could not afford it and he was returned to his jail cell. That night, Juan got into a conversation with his cellmate and told him "I sold drugs" and made other incriminating statements. The cellmate was actually an undercover narcotics officer. Which of the following is correct?

A) Juan's incriminating statements are admissible because any statements made to undercover agents in a prison or jail cell are admissible; suspects should be aware of the possibility that they are talking to undercover agents.

B) Juan's incriminating statements would have been admissible if the undercover officer had read him his *Miranda* rights.

C) Juan's incriminating statements are inadmissible unless Juan made the statement without any prompting from the undercover police officer.

D) Juan's incriminating statements are inadmissible no matter what the undercover officer did or said.

Question 197

A grand jury indicted Donovan for burglary. Officers found Donovan at Lucky's Bar and Grill because that is where he always hangs out. The officers placed him under arrest and took him to the police station. The next day, the judge set bail at $10,000 and Donovan's wife bailed him out. That evening, police called one of their informants —Izzy—who was a friend of Donovan. The officers told Izzy to go to Lucky's Bar and Grill and see if Donovan would make any incriminating statements. Izzy put on a recording device, went to the bar, and just hung out there next to Donovan while he drank a lot of beer. Izzy just sat there, never asking any questions. After about two hours, Donovan said, "I'm totally going to go to prison for this burglary. I never should have done that job." The prosecutor wants to use Donovan's confession against him. Is it admissible?

A) No, because Donovan never received his *Miranda* rights.

B) No, because Donovan was drinking heavily and cannot voluntarily confess under those circumstances.

C) No, because Izzy deliberately elicited a confession in violation of the Sixth Amendment.

D) Yes, because Izzy did not deliberately elicit a confession.

E) Yes, because Donovan was not subjected to custodial interrogation.

Question 198

Assume the same facts as Question 197. For purposes of this question, imagine that as Izzy and Donovan were sitting at the bar that Izzy said, "So why did the police pick you up?" Donovan responded, "For the burglary. I totally did it, but they'll never be able to prove it." Is Donovan's confession admissible?

A) Yes, because Donovan was not in custody and thus there is no Sixth Amendment violation.

B) No, because Izzy deliberately elicited an incriminating statement after indictment.

Question 199

Assume the same facts as Question 198. For purposes of this question, though, imagine that after Izzy asked, "So why did the police pick you up?" Donovan responded, "For the burglary. I totally did it, but they'll never be able to prove it. I hid all of the stolen property in the abandoned house on the corner of First and Main Street." Based on Donovan's statement, the police were able to recover a bag of stolen property that had Donovan's fingerprints on it. Assuming that Donovan's statement to Izzy is suppressed because it violates the Sixth Amendment, will the bag of stolen property also be suppressed?

A) Yes, because the fruit of the poisonous tree doctrine applies to violations of the Sixth Amendment right to counsel.

B) No, because the fruit of the poisonous tree doctrine does not apply to violations of the Sixth Amendment right to counsel.

Question 200

Police arrest Marv for the murder of his business partner. The officers place Marv in an empty jail cell. About an hour later they bring another arrestee to Marv's jail cell. The arrestee says his name is Jacob and that he was arrested for beating up his best friend. Jacob asks Marv, "You don't look that tough. You're probably in here for jaywalking. Hah. Seriously though. What did you do?" Marv responded, "I killed my business partner. Don't make me kill you, too." It turns out that Jacob had not beaten up his best friend. Jacob was actually an undercover cop. Is Marv's confession to Jacob admissible?

A) Yes, because the police complied with the Constitution.

B) Yes, because Marv poses a public safety risk since he is accused of murder and thus the deliberate elicitation was permissible.

C) No, because the police violated Marv's Sixth Amendment right to counsel.

D) No, because the police violated Marv's Fifth Amendment right to counsel.

Question 201

A grand jury indicted Steven for the murder of his neighbor after an altercation over who was responsible for pruning a tree on the border of their property line. The police arrested Steven and brought him to the police station. The next day, Steven appeared before a judge for arraignment, demanded a lawyer, and asked for bail to be set so that he could go home. The judge assigned a public defender to Steven's case, but denied bail on the grounds that Steven was too dangerous. The sheriff's deputy brought Steven back to the jail and left him in his cell. The next day, police officers went to Steven's jail cell and told him they wanted to ask him about some fraudulent business deals he has been involved in. The officers read Steven his *Miranda* rights and Steven waived. An hour later, Steven confessed to running a Ponzi scheme at work. Which of the following is correct?

A) Steven's confession about the Ponzi scheme is inadmissible because the police violated the Sixth Amendment by questioning him after he had requested a lawyer.

B) Steven's confession about the Ponzi scheme is inadmissible because the waiver is invalid since Steven had invoked his right to counsel.

C) Steven's confession about the Ponzi scheme is admissible because the police questioned him for a different offense than what he was indicted for.

D) Steven's confession about the Ponzi scheme is admissible because Steven cannot invoke a right to counsel with respect to the Ponzi questions.

ANSWERS TO MULTIPLE-CHOICE QUESTIONS

Answer to Question 196

Answer A is incorrect. Statements made to undercover agents in a jail cell are admissible in some circumstances. But this answer choice says "any" statements are admissible. This is overbroad. If the police deliberately elicit a statement from a defendant after adversary proceedings have begun, that statement is not admissible.

Answer B is incorrect. The *Miranda* doctrine is not applicable here because the question indicates that Juan has been indicted already. Thus, we are not in the *Miranda* world, but instead in the Sixth Amendment world. Giving the *Miranda* warnings would not solve any of the Sixth Amendment problems present in this question.

Answer C is correct. Because Juan has been arraigned, the Sixth Amendment right to counsel governs the outcome of this case. This answer choice correctly states the law. If a police agent (including an undercover officer) deliberately elicits a statement, that would violate the Sixth Amendment. However, if the officer only listens without prompting Juan to make a statement, that does not violate the Sixth Amendment.

Answer D is incorrect. This answer choice is too broad. If the officer did not prompt Juan to make statements about the crime and only talked with him about other unrelated matters (such as the weather) then the officer would not have deliberately elicited a statement from Juan in violation of the Sixth Amendment.

Answer to Question 197

Answer A is incorrect. The *Miranda* rights are not applicable in this situation. Donovan has been indicted already and thus we are in the Sixth Amendment world, not the *Miranda* world. Moreover, even if we were dealing with a preindictment situation, under the *Miranda* doctrine Donovan would not have been subjected to custodial interrogation since he did not know he was speaking with a police informant.

Answer B is incorrect. A confession is not involuntary simply because a person was drinking alcohol. As we discussed in Chapter 27, a confession is rendered involuntary by the actions of law enforcement. In this case, the officers did not prompt Donovan to drink alcohol.

Answer C is incorrect. Izzy did not deliberately elicit a confession from Juan. The question tells us that Izzy "just sat there, never asking any questions."

Answer D is correct. Izzy did not deliberately elicit a confession. When an informant (or police officer) just sits quietly and listens, that does not amount to deliberate elicitation.

Answer E is incorrect. This answer choice would have been correct if this were a *Miranda* question. A suspect who does not know they are dealing with a police agent cannot be in a coercive situation. Thus, the Supreme Court has concluded that the

Miranda warnings need not be given prior to an undercover agent trying to question a suspect in jail. But this question does not involve a *Miranda* situation. Donovan has already been arraigned and indicted. Accordingly, adversary criminal proceedings have begun and the situation must be analyzed under the Sixth Amendment right to counsel, not the *Miranda* doctrine. Under the Sixth Amendment, police cannot deliberately elicit a statement by using an undercover agent.

Answer to Question 198

Answer B is correct. It is true that Donovan was not in custody. He was in a public place and there did not appear to be any police officers present. No one could plausibly say that Donovan was under arrest or that his movement had been curtailed to an extent consistent with an arrest. But custody is not necessary for there to be a Sixth Amendment violation. Donovan has been arraigned and indicted, thus adversary criminal proceedings have begun. Acting at police direction, Izzy deliberately elicited a statement from Donovan by asking him why the police had picked him up. This is improper and the resulting statement should be suppressed.

Answer to Question 199

Answer A is correct. Izzy has deliberately elicited an incriminating statement from Donovan in violation of the Sixth Amendment's right to counsel. The statement must be suppressed. This question asks whether the fruit of the poisonous tree doctrine applies to Sixth Amendment violations. The answer is "yes." Just like the Fourth Amendment's protection against unreasonable search and seizure and the Fifth Amendment's protection against involuntary confessions, there is a fruit of the poisonous tree doctrine for violations of the Sixth Amendment right to counsel. (The outlier is *Miranda* violations, which for the most part do not have a fruit of the poisonous tree doctrine. See Chapter 34.) Because the fruit of the poisonous tree doctrine applies, the bag of stolen property must also be suppressed because the officers found it as a result of the illegally obtained statement.

Answer to Question 200

Answer A is correct. Although we are practicing questions in the Sixth Amendment interrogation chapter of this book, it is important to always ask yourself whether you are dealing with a Sixth Amendment or a Fifth Amendment fact pattern. For the Sixth Amendment rules to apply, adversary criminal proceedings must have already begun. This means an indictment, an information, a probable cause hearing, or an arraignment. This question does not reference any of those situations. Instead, it appears that the police have just arrested Marv and placed an undercover agent in his jail cell prior to any adversary criminal proceedings. This is therefore a *Miranda* situation, not a Sixth Amendment situation. But the *Miranda* doctrine does not apply to the use of undercover officers in jail cells because the suspect does not realize he is dealing with law enforcement. Accordingly, the trick employed by the police is perfectly lawful.

Answer B is incorrect. There is a public safety exception under the *Miranda* doctrine for imminent emergencies where police need to protect themselves or the public. This situation does not qualify. Many suspects are arrested for serious crimes that, if they committed them, makes them dangerous individuals. We do not suspend their constitutional rights, however.

Answer C is incorrect. Marv has not yet been subjected to adversary criminal proceedings. For example, he has not yet been indicted or arraigned. He has only been arrested. Accordingly, his Sixth Amendment right to counsel is not yet applicable and could not have been violated.

Answer D is incorrect. This answer correctly identifies the constitutional provision at issue—the Fifth Amendment right to counsel under the *Miranda* doctrine. However, it is incorrect to suggest that Marv's rights have been violated. Because Marv does not know he is dealing with a government agent, he is not being subjected to custodial interrogation. Accordingly, there can be no *Miranda* violation under the Fifth Amendment.

Answer to Question 201

Answer A is incorrect. Steven had requested counsel for the murder allegation he had been indicted for. Steven's Sixth Amendment right to counsel is offense-specific, though. In other words, his right to counsel is for the specific criminal charge—murder—that the State has charged him with. For other, unrelated investigations, Steven has not invoked his right to counsel. Accordingly, police can approach a suspect who has been indicted for one offense and seek to question him (and get a *Miranda* waiver) for a different, unrelated offense.

Answer B is incorrect. As described above, Steven has only invoked his right to counsel for the murder charge. After being read the *Miranda* warnings, Steven can waive his right to counsel for questioning about the separate crime of running a Ponzi scheme.

Answer C is correct. The Sixth Amendment right to counsel is offense-specific. When a defendant requests counsel (or is appointed counsel) under the Sixth Amendment, it is for the crime that they have been charged with. Police cannot approach the defendant about *that* criminal charge to seek a statement. However, for *other*, unrelated crimes, the police officers are free to read the suspect his *Miranda* rights and seek a waiver and a confession.

Answer D is incorrect. Unless the prosecutor has granted a suspect immunity (see Chapter 26) a suspect is always free to decline to answer questions. There is nothing in this question that would suggest that Steven cannot invoke his right to counsel.

CHAPTER 36

Eyewitness Identifications

THE RULE: Although there is no right to avoid being put in a lineup, individuals do have (1) a due process right that the identification procedure not be unnecessarily suggestive and (2) a right to counsel at live identification procedures if adversary proceedings have already begun.

Critical Points

- A suspect who was validly arrested does not have a constitutional right to avoid being put in a lineup.
- There are two *separate* constitutional rights at issue for identifications:
  - The right to counsel; and
  - Due process
- *The Right to Counsel Applies to Live Identifications Conducted After Adversary Proceedings Have Begun*:
  - The right to counsel at a lineup applies only after formal adversarial proceedings have begun. This means there must already have been an arraignment, indictment, information, or other judicial proceeding.
  - The right to counsel applies only to corporeal identifications. Usually this is a lineup, but it could also be a "showup" in which police bring only one suspect for the witness to identify. Both lineups and showups take place in person. The right to counsel does not apply when police show a witness a photograph. If the defendant is not being shown in person, the identification procedure is noncorporeal and there is no right to counsel.

  - If the police conduct an unlawful lineup in violation of the right to counsel or due process, the prosecutor may not present testimony about any identification made during the unlawful lineup. However, the prosecution can still have the witness identify the defendant in court. The in-court identification is based on an "independent source," namely that the witness saw the defendant while the crime was going on.
- *The Due Process Right Applies to All Identification Procedures and Requires (Subject to Exceptions) That They Not Be Unnecessarily Suggestive:*
  - Individuals have a due process right that the police not use an unnecessarily suggestive identification procedure. This is a separate, independent right that applies regardless of whether the individual also has a Sixth Amendment right to counsel.
  - An identification procedure does not violate due process just because it is suggestive. It must be *unnecessarily* suggestive. For example, if a witness is about to die, police can show the witness a single suspect because there is no time to create a full lineup. Showing a witness only one suspect is surely suggestive, but under the circumstances it may not be *unnecessarily* suggestive.
  - Even if the police conduct an unnecessarily suggestive identification procedure, the identification will still be admissible if the identification is likely to be reliable. In determining if the witness's identification is reliable, courts consider what happened at the time of the alleged crime. Relevant factors include: (1) how closely the witness paid attention to the perpetrator; (2) the accuracy of the description of the perpetrator; (3) the witness's level of certainty; and (4) the time between the crime and the witness describing the event.
  - The due process right against an unnecessarily suggestive procedure applies to *any* identification, not just corporeal (live) identifications. It therefore applies to situations where the police show a witness photographs of a suspect.
- Independent Source for In-Court Testimony: If a court excludes the out-of-court identification because the police violated the right to counsel or due process, it may still be possible for the witness to identify the defendant in court. The reason is that the in-court identification would be based on an independent source—the witness's memory of the crime. As explained in Chapter 23, the independent source doctrine is an exception to the fruit of the poisonous tree doctrine.

OVERVIEW OF THE BLACKLETTER LAW

There are five big-picture rules to understand about the law of lineups. First, if the police have lawfully taken a person into custody, they can force the person into a lineup or another identification procedure. Second, defendants have a right to counsel at live, in-person identifications, but that right only applies if formal adversary proceedings began before the identification procedure. Third, regardless of whether the right to counsel applies, individuals always have a due process right that the police use an identification procedure that is not unnecessarily suggestive. Fourth, if the police violate a person's right to counsel or their due process rights, testimony about the out-of-court identification procedure will be suppressed. Fifth, if a court suppresses testimony about the out-of-court identification, that does not typically result in suppression of an in-court identification because there is usually an independent source for the in-court identification. We will explore the second through fifth rules in more detail.

The Sixth Amendment right to counsel applies only after formal adversary judicial proceedings have begun. If police conduct an identification procedure before adversary proceedings have begun, there is no right to counsel. Most lineups, not surprisingly, occur right after arrest. An arrest does not qualify as a formal adversary proceeding. Therefore, the right to counsel does not apply to most lineups. For the defendant to have a right to counsel, the identification procedure must take place after an indictment, information, arraignment, preliminary hearing, or a later stage of the judicial process.

Another important point about the Sixth Amendment right to counsel is that it only applies to corporeal identifications. Corporeal means in-person identifications. If adversary proceedings have begun and the police conduct an in-person lineup or a showup (in which they only bring in one suspect), the right to counsel applies. By contrast, if the police show the witness a mug shot or another photograph of the suspect, the right to counsel does *not* apply. Photographs are non-corporeal—they do not involve an in-person observation of the defendant.

The rule that the Sixth Amendment right to counsel only applies to in-person identifications makes little sense. The role of the lawyer at an identification is to encourage police to modify unfair procedures to make sure the identification is fair, or to document unfair procedures so that the lawyer can cast doubt on the accuracy of the identification during trial. Non-corporeal identifications that rely on photographs can be just as misleading and unfair as in-person identifications. Indeed, using photographs is typically a less reliable way to conduct an identification than an in-person process. So a rule that guarantees a lawyer for in-person identifications, but not photo displays, makes no sense. Nevertheless, this has been the Supreme Court's rule for many decades.

Regardless of whether a person has a right to counsel, she still has a due process right that the identification procedure not be unnecessarily suggestive. Put differently, the due process protection against an unnecessarily suggestive identification procedure is a separate, different right than the Sixth Amendment right to counsel. Notably, the due process right (unlike the Sixth Amendment right) applies to photographic displays, not just to in-person identifications.

It is not easy for suspects to make out a due process violation, however. The individual must demonstrate that the police used a procedure that was both suggestive and unnecessary. If police place the suspect in a lineup with people who look nothing like him, then the procedure may be suggestive. Similarly, if the police show the victim only one suspect (a showup) or only one photograph, that is a suggestive procedure. But it must also be unnecessary. So, for example, if the victim is about to die and the police rush the suspect to the hospital for the victim to look at quickly, the suggestive procedure may be necessary because there is no time for a more elaborate procedure.

It is doubly hard for a suspect to make out a due process violation because even if he can prove that the identification procedure was unnecessarily suggestive, courts will still refuse to suppress the identification if it was nevertheless reliable. Courts will look at what happened at the time of the alleged crime, specifically: (1) how closely the witness paid attention to the perpetrator; (2) the accuracy of the description of the perpetrator; (3) the witness's level of certainty; and (4) the time between the crime and the witness describing the event. If these factors suggest that the witness's out-of-court identification was reliable, the court will not suppress it, even if the identification procedure was unnecessarily suggestive. Put simply, the Court's rules make it fairly difficult for a person to successfully challenge an out-of-court identification on due process grounds.

If a defendant can demonstrate a violation of his Sixth Amendment right to counsel or his due process rights, the court should suppress the out-of-court identification in which the constitutional violation occurred. However, that does not mean that the court will forbid the witness from identifying the defendant *at trial*. The independent source doctrine (which we covered in Chapter 23) applies not just to the Fourth Amendment, but also to identification procedures. If the prosecution can demonstrate that a witness will testify in court based on her observations from the crime, rather than from the unconstitutionally conducted lineup, then there is an independent source for the witness's testimony and the witness will be permitted to make an in-court identification.

For example, imagine that a victim was kidnapped and held by the perpetrator for three days. During those three days, the victim caught a glimpse of the perpetrator on several occasions and was able to make a mental note of his appearance. After the perpetrator was arrested and indicted, the police put him in a lineup without a lawyer present and the victim identified him. That out-of-court identification violated the defendant's Sixth Amendment right to counsel and should be suppressed. But the same witness could come to court during the trial and identify the defendant as the perpetrator not based on her recollection of him from the lineup, but instead based on her memory of him from the kidnapping when she had several glimpses of his appearance.

EXAM TRAPS TO AVOID

- Do not conflate the Sixth Amendment right to counsel and the due process right that an identification procedure not be unnecessarily suggestive. They are two *separate* rights. One right may be applicable even if the other right is not applicable.
- For the right to counsel, look for words such as arraignment, indictment, information, or preliminary hearing. These words signal that formal adversary proceedings have begun and that the Sixth Amendment right to counsel applies to in-person identification procedures. If the question only says that the suspect has been arrested, the Sixth Amendment right to counsel does not apply.
- It is rare for courts to find identification procedures to be so unnecessarily suggestive as to violate due process. It does happen, though. If the other people in the lineup look nothing like the suspect (because of height, weight, race, hair color) that may be unnecessarily suggestive. In addition, if police have no good reason for showing a witness only one suspect, that can also be unnecessarily suggestive.
- If the police violated the Sixth Amendment right to counsel or the Due Process Clause, that will result in suppression of the flawed out-of-court identification. But that does not mean the witness will be prohibited from making an in-court identification. To the contrary, there will almost always be an independent source (the witness's experience during the crime) for an in-court identification.

MULTIPLE-CHOICE QUESTIONS

Question 202

The police arrested Paul for robbery and immediately placed him in a lineup with five other people. Paul is 5'10" and weighs about 200 pounds, with thin brown hair. The other five people in the lineup ranged from 5'8" to 6' tall, weighed between 180 and 220 pounds, and all had brown hair. Police never read Paul his *Miranda* warnings and didn't appoint a lawyer for him. The witness picked Paul out of the lineup. Was the lineup unconstitutional?

A) Yes, because the police never read Paul his *Miranda* rights.

B) Yes, because Paul did not have the assistance of counsel.

C) No, because it was not unnecessarily suggestive and did not violate the right to counsel.

D) No, because lineups are non-corporeal and thus individuals have no due process protections.

Question 203

Assume the same facts as Question 202. For purposes of this question, though, assume that Paul was arrested on January 1. On January 8 he was indicted for robbery, and on January 10, the police conducted the lineup. Paul was never read his *Miranda* rights and he had no lawyer present at the lineup. Can Paul now successfully challenge the lineup as unconstitutional?

A) Yes, because he has been denied his right to counsel.

B) Yes, because the officers' actions violated Paul's due process rights through the identification procedure they set up.

C) Both A and B.

D) No, because the police did not violate his right to counsel.

E) No, because the police violated his due process rights through the procedure they set up.

Question 204

Assume the same facts as Question 203, but for purposes of this question imagine that after Paul was indicted, he was provided with a lawyer. The lawyer objected to Paul being placed in any lineup, but the police said they would conduct a lineup anyway. Thereafter, Paul was placed in the same lineup as described in Question 202. However, for purposes of this question imagine that Paul is 6'4" tall, weighs 150 pounds, and is mostly bald. Was the lineup constitutional?

A) Yes, because this was a non-corporeal lineup.

B) Yes, because the police did not violate Paul's right to counsel.

C) No, because the lawyer objected to Paul being placed in any lineup.

D) No, because the lineup probably violated due process.

Question 205

Assume that a court found that placing Paul in a lineup with much shorter and heavier people violated his due process rights. The court accordingly forbid testimony at trial about the witness's positive identification of Paul at the lineup. The prosecution still plans to have the witness testify at trial, though. The prosecution has indicated that the witness will testify that she was one of the robbery victims and that she can identify Paul in court based on what happened to her when she was robbed. Paul has moved to prevent the witness from making an in-court identification. How should the court rule?

A) The court should forbid the witness from identifying Paul in court because it is fruit of the poisonous tree from the unconstitutional identification process.

B) The court should allow the witness to identify Paul in court based on the attenuation exception.

C) The court should allow the witness to identify Paul in court based on the independent source doctrine.

D) The court should allow the witness to identify Paul in court based on the inevitable discovery doctrine.

Question 206

Police receive a 911 call that a man had been violently attacked at 123 Main Street. When the police arrived the victim was in bad shape. The officers quickly got the victim to provide a description of the attacker before an ambulance took him to the hospital. Based on the victim's description, the officers believed that they knew who the attacker was. The officers went back to the station and found a mug shot photo of Kerry, who they believed to be the attacker. The officers rushed to the hospital and showed the victim the mug shot photo of Kerry. The victim said, "That's him. That's the person who attacked me." Unfortunately, the victim died the next day. Can the prosecution introduce the victim's identification at Kerry's trial?

A) Yes, because the due process clause does not apply to non-corporeal identifications.

B) Yes, because the officers had good reason to proceed quickly.

C) No, because the officers violated Kerry's right to counsel.

D) No, because the officers violated Kerry's due process rights.

Question 207

Assume the same facts as Question 206. This time, however, assume that the victim fell into a coma right after the attack. The police investigate the crime and, based on surveillance video, the officers think that Kerry is the perpetrator. The officers arrest Kerry and a grand jury subsequently indicts him for attempted murder. Thereafter, the victim comes out of the coma. The officers bring Kerry's mug shot photo, as well as the mug shots for five other similar-looking people to show the victim at the hospital. The police do not tell Kerry's lawyer that they are taking the mug shots to show the victim in the hospital and the lawyer is not present when the officers show the photos. The victim picks Kerry's mug shot photo out of the photo display. Should the victim's photo identification of Kerry at the hospital be admissible?

A) No, because the officers violated Kerry's right to counsel.

B) No, because the officers violated Kerry's due process rights.

C) Both A and B.

D) Yes, because the Sixth Amendment right to counsel does not apply to this identification procedure and there was no due process violation.

Question 208

Manny is the manager of a bookstore and last week he was robbed at gunpoint. The perpetrator came into the store in the middle of the day. Manny asked if the man was looking for a particular book and the robber spoke with Manny calmly for a minute about his favorite mystery novelists before stopping himself, pulling out a gun, and saying "I'm not here for books, though. I'm here for your money. Put all the money you have in this bag." Manny is a retired Navy Seal and he was therefore cool under pressure. Manny calmly put the money in the bag and watched as the robber fumbled to close it and slowly backed out of the store. When the robber was gone, Manny immediately drove to the police station to report the crime and describe the perpetrator. An hour later, a detective showed Manny a single photo of a man named Connor, who has previous theft convictions. Manny told the detective "That's him. Definitely him. He's got the same green eyes." Connor has challenged this identification. Should the court suppress Manny's identification?

A) No, because while the identification procedure was suggestive, it was necessary for the police to do so.

B) No, because while the identification procedure was unnecessarily suggestive, Manny's identification is reliable.

C) Yes, because this was an unnecessarily suggestive identification procedure that violates due process.

D) Yes, because this was an unnecessarily suggestive identification procedure that violates due process and also because the police violated Manny's right to counsel.

ANSWERS TO MULTIPLE-CHOICE QUESTIONS

Answer to Question 202

Answer A is incorrect. Police do not need to read a suspect his *Miranda* rights before placing him in a lineup. Indeed, a suspect has no Fifth Amendment right to refuse to be placed in a lineup.

Answer B is incorrect. Paul is not entitled to a lawyer at the lineup. The police arranged the lineup "immediately" after arrest. Because adversary criminal proceedings had not yet begun, Paul had no right to counsel at the lineup.

Answer C is correct. Even if it was too early in the process for Paul to have a right to counsel at the lineup, he will always have a due process right not to be subjected to an identification procedure that is unnecessarily suggestive. This lineup did not violate due process, though. The other individuals in the lineup were roughly the same height, weight, and hair color as Paul. Accordingly, the lineup is not unnecessarily suggestive.

Answer D is incorrect. This answer is wrong for several reasons. First, lineups are corporeal. The word "corporeal" refers to an in-person process, whereas "non-corporeal" means the identification process involved photos. So this was a corporeal, rather than non-corporeal, identification process. Regardless, the due process guarantee applies whether the identification process is corporeal or non-corporeal.

Answer to Question 203

Answer A is correct. Once a defendant has been indicted, he is entitled to counsel. By conducting the lineup without Paul's lawyer present (or without Paul waiving his right to counsel at the lineup), the police have violated the Sixth Amendment.

Answer B is incorrect. Although the police have failed to provide Paul with a lawyer in violation of the Sixth Amendment, that does not mean they have violated Paul's due process rights. There is no indication that the identification procedure was unnecessarily suggestive. Accordingly, there is no due process violation.

Answer C is incorrect. As noted above, Answer B is incorrect. Therefore, Answer C cannot be correct.

Answer D is incorrect. Because Paul had been indicted prior to the lineup, he had a Sixth Amendment right to counsel at the lineup. The officers proceeded without Paul's lawyer (and without Paul waiving his right to counsel). Therefore, this is a Sixth Amendment violation.

Answer E is incorrect. The lineup was not unnecessarily suggestive. Paul was placed in a lineup with people who generally had the same appearance. Accordingly, there was no due process violation.

Answer to Question 204

Answer A is incorrect. This was a corporeal lineup because Paul appeared in person, rather than the police using a photograph. Regardless, the issue in this question is whether the lineup was so suggestive as to violate due process. An identification process can be unconstitutional regardless of whether it was corporeal (in-person) or non-corporeal (involving a photo).

Answer B is incorrect. It is true that the police did not violate Paul's right to counsel. However, Paul *also* has a due process right that the lineup not be unnecessarily suggestive. It appears the police have engaged in a due process violation by including people in the lineup who all look markedly different from Paul.

Answer C is incorrect. The problem in this question is not that Paul was placed in the lineup, but that the lineup was unnecessarily suggestive. Paul has no constitutional right to avoid being placed in a lineup.

Answer D is correct. It appears that the police have engaged in a due process violation. Paul is 6'4," weighs 150 pounds, and is bald. The other people in the lineup are much shorter, much heavier, and have brown hair. There is thus a stark difference in appearance between Paul and the other lineup participants. This creates a situation that is probably unnecessarily suggestive and thus a due process violation.

Answer to Question 205

Answer A is incorrect. The fruit of the poisonous tree doctrine should not prevent the witness's testimony about what happened during the crime. The witness has an independent source—her observation of Paul during the crime—for her testimony.

Answer B is incorrect. The attenuation exception is for situations in which intervening events have occurred that distance the evidence from the police illegality. Here there is no attenuation. Nothing of consequence happened in between the unconstitutional lineup and the in-court testimony. Rather, the relevant exception is the independent source exception.

Answer C is correct. The witness has an independent source for her in-court identification. She would not be testifying that Paul was the perpetrator based on her identification of him at the flawed lineup. Rather, she would be testifying based on an independent source—her observation of him at the time he committed the robbery.

Answer D is incorrect. The inevitable discovery exception is for situations in which the police found evidence unlawfully, but *would have* found the evidence lawfully in the future. The inevitable discovery exception is not relevant here. Rather, as noted above, this is a case that falls under the independent source exception.

Answer to Question 206

Answer A is incorrect. The due process protections apply to all identification procedures. Police can violate the due process rights of a suspect by placing him in an unfair lineup. They can also violate the due process rights of a suspect by using a photograph in an unnecessarily suggestive way.

Answer B is correct. Showing the victim a single photograph and asking whether the person in the photo was the perpetrator is surely suggestive. But the test is not just whether the identification procedure is suggestive. Rather, the test is whether it is *unnecessarily* suggestive. Here, the witness was in "bad shape" and hospitalized. There was reason for the officers to proceed quickly. Therefore, the procedure was not unnecessarily suggestive.

Answer C is incorrect. Nothing in this question indicates that formal adversary proceedings had begun against Kerry. Accordingly, the Sixth Amendment right to counsel does not yet apply.

Answer D is incorrect. Under these circumstances, the officers have not violated Kerry's due process rights. While they used a suggestive procedure, they had good reason to do so given that the witness was in "bad shape" and hospitalized. The identification procedure was therefore not *unnecessarily* suggestive.

Answer to Question 207

Answer A is incorrect. Kerry has been indicted, which means the Sixth Amendment right to counsel could be applicable. However, this is a non-corporeal identification. In other words, it is not an in-person lineup or showup where Kerry stands in front of the victim. The officers have brought photos instead of people. There is no right to counsel when the police use photos.

Answer B is incorrect. While an in-person lineup is preferable to using mug shots, the use of mug shots does not violate due process if the mug shots were not unnecessarily suggestive. Here, the officers included mug shots for five other people who looked like Kerry. This photo display is therefore not suggestive and does not violate due process.

Answer C is incorrect because answers A and B are incorrect.

Answer D is correct. Even though Kerry has been indicted, the Sixth Amendment right to counsel does not apply because this is not an in-person lineup. The Sixth Amendment right to counsel does not apply when the police show photographs. Additionally, because the police used photos of five other people who looked like Kerry, the photo spread is not unnecessarily suggestive.

Answer to Question 208

Answer A is incorrect. There was no good reason for the police to show Manny only a single photo. This was both suggestive and unnecessary.

Answer B is correct. Showing Manny a single photo was unnecessarily suggestive. However, Manny's identification is reliable. He had a minute to view the suspect calmly before he knew he was going to be robbed. Manny also had an opportunity to view the suspect carefully as he fumbled with the bag and walked out slowly. The time between the crime and Manny's identification was short, and Manny has a high level of certainty. The question does not provide us information about the other relevant factor: the accuracy of Manny's description. Even without this factor, however, there is considerable evidence that Manny's identification is reliable.

Answer C is incorrect. Ordinarily this would be the correct answer. The identification is suggestive (by showing only one person) and there appears to be no reason why that procedure was necessary. However, as described above for Answer B, it appears that Manny's identification is reliable. Manny had a good opportunity to view the suspect under clear conditions. The time between the crime and Manny's identification was short, and Manny is very confident. All of these are factors that the Supreme Court has said are important in determining the reliability of an identification. The Court has made clear that an unnecessarily suggestive identification procedure can be overcome if the identification was reliable.

Answer D is incorrect. As noted above in the explanations for Answers B and C, the unnecessarily suggestive identification procedure can be overcome because the identification was reliable. Additionally, Connor did not have a right to counsel because formal adversary proceedings have not yet begun and because there was no live identification procedure.

Essay Questions

Exam Strategies for Essay Questions

How to Use Practice Questions to Study Effectively

Below you will find seven essay questions that I have used on real criminal procedure exams. After you read each exam question, it may be tempting for you to jump ahead and look at the answer to "see whether you got it right." Do not do that! This is really important, so let me say it again: ***Do not look at the answers right after reading the questions.*** Immediately reading the answer will not help you perform better on your real exam, which is your goal. Let me explain how I think you should use the essay questions and answer keys by first pointing out where students go wrong on law school exams.

Your criminal procedure exam will test your knowledge of the law we covered in the preceding 36 chapters. You have to know the law. But knowing the rules does not guarantee a good grade on your final exam. Students mess up their law school exams in four ways, only one of which relates to knowledge of the law. After grading thousands of essay exams, here are the biggest problems I see year after year:

1. Students misstate the law—they get the rules wrong.
2. Students fail to spot the important issues.
3. Students see the issues and know the law, but they organize their answer poorly and thus do not convey how much they know. In other words, students write down the right things, but not in a way that is easy to understand.
4. Students *think* they have written down the rules, the relevant facts, and their conclusions, but they have not actually put them on paper. In other words, as

they were taking the exam, the students thought of the right analysis in their heads, but they did not write it down and thus cannot get credit for it.

How do you solve these problems? Here are some strategies:

For #1 (knowing the law), you should read this book. You would not have been admitted to law school if you weren't smart. Between your class, your intelligence, and this book, you are very capable of learning the criminal procedure rules.

For #2 (issue spotting), you should make a skeleton outline of your answer after reading the essay question. In other words, before jumping into writing multiple paragraphs analyzing one issue, you should spend a few minutes outlining *all* of the issues that you saw in the fact pattern. Write each issue—in just a word or two—into your answer before you start writing in depth about any of them. For example, if the essay question tells you the police arrested a driver and searched a car without a warrant, you will likely have to analyze the automobile exception and the search of a vehicle incident to arrest exception. There might also be an inventory issue for you to discuss. Write down the words "Automobile Exception," "Search of an Automobile Incident to Arrest," and "Inventory" on your exam answer. Then underline each phrase so that you will remember to make each issue into a subheading. After you have listed all the issues you saw, then you should go back to the top and start writing your full answer. Writing down all of the issues on the page at the beginning of the exam will remind you to go back and fill them all in. In short, as you spot issues, immediately list them on the page so you don't forget about them.

For #3 and #4 (organizing your answer and getting it all on paper), this is where it is important that you use the practice essay questions the right way. If you read the essay questions and then immediately jump to reading the model answers, you will likely say to yourself "I know that" or "I would've put that down." But are you sure? Under time pressure, would you have actually written it down? And would you have organized your answer similarly to the model answer? You don't know how you would have answered the question until you have actually answered the question. So here is what you should do:

For each practice essay question, you should answer the question the same way you would on an actual exam. Give yourself the exact amount of time that is allocated for the question. After you read the question, make a skeleton outline (see #2 above) and write out your actual answer. In short, make yourself fully answer the practice question.

When you have finished your own answer, you can then look at the answer key I have provided. In doing so, you should be merciless when comparing your answer to the model answer. Do not give yourself the benefit of the doubt by saying to yourself "Well, that's basically what I wrote." Go back to your own answer and look carefully to see if you have included the same level of depth as the model answer.

For example, did you identify the controlling rule *and* also point to the facts in the essay question that are most relevant for determining the outcome? Did you actually reach a conclusion and say how the court is likely to rule? Or did you give a more wishy-washy answer that doesn't actually take a position on which outcome you think is more likely?

If your answer skipped over part of the analysis or missed key facts from the essay question, make yourself re-write that portion of the answer. Don't just say to yourself "Now, I get it." Instead, force yourself to re-write the answer to the portion of the question you missed. This will push you to phrase your answer more clearly and more completely the second time.

On the pages that follow, you will find seven essay questions. For the first essay, I have provided a detailed model answer. This model answer should help you to see the issues, the rules, the ideal organization, and how to get them all on paper in a reasonable amount of time. Reading model answers is time-consuming, though, and it may be hard for you to compare your answer to my model answer. So for the next six essay questions I make it easier for you to check your progress. I have provided the actual grading key that I used when I graded these essay questions. The grading key is in bullet-point format and it should help you to quickly see which issues are most important (because they come with the most points), and which rules and facts from the essay you should have discussed in order to write a good answer. Once again, you should not look at the answer key before you have written your own answer.

Finally, I should say a few words about the point totals that you will see in the answer keys for each question. I typically allocate one point for each minute of an exam. So, if the essay question is 90 minutes, it is usually worth 90 points. If you look carefully at the answer to Essay #1, you will see that I have listed 85 total points for a 90-minute question. This is intentional. I usually leave a few points unassigned to award to students who think of things that I did not consider or to award to a particularly well-written answer. I used the same approach for the other answer keys as well. So you should not be surprised if the point totals in the answer keys do not exactly add up to a round number. Not all professors follow this approach, but I suspect it is pretty common.

Professors also differ in how they grade essay exams. Some professors design their answer keys down to the tiniest issue, with very specific point totals for each issue or sub-issue in the question. These professors are looking for very particular answers and award points accordingly. Other professors are less focused on students giving an exact answer and are more interested in a bigger-picture assessment of how a student has performed. I have tried to provide you with examples of grading keys for both approaches. You will notice that the answer key to Essay #2 identifies specific point totals for every sub-issue. By contrast, the remaining essay keys list point totals by topic, rather than in granular detail. It is not possible for you to know how your professors will grade their exams, so you should not stress over that. Instead, you should use the point totals as a guide for what issues are most important on each exam.

Now go practice!

Essay Question #1

(90 Minutes)

Officer Stamp works on the narcotics task force of the local police department. On March 1, Officer Stamp received a phone call tipping her off to a "big drug dealer operating right under everyone's nose." The informant said that Richard Smith—a partner at the nationally renowned law firm of Alvin, Baxter, and Carth—deals drugs out of the back of his house on Thursday evenings. The informant said that "if you watch Smith's backyard, you will see a bunch of well-dressed young guys with briefcases come by around 11:00 p.m. and leave less than 10 minutes later." Although very skeptical, Officer Stamp followed up on the tip and conducted surveillance of the house. Sure enough, on Thursday evening, Officer Stamp saw three young, well-dressed men with briefcases come to Smith's backyard at 11:00 p.m. One of the men appeared to give Smith a small package and Smith then gave the man a different small package a moment later. The three men then immediately left Smith's house. The entire series of events lasted only a few moments.

Officer Stamp thereafter continued her investigation by looking up the biography of Mr. Smith that is posted on his law firm's website. The biography indicates that Smith has done pro bono work for an organization that advocates the legalization of drugs. It also says that Mr. Smith, who is about 65 years old, is divorced and has no children.

Believing she has sufficient evidence, Officer Stamp, along with her partner, Officer Blast, each drive their marked patrol cars to the street where Smith lives. Not seeing Smith's vehicle, the two officers just sit tight in their patrol cars in front of Smith's house. Around 9:00 p.m., the officers see Smith's vehicle approaching the house, but it abruptly stops and turns around a few hundred feet from Smith's residence. At that moment, the officers see that a woman had opened a window in Smith's house. Both events surprise the officers because: (1) they did not expect Smith's vehicle to turn around so close to his house and (2) they did not think that anyone else lived in Smith's house. The officers decide to split up. Officer Blast follows Smith's car and Officer Stamp decides to knock on the door to Smith's house.

After following Smith's car for about two miles, Officer Blast decides to pull Smith over and arrest him. Officer Blast first handcuffs Smith and places him in the patrol car. Next, Officer Blast searches the trunk of the car, where she finds an illegal assault rifle. Deciding that Smith might be dangerous, Officer Blast removes him from the patrol car and searches his person. Officer Blast finds a thin sealed envelope in Smith's jacket pocket. Upon opening the envelope, Officer Blast finds heroin.

While Officer Blast is arresting Smith two miles away, Officer Stamp knocks on the front door of Smith's house. The door opens and a young woman with a flashy diamond ring answers it and identifies herself as Meredith. Officer Stamp tells Meredith that she is investigating possible drug activity and asks whether she can look around the house. Meredith says she doesn't mind, and Officer Stamp begins to search the house. After 40 minutes of searching, Officer Stamp moved toward the master bedroom. Meredith opened the door to the bedroom and Officer Stamp began looking through it. Eventually, Officer Stamp located a large amount of cocaine in a dresser drawer beneath some socks.

After being charged, Smith moves to suppress all of the evidence. You are the judge assigned to decide the suppression motion. Explain whether each piece of evidence—(1) the illegal assault rifle, (2) the heroin, and (3) the cocaine—should be admitted or suppressed and why.

Essay Question #2

(90 Minutes)

Here are the characters in our story:

Anakin	The driver and owner of the vehicle
Padme	A friend of Anakin's who was sitting in the front passenger seat
Officer Kenobi	A City of Tatooine police officer who works with drug dogs
Officer Windu	Another City of Tatooine police officer
Captain Solo	The second-highest ranking police officer in Tatooine
Luke	A K-9 drug dog

Anakin was driving down Main Street at 6:30 p.m. with his friend Padme in his hometown of Tatooine, Virginia. As Anakin's car approached the entrance to I-95 (which runs up and down the northeastern corridor of the United States) traffic began to back up. Anakin turned to Padme and said, "What do you think is going on? There's never any traffic here." Padme responded, "Oh look, there's a sign that says 'Sobriety Checkpoint. Be prepared to stop.' " Anakin became annoyed because he was in a rush. Twelve minutes later, Anakin's car reached the front of the checkpoint and he rolled down his window to talk to the officer. The following exchange took place:

Anakin:	This is ridiculous. I've got places to go.
Officer Windu:	Calm down young man, this is important police business. There's a lot of criminal activity around this area. People drink. They transport drugs. We're checking it out. Have you been drinking? Do you have any drugs in the car?

Anakin:	Well I'm a resident of this town and you're wasting my time and it makes me angry. I'm getting out of the car because I want to talk to your supervisor. [Anakin exited the vehicle and shut the door.]
Officer Windu:	Well, Captain Solo isn't here. But he approved this investigation yesterday. He told us it was okay as long as we stopped every car and picked a good intersection. So this is what we chose. If you have a problem, you can write him a letter.

At this point, Officer Kenobi walked his drug-sniffing dog (Luke) around Anakin's car. When Anakin noticed Officer Kenobi and Luke walking all the way around the car, he became even angrier and let Officer Windu know about his feelings:

Anakin:	You can't walk a drug-sniffing dog around my car. That's illegal. It's outrageous.
OfficerWindu:	Calm down. You seem very angry. Have you been drinking?
Anakin:	I have not been drinking. I am going to get you fired for this. You are a disgrace to police everywhere.

At this point, Anakin was talking very loudly and his eyes were red with anger. Officer Windu decided to arrest Anakin and told him, "You're under arrest. I am charging you with the crime of disrespecting a police officer while he is performing his official duties." (In fact, there is no offense in the state penal code for disrespecting a police officer.) Officer Windu handcuffed Anakin, searched him, and found a gun in Anakin's jacket pocket.

While Officer Windu was arresting Anakin, Officer Kenobi walked Luke (the drug-sniffing dog) around the car one more time. When Luke reached the driver's side door, he put his nose inside the car's open window. At that point, Luke sat down next to the window, a clear indication that he was alerting to drugs. (The total time for Luke to make two laps around the car was approximately 90 seconds.)

Officer Kenobi asked Padme to step out of the car. Officer Kenobi then immediately searched the car. A few minutes later, Officer Kenobi opened the center console (the area under the arm rest between the driver and front passenger's seats). Inside the center console, Officer Kenobi found a large bag of cocaine. Officer Kenobi arrested Padme. Both Anakin and Padme were then taken to the police station and processed.

Later that day, a few additional facts became clear.

First, Anakin did not have a valid permit for the handgun.

Second, prosecutors learned that Padme and Anakin were known drug dealers and they sold drugs as part of a team. Accordingly, prosecutors decided to charge both Anakin and Padme with possession of the cocaine found in the center console of the vehicle.

Third, prosecutors learned that Luke's certification to detect drugs was from a well-known private company. While that certification was still current, the certification was not for cocaine in particular, just drugs in general. Additionally, while a state police agency does certify some elite drug dogs specifically to search for cocaine, Luke did not have that state certification. Finally, Officer Kenobi did not keep detailed logs of how often Luke correctly and incorrectly alerted to drugs. Officer Kenobi explained instead that "Luke is pretty good at this. He's only been incorrect three times this month."

Finally, Padme told the police that she is not related to Anakin and that they are not dating. Padme claimed she had only been in Anakin's car a few times before.

Prosecutors have charged Anakin with unlawful possession of the gun and with possession of the cocaine. Prosecutors have charged Padme only with the possession of the cocaine. Anakin and Padme are deciding whether to plead guilty. They have asked you to advise them about whether they have a good chance of having the evidence suppressed. In particular, they want to know the following:

1. What issues will a court have to address in deciding whether to suppress the gun? Please explain all plausible arguments that could be raised by the defense and the prosecution and the likely outcome of Anakin's motion to suppress the gun.
2. What issues will a court have to address in deciding whether to suppress the cocaine? Please explain all plausible arguments that could be raised by the defense and the prosecution and the likely outcome of Anakin's motion to suppress the cocaine.
3. You have already advised Padme that she will not succeed in arguing that the cocaine was not hers. Padme's only hope is to have the cocaine suppressed as a Fourth Amendment violation. Does Padme have a plausible argument to suppress the cocaine? When answering this question, there is no need to repeat all of your answers to the previous parts. Focus your answer only on the legal issue(s) most important to Padme's suppression motion. In other words, what issues should Padme concentrate on and what are her chances of succeeding?

Essay Question #3

(90 Minutes)

On May 1, the CEO of the Dunder Corporation placed a call to the FBI and provided them with the following information:

> Most of Dunder's employees use computers throughout the day to track customer account information. On April 27, the IT Department received a tip that a Dunder employee, Dwight Scott, was "doing something on his work computer that is against company policy." Thereafter, the IT Department began to monitor Dwight Scott's computer use. The IT Department discovered that Dwight had bypassed the company's firewall, and they believed that he may have looked at sexually explicit websites featuring child pornography.

The FBI told the CEO that they would investigate immediately and that they wanted to look through Dwight's office and his computer files. The CEO agreed to remain at the office late that night so the FBI could arrive after Dwight had left for the day. When the FBI arrived at 10:00 p.m., the CEO provided them with Dwight's computer password (which the CEO had gotten a few hours earlier from the IT Department) and with a master key that opened all of the offices in the building. The FBI asked who else had access to Dwight's office. The CEO responded that "the only people with day-to-day access to Dwight's office are Dwight, his secretary, and the cleaning crew—and, of course, I and the other members of the Board of Directors have keys but we've never used them."

The FBI Agents unlocked Dwight's office, turned on his computer, and used the password to access his files. Almost immediately, the FBI discovered a folder labeled "Images." The FBI opened the "Images" folder and found multiple pictures of child pornography, which appeared to be in violation of federal law as specified in 18 U.S.C. § 2252A.

After thoroughly reviewing the Images folder, the FBI continued looking through Dwight's computer files and located a hidden folder of email messages labeled "Dwight's Personal Documents." Inside the Personal Documents folder the FBI agents found an email, written from Dwight's personal (non-company) email address to a woman named Angela. The message said: "I can't wait until tonight. As you know, I always keep some good stuff in my car. Right after I pick you up, we can park somewhere and have a high time."

The next morning, the FBI waited in the parking lot of Dunder Corporation for Dwight to arrive for work. When he pulled into the lot at 9:00 a.m., the police approached his car and told him to get out of the vehicle. The FBI handcuffed Dwight, told him he was under arrest, and placed him in the back of a police vehicle. The FBI then proceeded to search Dwight's car. The FBI found a bag of marijuana underneath the spare tire in the trunk.

The FBI agents took Dwight to the police station, booked him, and then placed him in an interrogation room. The following conversation occurred between Dwight and two FBI agents (Agent Bunk and Agent McNulty):

Dwight: Look, I just want to post bond and get out of here.

McNulty: You're not getting out of here. Ever. I hate jerks like you who prey upon children. The only question we need to know the answer to is where you got the pictures.

Dwight: What are you talking about? I don't have any illegal pictures.

Bunk: Don't waste your time trying to talk your way out of this. We weren't born yesterday.

Dwight: Look, I'm not going to confess to something I didn't do.

McNulty: You're already trying my patience. We can do this the easy way or the hard way. You can tell us where you got the pictures or I can leave you sitting here for the rest of the day chained to the table.

Bunk: Don't pay attention to him. Just tell me where you got the pictures.

McNulty: Don't belittle me, Bunk. I outrank you and I'll leave this guy chained to the table all day until he tells me where he got the pictures. I'm not kidding. He won't be able to stand up straight for 12 hours.

Bunk: Don't listen to him. Here's the thing, Dwight. You can help yourself here. We're going to find the source eventually anyway. If we have to do it without your help and spend a lot of time on it the U.S. Attorney is going to be upset. She'll seek the maximum and that's probably about 30 years. I can guarantee it. If you help us out, though, we'll put in a good word for you. You'll get two or three years maximum, maybe you'll even do a little better. It's up to you. Do it the easy way. Don't make me walk out of here and leave you with this crazy guy.

McNulty: Are you calling me crazy? When I'm done with this no-good piece of garbage, you're mine next, Bunk. You hear me?

Bunk: Just tell me where you got the stuff, Dwight.

Dwight: All right, all right. I use the screen name Jim Halpert and my password is "big tuna." If you go to the website www.scrantonicity.com you can see my emails and who sent me the pictures.

Bunk: Now we're getting somewhere.

McNulty: You know, Bunk, did you give him the warnings before we started this thing?

Bunk: No, I thought you did.

McNulty: I thought you had done it.

Bunk: You've got to be kidding me. Our supervisor is going to kill us for this.

McNulty: Just do it now.

Bunk: Okay, okay. Dwight, listen to me. You've got the right to remain silent. You don't have to talk to us. Anything you tell us can be used against you. You have the right to an attorney at trial. If you can't afford an attorney one can be appointed for you. Do you understand these rights?

Dwight: Uh huh. I guess so.

Bunk: Okay, then, just so I'm clear. You use the website www.scrantonicity.com, correct?

Dwight: Yes.

Bunk: And you get on that website to search for pictures of underage children?

Dwight: That's not how I said it.

McNulty: Look, don't start backtracking now. That's what you said, right?

Dwight. No. And don't yell at me. I'm sick of you. I'm done talking to you, McNulty. I'm done with you badgering me. Maybe I should just have a lawyer here instead.

McNulty: You're not going to be done with me until you tell me what you do on that website. Do you get on www.scrantonicity.com to download child pornography?

#2

Dwight: Yes, I do. Now get out. I'm only going to talk to your partner. I don't want you in here anymore.

After the interview was over, McNulty and Bunk used Dwight's password to log onto www.scrantonicity.com. After surfing the site for 15 minutes they were able to find incriminating chat logs showing Dwight asking for child pornography.

Dwight has moved to suppress: (1) the child pornography found on the computer, (2) the marijuana found in the car, (3) his confession; and (4) the incriminating chat logs on www.scrantonicity.com. You are the magistrate assigned to decide the suppression motion. Evaluate *all* possible arguments for admitting or suppressing each piece of evidence.

Essay Question #4

(75 Minutes)

In 2019, Tiffany Talent (who is a celebrity) started dating Paul Piano (who is a famous musician). In 2020, Talent and Piano moved in together, had a baby, and got engaged. Their new residence is an enormous house in Park City, Utah, which they named the "Talano Mansion." (Talano is a not-so-clever combination of the names "Talent" and "Piano.") The Talano Mansion sits on 10 acres of land, known as the "Elite Estate." The website for the Park City Appraisal District (the government agency that records property deeds) does not specify who owns Talano Mansion or the 10-acre Elite Estate. Rather, the property is listed as being owned by "Current Owner." This type of property recording is common in Los Angeles, where celebrities try to hide their financial dealings from the paparazzi. The Elite Estate is completely surrounded by a 12-foot-high fence. The Talano Mansion sits at least 300 feet from the fence.

Shortly after the birth of their child, Talent and Piano began to give media interviews. In late 2020, the following interview aired on television:

Reporter: How do you manage to look so relaxed with a newborn baby at home?

Talent: Oh, it's the marijuana.

Reporter: Do you have a prescription for medical marijuana?

Talent: No, we actually grow our own in our backyard. Ha!

Reporter: Are you being serious?

Talent: [Pause for a few seconds] Um, no, not really. It's still illegal to grow your own marijuana, right? And it would probably be bad for the baby, right?

After the interview, there was a national uproar about Talent's comments. Most people didn't believe Talent was really growing marijuana in her backyard, but a lot of people thought she was smoking marijuana in the house near her baby.

A few days after the interview, TMI (a media company that follows celebrities for its website and streaming show) decided to get to the bottom of the marijuana scandal. TMI had been successful in the past by paying police officers to provide them with gossip and pictures. An executive at TMI therefore turned to one of its best agents, Officer Kris Mumphries. Officer Mumphries was employed by the Park City Police Department as a regular patrol officer with a daytime shift patrolling the same neighborhood where Talent and Piano lived. TMI offered Officer Mumphries $10,000 for a picture of Talent smoking marijuana or a picture of her marijuana plants.

On the evening of November 23, Officer Mumphries (who was dressed in his police uniform) walked up to Talano Mansion and rang the doorbell but no one answered. Determined to get a picture, Mumphries found a 10-foot ladder, set the ladder against the fence, and climbed onto the top of the fence. Sitting on the fence, Mumphries saw Talent standing about 200 feet away from the house and about 100 feet from the fence. Talent was standing next to a large marijuana plant. Mumphries took a picture with his high-resolution camera. TMI posted the picture to its website less than an hour later.

Shortly after the picture was posted on TMI's website, the uproar about Talent growing marijuana became even bigger. The Park City Police Chief decided she could not ignore the publicity, and she instructed her officers go to a magistrate to get a search warrant. The warrant (along with the supporting affidavit) specified as follows:

State of Utah, City of Park City
Search Warrant and Affidavit

AFFIDAVIT

Officer Harry Tevin swears under oath that he has probable cause to believe that marijuana, a substance that is unlawful pursuant to the Utah Penal Code, is located in the house of Tiffany Talent and Paul Piano at 4077 Park Street (otherwise known as "Talano Mansion").

____

Officer Harry Tevin

SEARCH WARRANT

The People of the State of Utah hereby instruct any Sheriff, Police Officer, or Peace Officer in Park City as follows: You are commanded to search Talano Mansion for marijuana plants and to return and inventory all items recovered and removed from the premises.

____

Judge Mila Austin

On November 24, just a few hours after Judge Austin signed the warrant, the police proceeded to execute it. First, police searched outdoors in the area where Talent was photographed. Although they did not find any contraband there, they did see a small greenhouse hidden behind some trees, about 500 feet from the house. Inside the greenhouse, under a tarp, the police found a dozen marijuana plants and seized those plants.

The officers then went inside the house to search. After 30 minutes, police entered what looked like an office and found a file cabinet that was engraved "T.T. Important Documents." Officers opened the file cabinet and saw numerous folders. One folder caught their attention because it was labeled "Sara Swann Revenge Plot." Sara Swann was a famous musician. The officers opened the folder and saw a handwritten note. The note explained that Swann's music was horrible and it detailed the desire of both Talent and Piano to murder Swann. Officers seized the note and arrested both Talent and Piano.

Talent and Piano have moved to suppress the evidence against them. You are the clerk for the judge who will decide the suppression motion. Explain all possible arguments for admitting or suppressing the evidence discovered by the police. In particular, explain:

1. whether the marijuana in the greenhouse should be admissible against Talent; and
2. whether the note in the file cabinet should be admissible against Talent and/or Piano.

Essay Question #5

(60 Minutes)

Jack loves Las Vegas. He particularly loves to gamble in a VIP-only section of the Vegas Gold Casino. In the VIP area, high rollers are served champagne while they play poker at the $1,000-per-hand tables. The VIP area is roped off so that the "ordinary" patrons of the casino cannot bother the high rollers. A Vegas Gold security guard stands at the entrance to the VIP area so that the ordinary patrons cannot get in.

Unbeknownst to Jack, the FBI had been investigating him for a recent string of armed robberies of jewelry stores. At the most recent heist, the jewel thief had left behind a tiny amount of genetic material when he caught his skin on a sharp corner in the jewelry shop. The FBI was excited when it found this genetic material because it was a large enough sample to feed into a nationwide DNA database of known criminals. Unfortunately, the FBI's hopes were dashed when the genetic material did not match any known criminals. The most the FBI forensic analysts could do with the genetic material was to say that it came from a Caucasian man, roughly 50 years old, who was suffering from a rare skin condition known as argyria. Based on this information, the FBI was able to narrow its list of suspects down to 150 people, one of whom was Jack. The forensic analysts told the FBI agents that they could make a definitive match if they could get a sample of Jack's DNA.

So on Friday, April 11, undercover FBI agents followed Jack to the Vegas Gold Casino. They saw him exit his black Lexus SUV that had the license plate "HI GM-BLR." The FBI agents observed Jack proceed to the VIP area, where he sat down at the poker table in a chair that had his name on it. For the next 30 minutes, the agents watched as Jack drank champagne and played poker. Thereafter, Jack got up to go to the bathroom and left behind his champagne glass. The FBI agents saw their chance.

One agent knocked the security guard to the ground. The other FBI agent ran into the VIP area, used a swab to take Jack's DNA off the champagne glass, and ran back out. Both FBI agents then sprinted for the closest exit and, as they were running, they saw that Jack was chasing after them. The FBI agents raced through the casino to the closest exit and ended up in the parking lot. Right in front of them in the parking lot was the black Lexus SUV with the license plate "HI GMBLR." As the agents caught their breath, the casino door slammed open and Jack came out yelling: "You guys can't steal from me, I've got a machine gun in the trunk of my car and I'm going to get it and shoot both of you."

Before Jack could take another step, the agents pulled out their guns and badges and told him to get down on the ground. Jack immediately complied. The agents then took the car keys out of Jack's pocket and unlocked the trunk of the Lexus. Inside the trunk they found a fully automatic machine gun that they knew to be illegal. The agents then unlocked the car doors and found a bag of cocaine in the unlocked glove compartment.

Subsequently, the FBI forensics lab tested the DNA from Jack's champagne glass and found that it matched the DNA at the jewelry store. Jack was indicted for numerous crimes and has moved to suppress: (1) the DNA from the champagne glass; (2) the machine gun found in the trunk of his car; and (3) the cocaine found in the glove compartment. You are the law clerk assigned to the case. Thoroughly explain *all* possible arguments for admitting or suppressing each piece of evidence.

Essay Question #6

(60 Minutes)

Police have spent the last two weeks investigating a gang that appears to be heavily involved in the local drug trade. The police believe that a man named Ollie is the leader of the gang. Ollie owns an old-fashioned Cadillac that has been registered to him since 1996. Other members of the gang include Carl (who appears to be the contact that drug buyers call to get drugs) and Sal (who appears to be the delivery guy). The police have never actually seen any drugs change hands, nor do they have any specific tips from informants, but based on the furtive activity that they have observed, they believe drug activity is afoot.

The officers' best guess is that the operation works as follows: A drug buyer contacts Carl to request a certain quantity of drugs. Carl then sends a text message to Sal with the requested quantity of drugs and the location of the buy. Sal then drives the Cadillac to the location and completes the sale. The Cadillac is owned by Ollie and registered to him. The police have often seen Sal and Ollie driving together in the Cadillac. However, the police have never seen Ollie present when any of the suspected drug deals have been done. During those times, Sal is driving the Cadillac, but Ollie is not in the vehicle and is nowhere to be found. The police suspect that Ollie is the brains of the operation and that he is smart enough not to be in the Cadillac whenever a drug deal is about to occur.

After two weeks of surveillance, the police apply for a warrant to arrest Ollie, Sal, and Carl, and a search warrant for Ollie's Cadillac. The magistrate denies the warrant applications because "you've never seen any drugs change hands and there's no support for your text message theory."

After the magistrate turned down their warrant request, the police continued their surveillance. The police followed Sal closely and saw him drive by himself to a house. The police observed Sal pull the Cadillac into the driveway, take out his cell phone, and begin typing a text message. A moment later, the garage door opened and Sal drove the car inside. The garage door then closed. Five minutes later the police saw the garage door open, and they watched Sal drive out of the garage and get back on the road. Once again, the police had not seen the transfer of any drugs.

One of the surveillance officers said, "Look, that judge wouldn't issue a warrant, and these guys are too careful to get caught. So let's just do this thing already." Moments later, when the officers saw Sal change lanes without signaling, the police turned on their siren and pulled Sal over. The police immediately arrested Sal, handcuffed him, and placed him in the back of the police car. The first officer opened the trunk of the car and looked around. Underneath the spare tire they found an illegal assault weapon.

Just as the first officer was looking in the trunk, the second officer was opening the front passenger door of the car. The second officer saw a cell phone that was sitting on the floor of the front passenger seat. Just then, the phone lit up. When the officer looked over, she could see that the phone was buzzing. The officer turned over the phone and saw that the front screen was lit up. A message had just come in and was on the front screen. It said: "I think the cops are onto us. Dump the stuff in the car. Make sure you get everything that's hidden in the gas tank too." The officer subsequently opened the lid to the gas tank, reached her fingers inside the gas tank, and found bags of cocaine taped inside. The officers subsequently got a warrant to search the cell phone they had found on the front seat. A search of the phone indicated that the cell phone belonged to Sal and that the message about dumping the drugs was from Ollie.

Sal has been charged with a weapons offense and possession with intent to distribute the cocaine from the gas tank. Ollie has been charged only with possession with intent to distribute the cocaine from the gas tank. They have both moved to suppress. You are the law clerk assigned to the case. Thoroughly explain whether (1) the assault weapon is admissible as to Sal; (2) the cocaine is admissible as to Sal; and (3) the cocaine is admissible as to Ollie.

Essay Question #7

(75 Minutes)

After testifying in court one morning, Officer Olivia walks out of the courtroom and notices a file folder lying on the floor. Officer Olivia picks up the file and reads what's written on the outside of the folder: "Danny Dennis case: Property of Carl Careless, Attorney at Law. Privileged and Confidential." Based on the outside of the folder, Officer Olivia assumes that Carl Careless is a defense lawyer and that he must have dropped the file. Although she has never heard of Danny Dennis, Officer Olivia is curious and opens the file. The top piece of paper in the file is Carl's handwritten notes, which say the following:

> Dennis is charged with aggravated assault. The case looks like a slam dunk guilty to me. I tried to convince Dennis to take the prosecutor's plea bargain offer and plead guilty. Dennis said the plea bargain offer of seven years was way too high and there's no way he'd accept anything over a five-year prison sentence. I told Dennis that the prosecutor might agree to five years and that I'd ask him to lower the offer next week. As a backup plan, Dennis authorized me to tell the prosecutor that Dennis works in a big drug ring and that he can provide evidence against a key drug dealer (Keith Kelly) in exchange for a lighter sentence. Dennis says Keith Kelly sells drugs to kids at school by dressing young (grungy clothes, long hair, wears backpack, etc.). Dennis said he didn't want to rat out Keith Kelly unless really necessary and that I should only mention it to the prosecutor if he won't reduce his plea bargain offer to five years. I probably won't need to say anything about Keith Kelly because the prosecutor handling the case is kind of soft and I think I can talk him down to five years. Dennis is out on bond, so I will wait until next week to talk to the prosecutor.

Officer Olivia closed the file and became concerned that Dennis might get the five-year plea deal without agreeing to provide information about Keith Kelly. Officer Olivia therefore went back to the police station and did some research on Dennis and Kelly. Olivia learned that Danny Dennis lives at 123 Maple Street and owns a red BMW with license plate XRX-123. She also learned that Keith Kelly lives at 456 Green Street.

The next day, Officer Olivia staked out 123 Maple Street and saw a man leave the house in a red BMW with license plate XRX-123. She followed the vehicle for most of the morning and eventually it stopped at 456 Green Street. A man came out of the house at 456 Green Street carrying a backpack. The man with the backpack (who Officer Olivia assumed was Keith Kelly) walked up to the BMW, and started to get in. Before he could get in though, the driver yelled at him, "Hey, don't put that backpack in the car next to me. Throw the stuff in the trunk. I've already got enough problems without you bringing that in here next to me." The man did as instructed and put the backpack in the trunk before getting into the BMW.

Officer Olivia followed the BMW as it pulled away. The BMW committed no traffic violations, but after two miles, Officer Olivia turned on her police lights and stopped the BMW. After ordering both individuals out of the car and checking their IDs, Officer Olivia determined that the driver was in fact Danny Dennis and the passenger was Keith Kelly. Officer Olivia handcuffed and arrested both Danny Dennis and Keith Kelly.

Officer Olivia then proceeded to search Dennis and Kelly. Officer Olivia found nothing on Kelly, but she found a small bag of cocaine tucked inside Dennis's wallet in between two credit cards. After she finished searching the individuals, Officer Olivia placed both men in the back of her police car so that she could search the trunk of the BMW. Upon opening the trunk, she found the backpack Kelly was carrying when he came out of his house. Officer Olivia unzipped the backpack and looked through its contents, but she did not find anything illegal. Officer Olivia put the backpack to one side and lifted up the floorboard of the trunk so that she could see the spare tire. Underneath the spare tire, Officer Olivia found an illegal machine gun. Subsequent analysis indicated that both Dennis and Kelly's fingerprints were on the machine gun.

The prosecutor plans to charge Dennis and Kelly with various felonies. Before doing so, however, she wants your opinion as to whether the evidence is admissible. The District Attorney has asked you to answer the following three questions. In doing so, consider all relevant facts, law, and possible arguments why each piece of evidence should be admitted or suppressed.

1. Is the cocaine found in Dennis's wallet admissible against Dennis?
2. Is the illegal machine gun found underneath the spare tire admissible against Dennis?
3. Is the illegal machine gun found underneath the spare tire admissible against Kelly?

Answer Keys

Professor's Answer to Essay #1

General Advice on Test Taking in the Context of Essay #1

Here, the question specifically lists each piece of evidence: (1) the illegal assault rifle; (2) the heroin; and (3) the cocaine. If the professor sets out that format in the call of the question, you should follow it. Begin your answer with an analysis of the admissibility of the assault rifle and then move on to the next piece of evidence.

Even if the call of the question did not list the three pieces of evidence, it is generally a good idea in a criminal procedure exam to organize your answer around each piece of evidence. Defendants ask courts to suppress evidence, so your answer should take each piece of evidence one at a time.

Some professors like to see the definitions of terms and tests. For instance, one key issue in this question is whether there is probable cause. If your professor has indicated that she thinks the textbook definition of probable cause is important, you should explain in your answer that probable cause is defined as "the facts and circumstances within the officers' knowledge and of which they have reasonably trustworthy information are sufficient. . . ." If your professor has indicated that such definitions are not important, then you should not take up time writing the definitions in your answer.

Avoid the temptation to talk about things you spent a lot of time on in class, but that are not relevant to the question. For example, you likely spent multiple class sessions on whether or not something is a search. That topic was one of the longest chapters of this book, because it is a big deal. But the "search" issue is not present in Essay #1. This essay involves police looking through a trunk, an envelope, and a sock drawer. There is no plausible argument that these actions are not searches. As such, do not spend time explaining that the police have searched by looking in these locations.

And do not take the time and space to describe that a police action becomes a search if it invades a subjective expectation of privacy that is objectively reasonable. Move straightaway to the issues in dispute.

Avoid the temptation to cut and paste. In this question, you will have to analyze whether there is probable cause to arrest Smith, and also whether there is probable cause to search his car. Professors really don't like it when you cut and paste one section of your answer and drop it into another section. If the exact same analysis applies to both issues, it is fine to say "As I discussed above . . ." But be careful before you do that. Sometimes the analysis will be different. In this question, there is a better case for probable cause to arrest Smith than there is for probable cause to search his car. Be sure to take each piece of evidence or each person separately because the analysis can differ.

Remember to use paragraphs and subheadings to organize your answer. The better organized your answer, the more points you will get.

The model answer is below. You cannot expect your answer to be this polished. I wrote the question and therefore I had an idea of what the answer should be from the very beginning. Also, I was not limited to the 90 minutes allocated for the question. I had extra time to polish the writing so that it would be well organized for this book. Do not expect that your sentences will be perfect and free of typos. Of course, take a moment to run the spell check and to avoid glaring errors. But do not spend your time writing and rewriting individual sentences. You have limited time and you should devote it to identifying the issues and organizing them effectively.

MODEL ANSWER

Assault Rifle in the Trunk

Smith has moved to suppress the assault rifle in the trunk. For the rifle to be admissible the police must have had a lawful basis to stop Smith's vehicle and also a lawful basis to search the trunk of Smith's vehicle. As discussed below, the rifle should likely be suppressed as the product of an unlawful search.

Was the Vehicle Stop Lawful? **(15 points)**

To stop a vehicle, the police must have reasonable suspicion that criminal activity is afoot. Reasonable suspicion is a relatively low standard— even lower than probable cause. Here, the officers have received an anonymous tip that Smith is "a big drug dealer" and that an unusual number of men come to Smith's house late in the evening (at 11:00 p.m.) and stay a short time. While the officers cannot be certain that they saw a drug transaction, they were able to confirm that multiple men came to Smith's house late at night and left shortly thereafter. Confirming details—even arguably innocent details—suggests that the tipster has a basis of knowledge and is more likely to be correct.

In addition to the tip and confirming details of the tip, the officers observed Smith turn around only a few hundred feet from his residence. While it is possible that Smith turned his vehicle around for an innocent reason—such as forgetting to buy milk at the grocery store—there is also an incriminating reason why he may have turned around. The officers were sitting in marked patrol cars outside of his house. When a person engages in unprovoked flight from the police in a high-crime area, that alone may be sufficient to create reasonable suspicion. Here, Smith may not have engaged in "flight" because he just turned his car around. And given that Smith is a law firm partner who is likely well paid, it is unlikely that his home was in a high-crime area. But even if turning the vehicle around—by itself—does not amount to reasonable suspicion, it is still suspicious behavior.

In addition to the tip, the confirmed details, and turning the vehicle around near the police cars, we must also consider whether it was suspicious that the woman in Smith's house opened the window just as Smith was turning the vehicle around. One reasonable inference is that she may have been signaling to Smith that there were officers stationed outside the house and that he might get caught. Accordingly, while it is possible that the woman opening the window is completely innocent, it is also possible to consider the window-opening to be suspicious.

Finally, we should discuss—but probably not give weight to—the fact that Smith did pro bono work for an "organization that advocates the legalization of drugs." Lawyers regularly represent clients without endorsing the views of those clients. Just because a lawyer is providing legal assistance to an organization does not mean the lawyer believes in the values of that organization. And it certainly does not mean the lawyer is engaged in any actions—here, drug dealing—that the organization might support. A court should treat this fact as irrelevant.

Courts evaluate reasonable suspicion under a totality of the circumstances test. When we combine the informant's tip about drug dealing, the confirmation of the men coming to Smith's house late at night, the turning the car around upon seeing the police, and the possible signal by the woman when she opened the window, a court would likely conclude that there was reasonable suspicion to stop Smith's vehicle on the grounds that he may be involved in drug trafficking.

Was the Search of the Trunk Lawful?

Even if a court (as described above) will find the stop of Smith's vehicle to be lawful, we must still consider whether the search of the trunk that led to finding the illegal assault rifle was lawful.

Search Incident to Arrest **(5 points)**

The officer arrested Smith and then searched the trunk. Even if there was a lawful reason to arrest Smith (which is discussed below) the search of the trunk could not be justified as a search incident to arrest. There are two problems with invoking the search incident to arrest doctrine: (1) there was no reason to believe drug evidence would be found in the vehicle; and (2) a search incident to arrest cannot extend to the trunk.

First, the police may only conduct a search of a vehicle incident to arrest when the arrestee is unsecured and within reach of the vehicle, of if there is reason to believe evidence of the crime of arrest will be found in the vehicle. Officer Blast handcuffed Smith and placed him in the patrol car, so he is not unsecured. The legality of a search incident to arrest thus turns on whether there is reason to believe evidence of the crime of arrest would be found in the vehicle. Nothing in the anonymous tip referenced drugs in Smith's car. The tip specifically said that Smith deals drugs "out of the back of his house" and that if the police "watch Smith's backyard" you will see people coming to buy drugs late at night. The officer confirmed the late-night visits—that is, they confirmed suspicious activity at the house. The officers have no indication that Smith is dealing drugs out of his car or transporting the drugs in his vehicle. Accordingly, there is no reason to believe evidence of the crime of arrest—drug dealing—will be found in the vehicle.

Second, the Supreme Court has long held that police may not search the trunk of a vehicle incident to arrest. This rule may not make much sense in a world in which key fobs or even cell phone apps can open the trunk. But the Court has never overruled its decision excluding the trunk. Because the police searched the trunk, the rifle cannot be admissible under the search incident to arrest doctrine.

The Automobile Exception **(10 points)**

A court would next consider whether the illegal rifle found in the trunk would be admissible under the automobile exception. The automobile exception permits police to search a vehicle if there is probable cause to believe evidence is in the vehicle. It is very unlikely the police could demonstrate probable cause to believe drugs (or other evidence) would be found in the vehicle.

If police had probable cause to believe drugs would be in the vehicle, they could search anywhere in the vehicle to locate them. The automobile exception allows the police to search the trunk, because drugs could be hidden in the trunk just as easily as they could be hidden in the glove compartment, center console, or any other area of the vehicle. In short, the automobile exception gives the police a green light to search the trunk, but only if the police had probable cause to believe there were drugs in the car.

The key question therefore is whether police have probable cause to believe that there are drugs in Smith's vehicle. It would be difficult for a court to find probable cause. As noted above with respect to the search incident to arrest doctrine, there is no real evidence linking drugs to Smith's car. The anonymous tip said that Smith deals drugs out of his house and it encouraged the police to monitor his backyard. When the officers undertook surveillance and confirmed details (such as the young well-dressed men arriving for short stays at a late hour), all of the confirmed details related to the house.

Of course, Smith is driving his vehicle. Perhaps he always carries the drugs on him. Or perhaps he is able to sell drugs out of his house because he drives to his supplier and then brings the drugs back to his home. These theories are purely speculative, though, and police would have nothing more than a hunch, if that, that drugs would be found in the vehicle. A hunch does not establish probable cause.

Accordingly, a court should not find the illegal assault rifle to be admissible under the automobile exception.

Probable Cause for Lawful Arrest; Inevitable Discovery Exception and Inventory Doctrine

Although the assault rifle should probably not be admissible under the automobile exception or the search of a vehicle incident to arrest exception, there is a plausible case to be made that it would be admissible under a combination of the inevitable discovery doctrine and the inventory doctrine. In short, if the police lawfully arrested Smith for drug dealing, they would not have left his vehicle on the side of the road. The officers would have impounded the vehicle. If the department had an inventory policy that called for officers to inventory the contents of the trunk, the officers would inevitably have discovered the rifle when they opened the trunk. Thus, even though Officer Blast found the rifle through an illegal search of the trunk at the scene, the evidence would be admissible because it would inevitably have been discovered during an inventory search.

Lawful Arrest Requires Probable Cause **(15 points)**

To assess whether the police inevitably would have found the rifle during an inventory of the trunk, we must first be sure there was a lawful arrest of Smith.

Officers can arrest a person in public without a warrant so long as they have probable cause to believe the person engaged in criminal activity. The admissibility of the rifle therefore turns on whether there was probable cause to arrest Smith.

As discussed above, it is a close question whether there is probable cause. Here the evidence includes: (1) the anonymous tip about Smith dealing drugs; (2) the officers' confirmation of some of the details of the tip (i.e., that young, well-dressed men would arrive late at night and leave shortly thereafter); (3) the officers' observation of the exchange of packages, which could have been a drug deal (but might have been an exchange of lawful items); (4) the woman inside the house possibly signaling Smith that the police were on the street; and (5) Smith possibly turning his vehicle around upon seeing the police or the woman's signal.

If the police had only the anonymous tip there would likely not be enough for probable cause. The informant is completely anonymous and thus we have no idea about his or her reliability.

But, as noted above, the police have considerably more than just the anonymous tip. By confirming details in the tip, the officers have helped to establish that the informant has a basis of knowledge and seems credible.

While the officers never saw drugs and money change hands, the exchange of packages is potentially suspicious. Of course, there are non-suspicious reasons why a lawyer would exchange packages with law firm associates. The younger lawyers could have been giving Smith updated documents and Smith could have been providing them with edits on other documents. But in a digital world this could have been accomplished by email. Even if Smith were a night owl and only worked with hard copy documents, that would not change the fact that it is unusual for people to be exchanging documents in the backyard rather than at the front door. Finally, it normally would not take three lawyers to bring a senior partner a package of documents. All told, the police confirmed some innocuous details (such as the people being well-dressed) but also some suspicious details, as well as what could possibly appear to be a hand-to-hand drug deal.

Finally, it is hard to know exactly what to make of a woman waving out the window to Smith's car as he returns home and Smith turning his vehicle around only a few hundred feet from two marked police cars. There may have been lawful reasons for these events, but they also seem suspicious. At the margin, they enhance the case for probable cause.

One final point is worth noting. The fact pattern says that Officer Stamp "believ[ed] she has sufficient evidence." Officer Stamp's beliefs are irrelevant to the question of whether there is probable cause. The subjective intent of the officers does not control. Probable cause is determined objectively.

In short, we should ignore the fact that Smith did legal work for a group that advocates the legalization of drugs. And we should ignore the fact that Officer Stamp believed there was probable cause. The relevant considerations are the anonymous tip, the confirmed details, the officers viewing what could have been a drug transaction, the suspicious actions of the woman opening the window, and Smith turning his vehicle around within a few hundred feet of the officers' marked patrol cars.

Under the totality of the circumstances, these factors likely create probable cause to arrest Smith for drug dealing.

Inevitable Discovery Doctrine and Inventory **(10 points)**

Given that there is likely probable cause to arrest Smith and that no warrant is necessary for an arrest in public, the police will have conducted a valid arrest. When police conduct a valid arrest of a driver, they may choose to impound the vehicle.

Police departments typically have inventory policies to prevent false claims of theft against the department. Officers do not need suspicion to conduct an inventory, but they must follow the department's policy. If the department's policy instructs officers to inventory the contents of an impounded automobile, including the trunk, then the officers would find the illegal assault rifle during the inventory. Officers are free to seize contraband in plain view during an inventory. The officers would be lawfully present (because they are conducting an inventory pursuant to the department's policy) and the illegal assault rifle would likely be immediately incriminating (as long as the rifle's appearance indicated it was not lawful to own it). As such, the officers could seize the rifle under the plain view doctrine.

Of course, the officers did not in fact seize the rifle during an inventory at the police station. Officer Blast unlawfully searched the trunk at the traffic stop. But the rifle can still be admissible under the inevitable discovery doctrine. If Officer Blast had not conducted the unlawful search of the trunk at the traffic stop, the police inevitably would have found the rifle anyway when they properly impounded the vehicle and catalogued the contents of the vehicle during an inventory. Accordingly, the rifle should be admissible.

Heroin in Envelope

Smith has moved to suppress the heroin found in an envelope in his jacket pocket. The heroin would not be admissible under a *Terry* frisk, but it is admissible under the search incident to arrest doctrine.

Search Incident to Arrest **(5 points)**

As discussed above, there is likely probable cause to arrest Smith for drug dealing. Given that he is in public, the police do not need an arrest warrant.

If the police have probable cause to arrest Smith, they can search him incident to arrest. A search incident to arrest allows the police to open items, including closed containers, that the officers find on the person. The Court has authorized a bright-line rule allowing police to conduct a full-scale search incident to arrest. The rationale is to prevent danger to the officer and to prevent the destruction of evidence. Neither of those problems is really present here because the envelope surely doesn't contain a weapon and the officers are in a position to seize the envelope and prevent the destruction of evidence. But the fact that there is no danger to the officer or realistic chance of destruction of evidence in this case is irrelevant. The officers do not have to demonstrate that they face those problems in this case. The search incident to arrest is a bright-line rule and the police can always open containers on an arrestee, regardless of the facts of the particular case. Accordingly, as long as there is probable cause to make a valid arrest, the heroin in the envelope should be admissible under the search incident to arrest doctrine.

Terry Frisk **(5 points)**

If a court were to conclude that the police lacked probable cause to arrest Smith, then the prosecution could try to make the argument that the heroin in the envelope should be admissible under a combination of the *Terry* frisk and plain touch doctrines. This argument should fail, however.

Even without probable cause, an officer can stop a suspected drug dealer under the *Terry* doctrine to investigate further. To conduct a valid *Terry* stop, an officer must have reasonable suspicion that criminal activity is afoot. Because I have argued that there is probable cause to arrest Smith, I believe there should surely be enough suspicion to meet the lower standard of reasonable suspicion for a *Terry* stop.

If the police conduct a valid *Terry* stop, they can sometimes also engage in a *Terry* frisk of the outer layer of a detainee's clothing to check for weapons. To conduct a valid *Terry* frisk, the officers must have reasonable suspicion that the suspect is armed and dangerous. The police could argue that they are investigating Smith for drug activity and that drug dealers often have weapons. This argument is often persuasive to courts, although it might be less so here, where the suspect is an older lawyer and is suspected of dealing drugs to other well-to-do people. Moreover, he is not near the area (his home) where he is alleged to deal drugs. A court could go either way, but given that courts often defer to officers about safety risks and that drug dealers often have weapons, there is a plausible case that a *Terry* frisk would be permissible.

(The officers could try also try to argue that finding an assault rifle in the trunk creates reasonable suspicion that Smith would have a weapon on his person. This argument would fail, though. As noted above, the search of the trunk was unlawful and thus anything found as a result cannot be counted toward reasonable suspicion.)

If the officers conducted a valid *Terry* frisk, the remaining question is whether the heroin would be admissible under the plain touch doctrine. It is very unlikely the government would succeed on this argument.

If, during the course of a valid *Terry* pat-down, an officer feels an object that she immediately recognizes to be incriminating, the officer can pull it out and seize it. That is not what happened here, however. The fact pattern never says that Officer Blast immediately recognized the envelope as containing illegal drugs. Rather, the officer found the envelope and then proceeded to open it. The facts tell us that "upon opening the envelope, Officer Blast finds heroin." This recitation of the facts indicates that the officer only learned it was heroin *after* opening the envelope. Officers are not permitted to open items during a *Terry* frisk. The opening of the envelope was thus a search that can only be justified as a search incident to arrest or as a search requiring probable cause and a warrant. The heroin cannot be admissible under the *Terry* doctrine.

Cocaine in the Drawer

The police do not have a warrant to search the home. We therefore must explore whether an exception to the warrant requirement may apply. One possibility is that Meredith would have destroyed the drugs and that the police can claim exigent circumstances. This does not appear like a strong argument based on the facts. A second possibility is that the drugs are admissible because Meredith has provided valid third-party consent. The viability of consent is debatable, although there is a strong case for the drugs to be admissible under a consent rationale.

Exigent Circumstances **(5 points)**

Police can search a house under an exigent circumstances rationale if there is probable cause for the search and a risk that evidence will be destroyed while the police wait for a warrant. As described above, there is a compelling case for probable cause that Smith is dealing drugs out of the house. It will be more difficult for police to demonstrate the imminent destruction of evidence, however.

The government can make the argument that Meredith opening the window at the same time that Smith turned his car around so close to the patrol cars is a signal or communication for Meredith to destroy the drugs. Put differently, the government could argue that the officers had to enter without a warrant because Meredith was being signaled by Smith to destroy the drugs.

This argument is a stretch and not persuasive. The officers had been sitting outside the house before Meredith opened the window. Thus, if she were afraid of police entering and finding drugs she likely would have already destroyed them. Additionally, the idea that the open window and the car turning around were some type of signal is just conjecture.

Finally, although the subjective intent of the officers is not controlling, it is indicative of how a reasonable person would have perceived the situation. And the officers never rushed into the house. Officer Stamp knocked on the door and then took the time to ask Meredith for consent to look around. That does not suggest an exigent circumstance in which officers would be concerned about the destruction of evidence.

In short, the argument for searching the house (and admitting the cocaine in the sock drawer) on an exigency rationale is weak and should not succeed.

Consent **(20 points)**

A third party, like Meredith, can give consent if she has common authority over the property, or if a reasonable officer would have believed she had common authority. The facts do not tell us whether Meredith had common authority. Therefore, we should devote our attention to whether a reasonable officer could have believed she had common authority.

In determining whether a reasonable officer could have believed a third party had common authority, we look at what was known to the officers. While it might be illuminating for the officers to ask follow-up questions, they are under no obligation to do so.

Here, the officers knew that "Mr. Smith, who is about 65 years old, is divorced and has no children." An officer might therefore think that Smith lives alone. Indeed, the facts tell us that the officers were "surprised" because "they did not think that anyone else lived in Smith's house." These facts suggest it would not be reasonable to believe Meredith had authority to consent.

But other facts suggest a reasonable person could believe Meredith had common authority over the property. The officers thought Smith was divorced because his website bio said that. But his biography could be out of date. Or he could be divorced but have a girlfriend. Or perhaps his sister was living with him. Or he could have a roommate. Most importantly, the facts tell us that the events occurred "around 9:00 p.m." If Meredith was home alone at 9:00 p.m., that suggests she was not a transitory guest or a cleaning person. When people are left alone in a home in the evening, it usually indicates that they have some authority over the premises. Finally, when Meredith answered the door she had the opportunity to tell the police if she was a transitory guest. But she never did so. In short, while it is not a slam dunk, it would be reasonable for the officers to believe Meredith had common authority over the property to permit a search of the premises.

The hardest question is whether the officers could believe that Meredith had authority to consent to a search of a dresser drawer in the master bedroom. As noted above, police could reasonably believe that Meredith had common authority over the property because she was Smith's girlfriend, sister, or roommate. While any of those people could likely consent to the police entering the house and searching the common areas, it would be much harder for Smith's sister or roommate to consent to a search of the dresser in the master bedroom. If Meredith was Smith's sister or roommate, then she likely lived in a different bedroom in the house and the claim to have common authority over the master bedroom is much weaker. Thus, whether the officers could reasonably believe Meredith had common authority over the master bedroom probably depends on whether they could reasonably believe Smith was her boyfriend, fiancé, or husband.

We of course do not know whether Meredith was Smith's girlfriend, fiancé, or wife. But there are facts to suggest a reasonable officer could believe her to be. Meredith opened the door to the master bedroom with no prompting. This suggests that Meredith believed she was permitted to be in that room. Moreover, when Meredith first answered the front door the officer noticed that she was wearing a "flashy diamond ring," which suggests that she was engaged. Of course, Smith's sister or even his roommate could be engaged. But the existence of these possibilities doesn't change the fact that it would be reasonable for the officers to believe that Meredith—who was home alone late in the evening, let the police in, and opened the door to the master bedroom—had common authority over the entire house, including the dresser drawers in the master bedroom.

Accordingly, while a court would not be compelled to find that a reasonable officer could believe Meredith had common authority over the dresser, that conclusion is the most persuasive. Accordingly, the cocaine found in the dresser drawer should be admissible.

Professor's Answer Key for Essay #2

The Handgun

- Sobriety Checkpoint versus Drug Checkpoint
  - Primary purpose test to determine what type of checkpoint **2 points**
  - Drug checkpoints are unconstitutional **2 points**
  - Argument for this being a drug checkpoint **6 points**
    - Windu says "lots of criminal activity here"
    - Windu asks not just about drinking, but also drugs
    - Windu says Captain Solo "approved this investigation"
    - Drug Dog on the scene
    - 6:30 p.m. is early in the day and suggests drug rather DWI checkpoint
    - Near I-95 (a known drug corridor) suggests a drugs checkpoint
- If the Primary Purpose Was a Sobriety Checkpoint, Was It Lawful?
  - Factors to consider: **3 points**
    - Level of intrusiveness
    - Effectiveness
    - Minimal discretion of the officers (because all cars treated equally)

- Argument That This Is a Valid Sobriety Checkpoint **4 points**
  - Cleared by Captain Solo in advance
  - Stopped every car
  - Time speaking to the officer is short (90 seconds)
- Argument That This Is Not a Valid Sobriety Check-point **4 points**
  - Captain Solo didn't pick the location
  - No advance publicity to enable people to avoid the checkpoint
  - 12-minute backup to get to the front of the checkpoint

- Drug-Sniffing Dog
  - Not a search to walk dog around vehicle **2 points**
  - But the dog "put his nose inside the car's open window" looks like a physical trespass **2 points**
  - Legality of dog sniff turns on whether initial stop was lawful. **2 points**
  - Legality of dog sniff also turns on whether walking the dog extended stop. **2 points**
  - Total time of two laps (90 seconds) suggests no extension of the stop. **2 points**
  - Second walk around is closer question. **2 points**
- Stated Reason for Arrest Was Unlawful
  - Can't arrest for a crime that didn't exist. **2 points**
  - Can't search incident to arrest without valid arrest. **2 points**
- Inevitable Discovery
  - Arrest of Anakin invalid (no crime) so gun should be suppressed. **2 points**
  - The dog alert can give probable cause to search the car. **2 points**
  - But the dog alert might not be valid given that dog alerted right after putting his nose "inside the car's window." **2 points**
  - Search of the car falls under the automobile exception. **2 points**
  - If valid car search, Anakin would've been arrested for cocaine. **2 points**
  - Inevitable discovery because: **2 points**
    - Anakin would inevitably have been arrested
    - Items on Anakin, including the gun, would have been inventoried

- *Terry* Frisk **4 points**
  - Even if arrest was unlawful, gun might fall under *Terry* frisk doctrine.
  - Anakin is very angry and talking loudly
  - If officer thought Anakin was a threat, could argue for *Terry* frisk because of the possibility that he would be armed and dangerous.

Cocaine in Center Console

- Dog alert can create probable cause **2 points**
- Dog was certified; special certification unnecessary **2 points**
- Detailed logs for drug dog are not required **2 points**
- Three incorrect alerts is not fatal **2 points**
- If dog gave probable cause, can search under the auto exception **2 points**
- Problem: Nose inside vehicle could be a physical trespass **6 points**
  - If physical trespass to go through window, then it's a search.
  - No implied license to take a drug-sniffing dog on a house porch = no implied license for a drug-sniffing dog to stick its nose inside of a car window.
  - No probable cause for dog to put nose in the window.
  - Inevitable discovery/inventory won't fix this problem because there is no reason to impound the vehicle since arrest for disobedience is invalid.

Padme's Suppression Motion

- Padme has no standing to challenge the search of the car because they're not dating, and was only in car "a few times" **4 points**
- Padme does have standing to challenge the stop **3 points**
  - Can argue it was really a drug checkpoint
  - Can argue it was an invalid sobriety checkpoint
- Fruit of the poisonous tree: **4 points**
  - If checkpoint is invalid, Padme is being detained unlawfully
  - Cocaine is fruit of the poisonous tree
  - No attenuation because no time gap or intervening event
  - No independent source or inevitable discovery

Professor's Answer Key for Essay #3

Child Pornography on Computer

- FBI Entering Dwight's Office **4 points**
  - Does the CEO Have Common Authority to consent?
    - CEO has key
    - CEO says he never used key
  - Apparent Authority: Even if CEO lacks common authority, a reasonable officer could think he has authority
- Search of Dwight's Computer Under Consent **8 points**
  - Does CEO have common authority to consent to a search of Dwight's computer?
    - No indication that CEO has been on Dwight's computer before.
    - Unlike entering Dwight's office, there is no indication that the secretary, cleaners, board members, or the CEO have day-to-day access.
    - But the IT department does have Dwight's password.
    - Company policy might indicate that computers can be searched, but we have no information about the policy.
  - Apparent Authority: Even if CEO lacks authority to consent, could a reasonable officer think the CEO has authority?

    - Recognize that the legality of the computer search is a closer question than the legality of entering Dwight's office.

- Search of Dwight's Computer Based on Suspicion **4 points**
    - Does the tip from the CEO create probable cause?
        - Basis of knowledge: Tip is hearsay reporting what IT department found.
        - Reliability: CEO of a major company is likely reliable.
        - Totality of the circumstances approach suggests probable cause
    - No warrant: Even if there is probable cause, the police still need a warrant.

Marijuana in Car

- Search Incident to Arrest Doctrine Does Not Apply to the Trunk **2 points**
- Automobile Exception **6 points**
    - Probable cause: If search of computer was valid, then the email creates probable cause to search car for drugs.
    - Scope of search: If there is probable cause for drugs, police can search anywhere drugs can be found, which includes the trunk.
- Fruit of the Poisonous Tree Problems: **12 points**
    - Problem #1 (illegal entry): If consent was not valid to enter Dwight's office, then the email is fruit of the poisonous tree and there's no probable cause to search the car.
    - Problem #2 (illegal computer search): If consent is valid to enter Dwight's office, but not to search Dwight's computer, then the email is fruit of the poisonous tree and cannot be the basis of probable cause to search the car.
    - Problem #3 (illegal file search of personal documents): If consent was valid to enter Dwight's office and search his computer, it is still possible that the CEO lacked authority to consent to a search of Dwight's Personal Documents folder.
        - The government will argue that since the FBI agents had consent to look for child pornography, they can look anywhere on the computer.
        - But it is not clear whether the CEO can consent to the search of personal files on Dwight's computer.
            - More intrusive to look in folder labeled "Personal Documents"

- Email was clearly written from Dwight's personal email address
- We would need more information about whether employees had waived their privacy rights to all materials on company computers.

- The FBI would counter that they had already found child pornography and thus had probable cause to search all other files (because digital evidence can be hidden anywhere). But if the FBI wants to rely on probable cause, they would also need a warrant. (There are no exigent circumstances.) The police have no warrant.

- Inventory and Inevitable Discovery **6 points**
  - Impoundment is debatable
    - If car is lawfully parked in a private parking lot, there is usually no reason to impound it.
    - CEO is likely to fire Dwight and therefore order his vehicle removed.
  - If it is lawful to impound Dwight's vehicle, a search of the trunk is permissible if the Department's policy calls for items in the trunk to be inventoried.
  - Inevitable discovery: Even if there were no probable cause to search Dwight's car at the scene, the marijuana is arguably admissible because it would inevitably have been discovered during an inventory at the police station.

First Incriminating Statement

- *Miranda* violation because: **4 points**
  - Custody: Handcuffed and Interrogation Room
  - Interrogation: Express Questioning
  - No warnings given and no waiver
- Voluntariness of Confession: **10 points**
  - Argument for Involuntary
    - McNulty threatens to chain Dwight to the table for "the rest of the day"
    - McNulty again threatens to chain Dwight to the table and says, "He won't be able to stand up straight for 12 hours."
    - McNulty says, "We can do this the easy way or the hard way."

    - McNulty says, "You're not going to be done with me until you tell me what you do on that website."
    - Bunk guarantees that Dwight will get "two or three years maximum" as opposed to 30 years if he confesses.
    - Bunk threatens to leave Dwight with "this crazy guy," implying violence.
  - Argument for Voluntary
    - Very obvious that McNulty and Bunk are playing good cop/bad cop.
    - No force used against Dwight.
    - Bunk floating a lighter sentence for cooperation is not normally enough to render a confession involuntary.

Second Incriminating Statement

- Two-Step *Miranda* Problem **5 points**
  - Second confession is admissible if the two-step process was not intentional and the officers took curative measures.
  - No curative measures (such as telling Dwight that first confession was inadmissible).
  - No time lapse between the first invalid confession and second interrogation.
  - All we have to suggest it was an accident is the officers' word that they forgot to give the warnings.
  - Bottom line: Strong argument for suppressing the second confession as an invalid two-step scheme to circumvent the *Miranda* doctrine.
- Form of *Miranda* Warnings **3 points**
  - Bunk did not give the warnings correctly.
  - Bunk said there was a right to an attorney "at trial," suggesting that Dwight might not be able to get a lawyer for the interrogation.
  - This is probably not fatal because courts give officers flexibility on the form of the warnings as long as they key points are conveyed.
- Waiver of *Miranda* ("Uh huh. I guess so.") **4 points**
  - Express oral or written waiver is not required.

  - Look to course of conduct
  - Saying "Uh huh. I guess so" is sufficient to establish waiver.
  - But waiver can only be valid if it wasn't coerced. If McNulty's threats constitute coercion, there could be a waiver problem.

- Fruit of the Poisonous Tree from McNulty's Coercive Threat **4 points**
  - Giving the *Miranda* warnings in the middle of an interrogation will not break the chain of what started as a coercive interrogation.
  - Dwight's confession must be suppressed if McNulty originally threatened force.

- Invocation of silence: "I'm done talking to you, McNulty." **4 points**
  - Pro-invocation: "I'm done talking to you" means that Dwight does not want to be interrogated and that there must be at least a temporary halt.
  - Anti-invocation: Dwight has not clearly invoked his right to silence with respect to all officers. He's just indicated that he does not want to talk to McNulty.
  - This is not a clear invocation of the right to silence.

- Invocation of counsel: "Maybe I should just have a lawyer." **3 points**
  - "Maybe" is ambiguous.
  - Ambiguous statements do not constitute invocation.

Chat Logs **6 points**

- Fruit of the poisonous tree doctrine does not apply to *Miranda* violations. So even if the second confession violates *Miranda*, the chat logs are still admissible.
- Fruit of the poisonous tree doctrine does apply to coercive interrogations. So if McNulty's threat is coercive, the chat logs are inadmissible.

Professor's Answer Key for Essay #4

Marijuana in the Greenhouse as to Tiffany Talent

- Is Officer Mumphries a Private or Public Actor? **5 points**
  - Argument for public actor:
    - M is a police officer.
    - The estate was in M's patrol area.
    - M was dressed in his uniform.
  - Argument for private actor:
    - M worked the day shift.
    - M took the picture in "the evening" though
- Did Mumphries Search?
  - Physical Trespass: **10 points**
    - Police can conduct a search by physically trespassing
    - Leaned ladder against the fence.
    - M was sitting on the fence
    - M therefore set foot on the property.
    - But just because M was on private property does not mean M was on the curtilage.
    - The Talano mansion was "at least 300 feet from the fence."
    - M may have only trespassed on an open field, which would not be a search.

        - Best argument that M was trespassing on the curtilage:
            - Only one fence surrounded the entire estate, suggesting the entire area inside the fence was curtilage
        - Best argument that M was only trespassing on an open field
            - The estate was 10 acres, which is very large and he was far from the house

- *Katz* test: **10 points**
    - Can be a search under the *Katz* test even if no physical trespass.
    - *Katz* test is whether the officer invaded a subjective expectation of privacy that was objectively reasonable.
    - Key question is whether Talent had a reasonable expectation of privacy not to be photographed with high-resolution camera by the police.
    - Argument for this being a search under *Katz:*
        - Talent put up a 12-foot fence (clear evidence of subjective expectation of privacy)
        - Society expects that people will not put a ladder against another's property, climb up, and sit on the fence to take photos
        - Society expects that police will not use high-resolution cameras while sitting on their property.
    - Argument for this not being a search under *Katz:*
        - Talent is a celebrity. She can't reasonably expect privacy from photographers.
        - High-resolution cameras are very common.
        - Police could have acquired the same photograph from a plane or helicopter in navigable airspace or from a double-decker bus parked across the street.
- Conclusion: **2 points**
    - If Mumphries is a government actor and using the camera while sitting on a fence was a search, the evidence should be suppressed.
        - Talent's statement to the reporter was probably inadequate to create probable cause.
        - Officer Mumphries had no warrant.
    - If Mumphries was not a government actor, or if he did not search by using the camera while sitting on the fence, then the photograph can be used in the warrant application.

- Probable Cause for the Warrant: **6 points**
  - Assuming Mumphries was not a government actor or that he did not conduct a search by sitting on the fence and taking the photo, we should consider whether there was enough evidence to procure a warrant.
  - Talent's statement to reporter appears to be a confession that she is growing marijuana, but most people "didn't believe it."
  - M's photograph almost certainly creates probable cause.
- Warrant and Affidavit = Conclusory. Good Faith Exception Weak: **8 points**
  - The search warrant is likely invalid for lack of probable cause because the affidavit is conclusory. It just says Officer Tevin believes there is probable cause without any explanation of why.
  - Officer Tevin wasn't even the agent who gathered probable cause.
  - Good faith exception likely doesn't apply because the warrant appears to be facially invalid for lack of probable cause.
- Location: **10 points**
  - Search warrant is only for the Talano Mansion, not the Elite Estate.
  - No probable cause for the greenhouse (500 feet away).
  - Plain view: Searching under tarp is impermissible because the warrant doesn't authorize a search of the greenhouse and the marijuana is not otherwise in plain view.

Note in Cabinet as to Tiffany Talent

- The warrant is lacking in probable cause because nothing ties the marijuana to the house itself. **3 points**
- Search warrant is for marijuana plants, which couldn't be in file cabinet. **3 points**
- Can't read documents: Even if search for marijuana could extend to the file cabinet, that doesn't include reading documents. **3 points**

Note in Cabinet as to Paul Piano

- Piano Has Standing to Challenge Warrant for Lack of Probable Cause. **3 points**
  - Piano lives there because they "moved in together."
  - The name of house (Talano Mansion) might indicate some property interest.
  - The name of the land (Elite Estate) does not necessarily suggest ownership.

- Piano May Lack Standing for File Cabinet **5 points**
  - File cabinet is engraved "T.T. Important Docs"
  - Not married, so joint ownership of all property is debatable.
  - If no standing for filing cabinet, then he can't challenge that marijuana plants couldn't fit in file cabinet, or that cops can't read documents.
- Piano's Main Argument Would Be Fruit of the Poisonous Tree. **3 points**
  - If warrant were invalid, Piano would have standing (as a resident of the property) to challenge the illegal entry.
  - No search of the filing cabinet would have occurred if there had not been an illegal entry in the first place.
  - If the police entry was lawful, Piano probably loses because he likely cannot challenge the search of the filing cabinet.

Professor's Answer Key for Essay #5

DNA from Champagne Glass **12 Points**

- The first question is whether the police conducted a search when they swabbed the champagne glass for Jack's DNA.
- Facts suggesting Jack has a reasonable expectation of privacy in the champagne glass and that agents conducted a search:
    - Pro: Area guarded and roped off
    - Pro: Closed to general public
    - Pro: People don't expect their DNA to be taken off glass
    - Pro: Glass was at a special table and his name was on the chair in front of the table.
    - Pro: Compare *Bond v. United States*. Luggage in overhead rack can't be manipulated even though it's in public. This was Jack's glass, which suggests reasonable expectation of privacy.
- Facts suggesting Jack has no reasonable expectation of privacy and that the agents did not conduct a search:
    - Con: Glasses are interchangeable objects, especially where champagne is free. Jack (and other high rollers) would expect to get a new glass of champagne if the other is taken.
    - Con: Wait staff usually clean up glasses and return to public areas
    - Con: Jack left his glass and went to the bathroom
    - Con: Any high roller could pick up Jack's glass while he was gone

   - Con: Casino is open to public, very different from house.
   - Con: Lots of security cameras watch movements.
   - Con: Compare *California v. Greenwood.* Trash left on curb has no reasonable expectation of privacy. Glass was abandoned just like trash.

- If taking the DNA swab from the champagne glass was a search, the agents lack probable cause. Glass

  was not immediately incriminating. **2 points**
- Striking guard = Illegal, but that's not a Fourth Amendment violation relevant to Jack. **1 point**

Machine Gun in Trunk

- Fruit of the Poisonous Tree from Champagne Glass **4 points**
   - If the agents conducted an unlawful search by taking the DNA off the glass, then the machine gun could be fruit of the poisonous tree.
   - Attenuation: Jack's threat about shooting the agents arguably breaks the chain.
- Search Incident to Arrest **4 points**
   - Arrest is in public.
   - Only a valid arrest if threatening thief with gun is a criminal offense.
   - But can't search the trunk in a search incident to arrest.
- Inevitable Discovery **4 points**
   - Car probably can't be left at the Vegas Gold Casino, so agents will impound it. (But this depends on the Casino's policy for leaving vehicles.)
   - Inventory can extend to the trunk.
   - The department's policy must instruct the officers to inventory the trunk.
   - If inventory would have been valid, agents inevitably would have discovered the machine gun.
- Automobile Exception **6 points**
   - Information from the original DNA sample only indicates 1/150, which isn't enough for probable cause.

- No confirmation that Jack suffers from argyria skin disorder.
- FBI didn't get any further information to confirm hunch.
- Even if there is probable cause as to Jack, there is none as to the trunk.
- But Jack saying "I've got a machine gun in the trunk of my car" is enough for probable cause because machine guns are illegal.

- *Terry* Frisk **4 points**
  - Threatened officers with gun.
  - But agents can't frisk the trunk.

Cocaine in Glove Compartment

- Fruit of the Poisonous Tree **4 points**
  - From champagne glass (if the agents conducted an unlawful search).
  - From illegal arrest (if agents lacked a basis to arrest Jack).
  - From illegal search of trunk (if agents lacked a basis to search the trunk).
- Automobile Exception **4 points**
  - Machine gun in trunk doesn't give probable cause to search glove box.
  - DNA evidence doesn't give probable cause to search glove box.
- Search Incident to Arrest **6 points**
  - Recent occupant of vehicle is a stretch because Jack's been out of the vehicle for at least 30 minutes.
  - Need valid arrest, which is debatable due to gun threat.
  - Arrest can be based on machine gun in trunk, but there is possible fruit of the poisonous tree problem.
  - If crime of arrest is the illegal machine gun, there is probably no reason to believe evidence of that crime will be found in the vehicle.
- Inevitable Discovery **2 points**
  - Whether the car would be impounded depends on the casino's policy for leaving a vehicle overnight.
  - If the car were impounded, the cocaine would have been discovered during an inventory as long as the department policy specified logging items in the glove box.

- *Terry* Frisk **4 points**
    - Claims to have gun, which supports looking through car.
    - Claims gun is in the trunk, which hurts claim to open glovebox.

Professor's Answer Key for Essay #6

Weapon in Trunk

- Does Sal Have Standing to Challenge the Search of the Car? **8 points**
  - Argument for Sal Having Standing:
    - Driving car by himself when he was stopped.
    - Driven car by himself on previous occasions.
  - Argument for Sal *Not* Having Standing:
    - Sal doesn't own the car.
    - Sal only seems to drive by himself for illegal activity and with permission, but police don't know that for sure.
    - Sal possibly has standing as to the passenger compartment, but nothing indicates that he has a reasonable expectation of privacy in the trunk, especially underneath the spare tire.
  - Conclusion: As the driver and sole occupant of the vehicle, Sal seems to have a good case for standing. Reaching the opposite conclusion is possible, though.
- Consequences of the standing inquiry: **2 points**
  - If Sal does *not* have standing, then the gun is admissible even if the search was illegal.
  - If Sal has standing, the police must have had a valid justification for the search.

- Search Incident to Arrest: **4 points**
  - Valid to arrest for minor traffic infraction like failing to signal.
  - Fact that changing lanes was a pretextual reason for the stop is irrelevant.
  - But not reasonable to believe evidence of the crime of arrest (failing to signal) can be found in the vehicle.
  - Also, the search incident to arrest exception does not apply to trunk.
  - Conclusion: The search incident to arrest doctrine does not provide a valid basis for admitting the gun.
- Probable Cause and the Automobile Exception **15 points**
  - The initial case for probable cause to search the vehicle for drugs is weak
    - Police can argue that there is probable cause to look for drugs based on garage transaction, but no illegal activity witnessed.
    - Police can argue probable cause to look for drugs based on two weeks' surveillance, but no illegal activity witnessed.
    - Hard to claim probable cause when the magistrate rejected warrant application. Although just because magistrate doesn't believe there's probable cause doesn't mean the magistrate was correct.
    - Bottom Line: Case for probable cause to search the passenger compartment is pretty weak.
  - Cell phone message creates probable cause to search the trunk, but there is probably a fruit of the poisonous tree problem
  - The case for probable cause:
    - The text message surely creates probable cause to believe there is contraband (likely drugs) in the car.
    - Given their investigation, it is rational for police to believe "the stuff" referenced in the text message is drugs.
    - The "stuff in the car" could be anywhere, including under spare tire in trunk.
    - Thus, if the police were lawfully present when they saw the text message, that creates probable cause to search the trunk.
    - Inevitable discovery exception: Even though the first officer's search of the trunk was unlawful, the police would have found

the gun based on the probable cause that came from the text message.

- The case for fruit of the poisonous tree problem:
  - If the second officer was not permitted to flip over the phone, then the incriminating text message would not have been in plain view and could not be the basis for probable cause.
  - If the police have reasonable suspicion that Sal is dangerous and might be able to access a weapon from the vehicle, they can conduct a *Terry* frisk of the vehicle.
  - But a *Terry* frisk of the vehicle would not have permitted the officer to flip over the phone because it is clearly not a weapon
  - To seize the phone (or even to just flip it over), the officer would have needed probable cause to search the car, which the police did not have.
- Conclusion: Text message was found through an illegal search and cannot be the basis for probable cause to search the trunk.

- Inventory **6 points**
  - Proper to arrest for changing lanes without signaling (the Fourth Amendment allows arrest for any crime, even if it is minor).
  - Police were permitted to impound the vehicle because it could not lawfully remain on the side of the road.
  - Police can inventory the trunk if the department policy instructs them to.
  - If the inventory policy instructed the police to look in the trunk, then the police would have found the gun during the inventory.
  - The gun would therefore be admissible against Sal under the inevitable discovery exception.

Cocaine in Gas Tank as to Sal

- Standing **2 points**
  - If Sal has standing to challenge the search of the passenger compartment, he likely also has standing to challenge the search of the gas tank.
- Search of Gas Tank Incident to Arrest **3 points**
  - Search incident to arrest does not extend to inside of gas tank.
  - Arrest was for failure to signal and there is no reason to believe evidence of that crime would be in the gas tank.

  - Answer might be different if gas tank were open and within reaching distance, but the question says the officers had to open the lid to the gas tank.

- Automobile Exception to Search Gas Tank **4 points**
  - The text message creates probable cause to search the gas tank. Because it is part of the automobile, the police can search without a warrant under the automobile exception.
  - But, as discussed above, the police probably conducted an illegal search to see the message. The officer had to flip over the phone to see the message. The officer could not flip open the phone during a *Terry* frisk of the vehicle. As such, the text message was not in plain view and it cannot be used to create probable cause.
  - The automobile exception argument therefore likely fails.

- Inventory to Search Gas Tank **3 points**
  - As discussed above, the police would have impounded the vehicle and inventoried it pursuant to the department's policy.
  - But the inventory could not extend to the interior of the car, such as the gas tank.
  - Inventory argument will therefore fail.

- Bottom Line: **3 points**
  - Assuming police lacked probable cause to search the passenger compartment of the vehicle, they would not have seen the text message, and thus would have lacked probable cause to search the gas tank.
  - The cocaine should be suppressed as to Sal.

Cocaine as to Ollie **10 points**

- The analysis of the search incident to arrest, automobile exception, and inventory would be the same as set out above for Sal.
- The key question for Ollie is whether he has standing to challenge the search of the passenger compartment, specifically the flipping over of Sal's phone.
  - If Ollie lacks standing to challenge the search of the passenger compartment, the police can use the incriminating text message to create probable cause for the gas tank (even if the police were not lawfully present when they read the text message).

- Case for Standing:
    - Ollie owns the vehicle.
    - Owners of property usually have standing.
    - Ollie might have private items in the passenger compartment of his vehicle that he wants to keep from police view.
- Case for *No* Standing:
    - The reason that owners of property usually have standing is they are usually present.
    - Ollie was not present when the police searched the vehicle.
    - Ollie has temporarily given up possession of his vehicle by letting Sal drive it.
    - Analogy: When a landlord leases a house to another person, the landlord no longer has standing to challenge an illegal police entry.
    - Police have observed Sal driving the vehicle by himself to multiple locations. Ollie has not been in the car at all today.
    - By loaning the car to Sal and making the front passenger compartment accessible to him, Ollie has run the risk that Sal would allow others to view the property. Accordingly, Ollie should not have standing to challenge a search of the vehicle.
- No clear precedent: The Supreme Court has never said whether a person who temporarily loans a vehicle loses their standing to challenge a search of the vehicle. The argument against standing seems more compelling, though.
- Bottom line: If Ollie lacks standing to challenge a search of the passenger compartment of the vehicle, he cannot challenge the reading of the text message. The text message creates probable cause to search the gas tank. The cocaine is therefore admissible against Ollie.

Professor's Answer Key for Essay #7

Cocaine in Dennis's Wallet

- Standing to Challenge Olivia's Reading of File Folder **6 points**
  - The notes Olivia read in the file folder provided the initial basis to investigate Dennis and also the basis to stop the car and arrest Dennis.
  - The file folder belonged to Carl Careless, not Dennis. Normally Dennis would *not* have standing to challenge a search of the property of another person.
  - Here Dennis may have standing for the file folder, however, because a person who is represented by counsel works through their attorney. Dennis may have a reasonable expectation of privacy in the contents of the file folder.
  - Indeed, the document is labeled "privileged and confidential" and under the attorney-client privilege the contents are supposed to be shared only by Carl and Dennis.
  - Dennis thus has a good argument that he has standing to challenge Olivia's reading of the file folder.
  - If Dennis has standing and Olivia improperly searched by reading the file, then the contents cannot contribute to probable cause to stop the vehicle or arrest Dennis.

- Was the stop of the vehicle lawful? **7 points**
  - Officer Olivia needs reasonable suspicion to stop a vehicle.
  - The question tells us there is no traffic offense.
  - Arguably Dennis's statement to Carl Careless (as noted in the file folder) that Kelly is involved in drug dealing creates reasonable suspicion.
  - File notes say Kelly wears a backpack, so it might be plausible to think the backpack contains drugs.
  - Dennis's comment, "Hey, don't put that backpack in the car next to me. Throw the stuff in the trunk. I've got enough problems already without you bringing that in here next to me," suggests something illegal might be in the backpack.
  - Reasonable suspicion is a low standard enabling police to investigate further. It is probably met here.
- Search Incident to Arrest **8 points**
  - Requires a lawful arrest
  - If there is a lawful, custodial arrest the police can search everything on the arrestee, including his wallet.
  - Very weak case for probable cause to arrest Dennis, though.
  - Dennis was previously arrested for aggravated assault and has never been charged with drug dealing.
  - The information from Carl Careless' file folder suggests Kelly is involved in drug dealing and insinuates drugs might be in the backpack. Implication might be that Dennis knows because he is also involved in drug dealing. But that is speculation and does not create probable cause.
  - Dennis' statement "throw the stuff in the trunk" could imply that the "stuff" is drugs, but this is speculation. In any event, Dennis's statement indicates he does not want to be involved with whatever is in the backpack.
  - The case for probable cause to arrest Dennis is weak. Accordingly, the cocaine is probably not admissible under a search incident to arrest.

- Inventory Items on Person: **4 points**
    - If there is a valid arrest, the police will inventory Dennis's items when he is incarcerated at the jail.
    - If the police department's inventory policy instructs officers to open a wallet and log everything inside, the police would also have found the cocaine as a result of the inventory.
    - The key question, though, is the same as above. There must be a valid arrest in order to invoke the inventory doctrine.
    - As noted above, the case for probable cause to arrest Dennis is weak and as a result there probably is not a valid arrest and cannot be a valid inventory.

Machine Gun in Trunk as to Dennis

- Search Incident to Arrest Doesn't Apply to Trunk **4 points**
    - To invoke this exception, there must be a lawful arrest. As discussed above, the case for a valid arrest of Dennis is weak.
    - Even if there is a valid arrest, the search incident to arrest doctrine does not extend to the trunk.
- Automobile Exception: **12 points**
    - Police can search a vehicle without a warrant if they have probable cause.
    - Case for Probable Cause:
        - Dennis' statement to Carl Careless (in the file folder) about Kelly dealing drugs and carrying a backpack creates some reason to think that drugs might be in the backpack. This information, by itself, is pretty weak.
        - Dennis' statement to Kelly is more incriminating.
        - Dennis says "I've already got enough problems without you bringing that in here next to me." This suggests that the contents of the backpack could create problems for Dennis—that something illegal or incriminating might be in the backpack.
        - Dennis does not say "throw the backpack" in the trunk. He says "throw the stuff in the trunk." The word "stuff" in this context would seem to indicate drugs (or some other contraband) that is inside the backpack.
        - All of this information likely creates probable cause to believe there is evidence of illegal activity (probably drugs) in the backpack.

- Limits on Where the Police Can Search
  - If police have probable cause to believe a container (here, the backpack) contains evidence, they may search for the container and then open it without a warrant under the automobile exception.
  - But the police did not find the machine gun in the backpack. They found it under the spare tire.
  - We must therefore analyze whether there was probable cause for the police to continue searching after they found the backpack.
  - Kelly simply "put the backpack in the trunk." Officer Olivia was watching and it does not appear that she saw Kelly take items out of the backpack and hide them elsewhere in the trunk.
  - Having already found the backpack, there does not appear to be probable cause for Officer Olivia to look elsewhere in the trunk of the car.
  - Because Officer Olivia searched further by "lift[ing] up the floorboard of the trunk" and looking under the spare tire, it appears she has violated the Fourth Amendment by searching without probable cause.
  - In other words, Olivia had probable cause to find and search the bag, not to search elsewhere in the trunk. Once she found and searched the bag, she could not search further.
- Inventory **4 points**
  - If police had validly impounded the vehicle they might inevitably have discovered the machine gun when they logged items under the department's inventory policy.
  - This argument should fail, though, because, as explained above, there was no valid basis to arrest Dennis, who was the driver.
  - While finding an illegal machine gun in his car would create probable cause to arrest Dennis (and therefore impound his vehicle), the search that led to the discovery of the machine gun was unlawful.

Machine Gun in Trunk as to Kelly

- Standing for Stop of the Vehicle **5 points**
  - Even though Kelly is only a passenger, he has standing to challenge a stop of the vehicle. Just like Dennis, Kelly has been stopped.

- If the stop was invalid, the fruit of the poisonous tree doctrine will result in all subsequently discovered evidence being suppressed.
- As discussed at the very beginning of this answer, though, Officer Olivia likely had reasonable suspicion to stop the vehicle.
- So even though Kelly has standing to challenge the stop of the vehicle, he probably cannot point to any Fourth Amendment violation with respect to the stop, and this argument will fail.

- Standing for Search of the Trunk **5 points**
  - Kelly has a much weaker claim to standing to challenge the *search* of the vehicle.
  - Kelly certainly has a reasonable expectation of privacy in his own backpack. (Officer Olivia saw him bring the backpack out of the house and thus there is no dispute that the backpack belongs to Kelly.)
  - But the evidence was not found in the backpack. It was found under the floorboard of the trunk, beneath the spare tire.
  - The question is therefore whether Kelly has standing (a reasonable expectation of privacy) to challenge a search of Dennis' car (specifically the area beneath the spare tire).
  - As a passenger, Kelly almost certainly does not have a reasonable expectation of privacy in the spare tire area in the trunk of the vehicle.
  - Kelly has just gotten into the car. We have no information that he has been in the car before. And we certainly have no information to believe that he has stored objects in the spare tire area of the trunk and expected them to be kept private. In short, Kelly has no meaningful connection to the trunk of the vehicle (or even to the car itself) and thus cannot have a reasonable expectation of privacy.
  - Therefore, Kelly lacks standing to challenge the (illegal) search of the spare tire area.
  - Even though Officer Olivia likely committed an illegal search when she lifted the floorboard and found the machine gun beneath the spare tire, Kelly cannot have that evidence against him suppressed because he lacks standing.